More Than
They Promised

More Than They Promised

THE *Studebaker* STORY

Thomas E. Bonsall

Stanford University Press

Stanford, California

For H. Fairfield Butt IV

Stanford University Press
Stanford, California

©2000 by the Board of Trustees of the
Leland Stanford Junior University

Printed in the United States of America

Library of Congress Cataloging in Publication Data

Bonsall, Thomas E.
More than they promised : the Studebaker story / Thomas E. Bonsall
p. cm
Includes bibliographical references and index.
ISBN 0-8047-3586-7 (alk. paper)
1. Studebaker automobile--History. 2.
Studebaker-Packard Corporation--History I. Title.
TL215.S79 .B65 2001
629.222'0973--dc21   00-063564

Original printing 2000
Last figure below indicates the year of this printing:
01 03 05 07 09 08 06 04 02 00

Contents

Introduction, 3
1. The Wagon Years, 11
2. The Early Auto Years, 43
3. The Rise of Erskine, 85
4. The Fall of Erskine, 135
5. Back from the Abyss, 177
6. The War Years, 215
7. Studebaker Amnia Vincit, 233
8. The Packard Operation, 277
9. The Lark Ascendant, 313
10. The Swan Song, 349
11. Metamorphosis, 385
12. Postscript, 401
13. Why Studebaker Failed, 437
Bibliography, 473
Index, 479

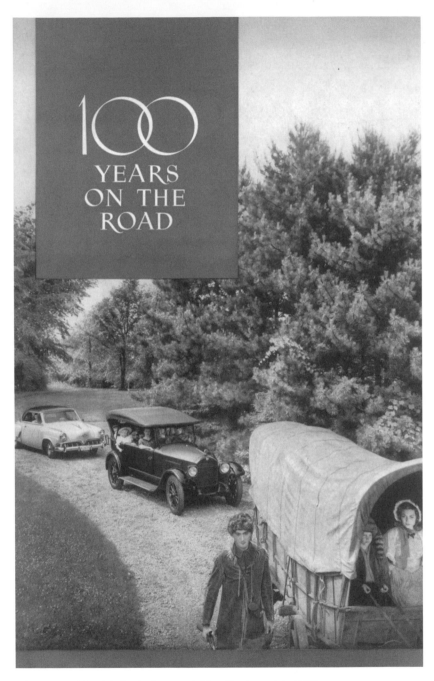

The cover of Studebaker's Centennial booklet issued in 1952.

Introduction

In his autobiography, famed designer Raymond Loewy made the following comment about Studebaker's final years as an automobile producer:

> My decades with the company were exhilarating and unforgettable, and my respect for its engineering department immense. I leave it to others to uncover the reasons why such a great, prestigious firm, having at last found its market, finally disappeared at a time when it was admired throughout the world and when the Avanti had just come out with a backlog of orders. It was an industrial tragedy.[1]

A tragedy it was, but if Loewy really didn't have a clue as to what had gone wrong he is almost unique among writers addressing the issue. Any number of books and magazine articles have set forth in numbing detail a wide variety of possible reasons for the sudden and seemingly unstoppable descent of this once great company in the years after World War II. This book will devote an entire chapter to the subject.

One question that arose several times during the research and writing of this book was the appropriateness of the title, "More Than They Promised." After all, the Studebaker car failed, did it not? Wouldn't "Less Than They Promised" be more fitting? No, I don't think it would—quite apart from the fact that there has already been a book published with that very title. "More Than They Promised" is an abbreviation of an informal slogan the Studebaker brothers used—"always give a little more than you promise"—and if anyone ever lived up to a slogan they did. Consider:

The Studebaker business started with two brothers, two forges and $68 (most of it borrowed). Within twenty-five years, the company could credibly claim to be the largest manufacturer of vehicles in the world. Throughout the one hundred twenty-six years of its independent life, the company survived fires, strikes, wars and financial catastrophes that would have destroyed many a lesser firm. It even survived fundamental shifts in the economy. When the end of the line approached for the horse-drawn vehicle industry, it diversified into automobiles and, when the automobile business began to fail, it diversified into industrial equipment and ended its days a highly successful, billion dollar conglomerate. And, all this from two forges and $68! More than they promised, indeed.

Given the public perception today, it is ironic that even the one-hundred-fourteen-year Studebaker vehicle story was mostly one of successes. Studebaker wagons and carriages were noted for their quality and value, and, later, so were Studebaker cars and trucks. The President series produced from 1927-33 is honored as a full classic by the Classic Car Club of America. The 1953 Starliner and the 1963 Avanti, designed under Loewy's direction, are widely regarded as being among the most significant designs in American automotive history. Studebakers are highly prized and avidly sought by thousands upon thousands of collectors the world over.

The status of Studebaker in old car circles is even more impressive when compared to that of its competitors. Since the dawn of the industry, there have been more than 2,000 brands produced in the United States. Several hundred achieved positions of some importance, at least for a time, yet most are almost entirely forgotten except by a few specialists and historians. It is a fact that of all the independent manufacturers only two have large and vibrant enthusiast followings today: Studebaker and Packard.

As is the case with any great enterprise, the Studebaker story was one of people and, for a company that was an important player in the auto business for two-thirds of a century, Studebaker was led by a remarkably small group of men. Albert Erskine ran the company for all but four years from the time it got serious about cars and went public in 1911 until it fell into receivership in 1933. His lieutenants, Paul Hoffman and Harold Vance, then assumed control and ran the show as a team from 1933 until the Packard take-over in 1954. James Nance, Packard's president, then headed the combined companies for two turbulent years until Harold Churchill assumed the helm in 1956. Churchill, in turn, was replaced by Sherwood Egbert, whose dynamic rule lasted from 1961 almost until the moment the factory in South Bend was at last shuttered in December, 1963. After that, Randolph "Bob" Guthrie manned the helm as the final Studebaker car rolled from the line in 1966. That makes for a total of eight men, in all, in sixty-one years—two of them operating as a team. Moreover, Erskine, Hoffman, and Vance between them held the reins for four continuous decades. This is a remarkable record of stability, yet the demise of the Studebaker car has led to a host of interesting questions for the historian.

Was Albert Erskine a visionary genius? Or, was he a short-sighted spendthrift who ran a great company into the ground? Were Hoffman and Vance the company's saviors? Or, were they the architects of its decline? Was James Nance a brilliant manager who performed heroically with the bad hand he had been dealt? Or, was he an appliance salesman out of his depth in the car business? Was Sherwood Egbert the automotive division's last chance? Or, was he an over-reacher who sealed its doom? Was Bob Guthrie a hard-nosed financier who cared more about the price of the company's stock than he did about Studebaker's rich transportation heritage? Or, was he a sober-minded realist who made a hard decision that was long overdue? And, ultimately, was the demise of the automotive division a result of homegrown failures in South Bend? Or, was it an inevitable conclusion quite beyond the control of those responsible for minding the company's affairs? The answers to all of the above questions are probably, at least to some extent, "yes." The Studebaker story may not be tidy—with easily identifiable heroes and villains—but it certainly is interesting.

Most of the key figures in Studebaker's history are poorly understood today. Erskine is remembered as the man whose fiscal policies in the early years of the Great Depression drove Studebaker into bankruptcy, but people forget that the first dozen years or so of Erskine's regime were ones of brilliant expansion in which he did practically everything right. Nor was he the only man who refused to believe the depression would last as long as it did. After all, no depression ever had. His fateful decisions in 1931 and 1932 weren't the work of a fool, but, rather, of a normally far-sighted man thrust into a life-threatening situation he didn't understand until it was too late, and who, consequently, followed a tragically wrong-headed course of action. Even then, facing a disaster of his own unwitting creation, it was he who devised a brilliant maneuver for saving the firm—merger with the White Motor Company—that came within a hairsbreadth of success. Had the merger been completed, as he had every right to expect, Studebaker (and Erskine himself) would have weathered the crisis, bloodied but intact. As it was, the fundamental strength of the Studebaker organization—for which Erskine was largely responsible—saved the firm.

Erskine had many successes in his eighteen years of undisputed leadership in South Bend. An objective examination of his career cannot help but leave the impression that he was a truly remarkable figure. Moreover, he, almost alone among the men running independent car producers, understood *and* took energetic steps to address the profound changes in the market in the 1920s as the industry matured. Alfred Sloan became celebrated for his "price step" theory of marketing, which he developed at General Motors in response to these same changes. Walter Chrysler achieved fame for successfully mimicking the same concept at Maxwell-Chalmers (which he transformed into Chrysler Corporation). Erskine moved heaven and earth to take Studebaker down the same road but, for reasons covered in this book, failed. Had he succeeded, we might be speaking of a "Big Four" today. To be sure, he had his fair share of other disappointments and mistakes, but nothing out of the ordinary in the auto business. In fact, he only made one critical miscalculation in eighteen years—failing to appreciate the full extent of the Great Depression and to take steps to preserve Studebaker's capital—but, alas, it was enough to bring down the company.

Hoffman and Vance are blamed for driving Studebaker to ruin in the early 1950s. And, they did. But, like Erskine, their first few years at the helm saw one masterstroke after another. They were the men who saved Studebaker from the calamity Erskine had unwittingly created, who hired Raymond Loewy, and who conceived the car that put Studebaker back on the map: the low-priced Champion in 1939. They were also the men who, in the years immediately following World War II, led Studebaker to its greatest era of production and prosperity. For the first fifteen years they ran the show, nearly every decision they made was right. After that, nearly everything they did was wrong. As with Erskine, we can't ignore the crushing mistakes, but we shouldn't forget the amazing achievements, either.

For his part, James Nance is seen as the man who took the mess Hoffman and Vance had created—and made it worse. To the contrary, my view is that Nance's instincts were generally right on target, but that he simply ran out of the time and money necessary to fix the nearly hopeless mess he had inherited. Indeed, Nance's biggest mistake may have been the decision to have Packard assume control of Studebaker in the first place, for it was mostly South Bend that dragged Studebaker-Packard down. Packard was viable as late as 1955, but Studebaker was already in desperate shape by the time Nance appeared on the scene and may well have been beyond resuscitation. It may have been too late for Packard, too, but that's a story for another book.[2] For our purposes it is sufficient to note that in 1954 Studebaker was unquestionably in the worst shape of the two and would probably have collapsed ten years sooner had Nance not come along.

While this book was being written, I drew on my research to publish an article on the 1953 Studebakers. It is my view that the product program taken as a whole was one of the worst conceived and executed in the history of the industry, and played an enormous role in destroying the company as a viable vehicle manufacturer. That article drew intense criticism from a number of Studebaker enthusiasts, primarily, I think, because it is almost impossible for many of them to reconcile their understandable love for this particular design with the catastrophic effect it had on the company. It is ironic that two of the three landmark postwar Studebaker designs were financial disasters, the other one being the Avanti. In a further irony, the one that was a huge success—the 1947 line—is often cited by Studebaker writers and enthusiasts as a strategic mistake, a judgment with which I emphatically disagree for reasons that will be discussed.

Others blame Egbert for the demise of the Studebaker car, reasoning that his ill-conceived Avanti program drained away funds that should have been used to redesign the bread-and-butter product line. As will be explained, Egbert came to South Bend after Studebaker's directors had already fired one president for proposing just such an investment. As far as they were concerned, Studebaker's automobile business was a dead letter before the presidency was even offered to Egbert, whose primary assignment was to diversify the company out of cars completely.

And, so it goes.

If this book does nothing else than clarify some of the misconceptions surrounding the men who ran Studebaker and the products they built, it will have accomplished a great deal. That is not, of course, the sole purpose of the present effort, and deciding what to cover, what not to cover, and what balance to give each facet of the Studebaker story, has been a major challenge. In fact, there are probably as many valid ways to write the history of Studebaker as there are writers capable of doing so.

There is no such thing as a "complete" history of a great industrial enterprise in the sense that every possible avenue is exhaustively explored. In this volume, there is a deliberate bias toward the business and marketing angles of the story, for, in the final analysis, it was the business and marketing acumen (or lack thereof) of those in charge that created both Studebaker's greatest triumphs and its most crushing defeats.

Yet, the critical hurdle when undertaking any publishing project of this scope, in my view, is to say something that has not been said before. The author and publisher must be satisfied that they can shed light on important aspects of the story not previous covered, or illuminate new angles that are important for a balanced understanding of the subject. This book, I am convinced, meets that challenge.

Baltimore, Maryland
July, 2000

Notes

[1] Loewy, p. 137.
[2] That other book would be, *The Fall of the Packard Motor Car Company*, by James Ward, also published by Stanford University Press.

Overleaf, final carriage inspection at the Studebaker factory in the 1880s.

ONE

The Wagon Years

The Studebaker story begins with the Studebaker family. It is, however, much more than the story of one family, for, if that is all it were, most of us wouldn't consider it terribly interesting or important. Yet, owing to the nature and contribution of that family, it is also in a microcosm the story of the industrial development of America, a story which is both interesting and important, indeed.

The hallowed life of the people of the earth has been long celebrated in American literature. This was the life that was supposed to be pure and simple and quintessentially American, the very bedrock of our civilization and of all the values for which Americans have lived, sweated and died since the founding of the Republic. Heart-warming though that may be, it doesn't happen to be entirely true. While American values may owe a good deal to our early agrarian experience, it was the sudden and rapid industrialization beginning in the middle of the Nineteenth Century that made America a great and astonishingly rich country. Without even realizing it at first, the Studebaker family found itself swept up by that development.

In truth, the Studebakers had always been industrialists in the sense that they made their living by manufacturing things, as opposed to growing things, i.e., in farming the land. Still, for more than a century after the family came to America, their manufacturing enterprises were tiny and unimpressive. This should not be surprising, for industry everywhere was tiny and unimpressive back then. When the Industrial Revolution hit full force, however—spurred on in no small measure by the Civil War, which, virtually overnight, transformed America from a predominantly rural-agrarian society into a predominantly urban-industrial one—the fortunes of the Studebaker family were transformed with it. This event was, in a very real sense, the Second American Revolution and the Studebakers, more-or-less by chance, found themselves in the vanguard. Therein lies the significance of the story which follows.

*   *   *

The Studebaker family's early history was, in most particulars, unremarkable. They first landed on the shores of the New World in the company of 388 mostly Dutch and German immigrants on September 1, 1736, having left Frefeld, Germany, some ten weeks before. The ship was the Dutch vessel *Harle* from Rotterdam, the place of arrival was Philadelphia and the name was Studebecker. According to surviving records, there were

John Studebaker.

five Studebeckers, in all: Peter, Clement, Henry, Anna Margetha and Anna Catherine. Like most immigrants, they were young. Peter, the oldest, was thirty-eight.

The family name was soon changed from "becker" to "baker" and they quickly embarked on what was to become a family way of life: blacksmithing and wagon making. It is known that by 1788 a Peter Studebaker, Sr., and his son, Peter, Jr., were established wagon makers living near York, Pennsylvania, about seventy-five miles northwest of Philadelphia. The family were Dunkards, too, members of a conservative religious sect that believed so firmly in a non-ostentatious way

The Studebaker homestead in Ashland, Ohio.

of life that they refused to put steeples on their churches. The Dunkards, or Dunkers as they were sometimes called, were part of the Brethren movement that also produced the Mennonites and the Amish. Although the Dunkards, despite their "plain" ways, found it easier to assimilate into general society than did the more conservative branches of the movement, it wasn't always easy for them, either—as the Studebaker family was to discover in due course.

As the family's westward migration continued, they settled near Getty's Town, later known as Gettysburg. Peter Studebaker, Jr., had a son John who was born there in 1799. In 1820, John married a German-American girl named Rebecca Mohler who hailed from Lancaster.[1]

As befit his new responsibilities as a husband and bread-winner, John Studebaker eventually bought property near Gettysburg—in 1830—and built a brick house with an adjacent workshop in which he continued the family's by-then-traditional business of blacksmithing and wagon making. According to family lore, he soon found himself in serious financial trouble owing to the unreliability of friends for whom he had signed notes. In any case, the family eventually pulled up stakes and moved on.

The early Nineteenth Century was the time of the great movement to settle the Ohio River Valley and John Studebaker became part of that population shift, moving his family to Ashland, Ohio, in 1835. The trip was made in three wagons, one these of the so-called Conestoga type, which we now call a "covered" wagon. It consisted of an enormous bed, or "box," drawn by four horses, while the top bows extended outward in a fashion characteristic of these vehicles and were covered with waterproof duck cloth. At least, the duck cloth was supposed to be waterproof, but, as one writer slyly noted, only the people inside actually were. Still, such wagons became an integral part of western folklore and they were used extensively by farmers and merchants back east, as well. John was accompanied on the arduous journey by Rebecca and the six children she had borne him. Two of the children were Henry and Clement, boys who were to grow up to play a central role in the story this book will relate.

As soon as they arrived in Ashland, John built a small house and shop very much like the arrangement he had had near Gettysburg. Above the shop, however, he erected a sign with the motto, "Owe no man anything, but to love one another." It was a motto the family would not always be able to honor in the early years, at least not insofar as the owing part was concerned. Life in the "Western Territories" proved difficult for many settlers, the Studebakers included. Rebecca was forced to do spinning and weaving to supplement the meager income her husband generated by blacksmithing and wagon making. The wagons were good, but money was scarce and the family remained in poverty.[2] Despite that, they were renowned for their hospitality and any traveler passing through who needed a hot meal and a place to bed down was sure to find it at the Studebaker home. On one occasion they managed to board sixteen nuns and it was small wonder a neighboring innkeeper groused that it was impossible for him to make an honest living while the Studebakers were around! As if that weren't enough, the Studebakers also regularly made their home available as a meeting place for Dunkard religious services.

Meanwhile, the number of Studebaker children had quickly increased to ten. John Mohler, Peter Everest, Jacob Franklin and a girl, Maria, were born after the family's arrival in Ashland. Maria was destined to outlive all her siblings. While big families were the norm in those days, the ten Studebaker children must have been a severe drain on the family's finances. Despite the fact that the boys were put to work as soon as they were old enough to help out in the family enterprises, the oldest boys also traveled around northeastern Ohio hiring themselves out as farm hands when money ran especially low. William B. Allison, a local politician who knew John Studebaker well, later wrote:

> He was a good old man who worked pretty hard at his anvil, but for all that had a constitutional tendency to financial prostration. He had some boys who were active young fellows who tried to help their father out, but in spite of all they could do and all the old man could do the blacksmith found himself more than once every year sued for debt before a justice of the peace...It was understood in the neighborhood that the old gentleman Studebaker owed nearly everyone in that part of the country and every merchant in the county seat whom he could induce to trust him. In the very same way about half of the farmers in the township owed him bills for sharpening plowshares, for repairing wagons and implements, and shoeing their horses. These farmers were too poor to pay and Studebaker was therefore unable to pay the merchants who had sold him supplies.[3]

Around 1850, when Henry and Clement came of age, John Studebaker encouraged them to leave the nest and establish themselves independently. This they did, moving westward to South Bend in Indiana.

South Bend, founded in 1831, was a promising place in the eyes of the young Studebaker brothers. It could already boast of a flour mill, abundant cheap water power from the St. Joseph River that ran through town, the Eliakim Briggs Threshing Machine Works and a fine local college that would ultimately evolve into famed Notre Dame University. Northern Indiana was also appealing to them because of the abundance of fine, hardwood forests suitable for inexpensively supplying the family woodworking profession. Indeed, in nearby Mishawaka, the Mishawaka Wagon Works already existed, as did an iron works. Perhaps best of all, there was an active local Dunkard movement. To Henry and Clem, South Bend seemed like just the place to settle.

At first, Clem went to work for Eliakim Briggs at the meager wage of

The H. & C. Studebaker factory as it appeared in 1858. The barn-like structure to the left was the original shop in 1852. The office and "repository," i.e., showroom, to the right were added later.

fifty cents a day. Later, he taught school. Henry, for his part, stuck to blacksmithing. Then, the two brothers made a decision that was to change the course of the family's life: They decided to go into business together.

H. & C. Studebaker was established on February 16, 1852, as a wagon-making business. The total capitalization was $68—$40 of which was said to have been a loan from Henry's wife—and two forges. From this humble beginning, the Studebaker brothers, Henry (then aged twenty-six) and Clem (aged twenty-one), launched an enterprise that was ultimately to become one of the largest manufacturers of horse-drawn vehicles in the world.

Business was slow at first, though. Only two or three wagons were built and sold that first year—one of which was still in daily service thirty-three years later—and the brothers were forced to scrape by with blacksmithing. That the Studebaker brothers knew how to make a good wagon was not a secret for long, however, and slowly the business began to grow by word-of-mouth advertising from their increasing numbers of satisfied customers.

Soon, a third brother, John Mohler, arrived in South Bend to join his older siblings. As fate would have it, though, he was soon lured even further westward by tales of gold in California. The nineteen-year-old John Mohler—known to his family and friends as "J.M."—decided to follow the thousands of hopefuls in the gold rush stampede to California to seek his fortune. He and his brothers built a wagon for the trip and J.M. traded it to a passing expedition in return for his passage. Five months later, in August, 1853—after he had lost virtually all his money playing his first-ever card game *en route* (three-card monte)—the group arrived in the center of gold fever in Hangtown.

Hangtown, a ramshackle burg of muddy streets, possessed a name that was inspired by the character of all-to-many of its inhabitants and the quick justice they often inspired in other citizens.[4] Half-a-century later, in 1912, at a celebration at the very site of his arrival, J.M. recalled:

> We were more than five months on the road, and landed here on this square in August, 1853, and I had but fifty cents in my pocket. Although that was my only earthly possession, my spirit was not daunted, for we were all led to believe that all we had to do was to go out on the morrow and dig up all the gold that the heart could desire.[5]

Surprisingly (at least to the new arrivals), the crowd that had gathered at the approach of the wagon train ignored all requests for directions to the gold. The only thing in which the citizens of Hangtown seemed to be interested was news of family and friends back east, about whom most had heard little or nothing for months. One townsman, however, wanted to know something else. J.M. continued:

> While the hubbub was going on, a man came up and asked if there was a wagon maker in the crowd of new arrivals. They pointed me out, and he asked, "Are you a wagon maker?" "Yes, sir," I answered as big as life, with my fifty cent piece in my pocket. He offered me a job in his shop, and I replied, "I came to California to mine for gold."
>
> After he had gone, a man stepped up very politely and said,

"Will you let me give you a little advice, young man?" And, upon my replying in the affirmative, [he] continued, "Take that job and take it quick." His manner impressed me. He said that there would be plenty of time to dig gold, it wasn't always a sure thing, and that the job just offered me was a mighty fine chance for a stranger. I was impressed, and decided to go to work for the wagon maker.[6]

It turned out to be a smart move. During the California Gold Rush, a lot more money was made selling picks, shovels and myriad supplies to the fortune seekers than was ever made digging gold. In J.M.'s case, he discovered that Joe Hinds, the wagon maker, wanted some help in manufacturing wheelbarrows to sell to the miners. Moreover, Hinds was willing to pay ten dollars a week for a qualified assistant. As J.M. was eminently qualified and, as the sum involved was a handsome wage, indeed, for a young man in 1853, it proved a profitable arrangement for both of them.

Again, as J.M. recalled it:

The tools were poor, and material only pitch and lumber. I stuck to the job, made many wheelbarrows, and put my money in the bank. I soon found that hundreds and thousands of the pioneers who tried the mines never made a cent, but those who stuck to steady jobs at good wages and saved their money were doing well. We worked many a night all night, frequently making miners' picks and repairing stage coaches, which came in late, and had to get out at six o'clock in the morning.[7]

J.M. became so proficient at making wheelbarrows that he earned the nickname, "Wheelbarrow Johnny." He was prospering, too. Within three years, he had saved $3,000. Hanging onto it proved a challenge on at least one occasion, though—and not because of the card games he had forsworn after his one and only sad experience on the trip west. He recalled:

When the Adams Express Company failed, I had $3,000 in the bank—all the money I had in the world. Hinds, my partner, had $22,000 in the same bank. I remember that it was two o'clock in

Hangtown, California, as it appeared in the mid-1850s.

the afternoon that the bank was closed, and we all knew that if it didn't open the next morning the boys would come in and tear up everything, provided they thought there was any money in the place. That's where Hinds and his level head came in. He knew that the express people would try to get their money out that night, for the failure was caused by lack of money elsewhere, and not at Hangtown. The bank backed right up against Hangtown Creek, and without saying a word to anybody Hinds made up his plan. He hid in the brush back of the bank just across the creek, and watched.

Sure enough, just as he expected, he saw the express people creep out of the building at about two o'clock in the morning with the bags of gold. He trailed them and saw them put the money in old Joe Douglas' safe. The rest was easy for Hinds. He waked me up and told me what had been done, and said he was going to levy an attachment on the safe, and from what he saw he was confident there was enough to pay us both, so he asked me if I wanted to stand in on the attachment suit. Of course I did, and we got out the papers bright and early. You can depend on it we didn't waste any time. Douglas, the old sinner, denied that the money was in his safe, but the officer found it and served the attachment, and as there was no defense we got the coin in short order, every dollar of it, while hundreds of others, after long waiting, received only fifteen to thirty per cent. Hinds threw that money into a wheelbarrow and trundled it through the streets of Hangtown.[8]

J.M. continued to prosper and, within five years, he had amassed $8,000—which he had stashed away, as he no longer trusted banks—a small fortune in 1858.[9] He kept in touch with his brothers in South Bend all this time. His letters frequently contained suggestions, based on his experiences in the rugged West, regarding ways in which Studebaker wagons could be improved. These suggestions were taken to heart by Henry and Clem, and, as a result, the reputation of the Studebaker wagon steadily grew.

Back in South Bend, however, H. & C. Studebaker was having a rough time. Financing was hard to find and without it Henry and Clem couldn't build enough wagons to maintain profitability. Then, in 1857, George Milburn, who ran a wagon factory in Mishiwaka, was unable to fill a large order for army wagons and asked the brothers to build one hundred of them as sub-contractors. This they did and their eyes were opened to the possibilities of running a large scale enterprise. Yet, without additional financing sustained growth was impossible. They had few tools, were forced to buy their materials at high prices as needed from the local hardware store and, worst of all, had to trade many of their wagons to farmers or take notes on which it proved difficult to collect. Their wagons were good and had a growing demand, but cash was hard to find in Indiana.

Another, and even more serious, problem that reared its head at about this time was a religious one. Those wagons that George Milburn had sub-contracted to the Studebaker brothers were intended for use in suppressing the members of the Church of Jesus Christ of Latter Day Saints, better known as the Mormons. Ironically, the Mormons had become good customers for Studebaker wagons, too. Their sins (in the eyes of Washington, at least) were the practice of polygamy and the widespread view that the Mormon church was conspiring to take over the Utah Territory and run it as a theocracy in violation of the separation of church and state mandated by the U. S. Constitution. There were also charges that the Mormons were harassing non-Mormon settlers passing through on the way to California and were destroying official records that were the property of the Utah territorial government. Upon subsequent investigation, most of these allegations proved to be either totally unfounded or greatly exaggerated, but, in the meantime, the army was dispatched to put an end to the "treason" running rampant out in Utah—by force if necessary.

In all, the Mormon War of 1857-58—also known as Buchanan's Blunder, after the president who ordered it—posed much more than a business dilemma for the firm of H. & C. Studebaker; it developed into a major religious crisis. The Dunkards were devoutly opposed to war and supplying combatants was deemed to be very nearly as reprehensible as personal involvement in the conflict itself. To make matters even worse for the Studebaker brothers, George Milburn had been accused of profiteering on his contracts to the War Department. So, when the deacons of the local Dunkard church paid a call on Henry Studebaker, the brothers suddenly found themselves at a crossroads. A biography of Clement Studebaker explained it this way:

> Under the influence of the persuasion of his Dunker brethren and yielding to the inclinations of his own heart, Henry expressed a desire to retire from the business which he and Clem had established...and to go into farming.[10]

In a nutshell, it had become clear that the "plain" ways of the Dunkards were incompatible with the ways of the business world. Faced with a choice between the two, Henry followed his family's traditional religious faith, while Clem—and, as it turned out, the rest of the brothers—found themselves increasingly alienated from the Dunkard movement. The business couldn't survive without growing and growth was impossible if the firm was restricted to the customers the local deacons approved. But, Clem needed money to buy Henry out. Barring that, the firm would be unable to take advantage of the only profitable business it had yet known. In a short time, Henry and Clem found themselves facing judgments against their firm from angry creditors and something drastic had to be done. So, five years after J.M. left for California, Henry and Clem wrote to him and begged him to return, buy out Henry and invest in the firm. He finally agreed.

J.M. had his $8,000 sewn into a leather belt, boarded a sailing ship at San Francisco bound for New York via the Isthmus of Panama and set off for home. Upon arriving in South Bend, he paid Henry $3,000 for his share and put the rest of his savings into the firm, while Henry, tired and discouraged, retired to the farming life. J.M. and Clem would run the firm from that point on, with J.M., twenty-four, in charge of manufacturing and Clem, twenty-six, managing the office. By that time, too, the firm had acquired a slogan and the evidence suggests that J.M. himself thought it up: "Aways give a little more than you promise."

Shortly after returning to South Bend, J.M. got married. His bride was

The Studebaker brothers, left to right: Clement, Henry, J.M, Peter and Jacob.

Abraham Lincoln's Studebaker carriage.

Mary Jane Stull, daughter of a well-to-do Dunkard family that farmed out-side South Bend. It was winter and they had intended to catch a train west to Chicago for their honeymoon. A blizzard stopped all the westbound trains, though, so they caught one going eastbound and spent their honey-moon in Goshen, Indiana, with J.M.'s younger brother Peter, who had be-come a successful merchant.

Even on his honeymoon, J.M. apparently couldn't stop talking busi-ness and, soon after his return to South Bend, Peter had erected a shed next to his store for the display of Studebaker wagons. It was the first Studebaker showroom outside South Bend and proved to be an instant success. Peter demanded more and more wagons to satisfy his growing clientele and his brothers were only too happy to supply them. Partly as a result, H. &. C. Studebaker grew rapidly. By 1860, the firm included a manufacturing shop, a paint room, a lumber yard and an office.

It was also about this time that the firm began to build carriages. As with the wagons, Studebaker carriages quickly earned an enviable reputa-tion. Within a short time, a Studebaker carriage was purchased by the White House, and it was this carriage that President and Mrs. Lincoln used to drive to Ford's Theater on the night of Lincoln's assassination in 1865.

Yet, the firm's sales were aided most significantly by the Civil War, which proved to be the true beginning of Studebaker's national reputation and real prosperity. This fact caused the Studebaker brothers quite a bit of discomfort, according to old accounts, owing to their religious views. While J.M. may not have been as strict as his older brother Henry, he had still refused to let his youngest brother, Jacob, join the Union Army. Business was business, though, and this was not the last conflagration in which Studebaker resources were to play a notable role. Shortly after the war began, government purchasing agents fanned out across the Northern states offering contracts to any business that could supply the Union's enormous need for military goods of almost any description. When the purchasing agents arrived in South Bend, the Studebaker brothers were ready for them. Noted a company history published in 1918:

> Ammunition, clothing, accoutrements, food, horses, saddles, harness, wagons, ambulances, and other things were immediately demanded by the United States Government. Wagons and ambulances were essential to the movement of troops and supplies. Where were they to be obtained in quantities? Where did the government look? According to the Bureau of Census report of 1870, H. & C. Studebaker were a most important source of supply. New buildings and equipment were provided, and many vehicles were furnished for war purposes, but the report says the Studebakers were unable to satisfy fully the demands made upon them. When the war ended, the reputation of Studebaker vehicles had widened to cover the East as well as the West, and the firm of H. & C. Studebaker had become an important factor in the industrial life of the nation.[11]

Studebaker wagons, it would seem, were appreciated by both sides in the war. A few days before the Battle of Gettysburg, a Confederate soldier wrote home with the following piece of news:

> We have burned parts of Chambersburg [Pennsylvania] and robbed the bank there. But best of all we captured a lot of blankets and food [and] sixteen Studebaker wagons into which we put part

of our powder train. It's summer and hot and the fruit is green. The farmers are well off and we shall be in Washington in a week at the most.[12]

It didn't quite work out that way, of course—the wagons ended up being used to evacuate Confederate wounded after the Southern defeat— but things were certainly working out well for the Studebaker brothers. The personal experience that thousands of soldiers had with Studebaker wagons during the war helped mightily to spread the company's reputation. By 1867, H. & C. Studebaker was turning out 6,000 vehicles each year, including wagons, carriages and buggies. The factory had expanded to four acres and 140 workers were employed at a payroll of more than $1,500 per week. The total assets of the company, which were valued at $10,000 when J.M. returned from California, had risen to an astonishing $223,269 and sales had reached $350,000 a year. Indeed, the company had grown so large that the brothers deemed it advisable to incorporate. This was done and, on March 26, 1868, the Studebaker Brothers Manufacturing Company was incorporated under the laws of Indiana with a capitalization of $75,000.

J.M. and Clem were joined in the corporation by Peter Studebaker. Peter, a gifted salesman, had decided there was more money to be made in

The Studebaker factory as it appeared in 1868. The original shop dating from 1852 had been torn down by this time to make way for needed expansion of the factory complex.

A Studebaker wagon.

wagons than in dry goods, and he was given the task of managing the sales and marketing effort for the company. Clem was named president, J.M. treasurer and Peter secretary (in addition to his sales duties), at annual salaries of $2,000 each. The combination of Clem, J.M., and Peter worked fabulously well right from the start. Just to make sure there would be no misunderstanding as to the working relationship between the brothers, though, Clem and Peter signed the following agreement:

> I, Peter Studebaker, agree to sell all the wagons my brother Clem can make.
> (signed) Peter Studebaker
>
> I agree to make all he can sell.
> (signed) Clem Studebaker[13]

Shortly after the incorporation, Peter began establishing sales and ser-

A Studebaker sprinkler.

vice branches around the country. The first was in St. Joseph, Missouri, near Kansas City. St. Joseph was an important way station and staging point on the main route of westward migration and the pioneers, who knew first hand of the unusual quality of the Studebaker wagon, spread the word with them. The Mormons, having reached a peaceful accommodation with Washington, continued to be large buyers. Additional branches soon followed in Salt Lake City, San Francisco, Kansas City, Portland (Oregon), Dallas, Minneapolis, Chicago, New York, Denver and other important cities. In this way, Studebaker became a business of truly national scope. As early as 1872, the brothers were proclaiming their company to be the "largest vehicle builders in the world." It may even have been true.

The fifth Studebaker brother, Jacob, joined the company in 1870 when the company employed 240 workers and was already the largest employer in South Bend. Under the combined efforts of the four brothers, the firm grew by the end of the century to immense size and profitability.

One of the interesting facts that can be ascertained from the financial statements of the company in the latter decades of the century, however, is the extent to which the Studebaker brothers plowed profits back into the business. Between 1868 and 1874, Studebaker Brothers Manufacturing Company reported sales of $4.3 million. Although profit figures are not available, the fact that the company soared from $360,619 in sales in 1868 to $761,116 in 1874 would certainly suggest that the firm was doing very well. And, yet, the brothers took dividends on their stock only once, in 1871, and then for a mere $107,587.48. After that, with annual sales on a seemingly unending upward course, they took modest dividends annually, but not until sales hit $4 million did combined dividends ever exceed $200,000.[14] Would that their successors had taken the same prudent approach.

It had not been an easy climb for the Studebaker brothers and they were not ones to blandly assume the good times would continue to roll. Indeed, they had their share of troubles even after the company hit the big time. In June, 1872, a devastating fire nearly wiped them out. The factory was soon rebuilt on an even grander scale and the surviving records barely show a blip in the sales curve. A second big fire in 1874 destroyed two-thirds of the works. This time, despite the devastation, the brothers rebuilt the factory even faster and made it even larger and better than ever.[15]

In 1876, the brothers celebrated their silver anniversary with a big dinner in South Bend. Clem made a speech. In it he noted a bit of the brothers' working philosophy of business:

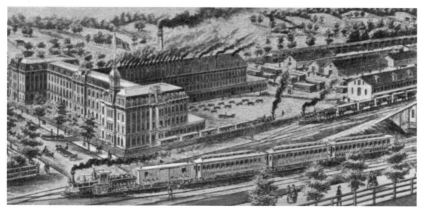

The Studebaker factory in 1872 as rebuilt after the first great fire.

The interest of the employer and the employee are identical. Capital cannot succeed without labor; nor can labor expect its reward without capital. What is to the interest of one is to the interest of the other.[16]

The following year, John Studebaker, the brothers' father, passed away at the ripe old age of seventy-nine. Following his death, J.M. and Mary finally dropped out of the Dunkard movement and joined the Presbyterian Church in South Bend.

In 1878, the company exhibited its wagons at the Paris Exposition and won a silver medal for excellence. Clem had even been appointed by the government to be the United States Commissioner to the exposition. It was an honor, he joked, that didn't even pay for his cigars. Back home, Studebaker carriages continued to grow in esteem with the best people (or, at least, with the people who *thought* they were the best people), and became increasingly popular with the nation's movers and shakers, as well. Presidents Grant and Hayes, for example, used Studebaker carriages, as had President Lincoln before them.

Even foreign potentates were desirous of being seen in Studebaker carriages, it seemed. It was at about this time that the Sultan of Zanzibar ordered two Studebakers. The order, from an aide to the Sultan named Peera Dewjee, indicated that the Sultan wanted them badly:

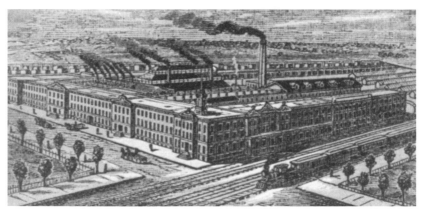

The Studebaker factory in 1876 as rebuilt after the second great fire.

I hereby beg to address you these few lines, and am glad to say that I have seen your illustrated catalogue of carriages, sent by one of my friends from England, from which I chose two for His Highness...Please send me a reply, as His Highness is anxious to have the carriages at once.[17]

According to some, the Studebaker brothers themselves were acting a little high and mighty by this time. Peter Studebaker, by all accounts an unusually affable and popular man, got worked up on the subject during the 1880 presidential campaign. He noted in a speech to Studebaker workers (whose number had by then risen to 890):

It is a favorite theme of the Democrats to abuse Republican manufacturers. Do they remind you that the American laborer can buy more flour, more meat and potatoes with his wages than any other laborer can in any other country on the face of the globe? Do they remind you that while a small profit on a large business will make your employer rich, at the same time a small loss on the same business will break him up? No! They tell you none of these things, but they try to impress upon you that your employers are tyrants and robbers!

Workmen, I know what it is to be poor. I know what it is to work for fifty cents a day and board myself. I know what it is to wish for the first white shirt. I know what it is to live week-in and week-out on mush and milk. I know what it is to sleep next to a clapboard roof and have the snow blow in and cover my head. I know what it is to stand on the outside of a circus tent and hear the music and the clown within, and wish I had a quarter to take me in. I know more. I know what it is to look wishfully in a show case, filled with gingerbread, and wish I had a penny to buy some. Knowing these things from hard experience, I say it makes my blood boil to hear any man say one word that will tend to encourage a man in a waste of time and idleness.[18]

A rumor was even circulated that the Studebaker Brothers Manufacturing Company would fire any worker who voted for the Democratic ticket. Peter was furious, blamed rival wagon makers for spreading the rumor and offered $1,000 to anyone who could substantiate it. No one tried to collect. In fact, J.M. himself was a Democrat (unlike his brothers), although he said he would vote for Garfield, the Republican candidate. Still, angry Democrats in the South threatened a boycott of Studebaker wagons in retaliation. Shortly before the election—which Garfield won—the good citizens of Dodd, Texas, sent the following letter to South Bend:

> Since the information that you threatened to disenfranchise your workers who have failed to vote as you directed, we have this day made arrangements to purchase one of your wagons, "coal oil" same and burn it in the presence of the voters of this precinct. The event will be duly advertised and published, with a request that the press of the state copy. We burn the Studebaker wagon without knowing who will be President. We burn it in the same spirit that the tea was thrown overboard in Boston harbor in 1776.[19]

In response, hundreds of Studebaker workers signed a statement in which they noted that most of them were Democrats and that they would feel free to vote against Garfield if they darned well felt like it. In a final comment on the affair, J.M. said that anyone who would burn a wagon was an "idiot," and recalled General Sherman's celebrated wisecrack: "If I owned hell and Texas, I'd rent out Texas and live in hell."[20]

Beginning in the 1880s, the uproar surrounding the 1880 election not withstanding, the factory continued to expand almost exponentially. New types of vehicles were added at a steady rate, many designed for local governments: sprinklers, flushers, sweepers, dump wagons and so forth.

In 1885, the Studebaker Repository was built on Michigan Avenue in the heart of Chicago. This building, a giant sales and service center, was then the one of the most grandiose structures in downtown Chicago. Later it was turned into a fine arts building, housing the Studebaker Theatre and the Studebaker Playhouse—both subsidized by the company. The Chicago Repository was the project of Jacob, the youngest brother, who died at forty-three shortly after it was completed. He was the first of the Studebaker

The Studebaker brougham built for President Benjamin Harrison.

brothers to go. Also in 1885, the factory in South Bend experienced yet another big fire. It was difficult to avoid conflagrations in a business that used so much wood and highly-flammable varnish, and the company was used to them by this time. The works were rebuilt in record time.

Dealer franchises were extended far and wide in the 1880s, largely under the leadership of Peter Studebaker. By the end of the century, the company had dealers in virtually every community of any consequence in the United States and in many foreign countries, as well. While there is some dispute as to whether the company was ever the largest manufacturer of horse-drawn vehicles in the world, it was clearly near the top of the pack by the middle of the 1880s.

Then, in 1887, Clem, flushed with success, built himself a house. He had owned houses before, of course, but none like this. In fact, no one in Indiana had ever had a house such as the one Clem built. Called Tippecanoe Place (after President William Henry Harrison of "Tippecanoe and Tyler, too" fame), it was a monstrous pile of limestone complete with vast lawns and luxuriant gardens—a veritable castle, in fact. It was supposedly the largest house ever built in Indiana (a claim that no one contested) and, in celebration of its completion, Clem decided to throw himself a house-warming party. Things were fated to get warmer than even Clem could have imagined, though. Two days before the scheduled date, Tippecanoe Place burned to the ground. Fires were becoming old hat for the Studebaker brothers by that juncture, though, and Clem, trouper that he was, held the party, anyway, in the blackened basement. Within a few months the entire pile had been rebuilt as good as new.

When Benjamin Harrison (grandson of William Henry) was elected from Indiana to be President of the United States in 1888, one of his first acts was to make sure the White House garage was fully stocked with Studebaker equipment. The itemized bill sent by the Studebaker Brothers Manufacturing Company listed the following:[21]

Landau	$1,600
Brougham	1,300
Victoria	1,500
Mail Phaeton	850
Mail Buggy	450
Set of double harness for landau	550
Set of double harness for brougham	350
Set of single harness	225
Robes, whips, coachmen's livery	300
Total	$7,075

By the 1890s, the brothers decided a new slogan was needed for the company. Their father's old slogan—"Owe no man anything but to love one another"—had long since passed into history. The other early attempts at a slogan for the Studebaker Brothers Manufacturing Company was, of course, "Always give a little more than you promise." Nothing wrong with that. Still, J.M. thought something classier was needed, something in Latin perhaps. So, the new slogan became, "Labor Amnia Vincit." There were various interpretations offered in English by J.M.: "Labor Conquers All," or "Work Always Wins." In fact, the slogan had been used in advertisements as early as 1867, but now—whatever it meant—it was official.

Peter seems to have had as much fun with words as his older brother. (Perhaps growing up with a name such as Studebaker encouraged a light-hearted attitude toward the language.) The most popular Studebaker buggy of the era was known as the "Izzer" buggy. The name, according to Peter, came to him one day while listening to a horse trader trying to sell a horse to a farmer. The trader boasted about all the blue ribbons the horse had supposedly won in past county fairs, but the farmer cut him off. "They're all has-beens," he snorted. "I don't want a wuzzer. What I want is an izzer!"

The Studebaker Brothers Manufacturing Company, which had survived wars and fires, was finally laid low by the financial panic of 1893. The en-tire nation was stunned by the sharp depression and, for a time, wagon orders all-but dried-up. The brothers were reluctantly forced to shutter the factory for five weeks. When a few workers were at last called back, they were asked to work at reduced wages. Sales fell from $2.3 million in 1892, to $1.9 million in 1893 and then to $1.6 million in 1894 before rising again. There was some worker unrest in this period—a first for Studebaker, where labor relations had been unusually good—and, in other industries, there were even riots and bloodshed. Addressing Studebaker workers, J.M. struck a conciliatory note that revealed much about Studebaker family values:

> I feel that you deserve the same right to be proud of the growth and prosperity of our institution that we [the brothers] have our-selves. I consider that every employee, so long as he gets his com-pensation, he gets his daily bread out of it, and that is all I get. God has enabled me, without being your superior, to reach a little higher power, to afford a little more luxury living, but that is all. Happiness and contentment make the true wealth of this world.[22]

In 1893, and for the first time since 1877, the brothers took no divi-dends. They had never believed in fat dividends, anyway, preferring to put as much money as possible back into the business. It was a thrifty, hard-nosed attitude they had come by honestly through the many vicissi-tudes they had endured. Looking back on their lives, the Studebaker broth-ers had a lot about which to be proud, of course, but they still could not forget the struggles they had had to face along the way. In 1897, when Clem spoke to a gathering of early pioneers in Ashland, Ohio, he spoke of the hard work and the hardship. It was a theme to which the brothers kept returning in public speeches, together with the lessons of industry and thrift that they had learned from their mutual experiences. As a Studebaker booklet published shortly after his death put it:

> In 1897, a reunion of former residents at Ashland, Ohio, was attended by 10,000 people, among whom were the three Studebaker brothers, it being their first visit since their removal nearly fifty years before. Clem was the spokesman for the family, and read a most interesting paper, reciting an unvarnished story of the early ups and downs of the family, its struggles and triumphs, and the poverty which had encompassed all. Seldom was told a more pathetic and realistic talk of the struggles of a pioneer family.

The week after the reunion in Ashland in 1897, Peter Studebaker died at the age of sixty-one. He was vice-president of the company and its general manager at the time of his death.

The Studebaker family had achieved national prominence by the time of Peter's death. They were particularly active in business and civic affairs

The Studebaker factory in 1890.

Frederick S. Fish.

in nearby Chicago, where their circle of friends and associates included such movers-and-shakers of the age as George M. Pullman (inventor of the railroad sleeping car), P. D. Armour (one of the founders of the meat-packing industry), Marshall Field (of department store fame) and Cyrus McCormick (the founder of the company that was to become International Harvester). The brothers also invested heavily in Chicago real estate and made a good deal of money in that sphere.

But, business went on as usual in South Bend—better than usual, in fact. By 1895, the panic was forgotten and the Studebaker factory was working twelve-hour shifts to try to keep up with the rush of orders. Sales returned to the pre-panic level of $2.3 million that year, then to $2.8 million in 1897, and to nearly $4 million in 1899, the final year of the century.

Even before the death of Peter Studebaker, the aging of the brothers had mandated the hiring and promotion of others outside the family to assist in the running of the company. Most notable among these individuals was Frederick S. Fish. A New Jersey corporation lawyer from a prominent Eastern family, he was active in state politics and had risen to the presidency of the New Jersey Senate by the time he married Grace Studebaker, one of J.M.'s daughters, in 1891.

After marrying into the Studebaker family, Fish found himself subjected to the "repeated insistence of J.M. together with Clem and Peter" that he pull up stakes and move to South Bend. He resisted at first, but soon gave in and began his career with Studebaker Brothers Manufacturing Company as general counsel. When Peter died, Fish was elected chairman of the company's executive committee and, in effect, took over day-to-day management. He quickly moved to modernize the business by restructuring it along corporate lines. In this way, the easy-going family enterprise was placed on a sound footing to enter the Twentieth Century.

The worldwide influence the company had attained was amply illustrated by the Boer War between Britain and the rebellious Afrikaaner settlers in South Africa. The British Government came to Studebaker to supply a large part of its needs for military wagons and ambulances. When the war ended, Lord Roberts, the commander of the British forces in South Africa, said in his official report:

> Wagons were imported from the United States, and they proved to be superior to any other make, either of Cape or English manufacture. The superiority of these vehicles was doubtless due to the fact that in America such wagons are largely used for the carriage of goods as well as for military transport. It may be added that they cost considerably less than Bristol pattern wagons.[23]

He was, it goes without saying (but we'll say it anyway), referring to Studebaker wagons. Nor had the United States Government forgotten where to find good wagons when the need arose. When the Spanish-American War erupted in 1898, the Army immediately ordered five hundred Studebaker wagons and, moreover, requested that they be shipped—complete with special paint and stencils—within thirty-six hours. They were.

In November, 1896, shortly before Peter Studebaker passed into history, the board of directors took a step that would have a far-reaching effect on the future direction of the company. Fish had been agitating for the company to test the waters in the fledgling automobile industry. He saw the start of something big, but the Studebaker board—and especially J.M. and Clem—were dead set against it. The wagon business was doing better than ever, while the auto industry would prove to be a passing fad or a rich man's toy—either way of no interest to Studebaker. Fish persisted, though, and finally a comparatively modest sum of $4,000 was appropriated for the building and testing of a "horseless vehicle." Reportedly, an experimental electric car was the goal, although little is known about it or even if a workable vehicle ever resulted.

Then, in 1897 or 1898, the company entered into a contract to build bodies for electric taxi cabs being produced by the Electric Vehicle Company, a firm that had been formed by Colonel Alexander Pope and others with the intention of monopolizing public transportation in the major metropolitan areas. In this pursuit, the Electric Vehicle Company was notably unsuccessful, but the venture did serve to introduce one of its key executives, Harold Hayden Eames, to Studebaker. This would have important ramifications later on.

Following that episode, Studebaker agreed to produce as many as a thousand bodies for an electric runabout manufactured by another company, although it seems highly unlikely that anything like that number could actually have been built. Later, in 1900, negotiations were entered into to purchase the rights to a steam car being developed in Detroit by Byron J. Carter. Carter, one of the most ingenious of the early auto pioneers, sold his steam car to another firm, though, and that was the end of that.[24] In the same year, rumors circulated that Studebaker was negotiating

A Hansom cab of the type Studebaker built for the Electric Vehicle Company.

to buy the Muson Electric Motor Company of La Porte, Indiana, but nothing came of that deal, either.

Then, in November, 1901, Clem Studebaker died at the age of seventy. His widow contributed funds for a new St. Paul's Methodist Episcopal Church to be erected in his memory in South Bend. Only J.M. among the five Studebaker brothers soldiered on.

Times were, indeed, changing and the old guard on Studebaker's board was dying off. Undeterred by past rebuffs and encouraged by the improved composition of the board, Fred Fish was more determined than ever to see the company enter the growing automobile field under its own name.

Notes

The most important resources drawn upon in the writing of this chapter include Albert Russel Erskine's *History of the Studebaker Corporation*, Stephen Longstreet's official company history, *A Century on Wheels: The Story of Studebaker*, Marvin Studebaker's *The Studebakers of South Bend* and Studebaker National Museum Archives in South Bend, Indiana. Periodicals used for important anecdotes and sidelights include the *Indiana History Bulletin*, the *Indiana Magazine of History, Pennsylvania Folklife*, and the *South Bend Tribune*.

1. The Mohler family eventually established a famous pipe organ factory in nearby Hagerstown, Maryland. Still later, they took a fling at the automobile business, as well, building a small number of very expensive cars under the Dagmar nameplate.
2. One of his wagons, built in 1830 before the move to Ashland, was a prized exhibit in the Studebaker museum years later.
3. Studebaker, pp. 79-80.
4. Hangtown is now known by the less evocative name of Placerville and is located about thirty-five miles due east of Sacramento.
5. Erskine, 1918, p. 17-19.
6. Erskine, 1918, p. 19.
7. Longstreet, p. 17.
8. Longstreet, p. 18-19.
9. Joe Hinds ran into hard times after the Gold Rush fizzled, and eventually

came to South Bend looking for work. He was hired by J.M. as an assistant foreman in the wagon works and later rose to the position of plant superintendent. He died in 1879.

10. Pennsylvania Folklife, Spring 1992, p. 121.

11. Erskine, 1924, pp. 18-19.

12. Longstreet, pp. 35-36.

13. Longstreet, p. 37.

14. All profit figures used in this book—unless otherwise noted—are computed after Federal taxes (where applicable) but before dividends were paid out, and, furthermore, are rounded-off to the nearest $100,000.

15. From $608,614 in 1871, sales rose to $687,963 in 1872, then to $820,019 in 1873, and dipped modestly to $761,116 in 1874. By 1875, it had soared again—to $1,032,040, Studebaker Brothers Manufacturing Company's first million-dollar year.

16. Longstreet, p. 45.

17. Longstreet, p. 55-56.

18. Longstreet, p. 48-49.

19. Longstreet, p. 51.

20. Indiana was the second state to adopt the so-called "Australian ballot" in 1889, i.e., the modern secret ballot. Prior to that time, voters in Indiana signed a registration book at the polling place and were given paper ballots for straight-party-line voting, i.e., a Republican ballot or a Democratic ballot.

21. Until 1909, Presidents of the United States were expected to supply their own transportation. William Howard Taft, who was inaugurated that year, enjoyed the first fleet of automobiles (or any other kind of vehicles, for that matter) purchased at government expense. Since, prior to that time, the president owned his own carriages and/or automobiles, he generally took them with him when he left office.

22. Longstreet, p. 60.

23. Longstreet, p. 63.

24. Carter, a close friend of Henry Leland, one of the founders of Cadillac, eventually founded a company to build the Cartercar, an odd friction-drive automobile that enjoyed a minor vogue in the latter years of the first decade of the century. William C. Durant was intrigued enough with the technology to buy the company following Carter's death in 1908 and make it one of the first divisions of General Motors. The friction-drive vogue, such as it was, proved to be short-lived, however, and the last Cartercar was built in 1915. Lamented Durant, "How was anyone to know the Cartercar wasn't the thing?"

*Overleaf, the E-MF chassis assembly room in the days before the advent of mass
production and the moving assembly line.*

TWO

The Early Auto Years

Although the modern-day perception is that the automobile put the horse-drawn vehicle manufacturers out of business, many of the early automobile companies were, in fact, direct or indirect outgrowths of the carriage industry. As the possibilities of the new technology became known around the turn-of-the-century, numerous carriage makers began offering as sidelines self-propelled vehicles of various descriptions, as Studebaker did in 1902. Many others got involved as suppliers of bodies with the pioneering companies that were developing the new mode of transportation, as Studebaker had as early as 1897. Still others got involved as partners with pioneering auto makers, as Studebaker was to do from 1904. This was perfectly logical, for the body work on those first automobiles drew heavily on carriage technology; i.e., they were horseless carriages in the literal sense of the term. William C. Durant, the founder of General Motors, got into the automobile business in this fashion, as did Charles Nash, Edward Murphy (of the Oakland Motor Car Company, later to become Pontiac), the Fisher brothers (of Fisher Body fame) and, of course, John Mohler Studebaker. The Studebaker Brothers Manufacturing Company, however, would be the only top-ranked carriage builder to make a direct transition to being a top-ranked automobile producer and, by all accounts, that achievement was due to the tireless exertions of Fred Fish, J.M.'s son-in-law.[1]

Fish, the president of Studebaker, was, in the parlance of the day, an "automobilist"—what we would call a "motor head" or a "car nut"—and also an enthusiast of early aviation. A true believer in the coming transportation revolution, he was determined to protect Studebaker's position as a major vehicle manufacturer by getting the company involved in the nascent auto industry. Wanting to do it and actually doing it were not the same thing, of course, and there were destined to be numerous false starts before he succeeded. Along the way, Studebaker was to have involvements both tangential and intimate with an amazing number men who played critical roles in the development of the automobile. Indeed, the story of Studebaker's search for the right car comes dangerously close to being a "who's who" of the early industry. If the story seems confusing at times, it never-the-less offers a fascinating glimpse into the amazing inter-relationships of the early auto companies and the key men who worked in them.

As was noted at the conclusion of the previous chapter, the company's initial experimentation began in 1896 with an electric-powered car. That came to naught, but by 1897 or 1898 Studebaker was doing a flourishing business as a body supplier to other manufacturers of electric vehicles. Then, in 1900, came the unsuccessful efforts to purchase Munson and the rights to Byron Carter's promising steam car. No serious thought, apparently, had yet been given to the internal-combustion gasoline engine, but that lapse would be rectified in due course.

The early years of the industry were ones of trial and error for everyone, filled with repeated failures and dead ends. The most promising ventures sometimes turned to ashes, while the successes often came from entirely unexpected quarters. As the new century dawned, it was not even clear what form of motive power the new-fangled automobile would use. Essentially, there were three main types: electric motors, steam engines and internal-combustion gasoline engines.

Studebaker's wide-ranging search for the right form of motive power is a reflection on the confused state of the automotive art that existed at the time, for each type of power had its strengths and weaknesses, and each attracted the attention of serious manufacturers. Indeed, it was not uncommon for a single brand to offer two or three different types one after the other, or even concurrently. As it turned out, Studebaker was to mount efforts involving all three, assuming one counts the Carter steam car affair, although only the electric and gasoline programs ever came to fruition.

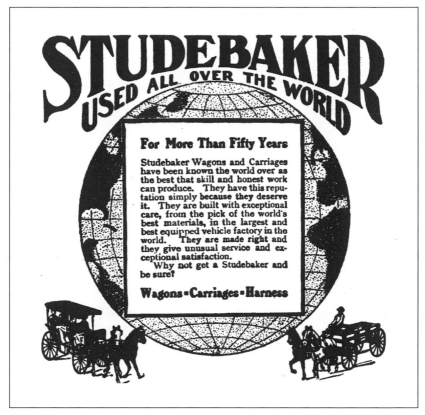

An advertisement for Studebaker horse-drawn vehicles, circa 1903.

Electric-powered cars were much favored even before the turn-of-the-century for taxi cabs in major urban centers such as New York City. Electric vehicles were clean, silent, reliable and easy to operate. They were also, unfortunately, heavy (due to the weight of the batteries), expensive (due to the cost of the batteries), and had very short range. The short range, in turn, was at least partly a by-product of the extreme weight of the batteries. Only a limited amount of energy could be stored and a disproportionate share of it was, owing to the weight of the batteries themselves, wasted lugging the batteries around rather than the car. One early motoring book estimated the weight-to-horsepower ratio of a typical electric car at 840 to 1—that is to say, 840 pounds of vehicle weight per horsepower—as compared with 185 to 1 for a gasoline car. That meant an electric vehicle was trying to move four-and-a-half times as much weight per unit of horsepower. (Steam cars, incidentally, were rated at 371 to 1.) In addition, recharging the batteries took, literally, hours, so transportation wasn't always there when it was needed and, on top of everything else, short battery life meant frequent and expensive replacement.[2]

While it was true that electric cars were considered by the urban social elite to be far more genteel than other types, one of Fred Fish's relations in New York City proved electric cars could still be dangerous in the wrong hands. According to a contemporary account:

> The lever which turned on the power was at the driver's side. All you had to do was to push the lever forward to go forward, back to go backwards, and upright to stop. This was considered simplicity itself, but the car's maker did not know Mrs. Fish.
>
> The first time she took the car out alone she started toward Third Avenue. Just as she got under way, a man crossed the street in front of the car. Mrs. Fish wanted to slow down, but she pushed the lever further forward, so the car kept going. It hit the man and knocked him down. She pulled the lever back—too far back—and the car slowly reversed and ran over the man again. This got Mrs. Fish really rattled. She moved the lever forward again—too far forward—and ran over the man a third time. Fortunately, the...man was not hurt much. Before Mrs. Fish had time to move the lever again, he got up and disappeared around the corner at high speed. Mrs. Fish managed to stop the car and left it right there. That was the last ride she ever had in it.[3]

Steam-powered cars, too, were clean, silent, reliable and easy to operate. They also suffered, to a certain extent, from a problem with range caused, in part, by weight—of the boiler, in this case—and they, too, tended to be rather expensive. In addition, there was the lengthy wait for the boiler to build up a head of steam after the car had been left sitting for a while. There was also a very real risk of fire with early steam cars. The boiler had to be lighted and there was always danger with an open flame. Gas stoves in homes sometimes blew up and so did steam cars, although not because of the boiler *per se*. On top of all that, in many states people who operated boilers of any kind had to be specially licensed. The State of New York, for example, saw no distinction under the law between the operator of a steam car and the operator of a giant steam railroad locomotive or a huge boiler providing steam heat for an office building. So, there were numerous drawbacks to steam power. Mostly, though, steam cars fell out of favor because people were afraid of them. With all that pressure, what if the boiler exploded? The fact that there was no known instance of a boiler exploding in a well-designed steam car failed to dampen the fears. Stanley, a renowned builder of steam cars, went to endless lengths to try to convince people that a boiler explosion was a practical impossibility, but to little avail.[4]

The internal-combustion engine seemed the runt of the litter at first. Early gasoline vehicles were noisy, smelly, crude, complicated, and by far the least reliable of the three types. They did, however, counter the perceived defects of electric and steam cars in significant ways. Full power was available more-or-less on demand (assuming the infernal contraption would start at all), speed far in excess of that offered by electric cars was

1902 Studebaker Electric.

generally available, refueling was as simple as pouring more gasoline into the tank, there was very little danger of explosion or fire, there were few legal restrictions on who could operate them, and gasoline-powered vehicles were (at least some of them) relatively cheap. From the perspective of increasing numbers of engineers, moreover, they held the greatest promise of easy development and improvement.[5]

The greatest influence on Studebaker, however, may have been the electric vehicle manufacturers with which it had become tangentially involved as a supplier of bodies. In any case, and whatever the reasoning behind its decision, the company finally took the plunge in 1902 after several years of experimentation and elected to do so with an electric-powered car. The sales catalog stated:

> As may be imagined, we have not been indifferent to the introduction of the horseless carriage. We have not, however, believed that it would be wise on our part or good faith toward the public to push upon the market an imperfect or immature product. We have expended a large of amount of time and money in experimenting and research conducted for us by experts in order that the machine of our adoption should be such that we could recommend and not discredit our standing in the vehicle world.

Reportedly, the first car was sold to F. W. Blees of Macon, Missouri, in February, 1902. The Studebaker Electric was a true horseless carriage sporting a body that was of obvious buggy design. The fenders and dashboard were made of leather, it used chain drive to transmit power to the rear wheels and a tiller for steering. The motor was a Westinghouse unit that was a standard for electric cars in the motor vehicle industry at the time, with the motor mounted underneath the body. Four forward speeds were offered and safety was enhanced by dual brakes. A Studebaker advertisement proclaimed ease of operation as its greatest virtue. "NO EXPERT CHAUFFEUR NEEDED," one ad screamed, "CAN BE RUN ANY DAY IN THE YEAR BY ANY MEMBER OF THE FAMILY." The top speed was around 13 miles per hour and the car had a forty-mile range between charges.

If the top speed of the Studebaker Electric seems ridiculously low, the standards of the time must be considered. Electrics were used primarily in urban areas—their range wouldn't permit cross-country touring, in any case—where their main competition was horse-drawn carriages and buggies. The latter had normal "cruising" speeds of four or five miles per hour and "high speed" capabilities of perhaps three times that rate for short distances. Gasoline cars did somewhat better. The first Cadillac, built in 1903, had a reported top speed of 35 miles per hour or thereabouts, but few people ever drove one that fast (and it was probably worth the lives of driver and passengers to do so). Furthermore, speed limits were very low in most urban areas—as low as four miles per hour in some major cities—and most of the roads of the day were primitive at best. In short, the Studebaker Electric was slow, but reasonably competitive in 1902.

A grand total of twenty Studebaker Electrics were sold that first year and one presumes that most buyers of electric cars, in general, had more luck than poor Mrs. Fish in the anecdote related above. For Studebaker, it was a start and additional models were added in subsequent years. Stanhope, victoria, four-passenger surrey and light delivery models were added in 1904, and the top speed was increased to a heady 14 miles per hour (with, according to some, the optional Edison battery of which more will follow). A four-passenger coupe and a stake truck came along in 1906.

The story behind the engineering of the Studebaker Electric is a confused one. If Studebaker's publicity in later years is to be believed, the car was designed by no less a figure than Thomas A. Edison, the father of the electric light bulb and an almost mythical figure in America by the turn of the century. It was also claimed that Edison took delivery of the second electric runabout produced. In fact, the truth seems to have been wildly inflated in this instance. Research indicates that Edison's involvement was both more interesting and more remote than the company's oft-related tale would have us believe.

Edison was one of the greatest inventor-geniuses of all-time, but he was the first to admit that his genius was, in his much-quoted phrase, "one per cent inspiration and ninety-nine per cent perspiration." His method was to seize upon a radical concept that intrigued him and then spend months or years in grueling trial-and-error work trying to find the solution that would make it a reality. Most of his celebrated discoveries were

Thomas A. Edison in his 1903 Studebaker Electric.

achieved this way, including the electric light bulb and the motion picture. Sometimes the perspiration worked, sometimes it didn't. This should hardly be surprising, although his triumphs are all that we remember.

It was around 1900 that Edison turned his attention to the fledgling auto industry. He became convinced that the automobile was going to replace the horse as soon as a cheap and reliable form of motive power could be developed. As a hard-headed businessman, he also realized the commercial potential for himself if he could get there first. The decision of which kind of motive power to develop was his first challenge.

After examining his options, Edison disagreed with the growing number of "experts"—a term which was at best relative given the state of the art of automobile engineering—and focused his attention on electric power. The crippling defect in electric cars, he realized, was the batteries then available, which were (as we have seen) too heavy, too expensive, incapable of storing sufficient charge, difficult to recharge and short-lived. Perhaps because he had been so stunningly successful with previous experiments with electrical devices, he became convinced that he could cure all these problems and, in so doing, revolutionize dry cell battery technology, revolutionize the auto industry and make a bundle for himself. Beginning around 1901, he and his associates spent two years doggedly experimenting.

An insight into Edison's methods was offered by a contemporary observer who happened to stop by the laboratory one day. Suddenly, there was an ear-splitting crash outside the window. The visitor was shaken, but Edison prattled on as if nothing were amiss. Shortly, a workman entered the office. "Second floor OK, Mr. Edison." Edison nodded. "Now try the third floor," he ordered, and only then bothered to explain to his visitor that he had directed his workmen to test cases for the new battery by dropping them from the windows of the building. "For a scientist," the visitor commented later, "Edison used some mighty peculiar methods."[6]

Toward the end of 1903, Edison announced that he had made the critical breakthrough and would enter production with his wonder battery in a few months. The news electrified the world.[7] Edison's battery breakthrough was greeted with enthusiasm in South Bend, as well. Significantly, though, the well-established chronology of Edison's research renders impossible Studebaker's later claim that he had designed their original electric car of 1902. In the first place, Edison never set out to design entire cars; he was only interested in the batteries. In the second place, his "revolutionary" battery did not enter production until well into 1904—at least two years after the first Studebaker Electric had been sold. In addition, while it is possible that Edison purchased the second Studebaker Electric manufactured, company illustrations of Edison at the wheel of what was alleged to be this "second" car clearly show the more curvaceous model that entered production in 1903 (and which was current in 1904), rather than the angular and austere original design of 1902. And, in fact, the only known photo of Edison in this car shows it bearing a 1903 New Jersey license plate.

What is known is that Studebaker was among the first companies to buy Edison's new batteries when they went into production. Unfortunately, the design failed to live up to its promise in actual use and Edison pulled the plug on the entire operation within a few months.[8] He did so, it should be noted, despite pleas from South Bend that he continue deliveries.

Studebaker's view of the situation, as related by Edison's biographers, was that while Edison's battery was less than hoped for it was an improvement over the batteries Studebaker (and, presumably, the other electric vehicle manufacturers) had been using up to that time. Edison refused Studebaker's entreaties, however, and that was apparently the end of Edison's involvement with Studebaker.

By 1910, Edison—who had doggedly continued his experimentation despite his initial disappointments (and, according to accounts, his considerable financial losses stemming from the failure)—did finally develop a battery that pleased him. Although it came too late to revolutionize the auto industry, it was used for a few years by several of the electric vehicle manufacturers still around at that juncture, including Detroit Electric and Baker Electric. It is unknown if Studebaker used this improved Edison battery, but there is no evidence that they did. In any event, Studebaker Electric production, which was never high, had been reduced to little more than a trickle by 1910 and ceased entirely by 1912. It must hardly have seemed worth the trouble to make a change so late in the game. A total of 1,841 electrics were built, in all.[9]

The debacle with the Edison battery notwithstanding, the electrics were never a big item for Studebaker, nor did it ever look as if they would be. Thus, since he first considered entering the auto industry, Fred Fish had tried electrics and steam cars (actually producing the former) and neither seemed to hold the promise the company sought. There was only one type of motive power left: the internal-combustion gasoline engine.

Accordingly, by 1903 at the latest—even before the Edison battery experience—Fish was pushing the idea of building gasoline cars as the only truly viable way of getting into the automobile business in a volume manner befitting a company that had long touted itself as one of the largest vehicle manufacturers in the world. He encountered predictably stiff opposition to this from the Studebaker board and, especially, from his father-in-law, whose views on the limitations of early gasoline cars were blunt— say the least. The gasoline automobiles at the turn-of-the-century were, in the deathless words of old J.M., "clumsy, dangerous, noisy brutes [that] stink to high heaven, break down at the worst possible moment and are a public nuisance."[10] In that, he had a point—certainly by the standards of engineering that existed in 1903—but it did not necessarily follow that gasoline automobiles were not the wave of the future. Fish, for one, had become convinced that they were. Indeed, by the time he began working to persuade his father-in-law toward this new direction for the company's automotive aspirations, it was becoming clear to most astute industry observers that the gasoline engine was going to win out in the end.

Still, while manufacturing the bodies posed no problem, Studebaker at this point possessed no engineering staff capable of designing any sort of gasoline engine. Even with the electric cars, Studebaker had built the bodies but bought the mechanical components on the outside, and electric car technology was simplicity itself compared to the challenges posed by building gasoline vehicles.

Basically, Fish had two options. Either Studebaker could buy components that could be assembled and sold under the Studebaker nameplate, or it could buy an existing producer of gasoline vehicles outright. It was not surprising that Fish sought to work out some sort of arrangement along the lines of the first option, but he was not adverse to pursuing the latter if the opportunity presented itself. In general, though, Fish appears at this stage to have been reluctant to commit Studebaker to manufacturing entire cars and this was understandable. Doing so upped the ante and the risk, guaranteed stout opposition from the old guard on Studebaker's board, and wasn't really necessary given the way the early industry was run.

Truth to tell, few automobile "manufacturers" of the day were manufacturers at all, but merely assemblers of components. This was true of all the most important producers, including Cadillac, Ford and Oldsmobile. Fish must also have understood that Studebaker's real strength was in its coast-to-coast distribution network, not in its manufacturing ability, which, insofar as automobiles was concerned, was embryonic at best. In short, Fish's prudent goal was to *sell* gasoline cars, not necessarily to build them.[11] Once the idea had taken root, a number of manufacturers were contacted, including the Garford Company in Cleveland, Ohio. The reason Garford came to Fish's attention was in all likelihood the presence on Garford's board of Hayden Eames, formerly of the Electric Vehicle Company, who served by reason of Albert Pope's investment in the firm. The time was the middle of 1903 and the course of events during the following year was

Hayden Eames.

destined to be confusing, indeed.[12]

Arthur L. Garford was something of a promoter; if there was a hot idea, he tried to run with it. He had made a fortune in the bicycle boom of the 1890s manufacturing bicycle seats for, among others, Albert Pope, and later capped his career by running for Governor of Ohio on Teddy Roosevelt's "Bull Moose" ticket in 1912. In 1903, he was convinced the automobile was the hot thing and was involved with Pope in an attempt to establish a manufacturing plant in Cleveland.

It seems likely that some sort of preliminary deal was reached with Studebaker by the late-summer of 1903. *Cycle and Automobile Trade Journal* announced a Studebaker-Garford tonneau (a two-passenger roadster with a detachable two-passenger section on the back) at that time. On the other hand, authorized Studebaker histories published in 1918, 1923 and 1952 all peg the summer of 1904 as the start of production for gasoline cars, as do other independently published Studebaker histories. In fact, there is no convincing evidence that a 1903 Studebaker-Garford ever existed.

Something, apparently, happened to delay the deal between Studebaker and Garford, and there is good reason to believe that the problem was turbulence in Cleveland. Garford, it was said, was trying to sever his relationship with Pope, whom he feared wanted to take over the company. At least one source contends that Fred Fish stepped in and offered to bankroll Garford's plans, but was summarily rejected because Garford had become determined to raise the money himself and go it alone without any backers who might be tempted to dispute his control.

Whatever the reason, Fish decided to look elsewhere and, within weeks, Studebaker had bought up another Cleveland auto maker, the General Automobile and Manufacturing Company, manufacturer of the General automobile. General was run by Rasmus Hansen, a Danish immigrant and his car, by all accounts, was a pretty good one. Available in single- and two-cylinder versions, production had reportedly reached a fairly impressive car-a-day by the summer of 1903. What happened then was that his investors backed out due to the company's inability to obtain a license from the Association of Licensed Automobile Manufacturers (A.L.A.M.). Why the A.L.A.M. refused to license the firm is unrecorded, and perhaps the license could have been obtained in time, but the withdrawal of financing caused immediate failure. The assets of the company, including the last twenty-five Generals, were sold in October of that year to Studebaker. The cars were at once shipped to South Bend and Fish now had an honest-to-gosh manufacturing facility for gasoline cars under his control.[13]

What transpired next with regard to General was...nothing. No one seems to know what happened to the last twenty-five cars and no use seems ever to have been made of the General Automobile and Manufacturing Company's facilities in Cleveland. Instead, Fish was suddenly engaged in serious negotiations with the machine tool making firm of Leland and Faulconer in Detroit.

Henry Martyn Leland remains one of the unsung heroes of the early American auto industry. He was already nationally renowned as the founder of Leland and Faulconer when he took on supervisory responsibilities for the Henry Ford Company in 1902, an action prompted by Ford's investors that immediately infuriated Ford. Then as later, Henry Ford didn't like anyone trying to tell him what to do. Following Ford's angry departure—to ultimately found the Ford Motor Company—the frantic investors in the enterprise implored Leland and his son, Wilfred, to take a major role in the firm. Although at first reluctant, Leland finally agreed to do so. And, since Ford's termination agreement had denied them the use of the Ford name, another had to be found. In due course, they decided to rename the company in honor of the founder of Detroit and, in this way, the Cadillac Automobile Company was born.

Almost immediately upon assuming a key role at Cadillac, Leland began to earn an international reputation for the extraordinary quality of his products. Most notably, under his direction Cadillac was the first auto maker to use fully interchangeable parts. This was a true watershed development without which the modern mass production techniques (pioneered, ironically, by Henry Ford) would have been an impossibility, and whose impact extended far beyond the confines of the auto industry. It is known from contemporary accounts that Fred Fish was deeply impressed by Leland's efforts in this area and pushed hard through the Society of Automotive Engineers (SAE) to spread interchangeability standards throughout the industry.

Curiously, though, Leland had no official capacity at Cadillac for several years after the departure of Henry Ford. Leland supplied most of the engines and chassis components through Leland and Faulconer. Cadillac's president, Lemmuel Bowen, was a big Leland supporter and even saw to it that Leland was elected to the board of directors and given some stock. Cadillac production remained steady at around 2,400 cars during 1904, which made Cadillac one of the largest auto producers in the nation.

All was not rosy in the Cadillac-Leland relationship, however, and that year there was a serious falling-out between Leland and some of Cadillac's stockholders (although not Bowen). The contract between Cadillac and Leland and Faulconer was nearing expiration, and there were rumblings that Cadillac was paying too much for its engines and other mechanical components. The controversy was sufficiently serious that Leland took the extraordinary step of looking for new business—just in case. Three horse-drawn carriage manufacturers were contacted in Ohio and Indiana. One of them was Studebaker and circumstances would strongly suggest that the contact was made during the winter of 1903-04—in other words, after the intial negotiations had fallen through with Garford and immediately after the purchase of the assets of Rasmus Hansen's General Automobile and Manufacturing Company.

The inescapable conclusion is that for some reason Fish had given up on the idea of manufacturing Generals (or Studebakers) using the facilities he had just bought. Was there a problem with the General car or plant? Circumstances would suggest the problem was under the hood, so to speak, for when Leland asked if Studebaker would be interested in buying gasoline car engineering and components from Leland and Faulconer, Fish responded at once with a firm commitment for 3,000 engines—Leland and Faulconer's entire annual output. What's more, Fish reportedly offered $15 more per engine than Cadillac was paying. Tempting as it was, Leland had to advise Fish that Cadillac had the right to renew and that any deal with Studebaker would have to await developments in Detroit. As it turned out, matters came to a head at a stormy Cadillac directors' meeting in March, 1904—while Bowen was reportedly in Europe—and, following heated discussion, the contract with Leland and Faulconer was renewed.[14]

The failure of the linkage with Leland and Faulconer was no doubt a keen disappointment to Fish (and, quite possibly, to Leland, as well). So, it was back to Cleveland and to Arthur Garford, who had by then freed himself from the clutches of Albert Pope. His company was already up and running and starting to supply its chassis to a variety of early auto makers who equipped them with bodies and sold them under their own nameplates. This list would eventually include Ardsley, Gaeth, Cleveland, Royal and Rainer—only one of which, Cleveland, had much impact. Swiss-born Louis Chevrolet raced Clevelands with some success in 1907-08, but, by 1909, Cleveland was bankrupt and Chevrolet went on to other ventures.[15] The Garford chassis seemed to be just what Studebaker needed, too, and Arthur Garford was delighted to have indirect access to the potential offered by Studebaker's nationwide dealer network.

At any rate, the first gasoline-powered, Studebaker-bodied cars were produced using the Garford chassis in the summer of 1904. The only body type listed featured a detachable tonneau. Called the Model C, it was a mid-sized car with chain drive and a two-cylinder engine rated at 16 horsepower. It had a wheelbase of 82 inches, a reinforced wooden frame, right-hand-drive steering and sold for $1,600. The first car was delivered in July of that year to H. D. Johnson of South Bend, J.M.'s son-in-law.

The Model C continued into 1905 as the Model 9502 and a five-passenger touring car was added to the range. The base price was lowered drastically to $1,250. Also new in 1905 was the much larger, 96-inch wheelbase, four cylinder Model 9503, which listed at $3,000. Available only as a five-passenger touring car, the Model 9503 was rated at 20 horsepower.

Although the cars built by Studebaker using the Garford chassis were generally known as "Studebaker-Garfords," they were sometimes advertised by the company as, simply, Studebakers. There is, understandably, some confusion among old car enthusiasts about this. While in the early years the cars seem to have been badged solely as Studebaker-Garfords, at

1904 Studebaker-Garford Model C.

least by 1910 they were being badged and promoted as Studebakers *per se.* The modern-day confusion over badging was certainly not helped by a decision on the part of Studebaker in 1912—after the Studebaker-Garford had been discontinued—to offer existing owners Studebaker badges that they could affix to their Studebaker-Garford cars. According to Studebaker financial reports, about half the owner body accepted the offer. Although it would be impossible at this juncture to determine how many Studebaker-Garfords were on the road in 1912, that number must surely have included most of the ones that have survived.

At any rate, the Model 9503 was carried over for 1906 as the Model E with few changes other than a price reduction of $400. The Model F was new, although similar to the Model E, except for its 104-inch wheelbase, 28 horsepower rating and $3,000 price tag. The top-end Model G was similar to the Model F, but boasted 30 horsepower and a $3,700 price. That was very expensive in 1906 and Garford's ideas were obviously not trending toward the "everyman's car" Henry Ford was trying to develop.

Still, things appeared to be going swimmingly. By 1906, Studebaker sales overall (including wagons) had risen from $4.1 million in 1902, the year the first Studebaker car was built, to $6.8 million.[16] For its part, the Garford factory in Cleveland was straining its capacity of about 500 chassis per year and Arthur Garford began to think expansively of a new plant that would raise output to 1200 or so and enable the company to firmly establish itself in the mid-price market segment with cars bearing the Garford nameplate unhyphenated with any other. Garford's idea was sound enough as far as it went, but he had made two grievous miscalculations. He had grossly underestimated a) the angry determination of his workers in Cleveland and b) the ruthless ambition of Fred Fish.

Arthur Garford ma9 have regarded himself as a forward-thinking progressive, but his attitude toward the working man was something else. He intended to build his new factory in nearby Elyria as a calculated way to get rid of his existing work force. As Garford saw things, the Cleveland labor pool was too expensive and too foreign. In a letter to a friend he extolled the quality of labor in Elyria:

> [It is] largely native and is constantly being augmented by
> the products of public schools and many young men of good char-

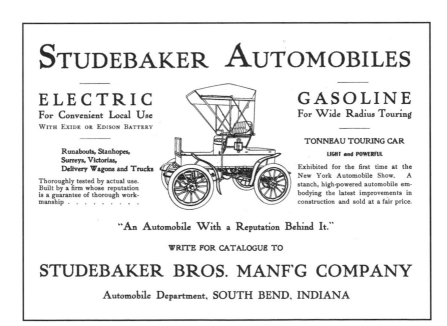

1904 Studebaker advertisement.

acter and eductation coming from surrounding farms. Substantially, no foreign labor is employed in Elyria of the Italian, Polish, or Hungaria~ type.[17]

Later, when the completion of the new factory was delayed by a serious construction accident, Garford dismissed it as being of little import because "only Italian laborers" had been injured. As for his existing labor force in Cleveland, he planned to dismiss them as soon as the Elyria facility was up and running, a prospect that had a predictable effect as soon as the workers in Cleveland figured out what was afoot. They responded in May, 1907, with a crippling strike that effectively shut the company down. Worse, Garford had now acquired a reputation for being hostile to labor and his efforts to hire qualified workers in Elyria proved so exceedingly difficult that there was little alternative to retaining many, if not most, of the existing work force after all. In the end, Garford was forced to settle with his Cleveland workers, but not before the strike had cost the company an estimated $50,000.

Meanwhile, Garford faced an even more shocking development on his own board. Back in the Spring of 1906 in order to fund his contemplated expansion, he had finally allowed Studebaker to become a minority investor, giving Fish three seats on the seven-member board. He did so on

1906 Studebaker-Garford Model G.

the assumption that he would continue to control the board with his majority of four. But, Hayden Eames soon went over to the other side and Garford found himself unexpectedly on the defensive.

By this point, even the economy seemed to be against Arthur Garford. The year saw the sharp recession known as the "Panic of 1907" that brought many healthy firms to ruin. The obituary list very nearly included Cadillac, one of the

1906 Studebaker-Garford engine.

industry's leaders, and it can't have made things any easier for Garford's company, which was already weakened by its labor troubles.

Then, Garford's general manager, C. E. Hadley, fell ill and had to resign. Chief Engineer James Heaslet was named to replace him. (A good man, Heaslet would later become Studebaker's engineering director.)

That wasn't the end of it, either, for Fish commenced maneuvering behind the scenes to acquire even more shares. By February, 1908, he had gained a majority and Arthur Garford suddenly found himself a minority shareholder in his own company. As if to drive the point home, literally, Fish had the "Garford" signs on the plant replaced with "Studebaker-Garford," and, for good measure, liquidated all customer relationships that competed with Studebaker or its dealers. That meant that dealers who were not Studebaker franchisees were summarily terminated. It also meant that remaining buyers of the Garford chassis, such as Cleveland and Rainer, were no longer to be supplied—and there would be no Garford car as such, either.[18] Many of the disenfranchised dealers sued, but it was a done deal: Fish now controlled Gardford's company and intended to run it solely for the benefit of Studebaker.[19]

As for the cars, which had almost been forgotten among the labor strife and the chaotic political maneuverings, there was little new to report. The 1906 Models E, F and G were carried over into 1907 with few changes, except that they were redesignated the Models L, G and H, respectively.

1908 Studebaker-Garford Model B in Washington, DC. President William H. Taft is the corpulent passenger in the rear seat.

Despite the "Panic," Studebaker's sales rose to $7.8 million in 1907. Most of this still came from horse-drawn vehicles, but, significantly, most of the *increase* was due to the sales of automobiles. Even J.M. was impressed by that. Indeed, J.M. may have been too impressed, for he apparently decided to unleash Fred Fish. J.M. gave his approval for Fish to begin pursuing an aggressive acquisitions policy and the first results involved in another automotive venture that was, at best, bizarre. This was the saga of the Tincher automobile.

Thomas L. Tincher had started building cars in Chicago as early as 1903. The cars he built were big and, even by the standards of the day, desperately expensive. Unable to make a go of it in Chicago, he moved to South Bend around 1907 and obtained financing from Studebaker for a new company to continue his manufacturing efforts. The company announced a capitalization of $200,000, most of which was reportedly contributed by Studebaker. The Tincher automobile was, by all accounts, a fine car. It used a massive (for the time) 127-inch wheelbase and was powered by an innovative, overhead-cam, four-cylinder engine rated at 50-60 horsepower. Everything about the Tincher was out-sized for the era, including the prices, which generally started at around $5,000 and went on up into the stratosphere from there. Unfortunately, no more than half-a-dozen seem to have been built in any one year and it was simply impossible to turn a profit on that level of volume (or lack thereof). So, the Tincher concern folded in 1909, taking Thomas Tincher—who filed for personal bankruptcy—and Studebaker's sizable investment with it.

Meanwhile, the most famous Studebaker-Garford product was announced for 1908: the Model B, often known as the "Forty." It boasted a 114-inch wheelbase and a 40 horsepower engine. The powerplant was of the T-head design and displaced 372 cubic inches (app. 6.0 liters), which was a pretty healthy size for a four-cylinder engine.

Yet, if Arthur Garford was understandably unhappy with the way things had turned out, so was Fred Fish. Fish was finding it impossible to attain the large volume of sales he wanted for Studebaker with Garford's pricey models and limited manufacturing facilities (not to mention Thomas Tincher's five or six cars a year). Although the Studebaker-Garford relationship would stagger along for another three years, only 2,481 Studebaker-Garfords were built in the entire eight-year association. Studebaker sold its interests to Willys-Overland in 1911 or 1912 and the

1908 Tincher.

last Garford car was built in 1913.[20]

It was around 1908 that Fish began casting about for a way for Studebaker to decrease its dependency on Garford and increase its sales, and the contentious relationship between Studebaker and Garford would seem like an innocent parlor game compared to the ensuing drama involving the company that was to play the central role in Studebaker's development as an important automobile manufacturer: E-M-F. As its name suggests, it was the product of three men—

B. F. "Barney" Everitt.

Everitt, Metzger and Flanders—but that was only the beginning of the story.

William Metzger was an especially fascinating figure. He was, one might say by way of comparison, the Lee Iacocca of his day. A master sales and marketing man whom many regarded as the best in the business, he was to play a central role in more than one pioneering car company. As early as 1898, when few people were even thinking seriously about automobiles, Metzger had opened the first retail dealership in Detroit. In time, he represented an impressive collection of notable early brands: Mobile (steam cars), Waverly Electric, Oldsmobile and Lozier. In 1902, he was offered the position of sales manager for the Cadillac Automobile Company. Although he accepted the offer, he continued to operate his dealership and dabble in other automotive enterprises, as well.

At Cadillac, Metzger wasted no time in seeking publicity. In one celebrated episode, he drove a Model A prototype up the steps of the Wayne County Courthouse in Detroit—located, not incidentally, on Cadillac Square—before several thousand onlookers. About a year later, the same stunt was repeated on the steps of the U. S. Capitol in Washington. In that case, the poor driver was reportedly gotten quite drunk, tied to the steering column, then dispatched to do his duty as a required part of a fraternity initiation! The police in Washington proved not nearly so tolerant as

William Metzger, left, and Walter Flanders.

those in Detroit and the man was arrested. Still, the ad showing the little Cadillac one-lunger chugging up the Capitol steps was a big hit. "A man drove a Cadillac up the steps of the Capitol at Washington," the ad read. "He paid for his fun, but it was worth the money to know the power of the Cadillac." Translation: It was certainly worth it to Metzger, who had masterminded the whole thing and had a fine advertisement to show for it, but one wonders if the poor fellow who did the driving was quite so enthusiastic when he sobered up in jail the next morning. This episode also points up another side of Metzger's character: a calculating coolness. One contemporary described him thusly:

> Billy was smart and had the marks of a gentleman. He was cold, too, and his smile was like that of a Spaniard wiping off a knife.[21]

Be that as it may, when Metzger had something appealing to sell, he certainly knew how to go about selling it. It was during the Cadillac's formal introduction at the New York Auto Show in January, 1903, in fact, that Metzger performed one of the greatest feats of salesmanship in the history of the industry. Accepting deposits for as little as $10, he sold out the entire year's production by the end of the week. Theodore MacManus, who later handled Cadillac advertising, recalled:

> Metzger, gray-eyed, tight-chinned, thin-lipped, and a sales-man, sold 2,286 Cadillacs at that show, receiving, on each ordered car, a deposit of ten dollars. This sum of approximately $23,000 served to plug part of the gap in the finances of the Cadillac company. The cars were built, thereby relieving Metzger from possible results of selling something he did not have.[22]

In this era, few motorists were hardy enough to consider winter driving. Consequently, all manufacturers depended upon the practice of "pre-selling" their products to the extent possible in the winter months in order to keep the lines going. Buyers, for their part, were content to order well in advance of delivery on the basis of deposits, which averaged 20 percent of the purchase price. There was a hard financial reason for this practice, too. The fledgling automobile companies were not considered "bankable" by major financial institutions because the industry was not yet regarded as stable. In order to obtain funding, the auto companies routinely demanded deposits for cars as yet unbuilt, then demanded cash-on-delivery.

The system worked well, but involved considerable risk. If a company was unable to deliver the cars in a timely way, or if there was a sudden collapse in demand requiring massive refunding of deposits—whether due to a downturn in the economy or to a decline in the reputation of a particular nameplate—financial ruin could quickly become a possibility.

This, incidentally, highlights a significant advantage Studebaker had over most of its competition in the early industry. Almost alone among auto manufacturer wannabes, Studebaker was a major company with a long-running track record of sound management and profitability. Furthermore, Fred Fish was an Eastern man, a lawyer who was well-connected with the New York financial establishment. Financing was not the obstacle for Studebaker that it was for most other firms trying to enter the industry, many of whom were broken by inadequate capitalization or even by temporary cashflow crises. Studebaker, as we are seeing, encountered many daunting problems in developing its auto business, but, significantly, cash was never one of them and this ready access to Eastern capital was one of the most important reasons the company was able to move so decisively to seize the "main chance" when it came around with E-M-F.

At Cadillac, as MacManus observed, Metzger had been forced to take some serious risks in order to compensate for his firm's inadequate capitalization. In fact, he had gambled in two ways at the 1903 New York show: 1) By taking so many deposits he had gambled that the company could produce a satisfactory product. And, 2) by taking "short" deposits of as little as 1.3 percent, he had gambled that the company would be able to do so in a timely fashion before its thin "capitalization" (the deposits) ran out. In short, Metzger was both a risk taker and a whiz at selling cars.

Still, no matter how much Fred Fish admired Henry Leland, Metzger discovered in time that Leland was not easy to work for. Rigid, uncompromising and never afraid to state his views in the most strident way, Leland ruffled many feathers and made a few notable enemies along the way. He tended to think that everyone should have the same opinions he did and could be extremely unpleasant when they didn't. By all accounts, he ran Leland and Faulconer and, later, Cadillac with the air of a benevolent tyrant. Owing to his fiercely held standards and enormous personal integrity, he was able to hold the loyalty and respect of many. But, by no means all. By 1908, Metzger, for one, had decided it was time to leave.

Walter Flanders, in some ways the most colorful of the three founders of E-M-F, had achieved renown as the highly gifted production manager for Ford Motor Company, even then the largest automobile manufacturer in the industry. By chance, he happened to be a machinery salesman upon whose route lay the embryonic Ford enterprise. He soon sold some machine tools to Henry Ford, who promptly complained that they weren't up to snuff. Flanders' response to that was to take off his coat, roll up his shirts sleeves and personally demonstrate to the automaker how the machines ought to be operated. Ford was so impressed he offered Flanders a job on the spot—that of shop superintendent and production manager. Flanders accepted and almost immediately began rearranging the shop layout for greater efficiency. When he was done, production of Ford cars had increased from twenty a day to one hundred fifty.[23]

B. F. "Barney" Everitt—described as "short, fat and jovial" by one contemporary—had made a fortune as a body supplier to the early industry, first with Oldsmobile and then with other manufacturers, including Ford where he met Flanders. Everitt also claimed credit for getting the Fisher brothers—later of Fisher Body fame—their start in the business. He introduced them to C. R. Wilson, another early body builder in Detroit, who hired them on. By the time the E-M-F venture got rolling, Fisher Body had been established and E-M-F became their first big account.

Metzger's partnership with Flanders and Everitt was part of a complex plan involving two different car companies. In the spring of 1908, Everitt took control of the Wayne Automobile Company in Detroit and brought Flanders in shortly thereafter.[24] Wayne was a respected producer of medium- and high-priced cars with sales of around six hundred units in 1907, which hardly seems significant today but was considered fairly substantial at the time. On August 4, 1908, the Everitt-Metzger-Flanders Company officially came into being. Meanwhile, Metzger had resigned as sales manager at Cadillac and purchased control of the Northern Manufacturing Company, a company with plants in both Detroit and Port Huron, Michigan. The Northern car had been founded by Charles King and Jonathan Maxwell in 1902 and, in October, 1908, Northern was brought into the Everitt-Metzger-Flanders Company.[25]

The car the company planned to manufacture was, as noted, to be called the E-M-F, the initials taken from the names of the three principals in the firm. On the face of it, there could hardly have been a more promising combination of talents. Everitt, who was named as president (and, not incidentally, was the chief financier of the operation), had proven management ability; Metzger, named as sales manager, was one of the finest sales and marketing men in the industry; while Flanders, named as general manager, was a noted production man. William E. Kelly, Wayne's highly-regarded chief engineer, remained with E-M-F in that capacity.

As for the E-M-F car, it was intended to be a high-volume item, although pegged at $1,150, a price point somewhat higher than Henry Ford's popular Model S and soon-to-be-famous Model T. The Model 30, as the first E-M-F was known, used a 30 horsepower, four-cylinder powerplant of L-head design. It also used thermo-syphon cooling, a primitive type that relied on heat convection to move water around in the engine. In addition, the Model 30 used beam axles, with semi-elliptic leaf springs in front and full-elliptics in the rear. A selective three-speed sliding gear transmission was rear-mounted by means of a transaxle. Except for the transmission and the transaxle, the basic engineering of the Model 30 was remarkably similar to the Ford Model T—as was the general appearance—although on a somewhat larger scale. A schedule of 12,500 cars was announced for the first year, with production to commence in September, 1908. In comparison, Ford built around 10,000 cars in 1908, including early Model Ts, so the E-M-F projections were ambitious, indeed.

Things got off to a slow start, though. According to one account, only 172 cars had been built by the end of 1908. At the Chicago Auto Show in February, 1909, Metzger admitted to reporters that the new company was far from reaching its announced goals "due to our determination to have our cars right" and to the fact that "we closely scrutinize each machine before it goes on the market."

If the E-M-F was proving to fall short of Metzger's commercial ambitions, his comments hinted that it was also falling far short of the Cadillac quality standards to which he had been accustomed. All too soon, disgruntled owners sneered that the initials stood for "Every-Mechanical-Fault," "Eternally-Missing-Fire," "Easy-Mark's-Favorite," or "Every-Morning-Fixit"—and in all likelihood a few more that aren't printable.

Alas, it was true. The Model 30, despite its strong sales appeal, so disappointed many of its early owners that one has to wonder if the car's reputation might not have sunk the company in time had not Studebaker come along. The thermo-syphon cooling system was a major cause for complaint, as chronic over-heating problems resulted. A water pump was designed and installed on later cars.[26] Worse, the rear transaxle used a housing of then-exotic aluminum to save weight, but the reliablity was dreadful and the problem wasn't fixed before the model was discontinued in 1912. Still, the Model 30 was a good road car when it ran at all. It excelled in competitive events—hill climbs, tours and the like—that were a popular fixture of early motoring.

Another major problem faced by E-M-F, at least at first, was its lack of a well-developed dealer network. At Cadillac, Metzger had demonstrated a flair for dealer development, but Cadillac had never had the volume

1909 E-M-F Model 30.

ambitions that Everitt, Metzger and Flanders had. So, for the E-M-F trio, the appearance of Fred Fish must have seemed the answer to their prayers. Fish had sales ambitions just as high as they did and, what's more, had the network of some 4,000 Studebaker dealer to offer.

The original contract, made in September, 1908, involved Studebaker handling only a part of the E-M-F factory's output. Specifically, Studebaker was entrusted with all of the export business and Hayden Eames, by this point Studebaker's general manager, was given responsibility for the American South and West. Metzger was left with the Eastern sales territory.

The first signs were good. Studebaker dealers were elated with the popularity of the E-M-F and so was Fish. It seems clear that he soon had something more than a distribution deal on his mind, too, for within a few months Everitt and Metzger were publically castigating him for deliberately restraining E-M-F sales in order to drive down the price of the stock.

Unfortunately, the *mélange a trois* of Everitt, Metzger and Flanders was turning out not to have been made in heaven, either, and it wasn't long before E and M had had quite enough of F, as well. In fact, at a board meeting early in 1909, they accused him of being in league with Fish to sabotage the value of the company's stock so that Studebaker could more easily buy control. They also demanded that Fish stop his behind-the-scenes trickery and buy the company outright.

This is, in fact, what Fish had decided to do. Studebaker described the view from South Bend in a company history published years later:

> Being assured of the future of the automobile, [Studebaker]
> management now perceived the necessity of embarking into the
> business on a large scale commensurate with its position in the
> vehicle industry...Moderately-priced automobiles that could be
> built and sold in large quantities were the necessary answer to
> this problem.[27]

Increasingly, E-M-F looked to be just the ticket and so in April or May
of 1909 a three-year deal was reached for Studebaker to handle sales and
distribution for the entire production capacity of E-M-F. These moves put
Fish and Flanders in close proximity, and their relationship was destined
to be at least as turbulent as Flander's had been with Everitt and Metzger.

Despite his undisputed ability—Everitt later said he was "the greatest
executive mind I ever knew"—Flanders was, if contemporary accounts can
be believed, a very difficult colleague.[28] A tall, rough-hewn man, he had a
personality to match. He was loud, direct in manner (often to the point of
rudeness), was noted as a hard drinker and womanizer, and had a famous

The E-M-F plant in 1910.

temper. One of the celebrated stories within the early industry involved Flanders and Charles Fisher, of Fisher Body. The Fisher brothers of necessity had quoted prices to E-M-F before the car was launched. As E-M-F volume grew, however, a truer picture developed and Charles Fisher decided he had to pay a call on Flanders. Fisher began the conversation thusly:

> My brother, Fred, and I have been thinking this thing over. We want to talk over with you the matter of a price adjustment.

Instantaneously, Flanders' temper erupted and he shrieked at Fisher:

> Here I am, just getting my head above water and you fellow start gouging me! Holding me up! I won't stand for it!

The tirade went on in that vein for a while. When Flanders had finally cooled down enough to catch his breath, Fisher interrupted:

> It is not our purpose to *raise* the price. What I am trying to tell you is that we think we are charging *too much*. We are making a big profit on this type of job and we want to lower the figure.

Fisher went on to explain that he and his brother had had no idea the volume would be so large when the initial contract was negotiated and they thought E-M-F was entitled to a lower mark-up. Flanders was struck dumb. No one had ever done *that* to him before and he asked if the Fisher brothers were crazy. Charles Fisher replied:

> Not at all. We believe in a fair profit for our work. Father always did business that way. We intend to do the same.[29]

That was too much for Flanders. At the next annual New York Auto Show, the unofficial industry convention at which anybody who was anybody could be found, Flanders made it his mission to boost the Fisher brothers to anyone who crossed his path—whether they wanted to hear it or not. According to one contemporary account:

Flanders, drunk or sober, sung the praise of the Fishers to all who would listen. When he couldn't get them to listen in any other way he pinned them to the wall with his great hands, and forced into their ears and consciousness his belief that the Fishers were the squarest-shooting, most efficient, most completely satisfactory, and altogether "the damnedest finest bunch of men in the United States" with whom to do business.[30]

Meanwhile, Fred Fish was methodically moving in for the kill. On May 3, 1909, within days of the signing of the Studebaker distribution deal, it was announced that Clement Studebaker, Jr., and Hayden Eames had bought out Everitt and Metzger and taken their places on the E-M-F board of directors. At the same time, Everitt and Metzger left to form a new Metzger Motor Company to produce a car to be called the Everitt, taking Kelly with them. Thus, Studebaker now controlled about 36 percent of the stock in the Everitt-Metzger-Flanders Company. Flanders was elevated to the presidency of E-M-F in the shuffle.

Commercially, the link-up with Studebaker turned out to be just what E-M-F needed. Expansion was so rapid that, by the end of 1909, E-M-F was said to be Detroit's largest employer. Several companies were acquired in quick succession: the Monroe Manufacturing Company of Pontiac, a body builder; the Western Malleable Steel Company of Detroit; and the Pressed Steel Sanitary Manufacturing Company of Detroit. A Canadian subsidiary was also created. Production of E-M-F cars reached 8,132 in 1909, short of the 12,500 predicted, but still impressive and rising sharply.

During the summer of 1909, the De Luxe Motor Car Company was bought up. It is unknown how many cars De Luxe had actually built, if any, but its Detroit plant was the key to a plan Walter Flanders had in mind. As the Ford Model T began to take off in sales, Flanders, according to contemporary accounts, became exceedingly miffed that E-M-F's thunder was being stolen—and by a company that used a production system he himself had set-up, no less. Determined to beat the Model T, Flanders convinced Fish to have Studebaker buy the defunct De Luxe plant for a car that Flanders wanted to build to under-price the Model T and, thus, win sales leadership away from it. All the cars he built in this Studebaker-financed operation would be sold through Studebaker outlets.[31]

The car that appeared in the 1910 model year, called the Flanders Model 20, was a nice-looking roadster (with an optional two-passenger tonneau for the back) that employed many of the basic engineering concepts of the E-M-F Model 30, but on a cheaper scale. The engine was an L-head four-cylinder unit displacing 169.6 cubic inches and rated at 21 horsepower. It was built on a 100-inch wheelbase and, in most chassis specifications, was similar in concept to the E-M-F. Priced at $750, it was competitive with the Model T at first, but, as Henry Ford began cutting prices in order to widen *his* hold on the market, Flanders was unable to keep pace and so Flanders was never able to succeed in his primary goal of winning sales leadership away from Ford. Still, more than 30,000 Model 20s were built before the plant and car were folded into Studebaker in 1912.

Meanwhile, the relationship between Fish and Flanders was becoming choppy, indeed. In a company history published years later, Studebaker described what happened next in the relationship with E-M-F:

> Toward the end of the year [1910], Studebaker management made three decisions that would have far-reaching implications for the company. The first was to simplify the product range then being offered. The electric cars and the high-priced gasoline cars were discontinued. Production would henceforth be concentrated on the increasingly successful medium-priced gasoline automobile range.
>
> The second was to buy-out the E-M-F company.
>
> The third decision was to take the company public. This was motivated by two factors, the declining participation of the Studebaker family in company affairs and the need for additional capital for expansion in the automobile business.
>
> A new era for Studebaker was dawning.

Insofar as E-M-F was concerned, this explanation was too cute by half (at least). What actually transpired beginning in the latter months of 1909 was a naked attempt by Fish to force Studebaker's control—in other words, what we would call today an "unfriendly" takeover. Fred Fish had decided that the main chance was at hand and was determined to seize it regardless of the consequences. Nearing retirement age, he was convinced E-M-F was his last chance to install Studebaker firmly into a leading role in the industry he was convinced would define its future. So, he made a bold grab for control by refusing to accept further deliveries of cars, a move that spelled almost certain doom for a volume manufacturer that had no other retail outlets. Flanders would have no choice but to surrender to the inevitable and sell out to Studebaker on Fish's terms.

But Flanders, being the combative man that he was, declined to surrender to extortion and called Fish's bluff. On December 9th, he announced that he was canceling the contract with Studebaker for non-performance. In other words, since Studebaker refused to accept delivery of E-M-F cars, the deal was off. At the same time, he announced that he would accept offers from prospective dealers for E-M-F cars in order to replace the suddenly-disenfranchised Studebaker outlets. According to one account:

> Flanders sat down with a map, and such information as he had as to where most of the E-M-F cars had been shipped on Studebaker orders. He divided the country into four sections— East, West, Middle West and South. He wired a leading salesman in each of the four sections to come poste-haste to the factory. He gave each of them a distributor's franchise in his own area, together with a list of possible agents, many of whom were Studebaker men. A national sales organization was completed in two weeks, and E-M-F business continued without a shutdown.[32]

This wasn't the response Fish had expected, to be sure and he desperately counter-attacked by suing through the courts to force Flanders to honor the contract that Studebaker itself had breached! Flanders easily won that one, but the battle was far from over.

No sooner had the echo from the judge's gavel died away, than Fish decided to take advantage of Studebaker's huge financial resources to go behind the scenes and woo the former stockholders of the Wayne and Northern companies that still held stock in E-M-F. His plan was to buy enough to give Studebaker a majority and, thus, outright control. The J. P. Morgan and Company brokerage firm in New York handled the negotiations on behalf of Studebaker. On March 9, 1910, it announced what *Horseless Age*, the industry trade magazine, termed "the most sensational deal in months in the automobile industry." For an estimated $5 million, Studebaker had bought all of the remaining shares—including those owned by Flanders— and was now the sole owner of the Everitt-Metzger-Flanders Company.[33]

Flanders personally ended up with a small fortune from the deal, so he probably didn't feel too badly about the way things had turned out. Apparently, the relationship between Flanders and Fish had been patched up to a certain extent, too, for it was also announced that Flanders had accepted a three-year contract to remain on as president of E-M-F.

All that remained now was for Fish to consolidate his gains. The aging of John Mohler Studebaker, the lack of Studebaker family heirs able or willing to manage the business and the need for centralized control of the

Photographed in Studebaker-Garfords in October, 1908, at Tippecanoe Place in South Bend are members of the Studebaker family and visiting dignitaries. Vice-President Fairbanks and J.M. Studebaker are seated in the rear of the lead car.

company's far-flung properties all forced some serious soul-searching in South Bend. The upshot was a new corporation—The Studebaker Corporation—that would bring all the Studebaker enterprises into the same tent.

By 1910, Studebaker Brothers Manufacturing Company had been in business for forty-three years. In that time, it had manufactured more than a million horse-drawn vehicles and related equipment and just over 4,000 motor vehicles, that together had brought in $119 million sales.[34] Of that, fully $16 million was profit and the Studebaker brothers had taken only $6.8 million in dividends, preferring to reinvest the rest in the business.

In addition to that, the Everitt-Metzger-Flanders Company, which Studebaker Brothers Manufacturing Company now owned, had racked up an impressive $21 million in sales in its first two years and $3 million in profits. A total of 23,432 cars had been built: 8,132 through the end of 1909 and 15,300 in 1910. According to some sources, it had become the second-largest automobile manufacturer in the country. It was definitely the second-largest employer in Detroit with 5,700 workers. General Motors was first (10,000), Packard was third (4,640) and Ford was fourth (2,595).

J.M. Studebaker and his wife, Mary, celebrated their golden wedding anniversary during the final year of the existence of the Studebaker Brothers Manufacturing Company. For J.M., who was nearing eighty, it was a long way from Hangtown, but as he faced the sunset of his own life the company he had helped to build was about to enter a future that would contain both the best and the worst of times.

A new era was, indeed, dawning for Studebaker.

Notes

The most important resources drawn upon in the writing of this chapter include Albert Erskine's *History of the Studebaker Corporation*, Stephen Longstreet's official company history, *A Century on Wheels:* C. B. Glasscock's *The Gasoline Age* and Studebaker National Museum Archives in South Bend. *Men, Money and Motors*, by Theodore F. MacManus provided insights into the personality and career of William Metzger. The oft-related and wonderful story about Charles Fisher and Walter Flanders appears in its most complete form in *Birth of a Giant* by Richard Crabb. Matthew Josephson's

Edison, A Biography covered an important sidelight into the story of the Studebaker electrics. Periodicals used for important anecdotes and sidelights include *Special-Interest Autos* and *Scientific American*.

[1] Although the Durant-Dort Carriage Company in Flint, Michigan, along with Studebaker one of the top-ranked carriage builders at the turn of the century, did not make a direct transition itself, it served as a breeding ground for a number of important players in the early automobile industry. Foremost among them, of course, was Durant himself, who first acquired Buick and then parlayed it into General Motors. J. Dallas Dort later went on to start his own car company to produce the respected Dort automobile. Nash worked for the carriage company before leaving to accept a job with Buick, eventually rising to the presidency of General Motors before striking out on his own (and Walter Chrysler worked for him at Buick). Murphy came closest to following the Studebaker example. His Pontiac Buggy Company had been reasonably successful, but he saw the much greater potential of the automobile and wanted to make the transition. This he did by forming the Oakland Motor Car Company in 1907. The first Oaklands were built right in the buggy plant, but Murphy died within the year and Oakland was bought up by General Motors. Even so, Oakland never amounted to much until the Pontiac brand was introduced as a companion line in 1926. The Fisher brothers started out in the carriage industry, at least individually, although their major joint enterprise—Fisher Body—was a body supplier to the auto industry. E-M-F was their first big customer. Later, they, too, sold out to General Motors.

[2] Cohn, P. 44.

[3] Horsepower ratings in the early industry should be taken with a large grain of salt. Few manufacturers had access to dynamometers. Instead, an engine's horsepower was usually estimated by means of this or that mathematical formula based on cylinder bore or perhaps something else. The results were generally crude, at best.

[4] In 1907, Fred Marriott was killed attempting a world record speed run in a Stanley race car. The crash occurred at a reported speed in excess of 150 mph and the car was completely demolished—except for the boiler. Eventually, the range problem was resolved by adaptation of the condenser principle, which had been developed for use in railroad locomotives. Pilot lights and other devices were also added to reduce the initial warm-up time to a couple of minutes. Unfortunately, steam power was passé by then.

[5] This may have been debatable insofar as the steam car was concerned, but it was certainly true of electric vehicles.

[6] Josephson, p. 414

[7] Pun intended.

[8] Ditto.

[9] Electric vehicle technology has not advanced significantly since Edison's improved battery in 1910, and the problems that bedevil development of a practical electric-powered car today are exactly the same ones that killed electric cars way back then. The improved Edison battery did prove to be a modest success in stationary applications, i.e., operating machinery, etc.

[10] Langworth, p. 10.

[11] This concept was standard practice in many sectors of the economy at the time, such in as the flourishing piano industry, then nearing its all-time peak. Thousands of pianos were sold as "stencil pianos" by the major piano manufacturers. Any local music shop could order pianos from Aeolian or any of the major manufacturers and have the local music shop's nameplate—or stencil—put on the fallboard. Although the practice was less common in the auto industry, it was not unknown. In our own time, it has even enjoyed something of a vogue, as with the many cars built by Mitsubishi, Kia, and Daewoo that have been sold bearing Dodge, Ford, and Pontiac nameplates.

[12] In his memoirs ("Horseless Carriage Days"), Hiram Percy Maxim, one of the key pioneers in the early auto industry, provided the following unforgettable description of Eames: "No man who ever met him forgot him. He was one of those blue-eyed, handsome thoroughbreds they raise in the State of Maine more frequently than anywhere else I know of. He stood erect, looked you over in a stern way, and had you on the defensive in the first few minutes. He had graduated from the Naval Academy...was a great reader, remembered everything he read, and had the most amazing vocabulary ever bestowed upon mortal man. His emotions were just barely under control all the time. To hold himself in leash required a superhuman effort day and night. He was profane to a degree, but intellectually and poetically so; never was he vulgar. When he lost his grip on his emotions he would launch forth into an epic of profanity that was nothing short of inspiring. Many times have I listened to one of his profane perorations with the same enraptured feeling which I enjoy when listening to great music. Eames' energy defied description. He fairly boiled from morning to night. Until you became accustomed to him he would tire you out—it would wear you down to a nervous frazzle merely to be in his presence for half an hour."

[13] The role of the Association of Licensed Automobile Manufacturers (A.L.A.M.) was an inglorious one. It was the enforcer of the notorious Selden patent, which it wielded like a club over the early industry. George B. Selden was part visionary, part speculator. He realized as early as 1877 that a self-propelled vehicle was possible and applied for a patent for a crude but workable vehicle in 1879. Selden could have been the first automobile manufacturer in the world,

as Daimler and Benz didn't get started until 1885, and by sixteen years the first in the United States. In short, his name could have been writ large in history books the world over. His intention, however, was not to *build* such a vehicle but to wait around for someone *else* to do so and then cash in on his patent. Indeed, for years he kept revising his application in order to keep it pending before letting it be granted in 1895 (a stratagem that would not be permitted today). The delay had been necessary because it had taken that long for others to get the same idea and do the hard work necessary to get the industry rolling, and it was not until that year that the first company was organized to build automobiles, the Duryea Motor Wagon Company. A patent was only good for seventeen years and Selden was far too shrewd an operator to let his patent go through before there was an industry from which he could exact tribute. Yet, even when his patent did go through, Selden found it extremely difficult to get any of the new manufacturers to take it seriously. Eventually, he assigned his patent to the Electric Vehicle Company and let them assume the challenge of collecting the royalties. Albert Pope was one of the main sponsors of the Electric Vehicle Company, and his right-hand man was Hayden Eames. The Electric Vehicle Company, in turn, joined forces with Packard and Oldsmobile to establish the A.L.A.M. to license the gasoline vehicle manufacturers for the purpose. This took place in March, 1903, and it happened not because Packard and Olds thought the Selden patent was valid (they didn't) but because a) they were leery of the expense of fighting it and b) they saw the new organization as a perfect tool they could use to protect the rapidly growing automobile market for themselves by keeping new competitors out. So, from that point on, a manufacturer without a license was subject to the threat of ruinous litigation from the A.L.A.M. Not surprisingly, nearly all the manufacturers complied—or tried to, but licenses were not easy to get. It was mostly the "respectable" companies that were favored, i.e., those whose investors or managers were on good terms with the men who ran Packard and Olds or the Electric Vehicle Company. (This would include, of course, Garford and, by extension, Studebaker. Eventually, Eames went to work for Studebaker.) This is probably why the General Automobile and Manufacturing Company couldn't obtain a license, for, at almost the same time, the newly formed Ford Motor Company was similarly spurned. Henry Ford, however, had the gumption to fight back. He stubbornly refused to accept the validity of the Selden patent and, when he was sued, fought it through the courts to the bitter end. The final decision by the United States Circuit Court of Appeals in 1911—when the patent was almost due to expire—added a suitably curious twist to an already strange affair. The Selden patent was, indeed, valid, the court said, but it only applied to vehicles powered by *two-cycle* gasoline engines—which virtually no one was building, anyway! Thus, the patent was valid, but Ford was innocent—

and, for that matter, so was Rasmus Hansen, who hadn't needed a license after all. Alas, the news came eight years too late to do Hansen any good.

[14] In October, 1905, Leland and Faulconer was formally merged with Cadillac to form the Cadillac Motor Car Company, with Leland at its head. Cadillac was, in turn, sold to General Motors in 1910.

[15] The car company was bankrupt, not the city—the city came later.

[16] Of this figure, $368,848 came from the sales of automobiles.

[17] Critchlow, p. 53.

[18] This chain of events probably contributed to the bankruptcy of the company that built the Cleveland.

[19] The total amount of Studebaker's investment in Garford is difficult to ascertain, but, judging from later Studebaker Corporation financial reports, may have been as high as $750,000. This was a substantial sum in those days when half-a-million was enough to capitalize a major car company.

[20] Arthur Garford, for his part, had started manufacturing trucks around 1909 and that end of the business was not sold to Willys-Overland. The Garford truck continued in production, although under several owners, until 1933.

[21] Critchlow, p. 57. The Spanish were held in low esteem in those days. The American war with Spain had just ended, and the Spanish had been accused of all manner of ruthless and cruel behavior in the treatment of their colonies, such as Cuba, that America "liberated."

[22] MacManus, p. 3.

[23] Some writers have credited Flanders with the introduction of mass production at Ford. This is not correct. Flanders was a master at conventional shop practice, but true mass production—with its seminal concept of bringing the work to the workers via a moving assembly line, and so on—was not developed at Ford until three or four years after Flanders departed.

[24] Some sources say that Everitt had participated in the founding of Wayne in 1904 with Charles L. Palms.

[25] Some sources contend that Metzger had had an interest in Northern as early as 1902. It is possible; he seemed to have an interest in just about everything else. In any event, soon after the consolidation with E-M-F, Maxwell left to go into partnership with Benjamin Briscoe, and the result was the Maxwell-Briscoe Motor Company, which had the misfortune to end up as part of the United States Motor Company, a General Motors-like conglomerate that went bust in 1912. Maxwell tried to pick up the pieces, eventually merging with Chalmers. It was when Maxwell-Chalmers, in turn, was teetering on the brink of bankruptcy in 1922 that Walter Chrysler was brought in to rescue it. That he certainly did. Within two years, Chrysler had transformed Maxwell-Chalmers into Chrysler Corporation, but not before Studebaker nearly bought the company (see Chapter Three).

[26] Flanders may have brought the thermo-syphon idea with him from Ford. Henry Ford was an enthusiast of thermo-syphon cooling because of its simplicity, and installed it on every Ford until the Model A in 1928. Of course, wags also said the letters in "Ford" stood for "Fix Or Repair Daily," but Ford customers seemed to be a more tolerant lot than those who bought E-M-Fs.

[27] Erskine, 1918, p. 43-45.

[28] Glasscock, p. 188.

[29] Crabb, p. 303.

[30] Glasscock, p. 181.

[31] A number of figures have been reported for the cost of the De Luxe plant to Studebaker, but $800,000 is the most commonly accepted one.

[32] Glasscock, p. 188-189.

[33] As is all too typical with events in the early history of the industry, there is considerable disagreement over the exact figure Studebaker paid for E-M-F and over who got what. Estimates of the total price range as high as $7 million. As who got what, Barney Everitt later recalled that he received $1.8 million for his stock, while Metzger received $1 million and Flanders received $250,000 for a stock bonus that had been promised him but had never actually been paid. Some accounts place Flanders' total compensation in the deal at $1 million, in all. More confusing still, it is unclear what time frame Everitt meant. When he recalled the sale of his and Metzger's stock, was he referring to the May, 1909, purchase of minority interest by Studebaker? Or, did they, as seems likely, sell only part of their holdings at that time?

[34] Including Studebaker Electric and Studebaker-Garford cars only.

Overleaf, the Studebaker body line in 1923.

THREE

The Rise of Erskine

Studebaker Corporation was officially incorporated under the laws of the State of New Jersey on February 14, 1911. The assets of the Studebaker Brothers Manufacturing Company and the Everitt-Metzger-Flanders Company—$15.4 million, in all—were folded into the new entity. Almost immediately, additional capital was raised by selling $8.3 million worth of preferred stock, pushing total assets to $23.7 million. Since the preferred stock carried no voting rights, the Studebaker family retained undisputed control. John Mohler Studebaker—a.k.a. Wheelbarrow Johnny, a.k.a. J.M.— remained chairman of the new corporation, while his son-in-law, Fred Fish, continued to operate as president.[1]

And, although no one knew it at the time, the man destined to guide the corporation's fortunes for more than two decades would join the firm before the year was out. Even before Albert Erskine appeared on the scene, though, the year was an active one. New branch and sales offices were established throughout the United States and in some foreign markets. Additions were made to the Detroit manufacturing facilities, too.[2] Clement Studebaker, Jr., who, as first vice-president, signed the letter to stockholders in the 1911 annual report, had a lot to crow about. He availed himself of the opportunity:

> The volume of sales and trading profits from the Vehicle division of the business were fully up to the expectations of the man-

1912 Flanders Model 20.

agement. While the automobile has made inroads into the pleasure vehicle business there is a constant and large demand for the
more important vehicle products of the Company, such as Farm
Wagons, Delivery Wagons, Sprinklers, Flushers, Dump Wagons
and kindred lines...We expect to market without trouble the entire
output of automobiles which will be by far the largest output in
our history.[3]

Sales of automobiles increased to 22,555, including the E-M-F, the
Flanders and a smattering of Studebaker electrics. The relationship with
Garford had been terminated at the end of 1910. Total profits for the year
amounted to $1.7 million.

By the time Studebaker Corporation came into being, it was becoming
painfully clear that the Flanders was as troubled a car as the E-M-F. This
was saying a lot, but perhaps should not be surprising as it used similar
engineering. J.M. felt compelled at one point to issue a public statement:

Business ethics are the same regardless of product. For sixty
years, the Studebaker Company has backed up its goods with a
guarantee showing good faith. Its relation to those who bought

86-

and used its wagons and carriages has always been considered a binding obligation. We apply this principle to our automobile business.[4]

The upshot was that Studebaker was forced to dispatch hundreds of mechanics around the country to repair Flanders 20s and replace defective parts, including transmissions, exhaust manifolds, clutches, brakes and carburetors.[5] In short, the Model 20 was a mess and the repair work—which was done at no cost to the hapless customers—cost the company nearly $1 million in pre-World War I dollars. It was one of the first, if not the very first, factory recall campaigns in the history of the industry and it was done on an entirely voluntary basis. Of course, Studebaker's reputation was at stake, and there must have been growing doubts about the viability of both

A 1912 Studebaker bought by China's leader, Sun Yat Sen (seated in the rear).

the E-M-F and Flanders brand names at that juncture. Indeed, both were gone within the year, replaced by the Studebaker nameplate. Walter Flanders would be gone, too. He had proven he could produce lots of cars, but all-too-many of them were simply no good.[6]

The myriad problems of the Flanders 20 notwithstanding, Studebaker experienced another very good year in 1912. Sales of motor vehicles rose 10 percent and a total of 28,523 cars were built during the calendar year. The corporation was doing a big business in export sales by this time, as well. In 1912, Studebaker products accounted for 37 percent of all American cars shipped to foreign markets.

Overall, Studebaker Corporation recorded a $2.3 million profit for the year on sales of $35.4 million. The company ended the year with dealer contracts in hand for 40,000 cars for the 1912-13 season, which was a record. The wagon business continued to grow, as well. The horse was not dead yet, it would seem, for sales of horse-drawn vehicles registered a 24 percent gain, making the 1912 model year in that division the greatest in the history of the company. The electric car, however, was—dead, that is—at least insofar as Studebaker was concerned. The last Studebaker Electric was built in 1912. Commented the company:

> The production of electric automobiles at South Bend was discontinued...It had been conducted for nine years without much success, and the ultimate superiority of the gasoline car had become apparent.

The following year, J.M. celebrated his eightieth birthday with a series of events in South Bend. Studebaker employees were given time off from work to shake the old man's hand in a receiving line in which J.M. was flanked by seven workers who had been with the firm for more than forty years. A nationwide contest had been conducted in anticipation of the festivities to find the oldest Studebaker vehicle still in service. A Wisconsin man claimed the prize with a wagon that dated to 1865. J.M. himself got a prize: a huge, silver loving cup.

Old J.M. had already returned to his roots the previous year. On April 16, 1912, he arrived by car in Placerville, California—known in his day as

J.M. Studebaker relaxes at home on his eightieth birthday in 1913.

Hangtown—after having taken the train to San Francisco. Reported the *El Dorado Republican and Nugget*:

> More than fifty-nine years ago a gaunt youth of nineteen stepped down from an emigrant wagon and took his first look around at the country where he had come to make a fortune. In his pocket was a lone fifty cent piece. Today, a kindly-faced aged man stepped down from the tonneau of a luxurious automobile and looked around him at the country where he had laid the foundation for his fortune. It was J.M. Studebaker returning to take perhaps his last look at the scenes of his early struggles.
>
> The auto had drawn up in front of the Ohio House where, on the wooden porch, stood a score of grizzled men. As Studebaker stepped down from his auto, he spied a face in the crowd. "Hello, Newt, you around here yet?" he said, by way of salutation.[7]

J.M. was guest of honor at a dinner that night. The menu was a masterpiece of cracker-barrel humor. As one Studebaker historian has noted, Mark

Twain—on an off day—might have written it. Never-the-less, it sounds like quite a spread:

CHUCK LIST
Chili Gulch Rib Warmer
Sluice Box Tailings, Flavored With Chicken
High-Grade Olives
Spanish Flat Onions
Cedar Ravine Radishes
Coon Hollow Pickles
Sacramento River Salmon Paved With Cheese
Indian Diggins Spuds
Tertiary Moisture
Slab Of Cow From The States
Bandana Fries With Bug-Juice
Lady Canyon Chicken, Hangtown Dressed
Webbertown Murphys
Shirt-Tail Bend Peas
Dead Man's Ravine Asparagus
Cemented Gravel A La Emigrant Jane
Butcher Brown Fizz Water
Assorted Nuggets
Amalgam Cheese, Rifle Crackers
Mahala's Delight En Tasse
Texas Hill Fruit
Pay Day Smokes — Hard Pan Smokes[8]

A further glimpse of J.M. at the end of his long life was given in later years by Paul Hoffman, Studebaker's president after the receivership in 1933. He was a star salesman at the Los Angeles Studebaker dealership beginning in 1911 and won, probably around 1912, a trip to South Bend as an award. There, he was ushered into the august presence:

I was escorted into Mr. Studebaker's office on the fourth floor of the administration building. He was...seated behind an old roll-top desk, slitting envelopes and putting them all into a neat pile. He said, "The boys downstairs buy scratch pads—I think it is an extravagance, a useless extravagance." That, of course was a lesson in frugality. It was a lesson I hardly needed because my grand prize was just this visit, which itself was some evidence of frugality.

But, he gave me a second, more important, reason. He said, "You're just starting out in business, and perhaps you would like to know why I think we have been successful. It's because we always give our customers more than we promise. This way you hold customers and get more customers." He waited a moment, and then added, "But, don't give them too much more, or you'll go broke!"[9]

J.M. had finally come to accept the automobile as an inevitability, even if he was too much of the old school to be entirely sanguine about the hold the new mode of transportation seemed to exert over younger generations. He went so far as to publicly admonish potential customers to move carefully, which was certainly extraordinary advice from a man whose company depended increasingly upon the sales of automobiles:

The automobile, of course, has come to stay. But, when a man has no business, it is a rather expensive luxury, and I would advise no man, be he farmer or merchant, to buy one until he has a sufficient income to keep it up. A horse and buggy will afford a great deal of enjoyment, not to the great extent that an automobile will, but the buggy is not as expensive a luxury. It will pay the farmer who lives five miles from town and who has cows to milk to buy an automobile, as he can get up at four o'clock or five in the morning, milk his cows, bring the milk to town, dispose of it, and be back at his work at eight with his horses all in good shape. For this reason, I say that if a person has a business, a machine is a good thing to have, but if a person has no business and no income, I should say, go slowly. An automobile is a piece of machinery and has to be looked after. It is expensive and will wear out.[10]

With the semi-retirement of J.M., a reorganization of the company was mandated. Albert R. Erskine, who had been treasurer, retained that job and assumed Clement Studebaker, Jr.'s, old title of first vice-president. In effect, Erskine was running the company and would continue to do so for the next twenty years. Fred Fish remained president for a time and old J.M. retained the chairmanship of the board, but it was Erskine's show now, for better or for worse.

Albert Russel Erskine was born in Huntsville, Alabama, on January 24, 1871, and his family numbered its ancestors among the town's earliest settlers. His great-grandfather had been a first lieutenant in the Revolutionary War and the clan was considered around Huntsville to be a fine, upstanding family. Unfortunately, as with many fine Southern families, their fortune had been wiped out during the Civil War. As a child, Erskine used to play with the stacks of Confederate bonds and currency that represented the wealth the family once had. There was little about his early life that promised a great career. Until he was sixteen, he attended public schools in a variety of places—Alabama, Texas, Missouri and back to Huntsville again—as his father moved the family around looking for work.

Albert Russel Erskine.

Then, young Erskine himself went to work for the Mobile & Ohio Railroad as an office boy at the unremarkable wage of $15 per month. Two years later, he was making $10 a week as a bookkeeper, having learned accounting by assisting the regular bookkeeper. "I realized even then," Erskine remembered years later, "that the only way to get on was to learn to do better work." By the time he turned twenty-one, he had advanced to a position as bookkeeper for a wholesale paper firm at $75 a month. The following year, 1892, he obtained a similar position with a wholesale drug firm. After three years in that job, when he was still working for the same wage as when he started, another bookkeeper quit. Erskine decided a dramatic gesture was called for, so he went to the head of the firm and proposed a deal: "I'll do both jobs if you will pay me $100 a month; I'll make $25 and you'll save $50." Intrigued, if doubtful, his boss agreed. Erskine didn't stay long with the wholesale drug firm despite the raise he had finagled, but he was beginning to show the pluck and creativity that would become his hallmark as he matured in the business world.

When he was twenty-seven, Erskine got his first big break. He was offered a job as chief clerk with the American Cotton Company's office in St. Louis. After that, he was on the move. Within two years, in 1900, he had moved to New York City and to the position of general auditor of the firm and manger of its operating department, supervising three hundred cotton gins in the South. There, his flair for organization really began to tell. He developed detailed forms, reports and statements for use throughout the company for the purpose of showing regular performance in a reliable and detailed way. The American Cotton Company evidently needed just that sort of help, for it soon fell into receivership. When it did, Erskine was the only top executive of the company asked by the receivers to stay on.

Erskine was flattered, but his ambition precluded wasting time with a moribund firm that was unlikely to go anywhere. So, by 1904, when he heard of a position as treasurer of the Yale & Towne Manufacturing Company, he was determined to get it. He went to see Mr. Towne himself. At their meeting, Towne was non-committal until Erskine demonstrated the accounting systems he had devised for American Cotton. Towne, impressed, offered to let Erskine do the Yale & Towne books for 1904 and, if he completed them satisfactorily, promised that he would be made treasurer. Erskine did the books and, in addition, presented a detailed report to Towne showing how the current systems at Yale & Towne were "expensive, overlapping and not comprehensive," and suggesting practical improvements. As a result, Erskine not only won the treasurer's job, he was made a member of the executive committee of the firm.

Yet, Erskine was still looking for his personal brass ring. After a short stay at Yale & Towne, he went to Underwood Typewriter Company as a vice-president and director. While in that position, he was advised by a banker friend that Studebaker was looking for "new blood" and needed an experienced finance man. This was just the sort of opportunity for which Erskine had been preparing. Best of all, the job paid $20,000 a year to start. So, it was in the capacity of treasurer that he joined Studebaker in October, 1911. A decade later, Erskine recalled his first impressions:

> I took no office, not even a desk. I spent the first four months out in different departments. I went to the desks of the men in every department and asked them to show me what they were doing, how they were doing it, and why they were doing it. I thus investigated the methods employed all through the plant.
>
> Having learned the details of the financial and commercial ends of the business, and having already had experience in modernizing corporation methods, I set about installing simple, direct, and economical systems in these departments. I knew clerical operations that could be dispensed with, and also what employees should be removed.
>
> The departments were not organized on functional lines. For example, a great deal of accounting was done in the sales department and was duplicated in the accounting department. Now, sales departments exist to sell goods. Salesmen are not accountants. I divorced them from accounting entirely and scrapped most of the accounting and recording work they had been doing. The manufacturing department, the purchasing department, and other departments were similarly relieved of all record-keeping properly belonging to the accounting department.
>
> At South Bend and vehicle branch houses, I found 3,500 forms in use. I cut them down to about 1,500. New forms were substituted for old ones as old ones were used up and within six months every department was functioning smoothly on the new systems, without knowing that it had taken any medicine.[11]

In the process, Erskine quickly became a True Believer. Once, when an interviewer had the temerity to suggest that—at least in the eyes of Europeans—America had no traditions, Erskine shot back:

Has Studebaker no traditions? The name Studebaker has stood for all that is sound and honest and staunch and durable in vehicular transportation for seventy years. No business in America, no business in the whole world, has better traditions to live up to than we of the Studebaker Corporation have. Studebaker tradition, Studebaker reputation enters into the building of every car we produce.[12]

Sales rose to $41.5 million in 1913. Profits, however, were down to $1.8 million—something management never likes to have to tell stockholders—but Fred Fish was unusually creative in sugar-coating the bitter pill:

The directors believed that the standardization of the company's products [for the 1914 model year] and the volume of sales were more important than the making of large profits in the year of 1913, and are gratified to advise the stockholders that the effect of this policy, and of certain changes in the organization, is now bringing and insuring more profitable returns, one effect being that the winter production of the automobile factories is proceeding in record volume, with product in better condition, and the average number of employees 3,000 less than last year.[13]

The company again expanded its manufacturing facilities at Detroit and Walkerville (Ontario) to meet increased demand for Studebaker cars. The South Bend facilities were mainly supplying parts for the assembly plants in Detroit (and, to a lesser extent, Walkerville). Still, increasing numbers of parts were being made in-house and that put ever greater pressure on South Bend. The parts now being manufactured in South Bend included, among other things, springs, castings and bodies.

The 1913 model year marked the final emergence of the Studebaker brand as a major nameplate in its own right. The Studebaker-Garford line was long gone and, after 1912, so were the E-M-F and Flanders nameplates. The Flanders Model 20 was dropped entirely, but the E-M-F Model 30 was transformed into a Studebaker.

The man behind the development of the new line of Studebaker cars was James G. Heaslet, formerly of Garford and E-M-F, who had established Studebaker's first engineering department in 1911. Heaslet had also hired Fred M. Zeder, a University of Michigan graduate destined to become one of the most highly respected engineers in the industry. Together, they re-engineered the Model 30 for its new role. The basic design was continued, including the transaxle, but most of the engineering shortcomings were addressed and the Studebaker proved to be a markedly better car as a result. One of the significant features of the new line was the availability of electric starting and lighting. Boasted a Studebaker advertisement, "Press a button and the brilliant electric headlights illuminate the road."

Available with either four or six cylinders, the latter featured the first cast-in-block engine in the industry. This six, the Model E, was rated at 40 horsepower and rode on a 121-inch wheelbase. Prices started at $1,550 for the touring car, while the limousine listed for $2,500. The four came in two models, the SA, rated at 25 horsepower and the AA, rated at 35. With the fours, only the AA was initially offered with electric starting and lighting.

The 1913 Studebaker was the car that really began to build the Studebaker reputation as an automobile producer. In 1913 and 1914, Studebaker was the third- or fourth-best-selling brand in America. In the $625-$1,500 price class, Studebaker was running even with Buick and only slightly behind Willys-Overland. After that, the growing strength of Buick and Dodge—and the capacity restraints Studebaker suffered in the aging E-M-F plant—reduced it to a steady sixth or seventh place in the standings, but the fact that Studebaker had achieved a substantial presence in the industry was undeniable.

In general, the Fours were the price leaders, usually pegged at around $1,000. The dominant body style was the four-passenger touring car, but roadsters, coupes and sedans were offered, too. The Sixes were much more expensive and got the more exotic coachwork, including seven-passenger body styles. Of the almost exactly 250,000 Fours and Sixes built between 1913 and 1917, about 80,000 were Sixes. According to some sources, only three of Sixes are known to have survived, making it one of the rarest volume models in Studebaker history, if not, indeed, the rarest.

At of the end of 1912, more than 90,000 Studebakers, Studebaker-Garfords and E-M-Fs had been produced. Most, of course, had not worn

Studebaker radiator nameplates (or badges, as they are sometimes called) when new. Now that Garford was no longer allied with Studebaker and the E-M-F nameplate was being dropped, the company apparently sought to increase awareness of the Studebaker brand by offering existing owners Studebaker nameplates that they could affix to their Studebaker-Garford

Early automobile advertising art was often remarkable, as this rendering by Franklin Booth in the 1913 Studebaker catalog demonstrates.

and E-M-F cars. According to the company, 45,000 such "requests" were received during 1912. Although the company announcement didn't spell it out, it seems almost certain that the owners were responding to an offer from the company; it rather strains credulity to think that half of their customers suddenly thought up such an idea on their own.

A total of 35,410 cars were sold during calendar year 1913—around 11 percent below projections, although this number seems to have been just about the maximum plant capacity at the time. This was achieved despite a strike in June, in which 2,000 workers walked off the job in Detroit. The strike represented the most notable foray into the auto industry of the International Workers of the World (IWW). The IWW, whose members were known as "wobblies," was a radical-socialist union whose perceived threat to the established order was far greater than its small following would ever have justified. It later became a prime focus of the notorious "Red Scare" crackdown of 1919 in which most of its leadership was jailed at the behest of the Federal government.[14]

Meanwhile, export sales were a bright spot for Studebaker, comprising 16 percent of the company's output. Exports continued to be restrained, however, by demands in the domestic market. As in previous years, only those cars that could be spared over and above American demand were allocated for exports. The company also acquired all but 6 percent of the outstanding stock in the Canadian affiliate, making it virtually a wholly-owned subsidiary. The following year, the acquisition was completed.

In addition, the wagon business, defying the laws of gravity, continued to show strength. Perhaps to reassure stockholders who harbored doubts about how long that strength could continue, Fish remarked:

> Prospects for the ensuing year [for horse-drawn vehicles] are excellent. During the year [1913] we devoted considerable time to standardizing the line, eliminating unnecessary varieties and adjusting selling prices...so that we now have assurance of greater profit from this end of the business.[15]

One is left to wonder, however, how much "standardizing" could have been done, considering that, as Fish went on to note:

> Our vehicle products consist of farm wagons, trucks, carts, delivery wagons, passenger vehicles, sprinklers, flushers, sweepers, dump carts, bob sleds, ambulances, ammunition wagons, army wagons, hand carts, harness, and skeins. We have marketed these lines successfully for many years, and the business in them holds up very well.[16]

The 1913 Studebaker motor car line was carried over for 1914, although the larger Model AA four was dropped. The Model S Four, now rated at 30 horsepower, and the Six were offered at $1,050 and $1,575, respectively. This was the year the steering wheel moved to the left side, the gas tank was relocated in the cowl and there were minor styling changes to give the car a more stylish appearance. The company must have been doing something right, for production continued to strain factory capacity throughout the year, resulting in sales of 35,460 cars.

War in Europe erupted in August, 1914, and Fred Fish left almost at once for England to offer the company's services to the British Government. Orders soon came pouring into South Bend: 3,000 wagons, 20,000 sets of harnesses, 60,000 sets of saddles and blankets. Later, an order came in for 5,000 military trucks to be fitted with caterpillar treads instead of tires. These trucks were precursors to the tanks the British developed in the latter stages of the war and which were to redefine land warfare in the second European conflagration in the 1940s.

Perhaps in reaction to Studebaker's obvious tilt toward the Allied side in the intensifying struggle, a Studebaker facility in New Jersey was bombed. It was quickly put back in service, but Americans were not nearly so unified in their feelings during the first world war as they were to be during the second. The authorized Studebaker history published in 1952 fairly drips with anti-German hostility. Of the bombing, it states:

> England was popular in this country, and the [J. P.] Morgan loans were not yet called the only reason for our support of the true fighters for civilization. The Hun was butchering Europe with German skill, and in New Jersey a Studebaker plant was bombed and burned out. A week later it was back in business...[17]

1914 Studebaker Four.

Presumably, these were the same uncivilized Huns of whom five landed in Philadelphia in 1736 and, in time and with German skill, built the great Studebaker industrial empire.

Bombings and a marked slowing of horse-drawn vehicle production not-withstanding, overall sales for 1914—$43.4 million—proved to be an all-time record. Profits were up, to $4.4 million, thanks largely to some serious cost-cutting in the Detroit plants. Approximately the same number of cars had been built in both 1913 and 1914, but average employment was cut from 7,129 to 5,146. In fact, almost all of the increase in sales volume was due to early "war contracts" for the government. Government orders increased steadily throughout 1915 and were a disquieting harbinger of things to come as the nation moved ever more toward a war footing. Total "war contracts" in 1915 would amount to $13 million, or more than six times the figure in 1914.

In 1915, Albert R. Erskine was promoted from his former position as first vice-president and treasurer to president. John Mohler Studebaker retired to the newly created position of honorary president, while Frederick Fish moved up to chairman of the board. In addition, F. Studebaker Fish was named one of three assistant treasurers (and was now the only member of the Studebaker family still an active officer in the firm).

Under Erskine's leadership, Studebaker soon became one of the first automobile manufacturers to use wholesale and retail financing to stimulate sales. Erskine began fairly modestly by having the company deposit its money with banks that agreed to make loans in at least equal amounts to Studebaker dealers. The following year, a more ambitious arrangement was reached with Commercial Investment Trust, Inc., to provide nationwide wholesale financing—or, "floor planning" as it is known today—to the dealers. This enabled the dealers to carry larger stocks and, not incidentally, to buy more cars from Studebaker. Under the deal with Commercial Investment Trust, Studebaker agreed to make good any losses caused by dealer defaults. Studebaker worked with a variety of financing companies after that, but the idea was the same and it represented the beginnings in the industry of modern financing methods at the dealer level.

The Fours and Sixes were changed somewhat in appearance for 1915, were noticeably less boxy than before and sported a fender line that was a bit more flowing. Sales rose significantly. Of the 46,845 sold, 90 percent went to the domestic market as foreign demand began to dwindle due to the war raging in Europe. Of the number exported, around one-third went to foreign governments for war-related purposes. The fact that Studebaker automobile sales were up 32 percent was due mostly to drastic price cutting in the lower-priced four-cylinder models in the summer of 1915. The company explained the reasoning this way:

> These price reductions were made in conformity with our policy of keeping a fixed profit to ourselves and giving the public the benefit of all savings effected by the organization over and above this profit, in such items as reduced overhead expenses, improved methods, saving in buying material, etc., and although our prices were reduced, the quality and size of our cars was actually increased, so that ouf customers now receive better cars than ever before for considerably less money.[18]

This was notable for being similar to the farsighted policy followed by Henry Ford. (It was also notable for being typical of the dreary run-on sentence structure commonly used in Studebaker Corporation pronouncements, but that's another subject.) Ford kept finding ways to build his cars cheaper so that he could pass the savings on to his customers, secure in the belief that every price reduction would widen the appeal of Ford cars. Remarkably, this bit of good business sense was regarded as radical—if not downright subversive—by many of Ford's competitors. It is significant that Studebaker, under Erskine's generally enlightened leadership, made no bones about pursuing the same policy. Studebaker four-cylinder prices had been cut from $1,290 in 1913 to $1,050 in 1914 to only $885 by the summer of 1915. It was no accident that demand intensified. Unit sales actually rose 107 percent between 1911 and 1915 (from 22,555 cars to 46,845). Erskine confidently predicted unit sales of 60,000 cars in 1916, war or no war.

Another way in which Erskine's Studebaker Corporation was echoing Henry Ford was in enlightened labor relations. Unlike Ford, however, Erskine's efforts were far more progressive and far-reaching than the often superficial and self-serving—even, it must be said, deceptive—practices at Ford.[19] On November 1, 1915, the eight hour working day was instituted at Studebaker plants in Detroit and Walkerville, although the work week was still six days. Wages were maintained at the old level—i.e., the hourly rate was increased to compensate for the reduction in hours. It was also announced that effective March 1, 1916, the work week in South Bend would be reduced from 55 hours to 50, with, as in Detroit and Walkerville, overall wage levels maintained. Furthermore, as of July 1, 1915, all Studebaker employees in the United States and Canada were offered free life insurance without examination as to age or medical condition. In addition, all Studebaker executives—including managers, superintendents and foremen and their chief assistants—were included for the second year in a row in a profit sharing plan.

Studebaker Corporation sales reached another all-time record in 1916 despite few changes in the automotive product line. Remarkably, this growth was due entirely to growth in automobile sales, as war contracts actually plummeted by 80 percent. America had not yet joined the conflict raging in Europe, although the sinking of the *Lusitania* the year before had intensified war fever even on these shores. Despite the fact that President Wilson was campaigning on a "peace" platform, most knowledgeable Americans assumed their country would be dragged into the war sooner or later. For the time being, however, things were "business as usual" and—for Studebaker, at any rate—business as usual was unusually good.

Total sales in 1916 amounted to a record $61.9 million of which only $2.8 million was generated by war contracts and a profit of $8.6 million was also reported. In fact, the company was straining every nerve to meet demand for Studebaker cars, which may explain why changing the location of the gas tank (from the cowl to the rear of the car) was the only development of note that year. The main problem, according to the company, was a shortage of railroad freight cars to transport cars to the branches and dealers. A company statement issued in February, 1917, noted:

> Results would have been still better had not the nation-wide shortage of transportation equipment seriously handicapped us in filling dealers' orders and abnormally curtailed our volume in the last quarter of the year. Fortunately, this condition is improving, and milder weather is already allowing us to deliver automobiles under their own power from our factories and branches.[20]

Studebaker's leading cast of characters posed in this 1916 Model ED Six: In the front seat, J.M. Studebaker and, at the wheel, Chief Engineer James Heaslet; in the back, Fred Fish and Albert Erskine.

1917 Studebaker Six.

Also helping was a new assembly plant in Chicago. South Bend was assembling cars, too, as the company pulled out all the stops to disperse assembly and obviate the need for long-distance shipment of finished products. The company now had assembly points spread across the heart of the midwest, from Detroit (and nearby Walkerville in Ontario), to South Bend and on to Chicago. Despite the problems, the 6,500 Studebaker dealers actually exceeded the company's target of 60,000 sales in 1916. A total of 65,885 cars were sold and the company confidently predicted 75,000 for 1917.

It was becoming apparent, though, that another new assembly facility would be needed in order to keep up with demand. Accordingly, Erskine set his engineers to the task of designing a state-of-the art facility and this, in turn, sparked all sorts of rumors that Studebaker would abandon South Bend. (Up to that time, of course, most of the current Studebaker cars were being built in Detroit; in South Bend, the declining wagon business still reined supreme.) Erskine felt compelled to personally promise J.M. Studebaker that the new plant would be built in South Bend. And, it was. Ground was broken on December 12, 1916 for a new machine shop, forge and power plant. This set in motion a trend that, within a few years, would see all automobile production shift from Detroit.

The last of the original founders of the firm, John Mohler Studebaker, died on March 16, 1917. He was eighty-three. His daughter, Grace Studebaker Fish, and his son-in-law, Frederick S. Fish, built the Sunnyside Presbyterian Church in South Bend in his memory.

Unfortunately, the company's hopes for 1917 were dashed by America's entry into the war. In February, the United States broke diplomatic relations with Germany. It seemed as if a formal declaration of war would be only a matter of time, but even before that took place, Erskine telegraphed President Wilson to offer Studebaker's full cooperation:

> Studebaker facilities of course are at the disposal of the Government. Any orders given us will receive preference and clear right-of-way.[21]

Wilson sent his thanks in reply and the War Department immediately undertook negotiations that ultimately resulted in substantial orders. Indeed, by the war's end, Studebaker had, to the detriment of its automobile business, shifted over to almost a complete war-footing. War was finally declared in April. As the company's 1952 history hyper-ventilated:

> America was being drawn into the war...The balance of power was needed to defeat the Germans moving quickly to become a master race over a slave world. England had lost the best manhood of two generations, the French were sunk down under great losses. Russia was staggering under greed, corruption, and moronic rulers. The German U-boats were sinking neutral American shipping, sending women and children to the bottom with a disregard, as usual, of any humane ideals.[22]

Be that as it may, Studebaker was "in it" even before America was (at least officially) and to those who might have been tempted to interpret Erskine's offer as a naked scheme to profit from lucrative military contracts, the results proved otherwise. Total sales dropped to $50.1 million in 1917 and profits plummeted to $3.5 million as the production of civilian passenger cars was sacrificed to satisfy the growing demands for war goods upon which the company often made little or no profit. By the end of the year, automobile production was running at half the 1916 level. Somehow, the company still managed to sell 42,357 cars, but its ability to produce them was dwindling with each passing month.

A contributing factor was that increases in material, wages and selling expenses had forced a substantial increase in the retail price being charged for the four-cylinder models. This increase, unfortunately, priced the four-cylinder Studebakers out of the volume part of the four-cylinder market. In contrast, sales of six-cylinder Studebaker models remained strong and even surpassed the 1916 volume.

Certainly one of the most intriguing 1917 Studebakers was a gold-plated show car exhibited at the January New York Auto Show and at other shows after that. The chassis alone was plated, but this still involved some 3,000 parts and set the company back a reported $25,000. Yale & Towne, for whom Erskine had formerly served as treasurer, did the work.

Meanwhile, the war was having a major effect on the way in which the company made its money. In particular, it breathed new life into the horse-drawn vehicle end of the business. Government orders for horse-drawn vehicles increased from 56,000 units in 1916 to 73,000 units in 1917. Part of the reason for this was Erskine's afore-mentioned decision to place all Studebaker facilities at the government's disposal. The government responded by dramatically increasing its dependence upon the company's

1916 Studebaker one-ton express truck.

Studebaker's military production during World War I included gun carriages, top, and the Model A military tractor for the British, a precursor of the modern tank.

offerings, and particularly with respect to the Vehicle Division. By the end of the year, half of all Studebaker plant capacity had been shifted over to horse-drawn vehicle production, with a consequent decrease in automobile production capacity, while the Chicago assembly plant was leased to the government and ceased to be a Studebaker facility entirely. Erskine

Above, 1918 Studebaker Big Six. Below, the Big Six engine.

went so far as to warn stockholders not to expect a stellar profit performance from the company for the duration:

We feel gratified in having voluntarily met the issue and placed ourselves in position to serve our Government as long as the war may last, freely and without compulsion. Government work ought to provide reasonably satisfactory profit returns, but it should be stated that the large automobile operations and resulting profits of peace times are opportunities that will not be again open to us until peace returns.[23]

The company was, however, operating with one eye on peacetime automobile sales. In June, the engineering and manufacturing departments were thoroughly reorganized with a resumption of peacetime production in mind. Perhaps more importantly, Erskine had made a hard-nosed decision regarding the company's cars. The product he had inherited was, in essence, a vastly improved version of the old E-M-F. By this point, though, it had become obvious that the Studebaker car was becoming seriously dated. In particular, Erskine was getting an earful from his brilliant (and recently promoted) chief engineer, Fred Zeder.

Zeder had built a remarkable team that included Owen R. Skelton and Carl Breer. Skelton, a graduate of the engineering school at Ohio State University, came from Packard where he was noted as a transmission and axle specialist. Breer was a graduate of Leland Stanford University in California and had worked with Allis-Chalmers before coming to Studebaker.

Breer had been lured by Zeder to Studebaker in November, 1916. Before he left for Detroit from California, where he was then living, he visited a local Studebaker dealer and was mightily impressed by the list of engineering features touted in a brochure that he picked-up in the showroom. He recalled his initial reaction:

> This list gave me the impression that I looking at a high grade, dependable vehicle that represented the latest in engineering technology. What a surprise I received when I later learned firsthand how erroneous this impression really was.[24]

1918 Studebaker street flusher.

On the job in Detroit, Breer discovered a host of problems, starting with the "minuscule" size of the engineering facilities. The cars themselves were profoundly troubled with mechanical defects. The engines ran poorly and the transmissions were a constant source of grief. Oil consumption was dreadful, main bearings had a nasty habit of self-destructing in the field, engine noise was excessive due to faulty engineering of the valve train and the crankshaft, the carburetors were badly designed—in short, as Breer saw it, the E-M-F-cum-Studebaker car was an engineering mess of the first magnitude. Apparently, Erskine was brought around to this view, as well, for he did more than ask Zeder's crew to fix the existing product (although he kept them busy enough doing that), he ordered an entirely new line of Studebaker cars to be put into intensive development.

In mid-September, 1917, three hand-built prototypes were secretly loaded onto a boat in Detroit and shipped to Buffalo. There, they were off-loaded and subjected to an exhausting 20,000-mile road test through Canada and the United States. Following the completion of that phase of their development, they were taken to the Chicago Speedway and subjected to a grueling 30,000-mile, night-and-day, endurance run. Erskine was delighted with the results. He later crowed that these were the cars that "made Studebaker famous." They were introduced in November, 1917, for the 1918 model year.

The old Four was continued over for a few months as the Light Four. The new models that Zeder's team had developed were called the Light Six and the Big Six, and—together with the carry-over four-cylinder models—this meant that the new Studebakers were available in three ranges: the 112-inch wheelbase Light Four starting at $895, the 119-inch wheelbase Light Six starting at $1,295 and the 126-inch wheelbase Big Six starting at $1,695. A production goal of 3,000 units per month was announced—baring adverse effects, the company warned, from "freight congestion, fuelless days and other conditions beyond our control."

The two sixes marked a major advance for Studebaker as an auto producer. Other than the old electrics, they were, in fact, the first cars ever designed from scratch as Studebakers *per se*. Gone was the troublesome transaxle, replaced by a conventional three-speed transmission located behind the engine. The frame was revised to permit the introduction of

Hotchkiss drive in the rear. The styling, too, represented a distinct advance, and was more curvaceous and contemporary than the rather angular and boxy cars built since 1913. Windshields were actually set at an angle, rather than perpendicular. A variety of body styles were available on the Model EH Light Six, including touring, roadster, coupe and sedan versions. An attractive four-passenger club roadster, known as the Chummy, was offered, as well.[25] The Model EG Big Six, curiously, was only listed as a touring car despite its flagship status in the Studebaker firmament. With its long hood, it was easily the most distinctive Studebaker built. The headlamp bezels were another distinctive feature, being rounded-off squares in shape.

Mechanically, both sixes were similar, although the Big Six, with its 60 horsepower engine, was the more powerful. The main difference between them was the detachable head on the Big Six's engine. Otherwise, the Light Six was a somewhat, well, lighter edition of the same basic design.[26]

As it turned out, passenger car production continued to dwindle even below the company's modest projections due to wartime demands of the government. Only 23,864 cars were sold in 1918, the lowest number since the company went public in 1911. Sales increased slightly to $52 million but profits, as Erskine had warned, remained in the doldrums at $3.9 million. As the nation returned to a peacetime footing in 1919, however, both sales and, especially, profits rose sharply. Overall sales amounted to a record $66.4 million, while profits soared to a record $9.3 million.

Although Studebaker's horse-drawn vehicle production had run at virtual capacity in 1917 and 1918, its continued success was thanks largely to government contracts and the decision was made in November, 1918, to get the company out of that business as soon as the war was over. This occurred in 1919 and all horse-drawn vehicle operations were liquidated except for wagons, farm trucks and harnesses. The remaining operations were liquidated in 1920. The Studebaker name would never again appear on the type of vehicle that had given the company birth and brought it world-wide renown, but it was a shrewd move. Noted Erskine in an interview given several years later:

> We were lucky in liquidating our horse vehicle business in 1919-20, through regular trade channels, at full wholesale

prices...Everything was booming at that time and people couldn't get enough of anything. This gave us more room, more money, and more men of unusual skill for the production of motor cars, particularly closed bodies. Had we not sold out then, we would doubtless have had to close down that whole part of our works in 1921.[27]

To replace horse-drawn vehicles, automobile production was being slowly centralized in Indiana. Of the $8.2 million the company spent on new plants and facilities in 1919, 90 percent was spent in South Bend. An entirely new automobile plant was under construction, including a forge shop, a stamping plant, a machine shop, a power house, and various storage and assembly facilities. This plant, designated Plant 2, cost $15 million and was to be dedicated to production of the new Light Six line upon which the company was placing much of it postwar hopes. The Light Six was scheduled for production in the spring of 1920.[28] It was also around this time that Guy P. Henry was appointed chief engineer, a position he would fill for six years. He replaced Fred Zeder, who had left in a huff after a dispute with Erskine. Zeder took Skelton and Breer with him and the three of them set-up shop as independent engineering consultants.

Sales of Studebaker cars soared to 51,474 in 1920 on the strength of a postwar economic boom, while income soared with it to another record: $90.7 million. This was the second-best figure in the company's history and almost matched the prewar high recorded in 1916. It was certainly strong evidence of both the wisdom of getting out of the horse-drawn vehicle business and in the design the postwar crop of Studebaker products, particularly the new Model EJ Light Six mounted on a 112-inch wheelbase. The 207 cubic inch engine used an aluminum head and was rated at 40 horsepower. Models introduced in the next several years included touring, roadster, sedan, coupe body styles. Curiously, styling was less rounded and more angular than before—"crisper," as the advertising copy writers might have put it—but more stylish, none-the-less. While it wouldn't be accurate to say that any Studebakers in this era were beautiful, there was a decided trend toward emphasizing aesthetics and the impetus for this had to have come from the top, in other words, from Erskine himself. The old

1920 Studebaker Special Six. The model shown is the four-passenger roadster, also known as the "Chummy."

Light Six was continued over with refinements as the new Model EH Special Six with tear-shaped cowl lights, while the revised Model EK Big Six continued as the flagship of the line.

The Big Six was little changed in basic specifications other than the addition of a single dry-plate clutch. It was much improved in appearance, however. A cowl vent, windshield wipers, a nickel-plated radiator shell, nickel-plated bumpers, spotlights, a motometer and optional disc wheels were all introduced during the two-year run. The Big Six model range was expanded in 1921, with the addition of sedan and coupe body styles.

Studebaker's sales performance in 1921 was especially impressive. In a year in which the nation underwent a short, sharp recession that nearly brought to ruin industry giants such as General Motors and Willys-Overland, and saw sales collapse for virtually all manufacturers, Studebaker experienced its all time record year to date: 66,643 cars were sold. Furthermore, this happened despite the fact that the Studebaker plant in Detroit was shut down in December, 1920, at the bottom of the recession and didn't reopen until the following January. The company took in $96.7 million in 1921 and posted a record $9.8 million in profits, a performance all the more noteworthy considering it was due entirely to automotive sales, the horse-drawn vehicle operations having been finally phased out.

Studebaker's stellar performance had apparently caught the eye of William C. Durant, the founder of General Motors. Durant had been forced out of General Motors for the second and final time in the latter months of 1920 and immediately set about creating another automobile company: Durant Motors. Development of a Durant car was quickly announced, but Durant was never one to aspire to the little leagues. By April, 1922, the *New York Times* was reporting Durant's intention to amass a rival to General Motors by merging Durant Motors with, among other companies, Studebaker and Pierce-Arrow. The rumor receded from the news as quickly as it had appeared, but Durant's interest in Studebaker continued. As late as 1924, he was still buying heavily in Studebaker stock and claimed, at one point, that he had turned a profit of $4 million in doing so. What Fred Fish and Albert Erskine thought about all this is unrecorded, and it is difficult to imagine either Durant or Erskine willingly becoming the subordinate of the other, but no official involvement with Durant or with Durant Motors ever came to pass.

Studebaker models were revised in appearance for 1922, with one-piece windshields featured along with cowl ventilation and nickel-plated headlamps. Disc wheels were optional and, throughout the line, these were the best-looking Studebakers yet. The Model EH Special Six and Model EJ

1922 Studeabker Big Six.

The Studebaker factory complex in South Bend in 1923.

Light Six were replaced with revised models designated EL and EM, respectively. The Big Six, designated the EK, also featured a cone-type clutch.

In 1922, with the nation's economy recovering, unit sales of Studebaker cars passed the century mark: 110,269 cars were sold. Sales, too, soared to $133.1 million. Indeed, the main problem for Erskine and his crew in this period seems to have been trying to create sufficient plant capacity to satisfy demand. In March, capacity was expanded to 440 cars per day, or about 130,000 cars per year (based on a six-day work week). For a company that had sold 22,555 cars as recently as 1911, the year it went public, this was definitely something to boast about. In that period, overall sales had risen from $28.4 million to $133.1 million. Profits had risen from $1.8 million to $18.1 million. The company also had 5,000 dealers (up from 1,500) and 17,663 employees. Of those 17,663 employees, moreover, 63.7 percent had qualified for profit sharing and 17.3 percent were stockholders in the corporation. The future certainly looked bright.

Automobile production was being shifted from Detroit with a vengeance at this juncture, with nearly all the capital spending for the past several years relating to the automotive operations having been spent in South Bend. In 1922 alone, six major plant buildings had been erected, including a closed body plant comprising around 350,000 square feet of floor space, and a shipping and car storage building comprising around 180,000 square feet of floor space. Over a million square feet of new facilities were built, in all, and the vast majority of that investment went into South Bend.

Studebaker reached a high watermark in 1923, with record sales of $166.1 million and record profits of $18.4 million. Allowing for inflation, these figures would never again be equaled in the company's history. This was accomplished on the basis of 145,167 cars sold, which represented just over 4% of industry sales that year and also would be a record that would stand for many years. In fact, more money was spent by consumers on Studebaker cars in 1923 than had been spent on all horse-drawn vehicles during the entire sixty-eight years in which horse-drawn vehicles had been produced by the company. Erskine, obviously feeling his oats by this time, boasted to a reporter from *Barrons*: "We eat obstacles for breakfast."

Indeed, it seemed to be true. Studebaker Corporation had been on the move since the end of the war. An impressive $39.4 million had been spent in capital improvements, such as new plants and facilities for automobile manufacture. Capacity had been increased from 50,000 cars per year to 180,000. The company was now manufacturing its own bodies, castings and other key components. Erskine, never one to be shy about Studebaker's accomplishments, bragged about this, too:

> No other individual manufacturer, except Ford, can produce as many closed bodies as we can and no manufacturer can make them better, because we have experienced wood workers and trimming craftsmen who used to make Studebaker carriages. In fact, with these new plants we can produce closed bodies at South Bend ten per cent cheaper than they can be made in Detroit. Therefore, we can sell closed cars cheaper than anybody in the industry.[29]

Erskine's reputation was growing apace in this era. *Motor Age* called him "a rare combination of master financier, manufacturer and salesman" and predicted: "As long as he stands at the helm, watch Studebaker!"

Erskine had his detractors, though. He could be rude and arrogant, and was known to harbor grudges. According to historian Maurice Hendry, Erskine once caused Studebaker's advertising agency to be fired as a result of a dispute over a poker game. Sometimes, too, his high-handedness re-

Will Rogers and Albert Erskine camping it up in front of a 1925 Standard Six.

bounded against him, as, apparently, was the case with chief engineer, Fred Zeder. Zeder had departed shortly after the postwar models were introduced, angrily claiming Erskine had broken promises to him and to his two able assistants, Owen Skelton and Carl Breer.

Then, early in 1925, Erskine's picked a fight with a candidate for the Federal judiciary. When Thomas W. Slick was nominated for a vacancy on the local circuit, Erskine vehemently opposed him, accusing him of having engaged in a stock swindle that Erskine described as "one of the rottenest things I ever saw." Slick was confirmed anyway, but the antagonism engendered would have critical repercussions down the road.

Erskine's attitudes on race were something less than enlightened, as well, as one might have expect from a white Southerner of his generation.

In a letter to Herbert Hoover, whom he actively supported for president in 1928, Erskine commented on the "Negro problem":

> Southerners will always maintain that the South is a white man's country...The Negro problem is the greatest peril which confronts America today. It daily grows worse. Our great cities are being crowded with hordes of Negroes demanding equality in boisterous and insulting terms wherever you meet them.[30]

Erskine, in short, was a man of extremes, in whom the virtues and the flaws often loomed equally large. The same man who could fire a key supplier over a card game and rage against the Negro could also take a leading role in the industry in improving conditions for the average worker.

Studebaker workers were of a somewhat different breed than those working for other auto manufacturers, too, owing to the composition of the local labor pool. When the Studebaker brothers set up shop in 1852, South Bend had been a town of 1,700. By 1920, some 70,000 people were counted in the census. Most of the population growth had come from Eastern Europe—Poles, Hungarians and so forth—and, as late as 1920, one out of five residents had been born abroad. Many still did not speak English; in the inbred Polish and Hungarian neighborhoods it wasn't necessary.

Erskine was proud of his workers, and of the nationwide reputation Studebaker was gaining as being a caring and liberal employer. This stood in marked contrast to many other auto companies that were considered to be little better than sweat shops. Henry Ford, who was once the darling of those seeking improvement in working conditions, had already become a symbol for the reverse. In an "autobiography" published under his name in the early 1920s—but almost certainly written by one of his public relations retainers—Ford outlined in no uncertain terms his ideas regarding the cold-blooded role of industrial management:

> It is not necessary to have meetings to establish good feelings between individuals or departments. There is not much personal contact [at Ford Motor Company]—the men do their work and go home. A factory is not a drawing room. We do not believe in the

"glad hand," or the professionalized "personal touch," or "human element." I pity the poor fellow who is so soft and flabby that he must always have an atmosphere of good feeling around him before he can do his work.[31]

Erskine's view could not have formed a starker contrast. In an interview given in 1925, he stated:

> The first duty of an employer is to labor. By labor I mean any man that does what he is told. It is the duty of capital and management to compensate liberally, paying at least the current wage and probably a little more, and to give workers decent and healthful surroundings and treat them with the utmost consideration. If management cannot do this, then something is wrong...
>
> In March, 1917, we inaugurated dividends on wages. Like other companies, we had had a very heavy labor turnover. There have always been millions of migratory workers, men who will not settle long enough anywhere to accomplish really effective work. We sought to provide a strong inducement to all our workers to say with us. We announced: "Nobody will pay you more or will treat you better than Studebaker. We are your friends. Come to us when you are in trouble and we can help you. No Studebaker employee can fail to be successful if he will stick with us and be industrious..."
>
> What is the result? Our men build their very souls into the Studebaker cars. They don't soldier on the job. They do honest work. The cars show it...
>
> No competitor ever takes away from us a Studebaker man we want to keep...We are all partners. There is no politics from top to bottom of our organization. Every man eats and thinks and dreams Studebaker.[32]

Well, perhaps, but as we have seen Erskine lost three good men shortly after the close of the war—Zeder, Skelton and Breer—and, it is hard to believe he really didn't want to keep men of such talent. At the time the

Zeder, Breer and Skelton posed for this publicity shot during the early 1930s.

trio left to form their independent consulting firm, they did so with the long range goal of getting back into the automobile business on their own. Their ace in the hole in that ambitious endeavor was the design for a new car they had been secretly talking about for some time. Once on their own, they set about developing their engineering designs in earnest.

Eventually, in 1921, the trio found a home with Willys-Overland. Unfortunately, this was just about the time that firm nearly went broke in the sharp recession of 1920-21. Fortunately, Walter Chrysler was also out of work. Chrysler, who had just taken early retirement from General Motors after heading Buick for several highly successful years, recalled:

> I had no shop, no office, no regular job, no responsibility. I hung around the house. Men kept coming to see me about this and that. The place was always full of ashes and cigar smoke. After about three months of that my wife put me out of the house. I couldn't blame her.[33]

So, thanks to Mrs. Chrysler's well-timed insistence that her husband quit loafing around and get a job, Chrysler quickly accepted the call to go down to Toledo to try and save Willys-Overland. What's more, he accomplished the task in astonishingly short order and, in the process, fell under the spell of Zeder, Skelton and Breer. Actually, it seems to have been a mutual admiration society, but there was a problem. In order to raise cash, the factory in Elizabeth, New Jersey, in which the trio had designed their wonder car had been sold to William C. Durant. Durant knew about the car and wanted it in the worst way. Moreover, Durant reasoned that since it was done on what was now his property it belonged to him.

That Durant had a point was undeniable and the situation promised to get sticky until fate intervened yet again. This time, it was Maxwell-Chalmers that was on the ropes and needed Chrysler's magic act. Chrysler was amenable and convinced Zeder, Skelton and Breer to let Durant have their car, then come over to Maxwell-Chalmers and design an even better one. So great was their faith in Walter Chrysler that the three agreed. It was perhaps a year later that Albert Erskine got in the act.[34]

Chrysler didn't own, or even control, Maxwell-Chalmers; he merely ran it. Erskine, knowing full well the ability of the engineering trio, having heard about the second car they were developing for Chrysler and wanting to expand Studebaker into other markets à la General Motors—shades of Durant!—decided to buy Maxwell-Chalmers. On behalf of Studebaker, he approach a group of investors in New York who possessed enough Maxwell-Chalmers stock to exert control and, following negotiations, offered them $26 million. They indicated that they would accept. What Erskine may not have known, though, was that Walter Chrysler had already decided to name the new car after himself and would be thunderstruck by the turn of events. As Chrysler recalled his autobiography:

> I felt sick...It was clear that if Studebaker bought out [Maxwell-Chalmers], then Frederick S. Fish, chairman of Studebaker, would want to head up the combined enterprises with the Studebaker president, Albert R. Erskine. There would hardly be room for Erskine and Chrysler in one pasture lot. Happily for me, that deal fell through...[35]

Happily, to be sure, but Chrysler was being coy. The deal didn't fall, it was pushed. Who pushed it, however, remains unclear. Most histories of the period finger Chrysler as the man behind the effort to thwart Erskine. Norman Beasley and George Stark, two contemporary Detroit newspapermen (working for the *Detroit Journal* and the *Detroit News*, respectively) later wrote an account based on an interview with Fred Zeder that offers another view.[36] In their account, Zeder says that Chrysler was in favor of seeing the deal go through until he informed Zeder about it. Zeder, whose departure from Studebaker had been less than cordial, still bore a grudge against Erskine and railed:

> Walter, if Erskine wants to pay twenty-seven million dollars [sic] for brick and mortar and machines, all right. But, no automobile. Remember that. No automobile! I'm glad you remember that Zeder, Skelton, and Breer own the patents on the Chrysler engine. And, believe me when I tell you that I'll take a sledge hammer and personally smash the new models into bits before I'll let Erskine have them. I told you [before], and I'll tell you again, that I designed and built one car for Erskine...He welched on his promises to me, and to my associates. He can't have two of my cars. Never![37]

In the account, the alleged promises that Erskine make to Zeder, Skelton and Breer were not specified. Breer's memoirs, however, suggest the likely answer. In 1918, Breer briefly left Studebaker to go to war. When he returned, he found that a Materials and Specifications Division had been created, known as "M & S." The purpose of this new entity was to supervise and to pass judgment on, the work of Zeder and his engineering staff. Worse, M & S, in Breer's opinion, was run by men whose engineering ability was far inferior to that of Zeder, Skelton and Breer—which may sound immodest but was probably true enough since the three of them composed just about the finest engineering team in the industry at the time. M & S argued with the decisions of Zeder's team and created serious delays in getting important decisions approved by management, i.e., by Erskine. "This," Breer noted, "broke down our morale" and was doubtless a key factor in the team's decision to abandon Studebaker. It is easy enough to assume that Zeder thought (not unreasonably) that Erskine had given him

1924 Studebaker Big Six.

ultimate authority for engineering at the time he was promoted to chief engineer and was miffed (to put it mildly) when Erskine sicced the new watchdog department on him two years later. Zeder and his cohorts left Studebaker within months of the creation of M & S.

Whatever the motivation, Walter Chrysler, working with another group of investors, finally out-bid Erskine for Maxwell-Chalmers. The Zeder-Skelton-Breer wonder car was subsequently introduced at the January, 1924,

1924 Special Six featuring the "Duplex" roof.

New York Auto Show as planned (and to great acclaim) and was the first car to bear the Chrysler nameplate.

The episode was no doubt a severe disappointment for Erskine on a number of levels. It did, however, show the degree to which he was determined to expand Studebaker's presence in the market and the amount of money he was able and willing to spend in order to achieve that. For a decade he had run Studebaker and had brought the company to the greatest sales and market penetration it had ever known. At this juncture, however, Studebaker reached a plateau. Try as he might—and he tried mightily—Erskine was never able to push Studebaker to a better level of performance than it attained in 1923.

Meawhile, Erskine's building program went on unabated. Construction of a new iron foundry in South Bend in 1924 completed the postwar capital expansion plans of the company. A grand total of $48.8 million had been spent since the end of the war. According to the company, no further expenditures were planned for coming years, although Erskine would think of a few soon enough.

Financially, the year was one of retrograde motion. Sales fell to $135.4 million, while profits took a sharp drop to $13.8 million. Sales of Studebaker cars also plummeted by 24 percent to 110,240. This was due, perhaps, to the aging of the product line and a new range of Studebaker cars was an-

1925 Big Six.

The original "Our Gang" comedy troupe posing in 1925 with a couple of Studebakers: a 1916 bus and a 1919 Big Six, both belonging to the Roach studio.

nounced on September 14, 1924. It consisted of no less than fifteen models mounted on three chassis. Some two million prospects crowded into Studebaker showrooms across the country within the first three days the new line was on sale and dealers reported selling 9,000 cars during the first week. It is clear that Erskine was pushing hard for good styling, for Studebaker products seemed to improve year-by-year in that regard. More than that, they were starting to assume a leadership role in design that grew consistently until the end of Erskine's regime. This is all the more amazing when it is remembered that Studebaker never had a big-name designer on its staff in this era, such as Frank De Causse at Franklin, nor any sort of formal design department of the sort that Harley Earl was to establish at General Motors in 1927 and wouldn't for another decade.

An interesting new feature on the 1925 models was four-wheel hydraulic brakes. Similar brakes had been pioneered in America by Duesenberg and Rickenbacker (among a few others). They were instantly controversial and for a reason that would astonish us today: many people thought it was downright unsafe to stop that quickly. Moreover, Erskine was one of them. According to Breer, Erskine attempted to organize other automakers to oppose four-wheel brakes. When that failed, Studebaker resportedly spent something on the order of $1 million on its own in advertising against them, but, by 1925, had bowed to the march of progress and installed them in the Big Six. It was said this was made necessary by complaints from dealers who claimed they were losing sales because of the company's stance. At any rate, a four-wheel hydraulic system was announced for 1925 as a $75 option. The company was still dubious, though, and made sure that the greatest braking power was at the rear wheels, which defeated the purpose to some extent for when a car brakes the greatest stress is thrown toward the front.[38] General Motors, when it introduced four-wheel mechanical brakes on the Cadillac V-63 series in 1924 had equalized the braking power, front and rear, but arranged the system so that the rear wheels would lock-up first. This was a superior approach, but merely to have four-wheel brakes of any description no doubt answered the pleas of Studebaker dealers.

The Light Six was dropped for 1925, but a revised Model EQ Special Six made its appearance with distinctive drum-style headlamps. It was available in sedan, coach, Duplex phaeton, Duplex roadster, victoria, berline, brougham and sport roadster models. The Duplex models were, essentially, fixed hardtops with sliding side windows. In that, they anticipated the hardtop body style by twenty-five years. A special touring model, called the Sheriff, was announced with the Big Six engine as standard equipment. The Big Six was revised, as well, and was redesignated the Model EP with higher engine compression and full-pressure lubrication.

The big product news was the Model ER Standard Six line, which replaced the old Light Six. Based on a 113-inch wheelbase, it clung to two-wheel mechanical brakes. The bored-out 241.6 cubic inch engine was considerably larger than that of the old Light Six, with increased compression and, at a rating of 50 horsepower, about 25 percent more power. Body styles included: sedan, business coupe, coach (two-door sedan), coupe, phaeton and roadster. The last two types were also available as Duplex models with a fixed top and sliding side windows that anticipated the four-door hardtop styling of the 1950s.

Studebaker also took the step of foregoing annual model changes with the Standard Six. Improvements would be made as they came available. Whatever else its merits, this policy has caused a great deal of confusion for modern-day restorers. Studebaker was not alone in that approach, however. Many manufacturers of that era (Packard, Oakland/Pontiac and

Chrysler spring to mind) used highly individual series designations that failed to conform to any sort of model year as the term is understood today. As for the Studebaker Standard Sixes, many modern writers have stubbornly tried to cram them into something resembling modern model years, but this is difficult, if not impossible, to do.

Prices across the Studebaker model range were reduced effective January 8, 1925, in an effort to spur sales. It worked. A total of 134,664 cars were sold during the calendar year and overall sales also rebounded to $161.4 million. Profits came back, as well, to $16.6 million. If it was not quite equal to the record performance of 1923, it was a welcome development following the poor showing in 1924. In particular, the export business was booming, with sales up 64 percent. Employment for the year averaged 21,977.

A name that would loom large in Studebaker's future appeared on the official list of officers for the first time during 1925. Paul G. Hoffman was promoted to vice-president in charge of sales. The following year, Harold S. Vance was also to become a vice-president, in his case in charge of production. Although no one could have known it at the time, these were the two men who were destined to pilot the company for two decades following the conclusion of the Erskine regime a few years hence.

Paul Hoffman, while still selling cars in Los Angeles and before he

The 1918 Big Six that Paul Hoffman promoted on the auto show circuit in 1924.

Knute Rockne, Notre Dame's famed football coach, posed with a 1926 Standard Six for this Studebaker publicity shot.

moved to South Bend, had garnered a great deal of publicity from a Big Six that had racked up over 400,000 miles without a single engine rebuild. The 1918 model car quickly went through a couple of owners, including a Los Angeles newspaper distributor. Studebaker bought the car for display at the 1924 New York Auto Show, then sent it on a publicity-generating trek from New York to Los Angeles. After that, it was given a well-earned rest in the Studebaker museum in South Bend next to the first Studebaker-built Conestoga wagon and Abraham Lincoln's Studebaker carriage.

Ab Jenkins participated in a dramatic demonstration of the reliability of the Big Six in 1926. He drove one from New York to San Francisco in a record-breaking eighty-six hours and twenty minutes, shaving sixteen hours off the previous record time. His average speed was 40.2 miles per hour, and this in a day in which paved roads were still few and far between outside the major urban areas. West of the Mississippi, in fact, the roads were little better than rutted trails in many places.

In 1926, sales slumped again to 111,315 cars. Overall revenues of $141.5 million and profits of $13 million were solid if unspectacular. This was the year that the old E-M-F plant in Detroit was finally closed and all production was transferred to South Bend. Vance was in charge of the relocation.

Concurrent with the consolidation in South Bend, a modern engineering and research plant was built. It was also about this time that the Studebaker proving ground came into being. An 840-acre site with a selection of driving conditions and gradients permitted the full testing of new Studebaker models, it was constructed just outside South Bend and was the first such facility in the industry. It included a high-speed, banked oval track, numerous roads of varying surfaces, and recreational facilities.

From the two forges of the original H. & C. Studebaker firm, Studebaker Corporation by 1926 had 12,500 machines in use in 342 manufacturing departments. Supplies used every year totaled: 30,000 tons of pig iron, 130,000 tons of steel, 450,000 gallons of lacquers and enamels, 1,778,000 square feet of plate glass, 20,745,000 board feet of lumber, 7,500,000 gallons of fuel oil, 160,000 tons of coal and 275,000,000 cubic feet of natural gas.

Capacity had been expanded again and again, totaling $52 million in capital expenditures of that type since the end of the war. This allowed a maximum of 200,000 Studebaker cars to be built if demand warranted. It was not to be, however. The company seems to have become stuck in the doldrums, in which sales consistently fell into the 110,000-135,000 range, depending on whether it was a "good" year.

By 1926, though, Erskine was more determined than ever to get Studebaker moving upward again and his big project was another car. More than a new model, it was an entirely new brand planned for introduction the following year. As if that weren't enough, it was to be named for the man who, more than any other individual, had brought the company to the heights of prosperity and prestige.

Proclaimed an advertisement:

> Some two years ago, Albert Russel Erskine, President of The Studebaker Corporation, came to the decision that the world automobile market would shortly demand a car of European type, built to the standard of the American fine car...Because Mr. Erskine was primarily responsible for the development of this evolutionary new car, the board of directors of The Studebaker Corporation unanimously decreed that it should be named the "Erskine Six."

Those of a Biblical cast of mind, who recalled the old injunction about pride going before a fall, might have been struck by this. Be that as it may, Studebaker was about to enter a tumultuous period in its history.

Notes

The most important resources drawn upon in the writing of this chapter include Albert Erskine's *History of the Studebaker Corporation*, Stephen Longstreet's official company history, *A Century on Wheels: The Story of Studebaker*, C. B. Glasscock's *The Gasoline Age: The Story of the Men Who Made It*, B. C. Forbes' *Automotive Giants of America*, and Carl Breer's *The Birth of Chrysler Corporation*. Walter Chrysler's autobiography, *The Life of an American Workman*, and *Made in Detroit*, by Beasely and Stark, offered fascinating insights into the relationship between Zeder, Skelton and Breer, on the one hand, and Albert Erskine, on the other. Periodicals used for important anecdotes and sidelights included various issues of *Special-Interest Autos* .

[1] In the next few years, the members of the Studebaker family would gradually liquidate their holdings. By the time the depression hit in 1929, practically no Studebaker family ownership remained.

[2] One of the plants bought up was the Ford's Piquette Street plant as that firm accelerated its expansion into its new Highland Park facility.

[3] 1911 Studebaker Corporation Annual Report. In this era, "vehicles" generally meant horse-drawn vehicles.

[4] Longstreet, p. 78.

[5] What was left?

[6] Everitt, Metzger and Flanders got together again as the movers behind the Rickenbacker automobile in the 1920s. Flanders died in a car crash in 1923. Metzger died in 1933, while Everitt followed in 1940.

[7] Longstreet, pp. 75-76.

[8] Longstreet. pp. 76-77.

[9] Longstreet, p. 83.

[10] Longstreet, pp. 72-73.

[11] Forbes and Foster, pp. 66-68.

[12] Forbes and Foster, pp. 61-62.

[13] 1913 Studebaker Corporation Annual Report.

[14] The IWW was also hated by the older, more moderate unions. In addition, lingering fear of the IWW was one reason often cited by historians for Henry

Ford's dramatic decision to initiate the $5 day in January, 1914.

15 1913 Studebaker Corporation Annual Report.

16 1913 Studebaker Corporation Annual Report.

17 Longstreet, p. 85.

18 1915 Studebaker Corporation Annual Report.

19 Henry Ford's famed "$5 day" was announced at about the same time. On the surface, it promised unheard-of wages to Ford workers in an industry where the entry-level wage was then around $2-$3 a day. In fact, the $5 wage rate only applied to workers in Ford's American plants (Canadian workers could aspire to only $4), then only to married men (who were presumed to deserve it more than single men), then only to those who had been on the job for a statutory period of time (which automatically excluded thousands of workers in what was a "high-turnover" industry), and, finally, only then to those able to pass muster following an intrusive personal investigation (on-site examination of the worker's home, interviews with the worker's neighbors regarding his character, etc.) by Ford's Sociology Department.

20 1916 Studebaker Corporation Annual Report.

21 Erskine, 1924, p. 57.

22 Longstreet, pp. 86-87.

23 1917 Studebaker Corporation Annual Report.

24 Breer, p. 31.

25 Shades of the Izzer buggy!

26 The smaller six got detachable heads in 1920.

27 Forbes and Foster, p. 72.

28 Plant 1, also in South Bend, built components. Plant 3 was the Detroit facility, in which all Studebaker cars had been built up to that time.

29 Forbes and Foster, p. 71.

30 Critchlow, p. 216.

31 Forbes and Foster, pp. 105-106.

32 Forbes and Foster, pp. 73-76.

33 Chrysler, p. 166.

34 Zeder, Skelton, and Breer's "Willys-Overland" car was built by Durant under the Flint nameplate.

35 Chrysler, p. 182.

36 Beasley and Stark published their book, *Made in Detroit*, in 1957, although the style would suggest that Beasley did most of the writing. Both had solid credentials. Stark was the City of Detroit's official historian for a time, while Beasley was also noted as the biographer of William S. Knudsen, the former president of General Motors. In both books, Beasley's writing tends to be breezy, with a heavy reliance on anecdotes and an often casual regard for chronology. For example, the Zeder story recounted here was set in 1925—after the first

Chrysler had been announced and perhaps a year-and-a-half after Erskine's attempt to buy Maxwell-Chalmers actually took place. Such haphazard attention to dates was not at all unusual even in very good automotive histories of the time, for nit-picking the details was not done as stringently then as it is today. None-the-less, Beasley generally got his important facts right, while his anecdotes, even when they were obviously misplaced in time, were based on first-hand interviews with the people involved and were usually reliable as to their basic thrust.

[37] Beasley and Stark, p. 298.

[38] Unless, of course, the car is going backwards.

Overleaf, the body drop on the South Bend assembly line in the late-1920s.

FOUR

The Fall of Erskine

Studebaker celebrated its Diamond Jubilee on January 2, 1927 with a huge affair in South Bend. More than 1,800 people were in attendance. For a dozen years Albert Russel Erskine had been, in a practical sense, master of the House of Studebaker and, after the death of John Mohler Studebaker in 1917, had been very nearly undisputed in his power. During that time he had, with rare lapses, done a masterful job. Beginning in 1927, however, things would start to go wrong for Erskine and for Studebaker. At first, the failures would be mixed with successes, but, in a few years, a crisis would arise and nothing Erskine could conjure up would stem the tide.

The first unmistakable sign that Erskine was not infallible was a new brand of automobile he named after himself. The company's official history, published in 1952, described it this way:

> Studebaker introduced a new small car called the Erskine Six. Not in South Bend or New York. But in Paris. Europe was mad about small cars, with their small use of gas as an added attraction. The car was also shown in London. Twenty-six thousand cars were sold abroad. It did well in America, too.[1]

Would that this claim had been entirely true. In fact, the Erskine—nicknamed "The Little Aristocrat"—ultimately became something of a disappointment on both sides of the Atlantic.

The genesis of the Erskine dated back to around 1925. Studebaker had for years done a big export business and listened intently when European dealers complained that Studebakers designed for American conditions were not nearly so appealing overseas. Europeans wanted smaller cars and, moreover, higher-revving engines with smaller bores in order to take advantage of European tax laws. In addition, there was a vogue in small sixes at the time. So, Studebaker responded.

In theory, the Erskine Model 50 was just what the European market wanted. Designed by no less a figure than Ray Dietrich of custom coachbuilding fame, it was quite stylish compared to the norms of 1927.[2] It looked like just the thing for cruising down Knightsbridge Road or the Champs Elysée. Furthermore, it was small—at least by American standards for a car in the Studebaker class—and mounted on a maneuverable 107-inch wheelbase. The engine, bought by Studebaker from Continental, was a 146.1 cubic inch six-cylinder powerplant rated at 40 horsepower. A "stroker," it used a long-stroke, small-bore design.[3] A range of four body styles was offered: sedan, business coupe, club coupe and touring.

Unfortunately, the program didn't work out the way Studebaker expected. Although the Erskine did sell fairly well in European markets at first, it quickly faded over there and it never really caught on in America. For one thing, due to the Erskine's lengthy gestation, the European boom in small sixes had peaked long before the Model 50 made it to Paris. The key drawback on both sides of the Pond, however, was price. At $975 for the sedan, the Erskine was not, by any stretch, an inexpensive car. The Ford Model A, which appeared on the American scene a few months later and was roughly comparable to the Model 50 in general dimensions, sold for barely half as much. Going toward the other end of the price spectrum, a 1927 Buick—a nameplate that packed a lot more wallop then than it does today—could be had for only $1,195, which was not very much more money for a car that was a world apart in size and image.

An additional problem at home was the Continental engine. Continental was one of the leading suppliers of "proprietary" engines to a number of the smaller manufacturers who could not afford to engineer and produce their own—a category in which, it might be noted, Studebaker hardly belonged. Be that as it may, Continental never built a truly distin-

1927 Erskine Model 50.

guished powerplant and the Erskine six was no stand-out even by Continental's standards. Furthermore, Studebaker tried to compensate for the relatively low power of the engine by fitting it with a very high 5.13:1 rear axle ratio. The effect of this was to encourage over-revving and, thus, reduce engine life to levels far below what American buyers found acceptable. At least from the perspective of prospects on these shores, the Erskine soon came to be regarded as a pricey little car with a weak engine and there wasn't much appeal in that. The Erskine accounted for 23,137 cars sold in 1927 (about 20 percent of Studebaker volume), rose to 37,496 in 1928 (about 28 percent), then collapsed to only 11,500 in 1929 (about 12 percent) as its reputation for burning up engines began to spread.

Things looked better with the carry-over model range, where Studebaker changed its series designations in 1927. Gone were the Standard Six, Light Six and Big Six. In their places were the Dictator, Commander and President. Styling, too, was changed and all Studebakers had a more massive appearance. The radiator shell was more rounded, the beltlines featured wide, double-moldings and closed bodies were fitted with enormous sun visors that were extensions of the roof, not obvious add-ons of the type General Motors and other manufacturers were using.

If the Dictator name seems repellent to us today, it must be seen in the context of the time. Hitler was still virtually unknown outside a few Munich beer halls. Dictators then were people such as Mussolini, who was amazingly popular in intellectual circles in the United States where Fascism was widely regarded as a beneficial movement toward social restructuring and efficiency in government.[4] (Perhaps it struck a chord with Erskine, who was something of a dictator himself in South Bend, if contemporary accounts are to be believed.) At any rate, a dictator was still generally regarded as a positive figure, hence the choice of the designation for Studebaker's low-priced line.

The Model EU Dictator series was the first one to feature the "Atalanta" radiator mascot. It also boasted more comprehensive instrumentation, with temperature and gas gauges standard. Two-wheel mechanical brakes were standard, as well. The old single bumper of the Standard Six was replaced by a double-bar bumper design. Body styles included: sedan, business coupe, berline, coupe, victoria, touring and roadster. The touring car was also available with the Duplex fixed top and sliding side windows.

The Model EW didn't actually become the Commander until a few months into the model run, but, name-wise, it fit nicely in between the

Dictator and President. Built on a 120-inch wheelbase, it came standard with disc wheels and two-wheel mechanical brakes. The engine was a 353.8 cubic inch six rated at 75 horsepower. Body styles included: sedan, business coupe, coupe, victoria, brougham, touring and roadster. The roadster was available as a Duplex model.

The top-end President is regarded by many modern enthusiasts of the marque to be the ultimate prewar Studebaker—perhaps the ultimate Studebaker, period. Some of these cars built up through the 1933 model year are regarded as

Delmar G. "Barney" Roos.

classics by the Classic Car Club of America (CCCA) and are the only Studebakers to attain that standing. The President was engineered under the direction of Delmar G. "Barney" Roos, who became Studebaker's chief engineer in 1927, replacing Guy Henry who had held the post since Fred Zeder left. Born in 1888, Roos was educated at Cornell. He started his automotive career with Locomobile, then joined Pierce-Arrow in 1919. Unhappy with Pierce management, however, he left for Marmon, then ended up at Studebaker. Ironically, he was to find himself *de facto* chief engineer of Pierce-Arrow again within the year.

The Brooklyn-born Roos was regarded by nearly everyone who knew him as a brilliant engineer, perhaps even a genius. He was also excitable and famously short-tempered. The daughter of Clyde Paton, who worked with Roos later at Willys-Overland, described him thusly:

> He would come leaping up the stairs two or three steps at a time, burst into my father's office many a morning, rant and rave about some problem real or imagined, shout and wave his hands for a few minutes, and then finally calm down and leave. My father soon realized that he was Barney's relief valve. Once he came to accept that fact, Barney's tantrums didn't bother him much.[5]

Another Willys-Overland associate recalled:

> Barney was not the easiest man to get to know. Once you knew him, though, you found that he was a wonderful, wonderful man— extremely interesting to talk to, very well educated, very intelligent. But, of course, if you didn't know him, he could just as well call you a fool to your face as anything else.[6]

Remarkably, Roos and Erskine established an amicable working relationship. Perhaps, having similarly strident personalities, they simply understood each other. Regardless, Roos' next few years at Studebaker were destined to be unusually productive.

The 1927 President models were all built on a 127-inch wheelbase. Three body styles were offered: sedan, Duplex phaeton and limousine. This was the year Studebaker dropped its four-wheel hydraulic brakes on some models and substituted four-wheel mechanical units. It seems a retrograde move (and it was), but many collectors say that the mechanical brakes are actually superior in practice, if not in theory, to the hydraulics. The Model ES President shared the same six-cylinder engine as the Commander that year. From 1928 on, however, the President was given special treatment.

Yet, despite its fresh and innovative model line-up, the company's performance in 1927 proved to be a virtually repeat of the middling level achieved in 1926. A total of 116,740 Studebaker cars were sold, up slightly from 1926. Overall revenues were actually down, to $134 million and profits, too, slid to $11.9 million.

Sales and profits rebounded a bit in 1928 as the nation experienced the last boom cycle before the onset of the Great Depression. A total of 136,205 Studebaker cars were sold, while overall corporate sales reached $177.1 million. Most of this increase, however, was due to "external growth"— i.e., due to outside acquisition for, during the summer of 1928, Studebaker had acquired controlling interest in the Pierce-Arrow Motor Car Company of Buffalo, perhaps the most prestigious nameplate of the classic era. A total of 6,491 Pierce-Arrows were sold, making a total for the combined companies of 142,696 cars.[7]

Erskine, speaking expansively about Studebaker's new direction, crowed that the company "now blanketed the motor car field with a line of passenger cars from the Erskine, the Studebaker, to the Pierce-Arrow," and that the firm now "had something for everyone." After several years at a plateau, Erskine was clearly eager to launch Studebaker Corporation on another cycle of growth. The acquisition of the controlling interest in Pierce-Arrow was but one manifestation of that and represented the latest evidence of an effort to transform Studebaker into a full-line producer of automobiles along the lines of General Motors and the insurgent Chrysler.

That Pierce-Arrow was not in the best of financial health had been well-known in the industry for years; Pierce-Arrow was prestigious, not profitable. In fact, the Buffalo firm nearly went under during the recession of 1920-21 and had stumbled along in the period since. It clearly needed a partner with deep pockets if it was to survive. The company had made its name building damn-the-expense luxury rigs—prices in 1921 had *started* at $6,500 in a era when a new Ford could be had for less than $400—and changing conditions in the industry in the decade of the flapper saw the company fall farther and farther out of touch. As late as 1924, the company's engines still used the venerable T-head design, a technology that had already been dated when Fred Fish and Walter Flanders were duking it out over E-M-F back in 1910. So, while Pierce-Arrow still had a powerful name in 1928, it urgently needed help in order to recover the ground it had lost during years of inactivity. Enter Studebaker.

It was not, in fact, an outright purchase, but the exact figures are surprisingly difficult to determine from even a detailed examination of Studebaker Corporation financial statements. The information given is incomplete and misleading, although not *necessarily* by intent.[8] The initial purchase was of 230,125 shares of Class B stock for $2 million, giving Studebaker around 57 percent of the outstanding stock and effective control. Pierce-Arrow thus became a partly owned subsidiary, with plans for Studebaker to complete the acquisition of Pierce-Arrow stock at some point in the future. Over the next two years, 152,211 shares of Class A stock and 23,800 shares of preferred stock were acquired, giving Studebaker virtually complete control. The total cost came to $9,753,998—or, about double

1927 Studebaker Standard Six.

the figure a close reading of the corporation's financial statements would suggest. It is at least possible (and perhaps probable) that Erskine and the board were deliberately understating the cost owing to the sad state of affairs in Buffalo. Moreover, part of the original stock purchase agreement in August, 1928, reportedly involved a direct cash infusion of $2 million to the beleaguered luxury car maker, money that was to be used to completely revise the Pierce-Arrow line for the forthcoming 1929 model year.

Meanwhile, the Erskine Model 51 for 1928 continued to languish at far less than hoped-for sales. The "stroker" engine was bored out a bit for more power and the model line-up was revised. Sedan, club sedan and roadster body types were offered. Full-width bumpers were equipped for the first time.

The Dictator was revised as the Model GE series. It featured a mechanical fuel pump, double-fluted bumpers and a rounded radiator shell. The bumper and radiator shell design were modified a couple of times during the two-year span of the Model GE and a windshield visor was added toward the end of the run. Engine displacement remained as before, but horsepower was increased to 67.

The Model GB Commander got four-wheel mechanical brakes, along with a mechanical fuel pump and wooden artillery wheels to replace the

1928 Erskine Model 51.

1928 Studebaker Standard Six.

disc wheels that had been standard in 1927. Wire and disc wheels were options. The mid-year Model GH featured lengthened fenders and a winged radiator mascot. The engine in both cases remained as in 1927, although rated horsepower rose to 85. Body styles were changed quite a bit. Sedan, club sedan, cabriolet, victoria, coupe and roadster styles were now listed.

The President was available in Models FA and FB during 1928. Both lines were eight-cylinder-powered. The early FA offered a 313.1 cubic inch eight rated at 100 horsepower, while later FA and FB models used a bored-out 336.7 cubic inch eight rated at 109 horsepower. In this form the President eight-cylinder engine would continue through 1933, although horsepower ratings would rise to 122.[9] The FA used a 131-inch wheelbase, while the FB used a 121-inch wheelbase. This was also the first year for chrome plating, while the Atalanta mascot was used early in the model year and replaced by a winged mascot later on.

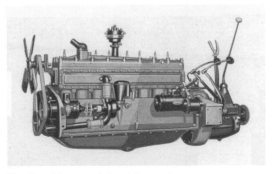

The President straight eight engine.

A Studebaker President (right) paced the Indianapolis 500 race in 1929.

Model availability included: sedan, berline, seven-passenger sedan, limousine, victoria, roadster and touring.

In order to achieve maximum publicity for its line, Studebaker organized a series of speed trials and attempts, resulting in a gratifying 160 official distance and speed records. Of these, 126 were American records that, a company advertisement boasted, included:

> ...every official record for fully equipped stock cars. No other manufacturer holds a single American fully equipped stock car record. Studebaker also holds 11 world records of cars of every kind, including racing as well as stock models, and 23 international records for cars classified abroad as stock cars. The most notable Studebaker world record is the one of 30,000 miles in 26,326 minutes elapsed time, or an average of 68.37 miles per hour. All of the Studebaker records were made on the Atlantic City Speedway under the sanction of the American Automobile Association which timed the cars and kept the records. The International Association of Recognized Automobile Clubs of Paris, the official international authority, certified the foreign records. Never before in the history of the automobile industry have the records held by any manufacturer approached the number now held by Studebaker.

It was true. When, in Atlantic City, New Jersey, three Commanders were run at a steady 60 miles per hour for 25,000 miles, it was more than a new record, it was a new category. The previous best continuous high-speed run had been for 15,000 miles. In addition, a President roadster was chosen as pace car at the 1929 Indianapolis 500. Studebaker had, in fact, been involved in Indy racing for several years. Back in 1924, Earl Cooper had nearly won the 500-mile race in a Studebaker Special. Tire trouble stole the victory, but Cooper still averaged 97.79 miles per hour for the race.

The impressive new line of Pierce-Arrow cars launched for the 1929 model year seemed to have turned that firm's fortunes around decisively, as well. Nearly 10,000 cars were built, which was by far the greatest number of Pierce-Arrows that had ever been produced in one year and a profit of nearly $2 million was recorded.

Historians and enthusiasts have debated for years the question of just how much "help" Studebaker supplied in terms of the actual building of Pierce-Arrow cars. It has been contended that the Pierce-Arrow straight-eight of 1929 was really a modified Studebaker engine, but the simple disparity in size—the Pierce-Arrow eight was 6-liters, the President eight (as designed) only a little more than 5-liters—would raise doubts about that. In fact, it has been well-documented that the Pierce-Arrow engine was under development long before the marriage took place. None-the-less,

1929 Pierce-Arrow Series 143.

Studebaker did cast the blocks following the takeover and Pierce-Arrow also benefited from a number of engineering developments emanating from South Bend in the years of Studebaker ownership, such as free-wheeling.

At any rate, Erskine's investment seemed to be paying off, after all, and, perhaps in celebration, stockholders' dividends that year for Studebaker Corporation reached an astonishing 129 percent of profits. Over the following months, Erskine authorized the purchase of an additional 15,400 shares of Pierce-Arrow stock, raising Studebaker Corporation's controlling interest to 91.7 percent.

The company now boasted of a range of nameplates—Erskine, Studebaker and Pierce-Arrow—that spanned the price spectrum from $895 to $10,000. In addition, a new subsidiary was planned for the production and distribution of Studebaker and Pierce-Arrow commercial vehicles. This proposed subsidiary was slated to use the recently vacated Detroit automobile facilities and have its own organization and dealers.[10]

In the view of many, styling for all of the company's brands was reaching an all-time high. In general, Studebakers were running a year or two ahead of styling trends in the industry at this time and, across the board,

1929 Studebaker President.

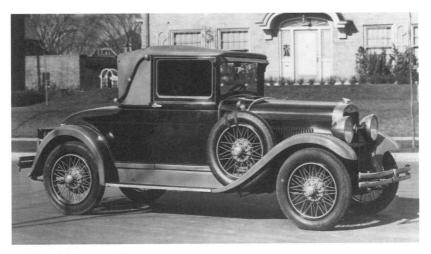

1929 Erskine Model 52.

had attained a classic beauty of line that they would be hard-pressed to beat in future years. This writer has long been fond of close-coupled sedans—which Studebaker called broughams—and the 1929 Studebaker examples of the type are among the finest ever designed. Particularly on the larger wheelbases in the late-1920s and into the early 1930s, Studebaker styling was so impressive that it rivaled many cars costing twice as much. Although the first Erskine in 1927 was the only car officially credited to Ray Dietrich, it has long been rumored that he acted as a professional design consultant on Studeabker and Pierce-Arrow cars from that point until the financial collapse in 1933. It makes sense, for Studebaker design suddenly went from mediocre to truly extraordinary. Top-notch designs don't just "happen" year after year and the company as yet did not have a professional in-house design staff. *Someone* with the master's touch had a hand in them and Ray Dietrich would appear to be the likely candidate.

The Commander series came in Models GJ and FD in 1929-30. The Model GJ was a 248.3 cubic inch six rated at 75 horsepower. The FD was the new 250.4 cubic inch eight, rated at 80 horsepower. In both cases, the engines were similar to those available in the Dictator, but with a slightly longer stroke for increased displacement, although the Dictator eight-cylinder engine would not be offered until 1930. Commander body style availability was changed again. Sedan, coupe, cabriolet, victoria, touring and roadster styles were now listed.

President designations were changed from Models FA and FB to FE and FH, respectively, and wheelbases were increased by four inches across the board. Horsepower, too, was increased: to 115. The use of a double-drop frame permitted lower and far more stylish body styling. The President line-up included: sedan, brougham, seven-passenger sedan, limousine, victoria, roadster, cabriolet and touring body styles.

Even the Erskine—now known as the Model 52—was upgraded a bit with a 109-inch wheelbase and the body types were changed yet again. Club Sedan, and two- and four-passenger cabriolets were listed in the catalog. In general, there was more styling resemblance to other Studebakers, which was not at all a bad thing.

Despite their acknowledged good looks, sales of Studebaker cars were on a downward slide at this point. Combined Studebaker and Erskine registrations in 1929 amounted to only 82,839 cars. The Great Depression had struck in October, 1929, and, by the time 1930 had staggered to a conclusion, it was clear that the bottom was rapidly falling out of the industry.

Still, the company managed to introduce an important new feature on Studebaker cars in 1930 when free-wheeling was announced. It was subsequently picked up by Lincoln, Pierce-Arrow and Hupmobile. The corporation had high hopes for its competitive appeal and boasted that "it bids fair to revolutionize the industry in America and abroad." This prediction, alas, proved to be wildly optimistic. Probably of more interest to prospective buyers, prices of Studebaker cars had been cut again and now ranged from $795 to $2,600. Studebaker commercial vehicles were similarly reduced in price and now listed from $695 to $4,375.

The Erskine entered the year as Studebaker's price leader, but was transformed at mid-year into, simply, the Studebaker Six. The Erskine name had never packed much punch, anyway. Both lines had the same Studebaker-built engine, a 205.3 cubic inch six rated at 70 horsepower. This was not only 62 percent more horsepower than before, it was a achieved with an engine of more normal bore and stroke design. The high-revving Continental-built "stroker" was gone and it is doubtful that many mourned its passing. The widest range of body types yet offered on an Erskine were listed for the final run: sedan, business coupe, club sedan, coupe, roadster and touring styles were available. When the Erskine name was dropped, so was the business coupe. A landau sedan was offered in its stead.

The two new Dictator series were the GL and the FC, which featured numerous changes. The wheelbase was increased to 115 inches and the six-cylinder engine on the GL was reduced in displacement to 221.4 cubic inches. Rated horsepower was actually increased to 68. The FC was an eight, but the displacement was actually less than the six: 221 cubic inches. Horsepower was rated at 70. The biggest change in the Dictator line was in appearance. As with all Studebakers, the Dictators were lower, sleeker and more stylish than ever before, partly as a result of a new double-drop frame similar to the type the senior models had been given the previous year. Body styles included: sedan, club sedan, cabriolet, coupe and touring.

Commander and President body style availability was essentially the same as in 1929 and, as before, Commanders were offered in six- or eight-cylinder form with full pressure lubrication. The 336.7 cubic inch President engine was the star, though. Rated at 115 horsepower, it was making quite a name for itself. Ab Jenkins set a new record with a twenty-two minute charge up 14,000-foot Pikes Peak in a President eight. Overseas, two Presidents won their class title at the 24-hour Brooklands Double Twelve race, beating out such celebrated names as Bentley and Alfa Romeo. This

1930 Studebaker Commander.

engine also powered a series of successful entries in the Indianapolis 500 between 1931 and 1937, adding additional laurels.

Despite the hoopla, Studebaker Corporation reported sales of only $86.1 million in 1930, the lowest amount since 1919 and profits plummeted to a mere $1.5 million, the lowest figure since the company went public in 1911. A total of only 67,269 cars for Studebaker and Pierce-Arrow combined were sold during the calendar year. In the years immediately to follow, however, the 1930 performance would seem heavenly. Actually, Studebaker's performance was worse even than the figures would suggest. Pierce-Arrow accounted for $18.8 million of total sales. To put it another way, Studebaker's sales alone came to only $67.3 million and, worse, only $382,281 of the reported profit came from the Studebaker side.

In his formal summation of the 1930 year, Erskine admitted the obvious but made a valiant (and not wholly unwarranted) attempt to put a positive face on matters:

> Last year [1930] was a very poor one for profit making in the automobile industry. An overly optimistic production in the earlier months, failing to find a ready spring and summer demand, had to be liquidated at cut prices, and following this, came the worst fourth quarter the industry had experienced in many years. From a commercial or competitive standpoint, much shifting of position occurred last year, but fortunately both Studebaker and Pierce-Arrow cars emerged with gains to their credit. Registrations of new passenger cars purchased by consumers in the United States in 1930 showed as follows:
>
> A decrease of 19.0 percent for Pierce-Arrow—the best showing of all.
>
> A decrease of 31.8 percent for Studebaker—the tenth best showing.
>
> A decrease of 32.3 percent for all makes—39 in number.
>
> The decreases ranged from 19.0 percent to 72.4 percent in the Pierce-Arrow field.
>
> The decreases ranged from 27.9 percent to 51.4 percent in the Studebaker field.[11]

Astonishingly, Erskine insisted on paying substantial dividends to Studebaker stockholders for the 1930 fiscal year. Although profits had all but evaporated, $7.6 million was paid out even though it was necessary to draw on capital reserves in order to do so. Erskine was apparently buoyed by company projections that earnings would rise to $4 million in 1931— assuming the same level of production seen in 1930 could be maintained.

One early casualty of the depression was the employee stock purchase plan, which had been in force since 1919. Under this plan, employees could purchase Studebaker Corporation stock on time, with the company acting as holder of the collateral interest until the stock was fully paid for. Owing to reduced employment levels in South Bend, with many workers going from full-time to part-time status (or no status at all, due to lay-offs), 56,368 shares were taken back by the corporation.[12] The corporation also bought back an undetermined number of shares acquired by directors in 1928 and 1929 under stock option plans, but which were rendered useless by the precipitous decline in the stock market.

If all the foregoing seems confusing, it can be simplified thusly: Studebaker workers who couldn't maintain their payments on their shares lost them, while directors, who had acquired shares with the intention of some quick profit taking, voted themselves a bailout. Life, as philosophers have noted, is not fair. It is not known how many directors' shares were involved, or how much the bailout cost the company, but it seems an inexplicable waste of the corporation's capital under the circumstances—especially considering that profit sharing for employees was discontinued as of August 1, 1930, effecting 5,209 eligible workers.

In fairness, the corporation was attempting to do right by its workers as it saw it. The dramatic increase in part-time workers was caused by the company's decision to "standardize" its work force by spreading the economic disaster equally, rather than by laying-off huge numbers of workers and keeping a relatively small number on the payroll full-time. Hourly wage levels were maintained at the pre-depression level, as well. In addition, the company lent nearly $100,000 to workers in need.

Meanwhile, styling in 1931 was a continuation and improvement on the basic themes so successfully established in 1929. The cars were sleeker and more elegant in appearance due to thinner moldings and new front

1931 Studebaker Dictator.

bumpers that dipped gracefully in the middle to accentuate the pronounced vee-shape of the radiator. Thus clothed, the Six was smart, the Commander graceful and the President truly imposing.

The six-cylinder Dictator was dropped for 1931 and the Studebaker Six bore an ever closer resemblance to its senior stablemates. Only the eight remained in the Studebaker line-up, redesignated as the Model 61. The wheelbase was reduced to 114 inches, but the horsepower was increased to 81. Body styles offered included: sedan, club sedan, landau sedan, coupe, roadster and touring.

The six-cylinder Commander was likewise dropped for 1931, but the 250.4 cubic inch eight continued over with an increase in horsepower rating to 101. This engine would continue to power the Commander through to the receivership, although it would be destroked to 236 cubic inches in 1933.[13] Cabriolet, touring and roadster body styles were deleted. Only sedan, coupe, brougham and victoria models were listed for 1931.

The President model designations went numeric, as with the Dictator and Commander that year. The Model 90 was mounted on a 136-inch wheelbase, the Model 80 on a ten-inch shorter length. Both were powered by the 336.7 cubic inch President eight-cylinder engine with an increased horsepower rating of 122. Body style availability was similar to 1930, except for the deletion of the cabriolet and the addition of a coupe.

For as long as anyone could remember, new Studebaker models had been announced in the late summer, generally August or September. That changed with the 1932 models and therein lies a tale. The modern concept of a model year with annual changes took effect with the announcement of the 1932 models and did so at the insistence of the government in Washington. This was an attempt to spur consumer interest in the depths of the depression. Washington's idea was that if all the manufacturers changed their cars every year (which many had not been in the practice of doing) and, moreover, introduced their new models at the same time, a national new car buying season psychology could be created. The New York Auto Show, held in January, became the semi-official launching platform for the nation's manufacturers starting in January, 1932. The idea worked, too, although it took a couple of years for it to start to produce significant results. Ironically, when "planned obsolescence" became a buzz phrase with many budding consumerists in the 1950s, few recalled that it was the government—not the auto makers—that concocted the system in the first place.

Studebaker styling reached the heights in 1932. Across the model range, these were some of the finest-looking cars Studebaker—or any company— ever offered. This is certainly true for anyone attuned to classic car design. The 1932 Studebakers are noteworthy, too, in that they represented the first serious effort on the part of the company to explore streamlining.

All top automotive designers in this era had set for themselves as a goal the eventual abandonment of carriage design with respect to automobiles. The typical automobile of 1930 was a conglomeration of different, often conflicting, design elements—hoods, fenders, bodies, sidemounts and so forth—that had been carried forward from the earliest days of the industry. What designers of the time were attempting to do—and the best of them were actually achieving—was to combine all of these elements into increasingly tasteful and harmonious envelopes from front to rear. The 1932 Studebaker line was a major advance in this respect. There were practically no straight lines. All corners were rounded, the A-pillar at the windshield swept gracefully down into the beltline as it flowed into the hood, head lamps had a more obvious bullet shape. Even the lower body swept up in an elegant curve as it met the frame.

Of course, part of the designer's challenge (as Chrysler was soon to learn from its Airflow) was in knowing how much in the way of design advancements it was safe to throw at consumers at one time. People, a music critic once complained, "demand novelty in everything, so long as it is always the same." Translation for purposes of the present discussion: Car buyers can only be moved along but so fast and knowing how fast is fast enough—but not too fast—is sometimes tricky, indeed. There is no indication that Studebaker ever stretched the envelope too far in this era, but it was certainly exploring the outer limits.

The Dictator continued over for 1932 as the Model 62. Its 221 cubic inch eight-cylinder engine was rated at 85 horsepower and it rode on a longer 117-inch wheelbase. The Dictator featured synchromesh for the first time, the Startix automatic starting system and safety plate glass. Styling was improved with a vee-d front bumper and pronounced angle to the windshield. Body styles included: sedan, St. Regis brougham, convertible sedan and roadster. The St. Regis brougham is considered by many to be the ultimate Dictator, but production was minuscule and chances of finding one are slim.

Commander body style availability was increased, as the line went from four models to five. The victoria was dropped, but convertible sedan and roadster models were added. As with the Dictator, the St. Regis brougham is regarded by many as the most desirable 1932 Commander body style, possibly excepting the convertible sedan.

The President went to a standard 135-inch wheelbase in 1932. The line-up included sedan, St. Regis brougham, coupe, convertible sedan, roadster, seven-passenger sedan and limousine body styles (and would remain unchanged for 1933).

The big news from South Bend, however, was another new brand of car. It was one that Erskine was confident would not only expand Studebaker into the low-priced field, but ensure the company's survival. The story of this car, which would make for a fascinating for a book in and of itself, began with two engineers, Roy E. Cole and Ralph A. Vail.

Cole and Vail had gotten their start in the industry in the early days with Oldsmobile—long before there was a Studebaker car as such, or even a General Motors. Yet, like another noted engineering team in years past—

namely Zeder, Skelton and Breer—1930 found Cole and Vail self-employed as engineering consultants and looking for a sponsor. Again, as with Zeder, Skelton and Breer, their hopes were seemingly fulfilled with a contract from Willys-Overland to design a new car, in this case to replace the company's aging Whippet.

Willys-Overland had had a roller coaster career in the auto business. When John North Willys joined the firm—then known as the Overland Company—in Indianapolis in 1907, it was on the brink of failure. He rescued it, added his name to that of the company and moved the operation to Toledo. There, Willys-Overland went from strength to strength until, suddenly, the crash of 1920-21 nearly wiped it out. After Walter Chrysler had miraculously restored its health and then gone on to other things, Willys-Overland soared again throughout the 1920s. In 1928, the company sold more than 230,000 cars, making it the third or fourth largest manufacturer in the industry and the little Whippet was the volume leader.

Alas for Cole and Vail, by the time they engineered and built two prototypes of their new car, Willys-Overland was again rapidly sliding to-

1932 Studebaker President.

Ralph Vail, left, and Roy Cole.

ward disaster, this time with no Walter Chrysler in sight.[14] The company's directors liked the car—liked it a lot, in fact—but there were no longer any funds available to put it into production. The two crestfallen engineers were paid for their work, though, and the Willys-Overland board graciously let them keep the two prototypes and all rights to the engineering.

It was at this juncture that Cole and Vail decided to take well earned vacations—the former to his hometown in Ohio, the latter to visit family in Michigan City, Indiana. As fate would have it, Vail had to pass through South Bend en route and, on the spur of the moment and despite that fact that it was a Saturday, decided to stop by the Studebaker factory. There, he found Erskine hard at work. Erskine agreed to talk with him, then agreed to look at the prototype, then agreed to take it for a spin. Before the day was out, Studebaker had not only bought the rights to the car, but had also hired Cole and Vail! Otto Klausmeyer, who was later named the first plant engineer for the Rockne, recalled many years later in an interview:

> Erskine got on the phone and called everyone in the place, including myself, and set about planning how we were going to quickly start this car in production. He decided that [this car] was

1932 Rockne Model 65, this one supplied to the Indiana State Police.

it, and he gambled the last amount of money that Studebaker had. He gambled everything to tool up this car. It was the last roll of the dice.[15]

Well, not quite, for Studebaker was hardly on the ropes at this point and Erskine was to demonstrate that he had one more spectacular roll of the dice left in him, but there is no denying the high stakes that were involved. This scenario also speaks volumes about the way decisions were made at Studebaker in those days and about Erskine's power. Yet, his actions were not quite as impulsive as they might seem, for he and Hoffman had been discussing the need to develop a new small car that might have volume potential and both were agreed that they probably need to hire someone from outside the company to do the job. It was at that moment that Vail serendipitously appeared, quite literally, on Erskine's doorstep.

The car was named the Rockne for South Bend's hometown hero, Notre Dame football coach Knute Rockne. Ironically, the Rockne's public debut in February, 1932, followed on the heels of the tragic death of its namesake in a plane crash in March of the previous year. If anyone in South Bend saw foreshadowing in that, they weren't saying so out loud. And, if Rockne seems to our modern ears an odd name for an automobile, it surely is no less appealing on its own merits than, say, Buick, and Knute Rockne was, indeed, a certifiable celebrity of the day and hero to many. Former President Calvin Coolidge was quoted in some of the initial advertising materials on the Rockne (and this *has* to be the only time Silent Cal was ever enlisted to sell automobiles):

> Fifty per cent would not do. His passing mark was one hundred. He required perfection. That was why men honored and loved him. That was the source of his power.[16]

Rockne had been associated with Studebaker for several years as an official spokesman and was slated to be named vice-president of Rockne Motors Corporation, the wholly-owned subsidiary Studebaker had created for the new marque. Rockne had decided to retire from football to take up a career in business, according to Erskine, although many scoffed at the notion. Rockne's ties to Studebaker were strong, though, and, in introducing the new car, Erskine wrote:

> Knute Rockne was more than a man of magnificent attainments in the world of athletics. He was well on the way to becoming an equally notable figure in the world of business...With characteristic energy, he brought to Studebaker the keen mind, the magnetic personality, and the indomitable persistence which had won him such high place in football. It seems to me highly fitting that the finest qualities of Knute Rockne, the man, should be so brilliantly reflected and recalled by the stamina, sparkle, and speed of the Rockne Six. It is a source of great pride to us and to his family that the Rockne Six will worthily honor his name and perpetuate his memory.

Rockne Motors Corporation was technically based in Detroit and the intention was to build all Rockne automobiles in the old E-M-F plant that Studebaker had vacated several years before. Erskine himself was chairman of Rockne's board, while Harold Vance was named president, both retaining their jobs at Studebaker (president and vice-president, respectively). George Graham, formerly head of sales at Willys-Overland, was named to take charge of the same responsibilities for Rockne. Cole was made vice-president of engineering; Vail was made vice-president of production. The three were just about the only notable personages on the Rockne board who weren't moonlighting from their real jobs at Studebaker. As it turned out, some cars would be built in Detroit and some in South Bend and the separate management was an obvious fiction, but Erskine was clearly determined to position the Rockne as an entity independent from Studebaker.

Why Erskine wanted to forego the established Studebaker name and develop a new one for this all-important car is an interesting question. Brand identity is a tricky thing to establish in the best of circumstances and the year 1932 was hardly promising to be the best of anything. The decision probably has to be seen in light of Studebaker's previous missteps. The Erskine was the first attempt to move downward. It failed to measure up to expectations and the renamed Studebaker Six wasn't setting the world on fire, either. Erskine must have assumed that the drawing power of the Rockne name and the selling power of the nation's Studebaker dealers would do the trick. In fact, the Rockne did far better than its brief life-span and reputation today as a failure would suggest.

The 1932 Rockne entered production in December, 1931, and was available in two model ranges, the 65 and the 75. The numbers may have referred (more or less) to the horsepower ratings—the 65 was rated at 66 horsepower, the 75 at 72—but could also have roughly referenced the top speeds. On the other hand, the actual model designations used within the company were 30 and 41, respectively. As is the case with much that involves the Rockne, the truth is hard to come by.

Both lines used Studebaker-built L-head engines, differing mainly in bore. The 65's engine displaced 189.8 cubic inches, the 75's displaced 205.3. The bodies, on the other hand, were entirely different between the two lines. The 65, which was built in Detroit, used its own body stamped by Budd, while the 75, built in South Bend, was a close derivative of the Studebaker Six in that regard and, according to some sources, would have replaced the Studebaker Six in due course. Four body types were listed for

Albert Erskine, right, and race driver Ab Jenkins pose with a 1932 Pierce-Arrow.

the 75: sedan, coupe, convertible sedan and roadster. Four body types were also listed for the 65: sedan, coach, coupe and roadster. Some sources also contend that the existence of the 75 was a sop to Studebaker's temperamental chief engineer, Barney Roos, who felt sidelined by the Rockne program. Letting him engineer the 75 gave him something to do, according to this line of thinking, although that didn't turn out to be very much.

There could have been little doubt at this point that Studebaker knew how to build a good car. The main drawback to the Erskine (other than its Continental-built engine) had been its relatively high price. This was a mistake the company did not intend to repeat, especially not in the teeth of a crushing economic depression. Prices started at $585 for the Model 65 and $685 for the Model 75. This was about $100 more than Ford and Chevy, but comparable to Plymouth. Moreover, the Rockne was wonderfully equipped. The humble little Model 65 came standard with free-wheeling, rubber mountings for the engine (dubbed "Floating Power" by Chrysler when it announced a similar system), synchromesh, key starting, a full compliment of gauges and, in sedan models, such luxury items as rear seat arm rests, foot rests and robe rails that were usually found only in far more expensive cars.

And, it worked. Of the 44,711 cars Studebaker built in calendar-year 1932, half of them—22,223—were Rockne's. Moreover, it was on the strength of the Rockne's reception that Studebaker (if Rockne is included) maintained nearly 92 percent of its 1931 sales volume. That was no mean achievement. In the entire American industry, only one nameplate increased its sales in 1932: Plymouth was up by 19 percent. The industry as a whole was down by nearly 43 percent over 1931 and Studebaker's performance brought it almost to a state of parity with the sales recorded by Buick and Pontiac. As it was, Studebaker missed attaining fourth place in national sales standings (behind Chevrolet, Ford and Plymouth) by fewer than 8,000 units—a level of success that in any year other than 1932 would have astonished the industry.

Partly due to the cash drain imposed by Erskine's reckless policy in continuing to deplete Studebaker's capital with dividends, though, the 1932 Studebaker models were carried over with few changes for 1933. There simply wasn't enough money left for major alterations. An exception was the Standard Six, which had been dropped entirely in deference to the Rockne. The Rockne's model range also had been pared back; the Model 75 was dropped, while the Model 65 was renamed the Model 10 (or 31 for internal use). Other than that, body styles and series availability was virtually the same in both Rockne and Studebaker ranges. Styling, too, was a general continuation of the highly effective streamlining introduced in 1932. The major development with the Studebakers was up front, where the grille—it was no longer a radiator shell—was angled aggressively and fenders were valanced in the manner pioneered in 1932 by Graham.

Five Studebaker Specials lined up before the 1933 Indianapolis 500.

The range of products built by Studebaker in 1933 is demonstrated by these photos. Top, the low-priced Rockne Model 10; middle, the Studebaker President; and, bottom, the landmark Pierce Silver Arrow.

The wonderful President chassis received its greatest accolade in this period when it was selected, in more-or-less stock form, as the basis of a series of Studebaker race cars especially built for the grueling Indianapolis 500. In 1932, five Studebaker Specials had been built. The top finisher, driven by Cliff Bergere, came in third and averaged 102.66 miles per hour overall —the first time a "stock" racer had cracked the century mark.

The following year, five new streamlined cars were built, again using essentially stock President mechanicals. Bergere posted a qualifying average of 115.64 miles per hour, and none of the five came in under 110 miles per hour. When race day came, all five factory cars finished, three of them "in the money." Counting two private Studebaker-based entries, Studebakers finished sixth, seventh, eighth, ninth, tenth, eleventh and twelfth. Anyone wishing to know how good the President engine really was could demand no more eloquent a testimonial. The company withdrew from racing after 1933, but Studebaker Specials in private hands were a presence on tracks around the country for several years thereafter.

Meanwhile, the most celebrated Pierce-Arrow of all-time was built for the January, 1933, New York Auto Show: the Silver Arrow. Designed by Phil Wright, it pioneered streamlining and was among the most influential cars of the decade, over-shadowed only slightly by the 1936 Cord. The decision to do the Silver Arrow wasn't made until the fall of 1932. This left an impossibly-short span of three months to hand-build five cars from scratch, so construction was shifted to South Bend in order to take advantage of the superior facilities available there. Work was conducted around the clock in shifts. Of the five cars, four are known to survive.

The success Studebaker had experienced in increasing its market share with its various lines in 1931 and 1932 may help to explain why Albert Erskine continued to feel so confident about his company. In the spring of 1932, despite the red ink that was now rising to flood crest in South Bend, Erskine declared a substantial dividend to the stockholders for the 1931 fiscal year just ended. As the company's 1952 history put it:

> Erskine...was honestly bullish on America...He believed in his country, his company, his job, and his cars...Erskine no longer expected things to be like the boom days. Things would level off.

The stock of the company must remain solid and healthy. He had the directors declare a dividend of $2,800,000. This cost capital but it kept Studebaker stock at blue-chip level. Erskine was a man of figures, of bookkeeping. Stock prices had special value to him, and those values must be kept up for the stockholders, for those who believed in Studebaker. Next year all salaries were cut again...[17]

In a similar vein, a contemporary account explained Erskine's actions in this way:

He was fundamentally an optimist. His own rise in the business world had confirmed him in that philosophy. His optimism was justified and stimulated by profits through a number of years. He refused to believe that the stock-market crash was anything more than a financial flurry, that the depression was more than temporary. He thought to do his part toward combating it by declaring more and greater dividends out of surplus and reserve, regardless of current profits or losses. The optimism of Albert R. Erskine required a lot of killing.[18]

It was tragic. In our own time, when a decline of 25 percent in the market is considered a cataclysm, it is hard even to conceive of a true depression. Between 1929 and 1932, the auto industry as a whole contracted by a staggering 72 percent. All auto makers were feeling the pain and did what they could to cope, but, by 1932, Durant, Jordan, Moon, Peerless and others were already among the departed. General Motors had scrapped Viking and Marquette (companion nameplates for Olds and Buick, respectively), as well as Oakland (for which Pontiac had been the companion line), and only one General Motors automotive division made money that year: Chevrolet. Such legendary luxury makes as Franklin, Marmon and Stutz were at or approaching bankruptcy. Cadillac, Lincoln and Packard would have joined them had they not had powerful companies behind them able to absorb their staggering losses. In addition, Hudson and Willys-Overland were both in desperate shape. Among American auto makers, only General Motors and Nash reported meaningful profits in 1932 and

Nash's, taken as a percentage of sales, was almost two-and-a-half times that of the mighty General. Charley Nash, who had been president of General Motors at one time, had evidently learned a thing or two about the car business along the way. As for his old alma mater, with all but one of its automotive divisions drowning in red ink, General Motors managed to report a profit in 1932 mostly through accounting legerdemain.[19]

Of course, no one knew how long the economic depression would last. While the country had never seen anything that bad, all previous depressions had been over and forgotten in a few months, or a year or two at most. The government, from President Hoover on down, kept insisting that prosperity was "just around the corner." The auto industry had vocal boosters for this view, as well, most notably Erskine. Unfortunately, Erskine put his money where his mouth was. Even as Studebaker lost millions, cash dividends paid to stockholders rolled merrily on.

In fairness to Erskine, it should be noted that most companies in the industry continued to pay dividends even after profits dwindled to the vanishing point around 1931 or 1932. There were a variety of reasons for doing this, not the least of which (it must be assumed) was that the directors of the various companies were generally major stockholders themselves and, therefore, personally dependent to some extent upon dividend income. There was also a legitimate need to maintain the value of a company's stock in order to influence the financial markets that determined not only a company's creditworthiness but also the cost of borrowing. The value of a company's stock was not the only factor that effected a company's credit, but it was certainly one of them.

Of far more importance, however, were a company's profitability and financial resources. Of course, few firms were profitable in 1932, but most of the successful ones still had sizable assets. Even before the depression hit, however, Studebaker's financial resources had been dramatically weaker than those of many of its competitors, weaker even than at similar Nash Motors where Charley Nash's legendary tight-fistedness is brilliantly apparent from the figures listed below. The chart is a comparison of Studebaker, General Motors and Nash in terms of after-tax profits, dividends and other relevant data for the four-year period from 1929-32. It is worth examining in detail, as it makes for fairly stunning reading.[20]

YEAR	SALES	PROFITS	CASH	DIVIDENDS	%*
NASH MOTORS COMPANY					
1929	202,723,252	18,634,302	42,011,405	1,635,600	9%
1930	78,992,453	7,618,245	38,845,514	13,606,900	179%
1931	38,426,377	4,850,979	37,014,105	9,453,500	195%
1932	23,346,527	1,022,485	33,150,351	3,990,200	390%
Total	343,488,609	32,126,011		28,686,200	89%
STUDEBAKER CORPORATION					
1929	119,090,434	7,903,450	6,431,999	9,956,564	126%
1930	67,311,983	382,281	8,502,653	7,551,981	1,976%
1931	52,262,434	1,186,869	11,830,698	2,566,700	216%
1932	38,172,827	-5,102,627	4,442,056	992,466	
Total	276,837,678	4,369,973		30,952,276	708%
GENERAL MOTORS CORPORATION					
1929	1,532,213,745	265,824,911	127,351,530	166,078,688	62%
1930	1,005,327,903	157,595,826	178,751,380	140,038,661	89%
1931	828,207,978	116,739,956	194,457,417	139,875,900	120%
1932	440,899,312	8,359,930	170,479,830	63,199,717	756%
Total	3,806,648,938	548,520,623		509,192,966	93%

As a percentage of profits. See Footnote 20 for a detailed explanation of these figures.

In the entire history of the Studebaker Brothers Manufacturing Company (1868-1911), the Studebaker brothers had voted themselves $6.7 million in dividends on profits of $16 million, or about 42 percent overall. For 1916, the last complete fiscal year before J.M. Studebaker died, dividends amounted to exactly $3 million on profits of $8.6 million, or about 35 percent. Then, the ratio began to climb, slowly at first, but with gathering speed after 1926. In 1928, Erskine ordered a 69 percent dividend and, from 1929 on, spent more on dividends than the company made in after-tax profits. From 1929-32, Nash spent 89 percent of its after-tax profits on dividends overall, General Motors 93 percent. Studebaker paid out an astonishing 708 percent—more than seven dollars for every dollar earned. Anyone wishing to understand how a company with Studebaker's long and successful history could have ended up in receivership need look no further.

If, however, one does look further, the figures provide additional interesting—and disturbing—insights. Bear in mind, too, that what we are examining here are the best and worst performances in the industry for the period in question. General Motors and Nash were the only auto companies to report a profit in 1932, while Studebaker was poised on the verge of the greatest industrial bankruptcy in American history up to that time. You wouldn't guess it from the sales figures, though. Between 1929 and 1932 Studebaker's sales fell by 62 percent. This was hardly good news, of course, but General Motors' declined by 71 percent and Nash experienced a gut-wrenching 88 percent fall, with sales collapsing to barely 12 percent of what they had been four years earlier.

So, one might reasonably ask, how did Studebaker show the best sales performance in this period of the three (and one of the best in the entire industry, for that matter) and end up as the only one of the three to lose money in 1932? A good question it is and the inescapable conclusion is that Studebaker was simply not as well run as the other two. There had been no natural disasters, or fires, or strikes that would account for it. Erskine's bullishness was likely the key factor. The same mindset that insisted on continuing dividends in the firm belief that a return to prosperity was "just around the corner" was no doubt also slow to enforce the sort of draconian belt-tightening that was going on at General Motors and at Nash.

The way in which the Rockne program was handled would seem to be good evidence of that. The whole purpose of the new brand was to increase the company's overall volume efficiency. Yet, production of the Rockne Model 65, which owing to its low price was projected as the sales leader, was assigned to the old E-M-F plant in Detroit rather than to South Bend where its sales really could have abetted that goal. As it stood in 1931 when the new brand was being planned, the factory in South Bend was operating at no better than 25 percent of capacity and the decision to split production between two plants was downright loony unless it was believed that the nation's economy was going to show a startling revival in 1932. When times are hard, you don't disperse your production; if anything, you consolidate it. In the end, both plants were doomed to struggle along at perhaps 15 percent of capacity in 1932 and there couldn't have been much chance of turning a profit under that scenario.[21]

The critical issue in Studebaker's life-or-death struggle as 1932 drew to a grisly close, however, was neither sales nor profitability, but cash. As any accountant knows, it is quite possible for a basically sound company to go bankrupt. A company goes bankrupt when it becomes insolvent, i.e., when it no longer has sufficient cash on hand to pay its bills, and this is not directly a function of profitability. In 1932, for example, Ford Motor Company posted a staggering loss of $72.4 million, while Chrysler Corporation lost $9.8 million—yet the solvency of these two firms was never seriously questioned because they had cash reserves that were more than sufficient to cover their losses. At Studebaker, in contrast, the cash position had been weak even before the depression hit. At the conclusion of business in 1929, Studebaker's cash on hand as a percentage of sales stood at 5.3 percent, as compared to 8.3 percent at General Motors and 20.7 percent at Nash. By the end of 1932, Studebaker's cash as a percentage of sales had fallen to a mere 1.2 percent, while General Motors' cash position had increased to 38.6 percent and Nash had amassed a truly amazing cash horde amounting to 142 percent of sales. As the depression deepened, Alfred Sloan, who ran General Motors, and Charley Nash had obviously been obsessed with liquidity—as well they should have been—while Erskine continued expending capital as if the national economic nightmare was hardly a matter worthy of serious attention.

It should be noted, too, that a company requires a certain level of liquidity simply to function. Generally, it is assumed that something on the order of 8 percent of sales should be on hand in the nature of liquid assets. A company needs to have a certain amount of cash around to cover the inevitable day-to-day ups and downs in its cashflow and be assured of being able to pay its bills on time, because if it can't pay its bills on time it risks becoming, by definition, insolvent. With that in mind, Studebaker's cash position at the end of 1932 was absolutely frightening. Of the $4.4 million listed in the chart, only $2 million was actual cash—the rest was demand notes or marketable securities—and the company, in addition to its normal cashflow requirements, had a revolving debt with the Chase Manhattan Bank in New York that had risen to $5.6 million and that had to be periodically refinanced. Were Chase Manhattan ever to demand that $5.6 million back, or were Studebaker ever to be unable for any reason to refinance it, that alone would be sufficient given its precarious cash position to force a bankruptcy. This is, in fact, precisely what happened—but we are getting a little bit ahead of our story. Suffice it to say that, as 1933 dawned, Studebaker was staring wide-eyed into the abyss.

It is apparent that Erskine belatedly realized the financial crisis into which his fiscal policies had brought the company. As a desperation move to head off disaster in South Bend, he orchestrated a deal in the latter part of 1932 to takeover Cleveland-based White Motor Company. The appeal of White was two-fold. First, White had a comprehensive line of medium- and heavy-duty trucks that nicely complimented Studebaker's product program. Second, White had $22 million in cash reserves. Which was the more important for Erskine is hard to say, but it is clear that by the summer of 1932 Studebaker urgently needed a cash infusion from somewhere.

White needed the deal, too. Its founder, Walter White, had died in 1929 and since then the company had been drifting. Despite its liquid assets, it was losing money and needed Studebaker's strong distribution system. Moreover, White had been taken over by Robert Woodruff, formerly with Coca-Cola, who was a fellow Southerner and long-time friend of Erskine's.

The plan itself was in equal parts brilliant and audacious and Erskine has been given far too little credit by most historians for what, by rights, should have resulted in a triumph. Had it succeeded, it would have averted disaster in South Bend, significantly broadened Studebaker's product coverage in the commercial vehicles field and done it all with a minimal infusion of up-front cash.

There were 625,000 shares of common stock issued for White. The first formal offer was made to White's shareholders on September 19, 1932, with a second offer following on October 19th. Shareholders in White were to receive for each share of their common stock the following: 1) one share of common stock in Studebaker, 2) $5 in cash and 3) $25 worth of 6 percent notes in Studebaker. The directors of White were in favor of the merger. So, obviously, were the directors of Studebaker, who saw it as their salvation. By the early part of 1933, Studebaker had succeeded in buying 594,442 of the White shares—or, 95.1 percent,—with a book value of $26.8 million for an outlay of slightly less than $3 million in actual cash. Although the stock-buying effort used up nearly all of Studebaker's remaining capital, it was the last piece of the puzzle. With those shares in hand, the merger seemed like a done deal. Then, a few of the remaining White stockholders objected.

The minority shareholders moved to block the merger for motivations that remain unclear. Studebaker partisans insisted they were trying to hold-up the deal in order to secure premium prices for their few remaining shares. Others, taking a more kindly view, said they didn't want to see White dragged down by a failing car company that was only interested in White's cash reserves. In any case, the protesting minority went to court citing a little-used Ohio law that prohibited out-of-state companies from merging with an Ohio company and taking that company's working capital out of state. The law was undoubtedly unconstitutional; the free flow of people and capital between states is one of the hallmarks of the American economic system. Yet, Erskine had taken that into account, too, and was planning to get around it by creating a new corporate entity—United Truck—to consolidate the Studebaker, Pierce-Arrow and White truck businesses, and almost certainly would have closed the deal if given enough time. Then, something happened that even Erskine hadn't anticipated...

Time for Studebaker had run out. Franklin D. Roosevelt was inaugurated as President of the United States on March 4, 1933, and almost immediately declared a surprise bank holiday.[22] In other words, he forced all of the nation's banks and other financial institutions to close in order to head-off a nationwide panic and give the new administration time to sort matters out. Suddenly deprived of their money supply, many businesses—even healthy ones—were forced to shut down for the duration. Studebaker's factories were shuttered almost at once, too, while Erskine and the board of directors desperately sought a way to temporarily refinance Studebaker's debt and keep the company going until the White takeover could be completed. Unfortunately, Erskine found all avenues of refinancing slammed shut by presidential fiat with no certain indication of when they would reopen. In the end, the bank holiday only lasted a few days, but it was too long for Studebaker.

The Chase Manhattan Bank was threatening to call its loan as soon as it was permitted to reopen. In order to stave off that threat and the likely attachment of its assets, Studebaker's board arranged for a small creditor in South Bend to move first and petition the Federal Court to declare the company insolvent and appoint a receiver. Studebaker purposefully declined to opposed the petition and it was promptly granted.

A Federal Trade Commission (FTC) report later noted, in typically dry government prose, what could be considered the official epitaph:

> Had this merger been effected, the funds of White Motor Company probably would have been sufficient to enable the consolidated company to continue to operate. However, when the proposed consolidation could not be consummated, the lack of cash caused The Studebaker Corporation to go into receivership on March 18, 1933, because the banking situation throughout the country was such that the necessary financing could not be done.[23]

Studebaker had always made a sound product and, most importantly, always made lots of money for its stockholders—or, at least it had done so while the nation's economic health remained robust. It was Erskine's blind devotion to dividends even as the nation slid ever deeper into depression that proved to be the company's undoing. The result was that while other companies were husbanding every nickel, Studebaker was willfully squandering its capital. The brilliant plan to merge with cash-heavy White almost saved the day, but the cash crunch, when it came, could be laid directly at the doorstep of Albert Erskine and, it must be said, of Studebaker's other directors, as well. (What were they doing, one wonders, while Erskine was playing fast and loose with the rent money?)[24] Studebaker, a basically sound company whose market share had actually increased by 73 percent since 1929, was forced into receivership on Saturday, March 18, 1933.

Beginning the following day, the fate of Studebaker was in the hands of receivers and, later, of trustees appointed by the Federal Court. The Federal Judge assigned to oversee the receivership was none other than Erskine's old nemesis, Thomas W. Slick. Erskine had expected to remain on as president under the receivership, but Slick would have none of it, so Erskine resigned and went home. Studebaker's elderly chairman, Fred Fish, who had long ago promoted automobiles as the way to ensure the company's future, resigned, as well.[25]

Erskine had flown as high as any industrialist in America, but now his life was in ruins. Not only was he out of a job, his Studebaker stock was worthless, he owed $350,000 in connection with personal real estate investments that had soured along with the national economy and, according to at least one report, owed more than $700,000 in back taxes. Bluntly, he was broke and had creditors he couldn't hope to pay. Worse, he was sixty-two and in failing health with a heart condition and diabetes, both far less treatable ailments then than they are today.

As he saw it, he had only one source of potential income left that would be sufficient to pay his debts and provide for his family: a collection of life insurance policies totalling $900,000 in value, none of which, as it happened, contained the usual "suicide" clause.[26] So, in July, having, as one contemporary phrased it, "analyzed the whole situation more accurately than he had analyzed the stock market," he set his final plan into motion.[27]

Keeping his own counsel, he invited his wife's family to come for a visit, so that she would have immediately at hand the support of her loved ones in her approaching time of need. He entertained them to a notably convivial dinner party, then all retired. The next morning his son—A. R. Erskine, Jr., known as Russell—found him dead, a bullet through his heart, still holding the gun wrapped in a towel to muffle the sound. They found a note addressed to his son, which read: "Russell, I cannot go on any longer."

Fortunately, the solution for Studebaker was less drastic.

Notes

The most important resources drawn upon in the writing of this chapter include Stephen Longstreet's official company history, *A Century on Wheels: The Story of Studebaker*, C. B. Glasscock's *The Gasoline Age: The Story of the Men Who Made It*, and Donald T. Critchlow's *The Life and Death of an American Corporation*. The financial analysis of Studebaker's bankruptcy drew on annual reports in the author's collection for General Motors Corporation, Nash Motors Company, and Studebaker Corporation (Indiana). The massive *Report on Motor Vehicle Industry* published by the Federal Trade Commission in 1939 offered invaluable details regarding the failed takeover of White Motor Company. Arthur Pound's seminal study of General

Motors, *The Turning Wheel*, published in 1934, provided further information and insights into the industry at the time of Studebaker's collapse.

[1] Longstreet, p. 91.
[2] Dietrich had been affiliated with both LeBaron, Inc., and Dietrich, Inc.
[3] Bore was 2.63 inches, stroke was 4.50.
[4] Mussolini was later supposed to have remarked, "It is possible to govern Italy...but what's the point?"
[5] Special Interest Autos, January-February, 1978, p. 41.
[6] Special Interest Autos, January-February, 1978, p. 41.
[7] Figures for the two companies were as follows:

	Units	Sales	Profit/Loss
Studebaker	136,205	157,692,207	13,947,181
Pierce-Arrow	6,491	19,436,672	-1,293,029

[8] It must be noted, though, that this was in the days before the S.E.C. set down strict disclosure rules that had to be followed in preparing such statements.
[9] Horsepower ratings were 115 (1929-30), and 122 (1931-33).
[10] In addition to its respected line of automobiles, Pierce-Arrow had, for years, built a small number of medium- and heavy-duty trucks.
[11] 1930 Studebaker Corporation Annual Report.
[12] Employment dropped from 18,137 in 1929 to 11,733 in 1930.
[13] The horsepower rating would remain virtually the same, though: 100 hp.
[14] Although its days as a major producer of passenger cars were over, the Willys-Overland roller coaster would soar again after World War II on the strength of the civilian Jeep.
[15] Special Interest Autos, March-April, 1976, p. 40.
[16] Shortly after penning these words Coolidge himself died. ("How can they tell?" was Dorothy Parker's droll comment upon hearing the news.) The Grim Reaper did seem to be stalking the Rockne project.
[17] Longstreet, p. 96.
[18] Glasscock, p. 259.
[19] Or, "thanks mainly to our financial-control procedures," as Alfred Sloan, GM's president, dryly phrased it. Charley Nash, for his part, was a notorious tightwad and, in that, he could not have formed a more stark contrast to the free-spending Albert Erskine. Walter Chrysler, who worked for Nash at one point, recalled: "Sometimes when he turned his thumbs down on some expenditure...I'd tell him he was tighter than a barrel without a bung. 'Charley,' I'd say imploringly, in the manner of a little boy, '*please* show me the first nickel you ever earned. [They say] you've got it hidden somewhere.'"

[20] Nash was on a fiscal year that ended November 30th. Studebaker and General Motors were on fiscal years that ended December 31st. Profits are computed after Federal taxes; state and local taxes are not deducted. Pierce-Arrow sales and profit data are not included in the Studebaker figures. Dividends include amounts for both preferred and common stock, and are listed for the year they were paid (i.e., the bulk of the dividends declared for 1928 were paid in 1929, etc.). Cash here is defined very narrowly to include only cash and marketable securities, and even there it is difficult to determine the latter. The actual "marketability" of securities is usually extremely difficult to ascertain from company financial reports. It can be assumed that the companies involved have given themselves the benefit of the doubt on such matters. Moreover, it is common in standard accounting to include items such as receivables, inventory, and notes payable to a company as current assets. Capitalization commonly includes the value of plants and facilities (less depreciation), goodwill, patent rights, and so on. Particularly in bad economic times, however, receivables can go bad or be hard to collect, inventory can be a functional liability, and items such as a company's investment in plants and equipment are meaningless in the sense of liquidity. Goodwill and other such numbers are frequently fantasies. Also, notes payable to a company and "investments" are often accounting fictions in that they frequently involve money a company "owes" itself via its subsidiaries, such as, in Studebaker's case, Rockne and Pierce-Arrow. To that extent, they have little meaning. The only items that count when the bill collector comes knocking are liquid assets such as cash and marketable securities.

[21] The annual capacity in South Bend was 200,000 units; the capacity of the old E-M-F plant is harder to determine, but, based on past performance, must have been around 70,000 units.

[22] Back then, the inauguration ceremony took place on March 4th. Later, it was changed to January 20th. In his inaugural address Roosevelt proclaimed, "the only thing we have to fear is fear itself." He didn't know Albert Erskine.

[23] Federal Trade Commission, p. 800.

[24] Only one director, banker John F. Harris, had protested the dividend policy. He finally resigned in February, 1932, warning that "many perplexing questions will arise" from the board's actions. Curiously, Erskine's family blamed Woodruff for the debacle, although it is hard to understand why.

[25] Fish died in 1936.

[26] This was an enormous sum in 1933. Adjusting dollars from any given era for inflation is always difficult, but a multiple of 25 is probably not unreasonable in this case. That would give Erskine's insurance policies a value in 1999 dollars of perhaps $22,500,000.

[27] Glasscock, p. 260.

Overleaf, the body drop on the South Bend assembly line in the late-1930s.

FIVE

Back from the Abyss

Few companies the size of Studebaker Corporation had ever gone bank-rupt and emerged in one piece and no automobile manufacturer had ever done so.[1] This fact must be clearly understood before the events of the two years following Studebaker's descent into the abyss can be fully appreci-ated. On March 19, 1933, the money was gone, the factory was shuttered, employee morale had been dealt a body blow, and public confidence was quickly eroding. To survive, the company needed a miracle—and it got one. The miracle workers were named Hoffman and Vance.

Paul G. Hoffman was born in Chicago. A car nut even as a child, the only thing he ever wanted to do was be in the automobile business. By 1909, he was working for the Chicago dealer for the Halladay automobile. Halladay was a local product built about fifty miles west of Chicago in Streator, Illinois, and was well-regarded. "Every Day A Halladay," was the company's slogan—at least until the company went bankrupt in 1913. Eddie Rickenbacker worked for Halladay at one point, as did three of the Fisher brothers before they moved to Detroit and started Fisher Body. Hoffman started out at the dealer level as a mechanic in the shop, but was soon selling cars in the showroom. By 1911, he had moved to Los Angeles and gone to work for the Studebaker dealer there. It was with Studebaker that he began to gain a reputation as a whiz of a salesman. He was soon earning monthly commissions of as high as $1,000, which was a tremendous amount of money for a car salesman in the pre-World War I era. Eventually, he

Paul G. Hoffman, left, and Harold S. Vance.

became a dealer himself and, by 1925, had gone to South Bend to take on the responsibilities of vice-president of sales for the entire corporation.

Harold Sines Vance was born in Port Huron, Michigan. His first link with Studebaker was as an apprentice mechanic for the local E-M-F dealer. That was in 1910 and the wage rate was all of fifteen cents an hour. From that humble beginning, he advanced to the stock room of the dealership, managing the supply of parts. Soon, he moved up to the E-M-F factory in Detroit. By the time the old E-M-F plant was vacated and its production moved to South Bend in 1926, he had risen to become Studebaker's vice-president in charge of production.

Immediately upon the resignations of Fred Fish and Albert Erskine, Vance was named chairman of the board and Hoffman was named president. Amazingly, it was only the second changing of the guard at Studebaker in eighty-one years.[2] Although Erskine and Fish were gone and no member of the Studebaker family would ever again serve on the board of the company that bore the Studebaker name, most of the remaining directors and officers stayed on.

Almost at once, Hoffman and Vance scraped together enough funds to launch an advertising campaign in newspapers all across the country to proclaim their determination to carry on and their confidence in the future of Studebaker. Reportedly, Hoffman had telephoned Judge Slick at one o'clock in the morning to get permission to spend $100,000 on the ads which resolutely proclaimed:

> Studebaker carries on...Studebaker is still Studebaker in spirit, scope, and service. There has been no change, except for the better, in the policies and programs of the historic Studebaker institution...
>
> The great South Bend plants of Studebaker, closed since the announcement of the bank moratorium, will reopen Tuesday, March 21, under the direction of...seasoned automotive executives.
>
> This pioneering organization has already faced and fought and triumphed over more "depressions," wars and "bad times" than any other company in the automobile business.
>
> Studebaker now confidently carries on, assured that it can continue to offer the American public the kind of automobiles and service for which the Studebaker name is distinguished.[3]

Somehow, Hoffman and Vance had managed to get the lines rolling in South Bend almost as soon as they assumed the helm. During April, their first full month of operations, they sold 3,806 cars and made an operating profit of $20,000. It didn't seem like much, but any profit at all was cheery news in South Bend in the spring of 1933. By December, the profit had risen $54,000 and more good cheer was seen in on the banks of the St. Joseph. The overall loss for the year still came to $1.4 million, but that was 72 percent less than the blood bath in 1932 and was achieved despite a 10 percent drop in sales.[4]

Of course, the intense competition in the industry meant that Hoffman and Vance couldn't wait for a return to profitability to update Studebaker products. Even as they were struggling through the wreckage Albert Erskine had left behind in those dark days of March, 1933, they were forced to devote their attention to the forthcoming 1934 models. A popular story around South Bend had it that the two were so elated by the fact that they turned a $20,000 profit in their first full month on the job that they ordered the development of entirely new models for 1934. There may have been a kernel of truth to the story, but developing—much less paying for—new cars was no casual undertaking in the spring of 1933.[5] Still, it was done.

To save money, the Detroit plant was closed and Rockne production was shifted to South Bend. The move was completed on Easter weekend, 1933, according to the recollections of old-time Studebaker hands.[6] The initial intention was to continue the Rockne there for the 1934 model year, but in July it was decided to drop the Rockne brand and replace it under the guise of the revived Dictator in a broadened Studebaker model range. This was true in terms of price, at least, although the Dictator had neither the unique body shell nor the separate identity of the Rockne. None-the-less, consolidation was clearly in order given the company's financial circumstances, and so the decision to scrap the unique Rockne body and concentrate all resources on promoting the Studebaker brand name made sense. At the same time, the President was downgraded in size and price in order to reduce development and production costs and to widen its sales appeal.

Another decisive cost-cutting act by the new management team was to dump Studebaker's white elephant in Buffalo. Pierce-Arrow was sold to a syndicate of investment bankers in August, 1933, for a reported $1,000,000.[7] Thus, on the face of it, Studebaker's five-year ownership of Pierce-Arrow

1934 Studebaker President.

had lost the corporation $8.7 million on the purchase price of the stock alone. Actually, the loss was greater even than that, for Studebaker was forced to make good $150,000 in debts owed by Pierce-Arrow to White and to cover some $16,246 in costs involved in the complicated transaction. So, the loss rose to nearly $9 million and the cash raised declined to $833,754, or less than nine cents on the dollar.[8]

There can be little doubt that the takeover back in 1928 had been a good thing for Pierce-Arrow. Arguably, the finest cars the Buffalo firm ever built were produced from 1929-33 and the end would have doubtless come years sooner without financial support from South Bend as the depression deepened. What Studebaker got out of the deal is harder to discern. At first, of course, it basked in the reflected glow of the prestige of the Pierce-Arrow name and was able to tout itself as a full-line car producer on the order of General Motors or Chrysler. After 1930, however, Pierce-Arrow quickly turned into an albatross and there can't have been many executives in South Bend who didn't earnestly regret the purchase by the time Studebaker itself hit the wall in 1933.[9]

The new Studebaker models announced for the 1934 model year were the most modern ever. Fenders were more deeply valanced in front and, in the rear, forecast the "pontoon" look that was to be the new vogue throughout the industry within a couple of years. The grille had a more pronounced taper to the "vee" and projected forward at the base. Bodies and hoods were far more integrated than before, head lamps had more aggressive bullet shapes and sidemounts were enclosed in body-color covers, or eliminated entirely on increasing numbers of cars. The new styling was also less highly sculptured, with character lines suggesting what had been boldly stated heretofore.

By every objective measurement the new designs were an improvement. In subjective terms, on the other hand, the quality of Studebaker design took a noticeable dip. Periods in which design is shifting from one school to another always produce awkward transitional efforts and styling was, alas, another one of the casualties at Studebaker in 1933 as the 1934 models were being developed. Hoffman and Vance were reportedly displeased with the way the restyling had turned out (as well they should have been) and this may have been a factor in the departure of Barney

Roos, Studebaker's capable chief engineer, in whose province fell responsibility for body design. This was typical practice in the industry in the days before formal design staffs were organized and the only company that had a design staff *per se* worthy of the name in 1933 was General Motors. It wasn't long before Hoffman and Vance retained an outside design consultant—but more on that later.[10]

There may have been a couple of other factors that influenced Roos' departure. He and Vance had reportedly long detested one another, which couldn't have helped since Vance was now chairman of the board. Roos was also in the midst of a messy divorce. According to one account, Roos impulsively submitted his resignation one day and took off for California. By the time he arrived, he'd changed his mind, but Vance had already leapt at the chance to replace him. He was rehired by Hoffman as an engineering consultant, but soon found a home at Willys-Overland where he played a key role in developing the Jeep.

Roos was succeeded as vice-president of engineering by Roy Cole of Rockne fame. Ralph Vail, too, was working for Studebaker proper now, having already been elevated to the vice-presidency in charge of production. The two would run engineering and manufacturing for the next fifteen years or so.

As 1933 wore on, the situation seemed dire in the short term but, in the long-term, Hoffman and Vance were convinced that prospects were quite hopeful. The bankruptcy laws are strict, though. Once a company files, the court's main obligation is to the company's creditors, of whom any company filing for bankruptcy necessarily has all too many. Sentiment doesn't enter into it, although there must have been quite a lot of that in Studebaker's favor in the court system in Indiana.[11] For Hoffman and Vance, the first challenge was to persuade Judge Slick that Studebaker was salvageable, for without that belief the court would have no recourse under the law but to order liquidation. This was to be done by filing a plan for reorganization of the company's affairs that would demonstrate, 1) that the company could again achieve profitability and 2) that at least the minimum interests of the creditors could be protected. In December, 1933, Hoffman and Vance duly filed a plan to that effect. It involved the creation of a new Studebaker Corporation to be incorporated under the laws of

Delaware that would assume the assets of the old company and retire its debts. That was the easy part. It would take Hoffman and Vance fourteen months to make it work.

Judge Slick must have been greatly encouraged by what he saw, for as early as November 11, 1934, he appointed Hoffman, Vance and Ashton G. Bean (the chairman of White Motor Company) as official trustees to run Studebaker.[12] It was an eloquent indication of confidence in the company and its people, for, in being permitted to continue under essentially the same management, Studebaker was nearly unique among major companies forced into bankruptcy in that era.

A key to the reorganization was the selling of $6.8 million in new securities. Lehman Brothers, the New York brokerage house, agreed to handle the underwriting—if Hoffman and Vance could secure additional underwriting on their own. Doing so kept the pair, singly or together, on trains and planes between South Bend and New York for months where they were forced to go from door-to-door along Wall Street attempting to convince skeptical financiers that Studebaker was worth saving. Finally, when they were $200,000 short, Ernest Woodruff, an old friend of John Mohler Studebaker, chipped in. "I knew J.M.," he said simply. "Put me down."[13]

The new Studebaker Corporation was duly incorporated on January 26, 1935, under the laws of the State of Delaware. On March 8, 1935, the old corporation ceased to exist and its assets were assumed by the new Studebaker Corporation. It was official: Studebaker was back from the dead.

Part of the securities held by the old corporation, a small amount of cash and the remaining common stock of the White Motor Company were distributed to outstanding creditors. Creditors also received stock in the new corporation to compensate for inadequate reserves remaining in the old one. Holders of preferred stock in the old entity received stock in the new corporation. Holders of common stock were granted certain subscription rights. Essentially, though, the 19,000 holders of common stock got little or nothing and the stockholders in the new corporation were a substantially different group.[14] Walter Teagle, chairman of Standard Oil (New Jersey) was the only individual owning more than 1 percent.[15]

Briefly, the way it worked out in practice was like this: The holders of $14.9 million in notes (the notes that Erskine had mostly used to pay White

1935 Studebaker President Custom.

Motor Company stockholders as part of the aborted merger) were given 669,983 shares in Studebaker and 442,187 shares in White. The $3.6 million owed to various banks was wiped off the books with a payment of $299,197 in cash, plus 148,949 shares of Studebaker stock and 98,306 shares in White. Miscellaneous creditors of both the old Studebaker and Rockne corporations were given, to replace their $2.4 million in claims, $212,985 in cash, $425,969 in debentures, 80,285 shares in Studebaker and 53,319 shares in White. Finally, the holders of $5.8 million in preferred stock in the old corporation received 72,602 shares of common stock in the new one. At the bottom of the list, the 19,000 holders of common stock got nothing except those dubious subscription rights.[16]

After launching the new corporation, not much energy was left for anything else and the Studebaker range was only modestly restyled for 1935. The most noticeable change was the new "fencer's mask" grille, which made no pretense to being a radiator shell. Horizontal hood louvers also added a sense of streamlining and built-in trunks made their first appearance on some models. The most interesting new model by far was the Land Cruiser, a highly-styled sedan reminiscent of the 1933 Pierce Silver Arrow. From a design standpoint, it was the most impressive car the new regime had yet produced. (The entire line—Dictator, Commander and President— was advertised as the "Studebaker Champions for 1935," though, and this has caused some confusion among modern enthusiasts who mistakenly associate the slogan with the Champion series of 1939.)[17]

Despite its best efforts, the company still lost nearly $2 million in the approximately ten months it was in business in 1935, with revenues dipping to $33.8 million. A total 45,068 cars and trucks were sold. Much of the loss was probably due to the fact that the board had ordered a costly restyling of the existing car and truck lines for 1936. It explained its reasoning to stockholders in this fashion:

> The major problem confronting your Corporation when it began operations...was how to obtain the larger volume of business necessary to cover expenses and fixed charges. Your management believed that the necessary volume could not be obtained with the 1935 models then in production. Accordingly, designs were made and tools were ordered for a complete new line of passenger cars and trucks.[18]

The new cars were hardly trend-setters, but they were a distinct improvement over the awkward efforts of 1934-35. (Ironically, the 1935 Land Cruiser, which had been a notable exception to this, was dropped for 1936.) The fencer's mask grille was wider, head lamps were lowered almost to

1936 Studebaker Dictator.

the catwalk and full pontoon fenders were in evidence. The loveliest of the new body types was the three-passenger coupe.

As a result of the new look, Studebaker sales took a pleasant leap. A total of 23,873 cars were sold in the first four months of the model run, as compared to 16,096 during the same period with the 1935 models. Of course, the nation's economy continued to rebound, if slowly, and that helped. In addition, the company had bitten the bullet and elected to cut prices yet again, even at the expense of what it considered to be desirable margins. Dictator models now ranged in price from $665 to $775, while the top-end Presidents ranged from $965 to $1,065.

The biggest development in the industry at this time, however, was independent front suspension and if there was a single individual who could be credited with the concept it was Maurice Olley. Olley was a brilliant suspension engineer who had worked at the Rolls-Royce subsidiary in Springfield, Massachusetts, then got a job at Cadillac after the Springfield operation folded in 1931. One of Olley's delightful observations regarding the state of chassis engineering in those days was that in a chauffeur-driven limousine, the main function of the owner riding in the back was to serve as a harmonic balancer for the comfort of the chauffeur, who had the best seat in the car. The biggest problem was the rigid front axle, which transmitted road shocks rather than absorbing them, causing a whole host of problems from rough riding cars to potentially dangerous wheel shimmy. All manufacturers had fought doggedly to mitigate these problems, but with only limited success.

Olley and other engineers at General Motors decided that the only way to resolve the problem was by doing away with the solid front axle entirely. The result, called Knee-Action by all General Motors divisions, was actually two different independent front suspension systems available on every 1934 GM car, excepting only the cheapest Chevrolets. Independent front suspension became, almost overnight, all-but mandatory for other manufacturers and virtually all of them rushed to develop systems of their own—or, like Ford, to come up with truly creative reasons to try to explain to their customers why they hadn't.

Studebaker decided to jump on the bandwagon and got its version of independent front suspension in 1936, which it called "Planar Front Wheel

Suspension" and touted as "superior" to all other types. It, indeed, used separate suspension arms, but clung to the old-fashioned transverse leaf spring connecting the two wheels. In that, it was sort of a hybrid system. Still, it did do away with the solid front axle—that much could not be denied—and Studebaker and Packard were the only independents to develop serious alternative systems on their own. Planar Front Wheel Suspension was standard on the President and optional on the Dictator.

In 1936, the company reversed the financial picture recorded in 1935. A profit of $2.8 million was reported on sales of $68.9 million. This represented a sale of 91,999 cars and trucks during the calendar year. Studebaker automobile registrations were up 71 percent for the year, as compared to an industry average of 24 percent.

Meanwhile, the United Auto Workers (UAW) in this era was making its final push to organize the industry. Most companies fought the labor union tooth-and-nail. Henry Ford, destined to be the last hold-out, even resorted to violence against labor organizers before it was all over. Studebaker, in contrast, made no serious effort to oppose unionization of its plants and, in that, was virtually unique among automobile manufacturers. The UAW was formally recognized by the company on May 21, 1937, and South Bend UAW Local No. 5 was one of the first established in the nation. Noted the company's authorized history published in 1952:

> What Studebaker management saw, and others failed to grasp, was that where unionization was unopposed, even encouraged, then the union membership became truly representative of all the workers, and that when all the workers of a plant are taken together the majority are level-headed and approach all problems with a common-sense attitude. In plants where unionization was opposed by management, the level-headed, common-sense majority stayed out of the unions, leaving them to the control and direction of the radical fringe which exists in all plants.[19]

Perhaps. Studebaker was to demonstrate another truth in subsequent years, though: Management that fails to stand-up to its unions when necessary does neither the company nor, ultimately, the workers any favors.

Studebaker also benefited from the fact that Indiana was a "right to work" state in which compulsory unionization—i.e., the "closed" shop—was against the law, although each new Studebaker employee received a letter from Hoffman encouraging him to join.

The first labor contract called for an average wage of 90¢ an hour for Studebaker's 7,000 workers. The work week was set at forty hours, with time-and-a-half for overtime. A seniority system was enacted, as were the restrictive job classifications the union seemed to dote on.

Styling in 1937 was a close continuation of the 1936 look. Grilles were redone in thinly-spaced vertical bars that swept around the sides of the hood at the top, but little else was significantly altered. A Coupe-Express model was introduced. This was a passenger car-based pick-up truck and established the concept that Ford and Chevrolet would pursue with some success in future years with the Ranchero and El Camino, respectively. (Remember, Studebaker got there first.) The base price was $685.

Dollar sales increased slightly in 1937 to $70.1 million, though the number of vehicles sold remained virtually the same as in 1936: 91,475. Profits, on the other hand, tumbled to $811,874 due to a short, sharp recession that began in the late summer and sent the auto industry reeling. Unlike the usual economic downturns that hit different market segments with varying degrees of severity, this one seemed to hurt everyone equally. Olds, Pontiac and Dodge—Studebaker's main market segment competitors—

1937 Studebaker Suburban.

were similarly down.

Still, part of the reason for the company's poor profit performance was the increase in cost for parts and labor. Unfortunately, Studebaker management had elected to hold the lid on prices until the end of the 1937 model run, then raise prices on the 1938 models to compensate for the shrinking margins earlier in the year. The problem with that strategy was that the recession hit just as the 1938 models were launched. Studebaker sales in the final quarter of the calendar year were 37 percent below the same period the year before and there was very little profit at that volume.

The 1938 model year did, however, mark the start of one of the most famous associations in the history of Studebaker: Raymond Loewy had affiliated with the company. The Loewy-Studebaker relationship was destined to span a quarter-of-a-century and produce some of the most interesting—and frequently influential—cars in the industry.

The French-born Loewy had come to America in 1919 and established one of the first firms in the then-embryonic field of industrial design. Eventually, his hundreds of clients would include everyone from cigarette manufacturers to the Soviet Government. Along the way, he and his associates were called upon to participate in design efforts for such disparate items as dinnerware, postage stamps, corporate logos, ships, spacecraft—even Air Force One. And cars.

Always intensely interested in automobiles, Loewy wrangled his first automotive assignment in 1931 from Hupmobile, a respected producer in the Buick price class. The result was the beautiful "cycle-fender" Hupps of 1932, so-called because of the unique shape of their fenders. Loewy's next Hupp, the aerodynamic range of 1934, was less successful—it was another one of those awkward transitional designs—but Hupp was in its final decline, anyway, and Loewy was soon looking for another auto manufacturer. Enter Studebaker.[20]

It was at about the time Hupmobile started going under that Hoffman and Vance decided Studebaker needed some help in the design field. Loewy was approached and the first fruits of that association appeared as the all-new Studebaker line for 1938. Loewy reportedly took his inspiration from a streamlined diesel locomotive his firm had designed for the Pennsylvania Railroad. The finest of the new model range, and the body type most

1938 Studebaker President.

eagerly sought-after by modern collectors, was the four-door convertible sedan. Built in both Commander and President versions, production was limited and the type only lasted two years, but it was one of the most impressive cars available in the industry in 1938. It did much to burnish Studebaker's image, though the 1938 Studebakers across the board were trend-setters. The nearly full-width bodies were a year or two ahead of most of the competition, while the oval head lamps that blended into the front fenders on President models were among the more ingenious treatments of the era.

Loewy's working style bears some comment. Like Harley Earl at General Motors, Loewy was more of a manager—at least by the time he landed the Studebaker contract—than a yeoman designer. As such, he rarely did the actual designing himself. His strength, by all accounts, was two-fold: 1) he had a wonderful eye for good design, combined with the ability to spot important trends in their early stages and 2) he had an extraordinary flare for selling radical concepts to the often staid managements to whom he contracted his services. The last part of the equation was no less important than the first. There were (and are) many top-flight designers who have little ability to communicate their ideas to management and, without that ability, even great designs are often compromised or rejected altogether.[21] In the 1970s, Loewy recalled:

That phrase, "promoter-designer," is often used by my critics. It admit to it. I had to be exactly that. When I started fifty years ago, nobody knew what I was talking about. Design talent was not enough by itself. Executives, engineers had to be sold some way. It was very difficult and in order to convince them I had to acquire a new type of salesmanship, simple ways to make my points clear, to overcome doubt and, sometimes, antagonism. In order to succeed, I had to develop an effective type of "sell," unusual and unexpected. It was a great help. And, if there are now 20,000 industrial designers all over the world making a good living, it is because a few of us—the pioneers—had to blend talent with salesmanship.[22]

The lengths to which Loewy was willing to go to sell his ideas is illustrated by the story of the cycle-fender Hupps. Hupp management knew it needed better designs, but remained unconvinced of Loewy's ideas. So, Loewy went to the expense of building a prototype on his own. Loewy realized that many businessmen aren't abstract thinkers; they often have trouble imagining what something will look like until they see it in the flesh. So, Loewy showed it to them, won them over and won the contract.

1938 Studebaker K10 truck.

Loewy also had a rare talent for spotting talent in others. It has been said that nearly every American automobile designer of any consequence in the 1930s and 1940s worked with either Earl or Loewy (or both) at some point. Loewy's associates in his early years with Studebaker included such stars as Virgil Exner (who directed Chrysler Corporation design in the 1950s), Robert Ebstein (who was to play a key role in the designing of the Avanti), Holden "Bob" Koto (who would design the all-important first postwar Fords), John Reinhart (who would do the first—and, as it turned out, only—postwar Packard), Robert E. Bourke (destined to be a key influence on the celebrated 1953 Studebaker coupes) and Gordon Buehrig (who had designed the famed Cord 810/812).

The 1938 Studebakers went into production on August 30, 1937. Overall industry units sales of passenger cars were off by 55 percent in 1938. Total unit sales for Studebaker Corporation slumped to 52,605 cars and trucks—off by only 43 percent, thanks to the appeal of the new Loewy styling—while cash sales fell to $43.8 million and a loss of $1.8 million was reported. The situation was of sufficient concern to the government that President Roosevelt met with the beleaguered auto makers in January. Still, the Federal government picked this moment to assess Studebaker for "excess profits" earned in 1935—a year in which the corporation reported a loss of nearly $2 million—and demanded $1.2 million in payment! The contention arose over the way in which the company's securities and inventory had been valued at the time of its incorporation.

A study ordered by the Federal Trade Commission (FTC) in 1938 included much information about Studebaker.[23] An example of this was an interesting comparison of the value increase in Studebaker automobiles between 1925 and 1939.

Cars, in general, were offering more and more of everything for less and less money, partly due to pressures created by the depression and partly due to the advance of technology throughout the industry. This is one of the factors that killed off the great classics. For the comparatively modest price of a Buick or a Studebaker in 1939, a buyer could get, in most objective ways, a better car than the typical Packard, Pierce-Arrow, Cadillac, or Lincoln of only a few years earlier. The FTC comments with regard to Studebaker bear quoting:

A [1925] Model ER [Big Six] Studebaker four-door sedan on August 26, 1924, sold...for $1,655.61, while the [1939] Studebaker model 9A [Commander] four-door sedan, announced September 12, 1938, sold...for $946.83. This represented a decrease in the price in the four-door sedan of about 43 percent, or $708.78 less than in 1924. In terms of price per pound of car there was a reduction from 50.8 cents in 1924 to 29.6 cents in 1938, or a decrease of about 42 percent. The length of the wheelbase increased from 113 inches in 1924 to $116^1/2$ inches in 1938, while maximum brake horsepower increased from 50 to 90, or, in terms of price per horsepower, there was a decrease from $33.11 in 1924 to $10.52 in 1938, or about 68 percent.

The government investigators were, of course, only concerned with data that could be measured statistically. Had they entered the realm of subjective comparison, they would have had a field day comparing the beauty of the 1939 Loewy styling with the angular awkwardness (in relative terms) of the 1925 car, and they would have noted the astonishing increase in comfort, luxury and ease of operation achieved in a mere fourteen years—all for dramatically less money.

The Commission's report also included a detailed investigation into the way in which the major auto producers treated their dealers. It found an amazing variety of abuses, mostly involving methods the manufacturers used to force dealers to take more cars than needed or to accept unpopular body styles. Cited as typical was the response of an unnamed Packard dealer:

In the spring and early summer of 1937, we were oversupplied, and during August and September, it was necessary to make excessive over-allowances to move them. Because of this we built up too large a used-car stock, and, in November and December, we had to mark these down to move them and, as a result, lost all the money we had made in the first nine months.

A Hudson dealer voiced a similar complaint:

"Pressure" is constantly applied. In fact, within the last week, just about everything was used by the district sales manager to induce placing commitments for cars for the next six weeks larger than this company would entertain. The reasons constantly used recently are that factory labor relations require the employment of labor continuously, and the factory, of course, could not think of building up cars that are not sold.

In contrast, Studebaker dealers appeared to be a generally contented lot. Noted the FTC report:

Most of the...Studebaker dealers [contacted] made no statements indicating that they had been subjected to pressure to take new cars that they did not need. Some, however, made statements of which the following is typical:

"The roadman told me they had so many cars for my territory and if I didn't take them somebody else would."

Regarding receiving unordered cars, this dealer stated:

"Only once in 1937, I think October, they shipped me four cars that I did not order."

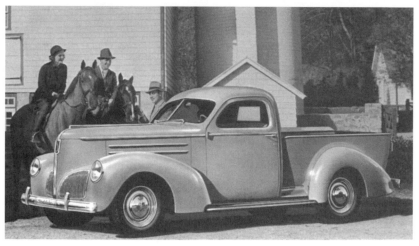

1939 Studebaker Coupe-Express.

Significantly, that would have been during the first weeks of the sudden, sharp recession of 1937-38. It was, of course, the thankless task of the field representatives of the various manufacturers to push as many cars as the home office wanted them to push. This number was often excessive, especially during unexpected downturns in the economy, and contention was the almost inevitable result. Still, it would seem that Studebaker played a fairer game than most.

The big 1939 Studebakers went into production on September 5, 1938. Commander and President models featured twin waterfall grilles mounted low in the catwalks. (The Lincoln-Zephyr featured a front end design that was remarkably similar.) Studebaker's major effort, however, came in the spring of 1939 with the introduction of the entirely new Champion. The Champion was a light-weight car designed especially for the numbing competition of the low-priced field, a field in which most of the automotive sales were made, but in which Studebaker had never had much success.

The basic motivation behind the Champion was simple: volume. Hoffman and Vance realized, as had Erskine before them, that Studebaker had to have more volume to survive. With the major producers getting bigger, Studebaker had no future as a producer of fewer than 100,000 car per year. Later, Vance admitted as much:

> Yes, some thought we were taking a risk. A lot of our ready capital went into development of that car. But...low price meant high volume, and volume is the priceless ingredient of growth. Most of us felt the Champion was the best investment we could possibly make against risk in the future. We had a loyal body of Studebaker owners. What we set out to do, and did, was to expand that number of owners as fast as possible.[24]

In announcing the impending arrival of the Champion to Studebaker stockholders, Hoffman and Vance described it as follows:

> Shortly after your corporation commenced operations in March, 1935, engineering work was begun on a new car calculated to give Studebaker and its dealers an opportunity to com-

Raymond Loewy, right, works on a clay model of the 1939 Studebaker Champion.

pete in the so-called "low-priced field." Approximately two-thirds of the passenger cars sold by the industry are in this field where your Corporation has been without representation. By May, 1938, development work had been substantially completed and your board of directors authorized the necessary expenditures for the production...The addition of this model should strengthen materially the position of Studebaker dealers and distributors, giving them a complete line of medium- and low-priced cars.[25]

Throughout the 1930s, the very nature of the automobile business had been changing in such a way as to make increasingly problematical the continued viability of all but the largest competitors. The chief villain was modern technology. The evolving automobile was becoming more and more complex. It was, consequently, costing more and more to produce cars and more and more of them had to be sold to defray those costs. The advent of the all-steel body, with the vast capital expenditures required for new machinery, had probably done as much to thin the ranks of the independent producers as had the economic depression and there were certainly more such threats on the way. General Motors, Ford and Chrysler would always be able to market sufficient numbers of vehicles to afford the enormous, and geometrically expanding, costs of research, development and tooling, but how would an independent manage to compete?

Still, at the time of the reorganization, Hoffman and Vance were not without significant advantages that could be exploited to Studebaker's benefit. The most important of these—at least potentially—was the company's image as a manufacturer of high-quality medium-priced cars. As soon as the national economy began to rebound, the medium-priced field was where the shrewd money knew the sales growth would be greatest. Yet, Hoffman and Vance also became convinced that medium-priced sales alone wouldn't give Studebaker the volume it needed.

Enthusiasts tend to believe that building good cars is enough and, as a corollary, that if a company goes under it must be because of deficiencies in the product. If that were true, people would still be buying Hupmobiles.[26] In its death throws, Hupp actually resorted to the slogan, "Hupp has always built a good car." No one denied it, but, sadly, building good cars was *not* enough. It was necessary to sell them to someone and, in order to do that, a keen appreciation of the realities of marketing strategy was needed. An examination of Studebaker's efforts in the 1930s demonstrates that Hoffman and Vance understood quite well where the challenges and opportunities lay for Studebaker.

Essentially, there were four basic target groups of potential car buyers available to any car company, including Studebaker: 1) existing customers; 2) customers graduating up from less expensive brands sold by the same company; 3) customers graduating up from less expensive brands sold by other companies; and 4) customers "captured" from other brands in the same price segments. Indeed, these categories are still valid today. One by one, Hoffman and Vance moved to target Studebaker products toward all four groups:

Of the four categories, the first is the Mother Lode. An old axiom in the marketing profession is that "a customer is yours to lose," i.e., once someone is buying your product or service, he or she is going to tend to continue to do so until given a compelling reason to change buying habits. Ironically, Studebaker started out in good shape here. While Erskine had been squandering the company's cash assets in the early 1930s, the Studebaker brand had, none-the-less, been recording substantial increases

1939 Studebaker Champion.

in market share. Studebaker may not have had any money in the spring of 1933, but it had a large and loyal group of existing owners who could be counted on to continue buying Studebakers in coming years—assuming Hoffman and Vance could keep them competitive. The repeated restylings from 1934 to 1942 and the retaining of Raymond Loewy, among other actions, were evidence of their intelligent effort to do that.

The second category—customers graduating up from less expensive brands sold by the same company—was less hopeful from Studebaker's

The Studebaker Champion engine.

perspective. Its one effort to launch an inexpensive brand with the Rockne had never had a chance to generate many customers. The Champion was a far more ambitious—and successful—effort in that direction. As a result, starting in 1939 Studebaker began building a base of low-priced customers who could be expected to fuel sales of medium-priced Studebaker lines in future years as these buyers became more prosperous.

The third category—customers graduating up from less expensive brands sold by other companies—was another one in which Studebaker stood to gain. Assuming the Studebaker product remained competitive in the medium-priced field, it would be an attractive alternative for buyers of low-priced cars built by Studebaker's competitors. In particular, Ford neglected the medium-priced field almost entirely until the Mercury was introduced for 1939; until then, virtually 100 percent of Ford owners seeking better grades of transportation had no choice but to go outside Ford Motor Company at trade-in time. With competitive products (see category number one), Studebaker could expect to garner its fair share of those sales.

The fourth category—customers "captured" from other brands in the same price classes—was also one in which Studebaker's prospects were as bright as its competitiveness allowed it to be and the Champion added a second price class in which conquest sales could be made.

The Champion entered production in February, 1939, was previewed to the media on March 4th and went on sale in April. The new line was brilliantly engineered and Studebaker's market share immediately jumped a full percentage point, from 2.28 percent in 1938 to 3.28 percent in 1939. The factory had to extend the work week to five-and-a-half days to accommodate demand. The Champion also did quite a bit to give Studebaker a

A Studebaker cab-forward car hauler delivering a load of 1939 Champions.

more dynamic image with the public, a considerable advantage in a business in which appearance is often more important than reality.

More than that, the Champion heralded a new era in Studebaker design and engineering. It demonstrated the company's dedication to building lighter and more efficient cars. Loewy was largely responsible for this, as the elimination of needless weight had long been an obsession with him. As soon as he established the styling section in South Bend, he had signs put up admonishing: "Weight is the Enemy!" The Champion certainly proved the merits of that concept. It weighed about 15 percent less than the typical Ford or Chevy, resulting in better fuel economy and less wear-and-tear on components, but offered comparable room and comfort. On the strength of the miserly Champion, Studebaker swept the Gilmore Economy Run in 1940, winning every class in which it was entered.

Studebaker sold 114,196 cars and trucks in 1939, or better than double the total in 1938. The Champion was largely responsible for most of the gain, although the economy rebounded somewhat, too. The Champion reached nearly 4 percent of the market for low-priced cars and accounted for around 60 percent of Studebaker unit sales. Revenues soared to $81.7 million and the company reported a profit of $2.9 million. Good times, it seemed, had finally returned to South Bend. Indeed, Hoffman and Vance assured stockholders that the good times were just beginning:

> Largely because of the introduction of the Champion, the domestic distributor and dealer organization increased 43.6 percent in 1939, from 2,180 outlets at the beginning of the year to 3,130 outlets at the end of the year. The opportunity afforded by the Champion to extend Studebaker retail representation, particularly in smaller communities, is by no means exhausted, and it is anticipated that substantial additions to the dealer body will continue to be made in 1940. One of the most gratifying phases of the success of the Champion in its first year is the high degree of satisfaction which all reports indicate that the car is giving to its owners, because owner satisfaction leading to the development of a clientele is an important and a necessary factor in the program of your corporation.[27]

Years later, when Studebaker's production efficiency came under scath-
ing criticism, it might have been useful to know that the company had at
one time, at least in the view of some observers, been leading the pack.
Noting that the Champion had been "launched at a cost of $3.5 million for
new equipment and tooling alone," *Automotive Industries* commented:

> Visualization of the machine shop lay-out and equipment from
> the factory routings must indicate to the seasoned factory execu-
> tive that the manufacturing scheme ranks with that of the most
> advanced plants of the industry. In fact, Studebaker shopmen are
> inclined to believe that not a few of the operations mark a definite
> contribution to machine shop practice.
>
> Nor is the machinery the only feature of the lay-out. Efficient
> mechanization has been carried through to encompass materials
> handling—gravity roller conveyor lines for machine lines, fitted
> with turntables, with roll-over fixtures at various points, and the
> first use we have noted recently of large hinged sections of the
> conveyor at strategic points to provide free movement of men and
> materials through the lines.

Surprisingly, Studebaker sales stagnated in 1940. The senior 1940
Studebakers, which went into production on August 14, 1939, and were
formally announced on September 26th, were refinements of the successful 1938-39 design, but the Champion was nearly near new. Furthermore,
Studebaker's dealer body had grown 15 percent to 3,598 and it was a boom
year for the industry. A total of 119,509 cars and trucks were sold (up only
4.7 percent from 1939). Income rose slightly to $84.2 million, while profits
actually dipped 27 percent to $2.1 million. Studebaker management was
silent on the middling unit sales, but explained the poor profit picture thusly:

> Throughout the first seven months of 1940, cars were sold a
> prices established at the beginning of the model season in August,
> 1939, although subsequently there were progressive increases in
> cost of material, labor, and expense, including taxes. At the end of
> August, 1940, with the introduction of new [1941] models, prices

The Studebaker display at the 1940 New York World's Fair.

were advanced as much as we believed the competitive situation would permit...however, these price advances on 1941 models were not sufficient to overcome the effect of the lower-margin 1940s models which prevailed during the first seven months of the year. The trend of costs is upward, and to what extent the average margin per car may be affected in 1941 is unpredictable.[28]

The question of the effect that the war in Europe would have on passenger car production in the United States was already becoming a constant topic for discussions and rumors within the industry, as well. World War II broke out in September, 1939, although America would not be dragged into it for more than two years.[29]

Bodies were new for the Commander and President lines in 1941. The designs had a pronounced General Motors "look" to them and this cannot have been a coincidence. Virgil Exner, who had joined the Loewy's in-house styling staff in 1938 after a brief career at General Motors, was in charge of their design. Furthermore, the design concepts coming out of Harley Earl's styling staff at General Motors were leading the industry at that point, as evidenced, in particular, by the design of the landmark 1938 Cadillac Sixty Special that had been in the works while Exner was laboring away in the Pontiac studio down the hall.

The Sixty Special is justifiably considered to be one of the most significant American designs of all time. Loewy, who was sensitive to important design advances in any field and Exner, who was a General Motors alumnus, must have been deeply impressed, for the 1941 senior Studebakers were clearly derivative the basic Sixty Special concept. The Sixty Special had the sporty appearance of a "hardtop convertible," although long before that term was coined. The hood line swept back and merged with the beltline roll that formed the exterior sill for the side windows, and then flowed on back to an extended rear deck. In that, the Sixty Special was the first production car from a major manufacturer to have what would later become known as "notchback" styling, with a long and fully integrated trunk. And, because the car was arrestingly low by the standards of the day, no running boards were needed. The total package was wonderfully exciting and youthful—a true sport sedan for the emerging executive class.[30]

The low-mounted 1941 Studebaker grilles, for their part, were probably influenced by Lincoln and/or General Motors. The Lincoln-Zephyr, announced in 1936, had used a V-shaped grille that tapered so markedly toward the base that it restricted air flow to the radiator. Thus, the early Zephyrs had over-heating problems. In response, E. T. Gregorie, Edsel Ford's design chief, devised low-mounted horizontal grilles for the 1938

1941 Studies on the line: Skyway Commander Land Cruiser, left, and Champion.

models. In addition to promoting engine cooling, they were a radical design departure from the traditional high, vertical grilles almost universally used in the industry. The 1938 Zephyr inspired Harley Earl to order his minions to do something similar on the full 1939 General Motors model range. This group included Exner, one of whose last renderings for Pontiac featured a grille that was not only stunningly low and wide, but an integral part of the front bumper. By 1941, designers at most other manufacturers were eagerly exploring the horizontal look, too.

The foregoing may irritate certain enthusiasts who like to think that Studebaker in this era was creating its designs out of whole cloth, influencing others but influenced by no one. As is the case with artists in any field, though, automotive designers are keenly attuned to what their colleagues are creating at other companies and it rarely takes long for a compelling concept to make the rounds. The Sixty Special, after all, had been heavily influenced by both the exciting Buehrig-designed Cord and by an earlier French design for the 1934 Panhard Panoramique. With Buehrig and Exner now at Studebaker, the situation had, in a sense, come full circle.

What is unique is the way in which designers adapt ideas to their own purposes and, in that, the 1941 Commander and President were admirable, indeed, and especially with regard to the new Skyway series that was announced in April. The Skyway models attained a level of design brilliance unsurpassed by any prewar Studebakers, excepting only the classic era masterpieces of the 1932-33 period. The astonishingly spare use of bright work was one feature that stands out and anticipated the "less is more" school of automotive design by two decades. The tasteful use of bright trim moldings around the side windows was another advanced feature worth noting. Even the low-mounted twin grilles were far lower and more aggressively horizontal in appearance than any other manufacturer dared to attempt at the time. The overall result was a *tour de force* for Studebaker and the fact that the individual elements may have been inspired by previous designs in no way lessens the credit due to Loewy and his associates.

The company did a big business in 1941, in general, and it proved to be the best year for Studebaker since the onset of the depression. A total of 133,855 cars and trucks were sold, rivaling the best year in Studebaker's history in that regard. Cash sales rose to $115.7 million and profits soared

1941 Studebaker Skyway President with one-piece curved windshield.

to just a few dollars shy of $6 million. Now that there was more money coming in than going out, an incentive compensation plan approved by stockholders in 1940 began to kick-in. Unlike the broad-based pre-depression plan, however, this one was limited in scope to twenty-eight top executives. A total of $288,454 was "earned" by those eligible in 1941.

By the time the 1942 models entered production in August, 1941, it was obvious to most Americans that the war in Europe would eventually involve the United States in a direct way. (The visit by the Japanese at Hawaii came as a bit of a surprise, though.) It was not known what the entry of the United States into a full-fledged war would mean to Studebaker and to the auto industry, but the impact was already being felt in the scramble for scarce items and the need to find suitable substitutes for a growing list of strategic materials that the American government ordered reserved for military application. There was, in fact, considerable concern among prospective car buyers regarding the effect of all these substitutions and shortages on the quality of the soon-to-be-introduced 1942 models. It was widely feared that they would be inferior, but history proved these fears misplaced as hundreds of thousands of 1942 cars from all manufacturers gave excellent service during the period approaching.

As was the case with most manufacturers, the 1942 Studebaker passenger car line was essentially the same as that offered in 1941. The Champion continued to be built on its own body shell distinct from that of the senior models, although there was more attempt at a family "look" than had always been the case in previous years. All Studebakers received massive one-piece grilles of a pronounced horizontal design.

The Federal government, for its part, was taking great pains to demonstrate its ability to sow confusion with some of its regulations regarding allocations and restrictions. In a market in which almost literally anything on wheels could be sold to an increasingly car hungry public—"desperate" might more accurately describe the mood in the latter months of 1941 when production cutbacks began to bite and total war seemed ever more imminent—the government became unaccountably fearful for the fate of certain manufacturers who had been unable to obtain adequate quantities

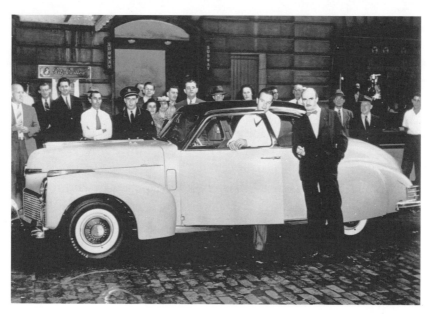

Bob Hope, left, and Harold Vance with a 1942 Studebaker Skyway President.

of scarce chrome. Accordingly, it drastically restricted the use of chrome by all manufacturers so no company would have an "unfair" competitive advantage. At General Motors, where ample supplies of chrome trim parts were on hand, this policy reached the point of absurdity. GM was actually forced to paint over the chrome before the parts could be used.

The "blackout" car was thus developed to deal with chrome shortages, both real and government-fantasized. The regulations specified that most normally chromed trim parts, except bumpers, would have to be painted on cars built after December 15, 1941. Each manufacturer handled this in its own way; some developed a series of two-tone schemes to try to dress up the chromeless cars as much as possible (with the painted trim parts harmonizing with, or contrasting to, the body color), while others just got as close to chrome color as they could by painting it all gray. Surviving factory photos of actual blackout 1942 Studebakers suggest the chrome-gray scheme was employed in South Bend.

On September 13, 1941, the government established quotas for each manufacturer for civilian passenger car production in the August-November period. On October 24th, December quotas were issued. January and February, 1942, quotas were subsequently issued, then repeatedly reduced. On December 24th, as a conservation measure, it was forbidden to equip cars with spare tires; new cars were to be shipped with four tires only.

Effective January 1, 1942, civilian sales of passenger cars was halted pending establishment of a rationing system, although production continued under strict quotas for each manufacturer. On January 6th, the manufacture of anti-freeze was prohibited. On January 14th, the rationing of tires was ordered. By the time the government set February 10th as the date for final production of passenger cars, it was a struggle for many companies to keep the lines going. On January 24th, Willys-Overland was the first manufacturer to cease production. Dodge followed on the 29th, while Lincoln, Chrysler and Studebaker stopped the lines on the 31st. Olds, Buick, Cadillac, Hudson and Nash lasted until February 3rd. Chevrolet quit on the 6th. Ford and Packard made it all the way to the 9th. Only Pontiac hung in there until the very end. The last 1942 Pontiac—and the final 1942 American car—rolled off the line on February 10, 1942. It would be nearly four years before volume manufacture of American automobiles resumed.

Studebaker's official January quota had been approximately 8,000 cars, although somehow 9,285 were built. All of these were frozen in company inventory when the lines stopped on the 31st. Their disposition awaited directives from the government's Office of Price Administration (OPA), which was attempting to develop plans for them and for the several hundred thousand cars in the hands of other manufacturers. In March, a convoluted rationing system was inaugurated to dole out cars to buyers with priority needs: doctors, people engaged in key defense work, government agencies, the military, etc. So parsimonious was the OPA that thousands of cars remained frozen when the war ended three-and-a-half years later. Commented the company in its annual report issued to stockholders in March, 1942:

> In addition to these finished cars, the Corporation had in inventory, or in the hands of vendors ready for deliver, parts and sub-assemblies estimated to have a value of approximately $2,800,000.00 which in large part appear to be frozen for the duration of the emergency. Because no retooling for the production of passenger cars and light commercial cars can be expected during the war period, it is anticipated that when production of passenger cars and light commercial cars can be resumed, Studebaker and all the other automobile manufacturers will, of necessity, start production again with substantially the same models as are now current.[31]

That proved to be a prophetic observation. For the next three-and-a-half years, however, the men and women of Studebaker devoted all their energies to government war assignments and were to compile a truly enviable record in that regard.

It has become fashionable to dismiss Hoffman and Vance for the many mistakes they made after World War II. Much of this condemnation is warranted, to be sure, but it is also necessary to remember that their leadership was extremely adept—if not brilliant—before the war. Against heavy odds, they saved Studebaker from probable liquidation in 1933. Then, between 1933 and 1942, Studebaker was, thanks largely to their efforts, an aggressive company that rarely made a serious mistake or let a meaningful opportunity go by.

Notes

The most important resources drawn upon in the writing of this chapter include Stephen Longstreet's official company history, *A Century on Wheels: The Story of Studebaker*, and C. B. Glasscock's *The Gasoline Age: The Story of the Men Who Made It*. The financial analysis of Studebaker's bankruptcy and reorganization drew on Studebaker annual reports in the author's collection as well as on the massive *Report on Motor Vehicle Industry* published by the Federal Trade Commission in 1939.

[1] Willys-Overland also went into receivership in 1933 and survived, but never re-emerged as a significant automobile producer.

[2] John Mohler Studebaker—along with his brothers, and, later, his son-in-law, Fred Fish—had run the company from 1858-1915, and the first changing of the guard took place at that time. Albert R. Erskine had run the show from 1915-33. Erskine had also been president of Pierce-Arrow. Arthur J. Chanter, formerly vice-president of Pierce-Arrow, was named to head that firm. Ashton Bean remained head of the White Motor Company.

[3] Longstreet, p. 98.

[4] Operating profits (or losses) are substantially different from the overall figures reported as profits or losses at the end of the year. There are different ways to compute them, but operating profits generally do not include capital investment, depreciation, taxes, and so forth. In essence, they reflect the profits or losses sustained on the day-to-day operations of the company. For this reason, it is quite possible to show an operating profit and still report a loss for the year, as Studebaker did in 1934. Without operating profits, though, there would be nothing left over at the end of the year to fund capital investments for items such as new product development, and this is why Hoffman and Vance were so cheered by Studebaker's quick turn-around in April, 1933. It was, indeed, a significant development that boded well for the future—but it hardly meant that they were out of the woods.

[5] Even assuming the money could be found, a company in receivership would need the approval of the court to spend it for capital investments.

[6] Easter fell on April 16th that year.

[7] The group was headed by Arthur J. Chanter. He had transferred over to Pierce-

Arrow from Studebaker after the takeover in 1928 and had served as executive vice-president. In April, 1933, following Studebaker's bankruptcy, he had been named president of Pierce Arrow.

[8] In fact, it was worse even than *that*. Pierce-Arrow had made $1.2 million in 1930, which was almost five times as much as Studebaker made in South Bend, but, when production hit the skids, the results were, if anything, even worse in Buffalo. It isn't known if Pierce-Arrow made money in 1931, but odds are heavy that it didn't. By 1932, every other luxury car manufacturer in the country was awash in red ink. Pierce-Arrow sales were in a fatal slide, and, by 1933, had collapsed to barely 2,000 cars—one fifth the number produced in 1929. There couldn't have been much money in those numbers, and it is known that Pierce-Arrow had "borrowed" an unspecified amount of money from Studebaker to subsidize its losses as the depression deepened. Because of this, some of Studebaker's creditors tried to seek redress from it on the not unreasonable grounds that it was sitting on at least some of Studebaker's assets. Not only did these creditors fail to get their money back, neither could Studebaker. The terms of the sale involved forgiving those debts, so the total loss Studebaker took on the deal was certainly far higher even than the $9 million noted here.

[9] Pierce-Arrow struggled along for several years until it, too, fell into bankruptcy in 1938, yet Pierce-Arrow cars continued to represent the highest standards of quality until the very end. Two of its last cars were bullet-proof limousines built for F.B.I. Director J. Edgar Hoover. It has been a point of pride for Pierce-Arrow enthusiasts that the company never cheapened its name with a lesser product, as did Cadillac (with the LaSalle), Packard (wth the One-Twenty), and Lincoln (with the Lincoln-Zephyr). That is true, but it also goes a long way toward explaining why the nameplate failed to survive, for cars in the traditional Pierce-Arrow mold were doomed. In a curious twist, the name was very nearly revived in 1962 for the car that became the Avanti. It was reportedly Raymond Loewy's personal choice, and most of the early Avanti designs bore Pierce-Arrow nameplates or insignia. In the end, Studebaker made the decision to go with a name that looked to a future it did not have, rather than to a past it could not recreate.

[10] Roos' engineering credits included the mechanical fuel pump, ball-bearing spring shackles, and free-wheeling. He was far from finished when he lost his berth at Studebaker. He went to Willys-Overland and was instrumental in the development of the Jeep. He died in 1960.

[11] Eagle-eyed readers may object here that bankruptcies are handled through the Federal court system, not the state court systems. This is entirely true, but even the bankruptcy courts are staffed by well-connected political appointees selected from the local area. In other words, the bankruptcy court in South Bend was doubtless run by lawyers from South Bend whose staff would also

be drawn from there. These were people who had firm ties to the local community and, in many cases, no doubt had family and friends dependent upon Studebaker's survival.

[12] Bean made a good team with Hoffman and Vance, according to all accounts. He died on July 19, 1935.

[13] Longstreet, p. 100.

[14] The specific terms of the pay-out were as follows: The creditors and bondholders of the old company received four shares of common stock in the new entity and two-and-two-thirds shares of White Motor Company common stock for every $100 they were owed, plus subscription rights to debentures and common stock. The creditors of Rockne Motors Corporation received the following for every $100 owed them: $25 in cash, $50 worth of debentures in the new entity, one share of common stock in the new entity, and approximately seven-tenths of a share of common stock in the White Motor Company, plus certain subscription rights. Holders of preferred stock in the old entity were given one-and-one-fourth shares of common stock in the new entity, plus certain subscription rights. Holders of common stock in the old entity got nothing save those subscription rights. The Studebaker family, incidentally, which had controlled a majority of the stock until John Mohler Studebaker's death in 1917, owned very little by the time the company went into receivership.

[15] Teagle, in fact, owned 32,075 shares amounting to about 1.5%. There were five investment houses that also controlled more than 1% each, but all six of the owners of more than 1%—including Teagle and the investment houses—only controlled 13.8% of the stock in the new corporation.

[16] At this juncture, it is not clear what the subscription rights were. Probably, they entitled the holder to buy stock or notes issued by the corporation at presumably favorable rates in future years—rather like stock options or warrants. If so, it might have been possible for the old holders of common stock to recoup at least some of their losses, assuming they were in a position to spend even more money exercising their subscription rights at the appropriate time.

[17] It does offer a likely indication of where the Champion name came from, though.

[18] 1935 Studebaker Corporation Annual Report.

[19] Longstreet, pp. 102-103.

[20] Hupmobile shut its doors in 1936, then, reorganized, and struggled along until 1941. Its last effort was the Hupp Skylark, which used the body dies of the Cord 810/812. The "coffin nose" Cord was a lovely car, even in Hupmobile form, but was unable to save Hupp as an auto producer.

[21] To cite one example, Gordon Buehrig, who worked with Loewy at Studebaker, had seen his landmark concept for the "coffin nose" Cord rejected while he was a designer at General Motors.

[22] Loewy, pp. 8-47.

[23] Federal Trade Commission; the quotes cited here appear on pp. 210-211 and pp. 795-823.

[24] Longstreet, p. 109.

[25] 1938 Studebaker Corporation Annual Report.

[26] Or, for that matter, Pierce-Arrows. The finest cars Pierce ever built were arguably built after the Great Depression doomed the company.

[27] 1939 Studebaker Corporation Annual Report.

[28] 1940 Studebaker Corporation Annual Report.

[29] Canada, as a member of the British Commonwealth, declared war in September, 1939.

[30] The Sixty Special exerted enormous influence on the industry beyond Studebaker. Nash and Packard late-prewar products, in particular, were obviously inspired by the new design school. As for General Motors, it knew it had a good thing and stuck with it. The Sixty Special became the design prototype for nearly every major General Motors product built through 1949.

[31] 1941 Studebaker Corporation Annual Report.

Overleaf, the assembly of radial engines for Flying Fortress bombers.

SIX

The War Years

Considering that the company had been founded by a pacifist Dunkard family, Studebaker had a remarkable number of brushes with war. In fact, it might fairly be said that the Civil War *made* the company in that it provided the first real prosperity it had ever known and fostered the Studebaker name by spreading it from one end of the country to the other. The lasting fortune and reputation of Studebaker can be dated from that experience.

Studebaker was destined to have intimate involvements in all of America's subsequent conflicts, including the Spanish-American War and World War I. It even participated as a major supplier to the British during the Boer War. The company's lengthiest and most complex war experience, however, came with the outbreak of World War II in 1939.

The conflagration first made itself felt in South Bend when, in November, the French government placed a much-publicized order for 2,000 trucks. It was but the first of many war assignments to come and, if many of these trucks were to end up in the hands of the Germans following the precipitous fall of France in June, 1940, no one could have predicted it at the time. By then, the United States Government was actively preparing for the possibility of direct involvement in the war. As early as March, 1941, Hoffman and Vance addressed the issue in a message to Studebaker stockholders:

> In October, 1940, at the request of Mr. William S. Knudsen,
> now director general of the Office of Production Management,[1]

the automobile industry announced that it would subordinate its tooling requirements for new models in 1941 to the needs of the Defense Program.[2] Subsequently, at Mr. Knudsen's request, the industry has undertaken to make changes in design and specifications to conserve zinc, nickel, aluminum, and other critical materials. Announcement of these measures has led, quite naturally, to speculation as to the extent to which industry generally, and the automobile industry in particular, must ultimately subordinate its normal business to the requirements of National Defense. That defense needs come first admits of no argument, but it does not appear as yet that a restriction of automobile production is necessary for that purpose.[3]

That would happen in due course. Already, in January, 1941, contracts had been signed with the War Department to build aircraft engines on a cost-plus basis. Three plants in South Bend, Ft. Wayne and Chicago with a total of 1.5 million square feet of floor space were to be turned over to this effort. It was estimated that 9,400 workers would be initially employed. The War Department was going to pay for the cost of the plants and equipment through its Defense Plant Corporation and then lease them to Studebaker. In addition, Studebaker had built prototypes of new, heavy-duty military trucks. As soon as these prototypes were deemed satisfactory, contracts were signed by the War Department for them, as well.

Of course, none of this was bad for business. As the 1941 annual report, issued in March, 1942, predicted:

> Despite interruption of its normal activities, Studebaker has been successful in maintaining employment and dollar volume at a high level. It is fortunate that the war production activities of this organization were started early enough so that today a substantial portion of the manufacturing facilities in all of its plants is engaged in the production of a variety of war materials. As a result of this early start, it is anticipated that by the end of March [1942] increased employment in war activities in all plants will have offset the reduction in employment occasioned by the stop-

page of passenger car production...When Studebaker reaches capacity production on its present commitments for war materials, it is estimated that the aggregate employment in all plants, as well as the Corporation's total dollar volume, will be at a rate of at least two-and-one-half times that for 1941.[4]

That proved to understate Studebaker's ultimate achievement by 40 percent. In fact, before the war ended Studebaker alone completed $1.2 billion in war contracts. While the money was good, what the American auto makers, including Studebaker, were mostly making was a daunting amount of material for the war effort. If, as the Duke of Wellington once noted, the Battle of Waterloo was won on the playing fields of Eaton, it can with equal justice be said that World War II was won by William C. Durant, Henry Ford, Alfred Sloan, Walter Chrysler, Albert Erskine and other dynamic pioneers who labored with such foresight to build the American automobile industry into the greatest industrial machine the world had ever known. It was American guns, tanks, trucks, ships, aircraft and bombs that turned the tide both in Europe and in the Pacific, and the American auto industry, together with its Canadian subsidiaries, did far more than its fair share to supply that need. When the end of the conflagration was at last in sight, *Ward's*, an industry trade magazine, observed with entirely justifiable pride:

> The presence and availability of the automobile industry's mass production facilities...saved the Allied Nations tens of thousands of fighting men's lives and shortened the prospective war period by years, if it did not save the peace-loving nations from complete defeat and obliteration at the hands of blood-thirsty warmakers obsessed with a lust for power. This, history must and will record, has been the automobile industry's outstanding contribution to civilization's progress.[5]

Studebaker's primary contribution to the cause was in the works when America entered the war. The company was already producing ever increasing quantities of the military trucks it had designed specifically for

Studebaker trucks awaiting shipment during the war.

the government in 1940. The cessation of automobile production released additional facilities for truck production and, by 1944, Studebaker had become the second-largest producer of two-and-a-half ton trucks for the armed forces (and, most likely, in the world). Studebaker trucks were supplied through Lend Lease to the Soviet Union and also served in the Pacific Theater, where some 5,000 Studebaker trucks transported supplies into China along the famed Burma Road and where the Chinese Red Cross used Studebaker equipment exclusively.

Studebaker's facilities for Cyclone aircraft engine production intended for the Flying Fortress bomber were also nearing completion by the time civilian vehicle production stopped in January, 1942. Production attained a level of 8,000 units in 1942, but soared to 22,000 in 1943. The Flying Fortress was to prove invaluable in the air war over Germany.

In addition, by the latter months of 1942 the company was building an amphibious personnel carrier known as the Weasel. Known officially as the M-29 cargo carrier, the Weasel was powered by the Champion engine and was sort of an amphibious Jeep with tracks like a tank. It was designed as a small vehicle that could go anywhere in the transport of soldiers or supplies and was first used in the campaign against the little-known Japanese invasion of the Aleutian Islands in 1942.[6] Later it achieved note in the Italian campaign in Europe and in the all-important Normandy invasion. Still later, upon his much-promised return, General Douglas MacArthur used a Weasel as his personal vehicle in the Philippines campaign.

Yet, Studebaker's most significant participation proved to be on the Eastern Front where Soviet soldiers and tanks waged a bitter yard-by-yard, mile-by-mile battle with the Germans for four years. American and British histories of World War II in Europe tend, not surprisingly, to focus on those battles in which Western forces predominated. The much-romanticized North African campaign is one, in which Rommel, "The Desert Fox," was pitted against Montgomery and, later, Patton. The numbingly complex D-Day invasion of Normandy is another. The great battles on the Eastern Front are given far less attention, although they were arguably more important in a military sense. The decisive Battle of Stalingrad in the Winter of 1942-43 was, in fact, the turning point of the European war against the

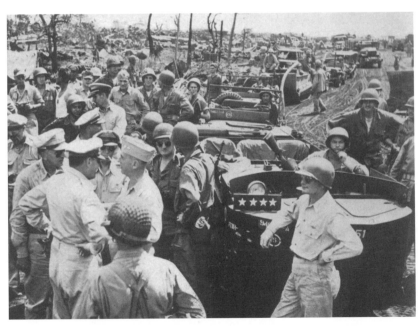

General MacArthur, left, with his Studebaker Weasel in the Philippines.

Germans in the view of military historians, just as the Battle of Midway in the late-Spring of 1942 was the turning point in the Pacific war.

Stalingrad has received some notice in the West, of course, although not nearly as much as it deserves, while the epic Battle of Kursk the following July is almost unknown in the West except by military historians. The latter was the largest massed tank battle in history and broke the back of the German military machine. From that point, the resolution of the war in Europe was preordained and it was just a matter of the Red Army keeping up the pressure and pursuing the retreating Germans to Berlin.

The Soviets angered many Westerners in later years by doggedly insisting that they had won the European war—"The Great Patriotic War," as it is known in Russia—almost single-handedly. While that view was clearly excessive, it was none-the-less true that the Soviet people bore the brunt of the carnage. Combined British, French and American losses in the war were in the hundreds of thousands of dead, while Soviet losses were in the tens of millions—so many, in fact, that an accurate count has never been possible—and virtually all of the Soviet Union's European territory was utterly laid waste. Yet, the Soviets could not have sustained such losses and fought the Germans to ultimate victory without enormous assistance from the Western Allies in terms of food and equipment. Indeed, it might be said with some justice that the European war was won by a combina-

The 100,000th Studebaker military truck in 1942 was "dead-icated" to Hitler.

A Studebaker truck on the Eastern Front.

tion of Russian blood and American materiel, and notable among the latter were Studebaker trucks.

Studebaker trucks began arriving by the tens of thousands via the Persian route in the latter part of 1942. No one really knows how many were sent, but the quantity was huge. According to one story at the time, Studebaker trucks became so ubiquitous that the Russians started using the word "Studebaker" to signify any truck. It may even have been true for, until Studebaker trucks began arriving, trucks of any kind had been scarce in the Soviet Union and the Red Army had been almost entirely dependent upon horses for transportation. As the Battle of Kursk was to demonstrate, the Soviets by then had the best tanks in the world (and probably the best tank commanders, as well), but had they been left to their own resources would have been fighting the war with a transportation system that dated back to the days of Napoleon.

Studebaker trucks first made their presence felt in the all-important Battle of Stalingrad where the mobility they gave Soviet troops enabled the Soviet generals, first, to encircle and defeat the army of von Paulus and, later, to effectively pursue and destroy the remaining German forces in retreat. A few months later at the Battle of Kursk it was German and

Soviet tanks that did most of the fighting, but it was Studebaker trucks that enabled the Soviets to respond quickly with support troops and supplies for a decisive battle that had been initiated at a time and place chosen by the Germans.

Joseph Stalin, the Soviet dictator, was so appreciative of the effectiveness of his Studebaker trucks that he sent the company a letter of thanks. His successor concurred. Nikita Khrushchev, in his memoirs, also singled-out the enormous contribution of these vehicles:

> Just imagine how we would have advanced from Stalingrad to Berlin without them! Our losses would have been colossal because we would have had no maneuverability. [7]

The German officer corps agreed with this conclusion. Erich Kuby, in his book, *The Russians and Berlin 1945*, noted that it was widely believed in the German military that "it was not so much the Red Army itself that had won the war, as the trucks they had received from the Americans."[8]

After the war, Studebaker trucks remained for many years the bulwark of the Red Army's transportation system. The anti-aircraft guns that ringed Moscow in order to repel any British or American air attack—which, after the start of the Cold War in 1947, Stalin expected at any moment—were mostly mounted on Studebakers until long after the aging tyrant died in 1953, while the Soviet Union's Eastern European satellites were using Studebakers almost exclusively for that purpose as late as the end of the decade.[9] Again Khrushchev recalled:

> After Stalin's death, it seemed that all of our artillery was mounted on American equipment. I remember proposing, "Let's turn all the automotive equipment we're producing over to the military so that the tractor-mounts in our parades will be Soviet made." Almost all the artillery in the GDR [East Germany] was mounted on American Studebakers. I said, "This simply won't do. It's disgraceful. Just look how many years have passed since the war ended, and we're still driving around in American equipment!"

In reading contemporary accounts of life in the Soviet Union published shortly after the end of the war, one finds frequent anecdotal evidence regarding the importance of Studebaker trucks in the devastated Soviet economy. John Fischer, an American who headed the United Nations food relief effort in Ukraine in 1946 and wrote a book about his experiences, noted not only the sheer volume of Studebakers on Soviet roads but hinted at their psychological impact:

> The [Soviet] press insistently assures the Russians that they are the happiest people on earth...Nevertheless, some doubts manage to creep in. Whenever a Russian looks at a...Studebaker Lend-Lease truck, he can't help but see that it is better than anything coming out of Soviet factories. Moreover, he looks at them often, since they make up nearly half of the road transport, and he may wonder how a "decadent" country [such as the U. S.] manages to build such a lot of undecadent trucks.[10]

To sum up the contribution of Studebaker and other American suppliers of war goods to the winning of the war on the Eastern Front, we turn again to Khrushchev:

> The Allies gave us this help neither out of compassion for our people, nor out of respect for our political system, nor out of hope for the victory of Socialism and the triumph of Marxism-Leninism. The Allies helped us out of a sober assessment of the situation. They were facing a matter of their own life or death. They helped us so that our Soviet Army would not fall under the blow of Hitlerite Germany and so that, supplied with modern weapons, we would pulverize the life force of the enemy.

That was, essentially, true. And, while there must be many "what ifs" in an event as overwhelming as a world war, it was also true that without those Studebaker trucks sent by the untold tens of thousands the war on the Eastern Front and, therefore, the war in Europe, might have ended quite differently. Meanwhile, back in America another tantalizing "what if" situation was playing itself out in relation to the composition of the auto industry itself and, again, Studebaker was in the thick of it.

By the time America was drawn into the war, Ford Motor Company was in dreadful shape. Indeed, it had been for many years. One is tempted to refer to this as an "open secret" in Detroit, except that there was nothing secret about it at all. Every intelligent industry observer knew that Ford was in a potentially fatal downward slide and also knew the reason: Henry Ford. The old industry pioneer, who had run the company with such brilliance in its first two decades, had completely lost touch with reality as the market matured. The products were dated, the only market segment in which the company remained a force was the low-priced field (and its influence there was rapidly waning), and management organization was an oxymoron in a billion-dollar company where the increasingly senile and tyrannical founder made all the decisions. Nearly all the really good managers had been driven out, leaving, for the most part, a tired bunch of thugs and second-raters.

In the opinion of most observers, the only thing that offered any hope for the company was the old man's remarkable son, Edsel. Edsel was universally regarded as an astute automobile man who understood the maturing market and the need for a modern management organization, and who was well prepared to lead the company out of the wilderness as soon as his father left the scene. Under the circumstances, Edsel's premature death at the age of forty-nine in May, 1943, caused shock waves—and not just in Detroit.

There was a war going on and, what's more, a war that had been far from won by the Allies. The vast Ford manufacturing facilities were regarded by Washington as essential to the successful prosecution of the war effort and there were many in the nation's capital who remembered Henry Ford's active opposition to American involvement in World War I. There had been much doubt at the start of the war regarding the reliability of Ford Motor Company as an active participant in the war effort and, as long as the old man lived, considerable concern remained in the highest government circles.

Even before Edsel's death, there had been talk of nationalization. If this seems far-fetched to modern readers, the case of the Japanese-Americans should be recalled. A government capable, in the name of prosecuting the war, of throwing tens of thousands of its own citizens into concentration camps for no reason other than their ethnic ancestry was capable of nationalizing a car company if it felt the need to do so.

It had mostly been the continued presence in the company of a few—and dwindling number of—respected men such as Charles "Cast Iron Charlie" Sorensen, Ford's legendary production chief, and Edsel Ford that kept Ford's enemies in Washington at bay. When, upon Edsel's death, Henry Ford announced that he would resume the presidency he had relinquished to his son in 1919, the gasps of disbelief could be heard all the way from the Detroit River to the Potomac and back again. Peter F. Drucker, one of the mid-century's most highly regarded writers and theorists on corporate management, recalled the episode as follows:

> Reality was such that the survival of [Ford] seemed improbable—some people said impossible. The best indication of the seriousness with which these chances of survival were viewed was a scheme proposed in responsible circles during those days in Detroit. The U. S. Government, it was said, should lend enough money to Studebaker—the fourth largest automobile producer but still less than one sixth the size of Ford—to buy out the Ford family and to take over the company. In this way, and this way alone, Ford would have a chance to survive. Otherwise, it was agreed, the company might well have to be nationalized lest its collapse seriously endanger the country's economy and its war effort.[11]

One would be inclined to dismiss this as just another rumor except that Drucker's credentials were impeccable and it just so happened that he was at that very point in time doing detailed research in Detroit for his monumental study of General Motors, *Concept of the Corporation*. His research involved almost unprecedented access to top industry leaders such as Alfred Sloan who certainly made it their business to know what was going on. Moreover, William S. "Big Bill" Knudsen, who had resigned from the presidency of General Motors to take a leading role the nation's domestic war effort, retained close ties to Sloan and other industry leaders.[12]

It has long been known that there had been talk of nationalization even before Edsel's death, so that much, at least, is an established fact. The very idea, though, must have sent shudders up the spines of men such as Sloan. The industry had fought Roosevelt's despised National Recovery Act (NRA) tooth-and-nail in the mid-1930s because it threatened limited Federal control over the auto industry. When Knudsen (himself a Danish immigrant) agreed to head the OPM in 1940, his patriotic decision was reportedly regarded as little short of treason by some of his "friends" at General Motors who refused to countenance any cooperation with the hated enemy in Washington—a.k.a. "That Man In the White House"—war or no war. So, it is easy to speculate that the talk of a Federally-financed buy-out of Ford was considered infinitely preferable by, or even promoted by, men such as Sloan as being perhaps the only way to keep the loathsome Roosevelt and his minions from gaining control of a key member of the auto industry.

A better question is: "Why Studebaker?" First, a takeover by General Motors would have been out of the question. It would have smacked of monopoly and, besides, General Motors hardly needed Ford's automotive brands or facilities. Chrysler would have been a better choice, but it already had four successful brands that spanned the market (Plymouth, Dodge, De Soto and Chrysler) and would have had little use for three more (Ford, Mercury and Lincoln).

The idea made sense for Studebaker, though. The Champion posed little real competition for the Ford brand and could easily have been phased out. The medium-priced Studebakers were in partial competition with Mercury, but that could have been dealt with by simply kicking Studebaker models up a notch or two to compete with Buick. The result could have been a potent automotive stable consisting of Ford, Mercury, Studebaker and Lincoln brands giving the new Studebaker Corporation rough parity with Chrysler Corporation and a serious shot at competing successfully head-to-head with General Motors.

Doubtless another factor—and one dripping with irony in light of the common view today—was that Hoffman and Vance then were seen as two of the best managers in the business. Hoffman and Vance had, after all, saved Studebaker from bankruptcy and put the company back on the map as a serious competitor. Indeed, Vance was so highly regarded that he had been selected to act as the auto industry's official liason with the OPM. In short, the general industry view of the Studebaker management team overall was that it was top-notch and, by extension, represented exactly what Ford so desperately needed.

A Studebaker takeover of Ford might have worked well. In the end, of course, nothing came of either the takeover or the nationalization talk. For one thing, it is clear in retrospect that the Ford family would have resisted any such efforts and, as events also demonstrated, the determination of people such as Eleanor Clay Ford (Edsel's widow) and her son, Henry II, was not to be taken lightly. A more important factor was that the war soon shifted decisively in the Allies' favor. By the conclusion of 1943, just about everyone in the know—including, as we later learned, even the German General Staff—realized that the United States and its allies were going to win and the sense of urgency in Washington regarding the situation at Ford quickly dissipated.

So, in the end, the idea of a Ford Division of Studebaker remained just that—an idea. After the war, Henry Ford II led a remarkable revival of his company's fortunes, and the first thing he did was hire a competent management team and reorganize Ford along the lines laid down by Sloan at General Motors. The result was one of the greatest revivals in American industrial history. As for Studebaker, it, too, would pursue an aggressive postwar strategy. Unfortunately, the results in South Bend were destined to turn out much differently.

But, Studebaker's star was still in the ascendant in 1943 and would remain so for a number of years. Certainly there was nothing in the company's wartime performance to give anyone cause for anxiety regarding its future. Quite the opposite was the case as the company built 197,000 trucks for the war effort, along with 64,000 Cyclone engines and 15,000 Weasels. Studebaker's dollar volume of sales peaked at $415.7 million in 1944—more than three-and-a-half times the 1941 sum. Profits that year reached a high of $19.8 million. If an outside observer had had a negative opinion of the company at that juncture, it most likely would have been that Studebaker was *too* successful and, in fact, it was financial results such as those in South Bend that lent credence to the popular belief that industry, in general, got rich on the war.

As a close examination of the 1944 Studebaker annual report makes clear, however, that the financial picture was not nearly as rosy as all that. Congress giveth and Congress taketh away, and Congress had enacted an excess profits tax even before the hostilities began for the United States specifically to prevent industry from making windfall profits off war contracts. This was understandable, given that the government, in its rush to put American industry on a full war footing as quickly as humanly possible, had assigned most war contracts on a cost-plus basis. In other words, competitive bidding—and even close scrutiny by government auditors— was thrown aside in the emergency. Companies were told to do whatever they had to do to meet government needs and, whatever they spent, they could tack a fixed percentage onto that for profit. The possibilities for abuse in this system were all-too obvious, hence the excess profits tax.

In Studebaker's case (which is revealing), the $19.8 million in profits in 1944 was subject to a normal $1.7 million in Federal taxes and then reduced by another $13.9 million in excess profits taxes. At the same time, the company was also forced by simple prudence to set aside funds for the projected cost of reconversion to peacetime production at the war's end. So, the final profit reported for the year was reduced to a shade more than $4 million. True, this was good money, but it was far from the rip-off that some people later pictured it. In fact, it represented only about 1 percent return on sales, a figure that would have been considered extremely poor by peacetime standards. The after-tax profit in 1941, for example, had been more than double that of 1944 as a percentage of sales.

In due course, negotiations with the government proved that Studebaker had earned no windfall profits at all on its war assignments in 1942-44 and more than $18 million in "excess" profits taxes were refunded to the company. Of total dollar sales in the period of almost exactly $1 billion, the company's net profit totaled $26.9 million, or about the same percentage of net profit on sales it had made in peacetime. [13] On the other hand, under the unexpectedly costly burden of reconversion, profits slumped to $3.6 million in 1945 and actually turned into a loss of $8.1 million in 1946. So, while it was true that Studebaker and other auto manufacturers were making sizable profits at the height of the war, they were hardly making a killing and much of the profit recorded during those peak years was expended in the huge, and largely unanticipated, costs of reconversion to peacetime production in 1945 and 1946. In the end, it seems unlikely that Studebaker's profits were much greater than they would have been during the same period had the war never taken place.

It is doubtful the company had any regrets. At the outset of the war, recalling its history, it had announced a promise to do everything in its power to aid the war effort:

> Studebaker has been called upon on numerous occasions to make its contribution in an emergency involving the United States. Studebaker vehicles saw active service in the Civil War, the Indian Wars, the Spanish-American War, and World War I. In the present World War, as in the first, Studebaker will produce a variety of war materials and will cooperate to the fullest extent in the nation's war effort.[14]

It is hard to see how anyone could deny that the men and women of Studebaker made good on the company's promise—and then some. As in so many cases in Studebaker's nine decades of operation, it had delivered more than it had promised.

Notes

The most important resources drawn upon in the writing of this chapter include Stephen Longstreet's official company history, *A Century on Wheels: The Story of Studebaker*, the company's annual reports to stockholders, and automobile industry yearbooks published by *Automotive News* and *Ward's*. The factionalized chaos in which the automobile industry operated and with which America waged and, ultimately, won the war is beautifully captured in Bruce Catton's *The War Lords of Washington*. Peter F. Drucker's *The Practice of Management* is the primary source for the tale of the proposed Studebaker takeover of Ford. The impact that Studebaker trucks had on the Russian Front is based mostly on company documents, but Erich Kuby's *The Russians and Berlin 1945* and the memoirs of Nikita Khrushchev and John Fischer added important sidelights.

[1] Knudsen resigned as president of General Motors to take the job.

[2] This referred, certainly, to the 1942 models that would be tooled during calendar year 1941, as the 1941 models were already tooled and on the road at that point.

[3] 1940 Studebaker Corporation Annual Report.

[4] 1941 Studebaker Corporation Annual Report.

[5] Ward's 1944 Automotive Year Book, p. 9.

[6] Little remembered today, the Aleutian campaign was a feint by the Japanese that was supposed to draw American naval forces away from Midway Island, which was the real strategic goal. The trick failed, and the ensuing Japanese disaster at the Battle of Midway is regarded by military historians as the turning point in the Pacific war. The Japanese did, however, succeed in occupying a few small islands on the uninhabited tail end of the Aleutian chain and in holding them for many months—mostly because the American military command in the Pacific Theater couldn't decide if it was worth the effort to dislodge them. When that effort was finally mounted, it was discovered that the Japaese had already left, apparently finding the barren islands so miserable it wasn't worth staying.

[7] This and the following quotes from Khrushchev are found in the first volume of his memoirs, p. 226.

[8] Kuby, p. 206.

[9] As late as 1959, New York Times reporter, Harrison Salisbury, commented during a tour of the Soviet Union on their use, as well.

[10] Fischer, p. 55-56.

[11] Drucker's The Concept of the Corporation was published in 1946. This quote is found in a later work, The Practice of Management, published in 1954.

[12] After starting out as head of the Office of Production Management, Knudsen served with the all-powerful War Production Board, and, still later, was a high-octane industrial production troubleshooter for the War Department.

[13] After deductions for the cost of war contract termination, projected postwar reconversion, and the addition of the $18 million refunded for improperly assessed excess profits taxes.

[14] 1941 Studebaker Corporation Annual Report.

Overleaf, welding bodies in the framing jig in the early 1950s.

SEVEN

Studebaker Amnia Vincit

The automobile industry entered the postwar era with an optimism born of the tremendous achievements accomplished during the war and of the knowledge that a prosperous nation, deprived of cars for nearly four years, eagerly awaited. As early as 1943, with war assignments still in high gear—but, in some cases, already beginning to wind down—the industry's thoughts had inevitably turned to the resumption of civilian production. The National Automobile Dealers Association (NADA) estimated that there was already pent-up demand for ten million passenger cars—twice the best prewar year on record—and the war still had two years to run.

In 1943, Studebaker engineers were quoted in *Ward's*, the industry trade publication, as saying that postwar cars would stress economy rather than "fanciful designs," and that styling would be evolutionary. There was no thought of producing an entirely new postwar car; there was no time to plan, develop, design, engineer and test one. Moreover, Studebaker, along with other manufacturers, still had millions of dollars tied up in parts and supplies from the aborted 1942 model run.

Reconversion would be a daunting task, as difficult as the shift to war had been. In its 1943 annual report, issued in March, 1944, Studebaker's board of directors addressed this issue to the company's shareholders:

> Although the end of the war is not in sight, the Corporation's management is increasingly aware of its responsibilities to stock-

holders and to employees with respect to the prompt and orderly transition of this business from a wartime to a peacetime basis. Generally speaking, the planning and development stages of our war production responsibilities are behind us, and so, a few men in our organization can be assigned to postwar planning without any detrimental effect whatever to our current war production. We believe that with the resumption of civilian production of passenger cars and commercial cars, Studebaker will have an unusual opportunity. We are planning boldly but carefully and thoroughly to take full advantage of it.[1]

That same month, the War Production Board appointed a committee of manufacturers' representatives to plan for peacetime conversion. As it happened, the plan worked out by Studebaker personnel became the standard for use throughout the auto industry. Known as the Studebaker Plan, it set out the physical, accounting and legal stages for terminating war contracts, disposal of war-related property, and also set out the government's contribution to the costs of reconversion.

By March, 1945, with the end of the war at last in sight, the company notified its stockholders:

> The implications of the German break-through on the Western Front in December, of the Russian drive which started in January, and of other recent military events, indicate how impossible it is to anticipate the course of the war to the point of putting a time table on the resumption of civilian production. However...the day will come when the full resources of the Corporation, in facilities, in manpower, in skills, will no longer be required for the prosecution of the war. Then, this organization will be ready to apply to the problems of speedy reconversion the same kind of effort which so quickly transformed our activities in the emergency following Pearl Harbor.

Noting the "greatly enlarged Studebaker business which we confidently expect in the postwar period," the company continued:

Our dealer organization, both at home and abroad, has been preserved and greatly strengthened. At no time in the past has Studebaker ever had the quality or completeness of sales representation which it now enjoys. Following the war period, Studebaker resumes its position in the transportation industry with that position greatly strengthened and improved. Studebaker is stronger financially; it is stronger in organization; and, particularly, it is stronger in public regard because of its accomplishments during the war.[2]

On May 11, 1945, the War Production Board announced that it would permit manufacturers to begin reconversion to civilian production on July 1st. The contract for Cyclone aircraft engines had already been terminated in May and the contract for trucks and Weasels was canceled in August. Gasoline rationing officially ended on August 15th and, on that same date, the War Production Board lifted all restrictions on civilian passenger car production. The race was on.

Ford actually managed to build its first 1946 car on July 3rd and another 359 cars by the end of the month, although they must have been assembled largely from leftover 1942 parts and supplies. Ford couldn't have reconverted the giant Rouge plant in two days. The second manufacturer to begin 1946 production, Hudson, didn't get the lines going until August 30th. The first 1946 General Motors product, a Chevrolet, didn't see the light of day until October 3rd. Unfortunately, everything came to a grinding halt for General Motors on November 21st before it had really commenced when the UAW struck in a job action that became the longest in General Motors history and which was not settled until March 13, 1946. In South Bend, the first postwar Studebaker rolled off the line on October 1st. Strikes in the plants of suppliers, however, restricted production to a trickle through the remaining weeks of the year. It was not until January 2nd that production began in earnest.

As of December 31, 1945, Studebaker had cash on hand in the amount of $33.6 million, compared to $16.9 million at the close of business at the end of 1941. Its overall assets stood at $64 million, its stock and capital surplus at $40.9 million. If Studebaker's financial position had strength-

1946 Studebaker Skyway Champion.

ened during the war years—and there could be little doubt that it had—the company was still tiny compared to the Big Three. While Studebaker's assets were comparable to those of the other independents, the assets of General Motors were *twenty-eight times* as great. Even Chrysler could boast of assets more than six times as large as Studebaker's.[3] It would be foolish to overlook such figures (and, goodness knows, few writers discussing this period have). On the other hand, it would be unwise to make too much of them. If Studebaker could never hope to rival GM on a balance sheet, it never-the-less had a lot going for it.

As it faced the challenges of the postwar era, the company was clearly in the best shape it had known in years. If the 1946 Studebakers would have to be warmed-over 1942s, it was unlikely that anyone would care; the pent-up consumer demand was huge. As the company subsequently noted in its 1946 annual report to stockholders, "accumulated demand, both here and abroad, was so great during [1946] that there was no apparent limitation to sales except that of production."

As early as 1944, Hoffman and Vance had taken steps to strengthen their dealer body when they canceled the traditional system of using distributors. The distributors acted as middlemen between the factory and the dealers. By cutting them out, the profit the distributors took could be passed along to the dealers. Naturally enough, the dealers applauded this decision. The role of the distributors was (and remains) controversial, though. Some historians contend that the distributor system was a benefit to the independents because it helped insure stronger dealers owing to the direct interest the distributors had in maintaining good-performing local outlets. The distributors were, in effect, autonomous profit centers in a way that factory zone offices never were and a distributor's profits were directly dependent upon how well or poorly his dealers performed. On the other hand, when the Big Three went on periodic dealer raids—which happened repeatedly in the early postwar era—a defecting distributor could take a whole region's worth of dealers with him, suddenly leaving the independent manufacturer with no representation at all. So, on balance, the decision to end the distributor system was probably a good one.

A key strength was the loyal worker base at South Bend. Of the total work force, 50 percent had been with the company for at least five years and a remarkable 18 percent had been there for more than twenty years—remarkable, in part, because of the severely reduced employment levels of the depression years. Of the 3,700 Studebaker workers who served in the armed forces during the war, fully 78 percent returned after the hostilities were over. By the end of 1946, total employment had reached 15,382. Studebaker would be almost unique among American auto makers in sur-

The first 1946 car driven off the line by Paymaster Bill Studebaker, one of the few family members still around, whose signature still appeared on company checks.

viving the tumultuous year of 1946 without a single day lost due to strikes in any of its facilities.

Nationwide, production time lost to strikes came to an astonishing 113 million man-days—and this did not count down time at companies such as Studebaker where there were no strikes but where significant production was lost due to strikes elsewhere.[4] It was estimated that the number of man-days lost in 1946 would have been sufficient to run all the nation's steel plants at full tilt for an entire year. What was happening was repeated clashes between an organized labor movement that had grown ever more powerful during the war years of easy labor policies during which costs were not a top priority, on the one hand, and industrial management which sought reassert its prerogatives and to get control of labor costs as a part of reconversion to a peacetime economy, on the other. Company after company gritted its teeth and endured sometimes lengthy strikes to force the issue, but Hoffman and Vance refused to follow suit. This would have serious consequences later on.

In any case, the first 1946 Studebakers that were announced to the public on October 23, 1945, were visibly little changed from those that had last rolled off the line in 1942. The main difference was in product deletions. As with most manufacturers, Studebaker sought to speed the reconversion by drastically limiting the number of models initially offered, so the 1946 range was limited to the Champion, redesignated the Skyway Champion. The most noticeable styling change consisted of a wide bright trim molding running along the rocker and the bottoms of the fenders. The overall result was a cleaner, more pleasing car that was fully in keeping with the prewar Skyway concept. Four models were offered: cruising sedan, two-door club sedan, five-passenger coupe and three-passenger coupe.

Engineering developments were no more cosmic than those coming from the design studio. Skyway Champions used improved leaf springs and air cleaners, an automatic choke and silent helical gears, and were powered by the 169.6 cubic inch six that had also been used in the wartime Weasel. For 1946, it was rated at 80 horsepower. Aluminum pistons, which had been dropped on the 1942 models due to wartime materials restrictions, were back.

The ambitious original calendar year 1946 production target of 265,500 cars and trucks was missed by a mere 144,737 units. For the auto industry, in general, it was a period of extreme frustration. Every manufacturer had planned for spectacular levels of production and had stumbled over the same obstacles of shortages, labor unrest and allocation restrictions. To say that the government, in particular, was becoming increasing unpopular in auto industry circles would be an understatement and Studebaker went so far as to publicly attack government policies:

> Materials shortages caused by strikes in 1946 were aggravated by government action. So much of the output of sheet steel and pig iron has been diverted from normal channels of distribution by government directives that all metal working industries, but particularly the automobile industry, have suffered severely and, in our opinion, to a great extent unnecessarily.[5]

In light of what it had had to overcome, Studebaker management was no doubt grateful for the 120,763 cars and trucks actually built in the stop-and-go 1946 calendar year. One thing that had expanded sharply in 1946, however, was the price of a new Studebaker; the least expensive 1946 Champion now listed for $1,002—up 35 percent from 1942. Despite the dramatic price increases at all companies, wage and price controls at the government level guaranteed—if unintentionally, to be sure—that the prices an auto maker could charge never quite kept pace with increasing wages and other costs. That fact, combined with the severely restricted ability to build cars early in the year, reduced profits to the vanishing point at many companies. Studebaker's revenues declined to $141.6 million for the year and a loss of $8.1 million was recorded, most of it in the especially troubled first two quarters. The company was able to apply for a refund on taxes paid in previous years, however, and, in this fashion, could report a net income of just under $1 million, but it was an accounting trick that couldn't go on indefinitely. Despite the actual loss for the year, though, $1.2 million in dividends was paid out to stockholders.

The big news, however, was not the warmed-over 1946 product line, the frequent work stoppages, or the company's hassles with the government. It was an entirely new line of products that would prove to be the major news story of the year in the industry. Historians have been debating how and why for decades. How did Studebaker move so quickly? And, why were Hoffman and Vance so determined to do so? Harold Churchill, then in engineering and later to head the corporation, explained it this way:

> Vance and Hoffman recognized the necessity for fresh styling and it could be done at a minimum cost in time because of the short changeover in our plants. Our principal war production was done in "war plants." The military trucks and Weasels built in the passenger car plants did not use passenger car production equipment except in the machine shop. Other space was the principal requirement and, therefore, conversion to "peace" production was fairly simple.[6]

The story of the development of the 1947 Studebakers has been as controversial in its own way as the cars themselves. The impact that the company made can be gauged by the fact that after the passing of more than four decades there are still people actively trying to claim credit for them, if not for themselves then on behalf this or that person involved in the process. ("Success has many fathers," as the old saying goes, "but disaster is an orphan." How many people are still trying to take credit for the Edsel?)

The key figures were Raymond Loewy, Virgil Exner, one of his designers, and chief engineer Roy Cole. The process became a highly political one and there were several dynamics involved. One was certainly a clash of egos between the three men and, it would seem, in particular between Exner and Loewy. Another was long-simmering tension between company "internals" such as Cole and the "outsider" Loewy. Finally, there was the natural competition that has always existed at virtually every automobile company between designers, on the one hand, and between designers and engineers, on the other.

Cole had, of course, distinguished himself (along with Ralph Vail) by creating of the Rockne. By all accounts, Cole was a solid "nuts and bolts" type of engineer who had little interest in design, except to the extent that the in-house design staff (loosely managed by Loewy) infringed on his prerogatives as vice-president of engineering. The antipathy between Cole

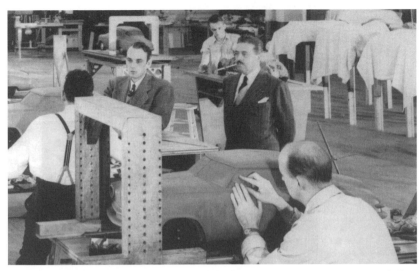

Raymond Loewy, right facing the camera, and Virgil Exner, left, in the Studebaker styling studio in 1945. Note the 1947 Studebaker clay model in the foreground.

and Loewy can be discerned from an interview that Loewy gave three decades after the fact in which he pointedly referred to Cole's "stuffy office" into which he (Loewy) continually tried to bring the fresh breath of contemporary European design, to which Cole's reaction was "usually...rather contemptuous," with Cole dismissing what Loewy regarded as the finest European cars as "freakish" products of a "nutty" and "half-baked" foreign automobile industry. The Cole-Loewy relationship was, to put it mildly, marked by neither mutual respect nor shared values.[7]

The Exner-Loewy relationship was hardly better. Both were master designers. Loewy had already established his credentials and reputation in that department, though, while Exner had not. In time, "Ex" would earn almost as big a name on the strength of his shattering Chrysler Forward Look cars of the late-1950s, but during his Studebaker years he was still working anonymously in the trenches and awaiting his big chance. Various reasons for Exner's antagonism toward Loewy have been advanced, and the tension was probably exacerbated by a basic clash of personalities, but the most likely explanation is that it boiled down to the natural resentment and creative suffocation that a gifted and ambitious artist would normally feel when compelled to live in someone else's shadow.

And, Loewy cast quite a shadow. As has been previously noted, he had a remarkable talent for spotting design trends, for selecting top-notch designers to do the yeoman's work required to bring them to reality, and for selling their work to the generally conservative management types who paid the bills. A major part of his sales pitch was his own name, which he assiduously built up. On one level this was merely good business. Yet, self-promotion does seem to have come rather naturally to Loewy, who never appeared to be embarrassed about claiming full personal credit for any design his minions might create. It was even alleged that he was not above signing his own name to their drawings, which is close to being a capital offense in the creative world.[8] Loewy's reasoning, no doubt, was that they were working for him and everything they did was a "Loewy" or "Loewy Associates" design by definition, but it would not be surprising if the more talented of his underlings saw it differently.

According to Bob Bourke, this was, indeed, the root of the contention. Years later, as Bourke recalled in an interview:

> The problem was basically a disagreement in philosophy and approach. Ex felt that a man was either a designer or promoter, but not both, and to make matters worse he felt Loewy received all the credit for Studebaker styling successes from both management and the public. Although I understood Ex's viewpoint, I still held [Loewy] in high regard, as I recognized the necessity of being a good salesman in this profession.[9]

All of this came into play during the development of the 1947 Studebakers. Early work began as soon as war demands would permit, perhaps as early as 1942, but certainly by 1943. Loewy Associates was retained to work up some postwar concepts with a South Bend-based team that was increased overall from twenty-eight people to thirty-nine for the project. Included were (among others): Exner, Gordon Beuhrig (of "coffin nose" Cord fame), Bob Bourke (later to be principal designer of the 1953 Studebaker), Bob Koto (designer of the 1949 Ford) and John Reinhart (designer of the 1951 Packard and the 1956 Continental Mark II). It was as brilliant a group of automobile designers as was ever assembled.

The idea of using a rear-engined "pancake" six was explored and quickly dropped, and all the evidence suggests that the essential design was in place by the spring of 1944. It was at this point that Exner was visited by Cole with a curious offer. Would Exner be willing to develop a competing design on his own time with under-the-counter factory assistance? Exner would, indeed, and was soon moonlighting in a make-shift design studio in his home.

What was going on? According to the recollections of Exner, Bourke and Koto, Cole was deliberately sabotaging the official Loewy team. He did this not only by hiring Exner on the sly to prepare an alternative design, but also, in order to make absolutely sure Loewy went down in flames, by giving a set of incorrect dimensions—or "package"—to the Loewy team so that when the two designs were finished the Loewy proposal would fail on purely objective grounds, if nothing else. And, presumably, that would be the end of Raymond Loewy at Studebaker. In short, Loewy Associates was sandbagged. It sounds almost too Machiavellian to be true, but stranger things have happened in corporate political wars. Moreover, too many sources confirm it. Koto, for example, recalled:

> For several months we were working individually on this...package. Unbeknownst to us and to Loewy, Exner was working on yet another package in his basement at home. All our separate models in the studio were cast and we had shows for top management, and meanwhile Exner and Roy Cole had Budd in Philadelphia build this full-size wooden mock-up of Exner's basement design. The Budd mock-up was shipped to South Bend and was shown, and management bought it—accepted it on the spot.[10]

Koto was referring to a meeting of Studebaker's board that was called late in 1944 to view the two proposals, the second of which came as a complete shock to Loewy and his other designers. Again, Koto recalled:

> What did the rest of us feel at the time? We all liked Exner...but it was kind of a shock. You can understand how Loewy felt...[11]

1947 Studebaker Champion.

One can certainly imagine. Years later, Loewy was still outraged as he described the incident:

> In my experience in over fifty years, working in more than a hundred corporations, I have never seen such a case of despicable behavior...I immediately fired Exner for disloyalty and unprofessional behavior.[12]

According to Loewy, Cole, in turn, was "furious" about *that*. (Is it really possible that Cole didn't anticipate Loewy's reaction?) In any case, Cole rehired Exner as an employee on the engineering staff, but Loewy refused to allow him to come near the styling department, which remained under Loewy's control. It was not a pretty situation, but the final car, according to most evidence, remained more Loewy than Exner. Exner's influence was exerted primarily on the front end, with its high hood that was in marked contrast to the rounded, sloping hoods Loewy preferred. The rest of the design adhered closely to the Loewy team's design, although it had to be reworked to fit the new dimensions Cole had laid down.

The actual production models were divided into two series, the Champion and the Commander. The Champion, starting at $1,446, was built on a 112-inch wheelbase and was available in both DeLuxe and Regal trim. The Commander was built on a 119-inch wheelbase, except for the Land

Cruiser sedan, which used an extended 123-inch wheelbase. Base Commander prices began at $1,661 and topped out at $2,043 for the Land Cruiser. The Champion's six-cylinder engine was a carry-over, while the Commander used a revived version of the 226 cubic inch six rated at 94 horsepower that had originally been developed for the Rockne. There were five basic body styles available in either Champion or Commander form: three-passenger coupe, five-passenger coupe, two-door sedan, four-door sedan and convertible. In addition, the long-wheelbase Land Cruiser sedan topped out the Commander line.

At the time of their introduction in the late-Spring of 1946, the 1947 Studebakers were the first all-new postwar body designs to come from any American manufacturer. That would have been startling enough to the competition, but the Loewy / Exner design was startling in its own right. The five-passenger coupes with their wrap-around rear windows caused the most commotion. They were quickly dubbed the "which way" cars because people claimed it was impossible to tell whether they were coming or going. This was an exaggeration, to be sure, but the design grabbed popular attention as few automotive deigns had in recent memory. From the perspective of design professionals, the cars were hailed for their unusually clean lines, good proportions, fenders that flowed gracefully into

1947 Studebaker Commander Land Cruiser.

the beltline and admirable lightness for their size.

As aggressive as the design was, though, it was only part of an ambitious plan for postwar expansion in South Bend. Indeed, Hoffman and Vance acknowledged this much in a letter to stockholders:

> For Studebaker, 1946 was in a very real sense a year of decision. Despite all of the problems that it involved, the company's management determined to go forward with the program it had developed before the close of the war, which provided for (1) the introduction at the earliest possible date of genuine postwar passenger cars and (2) the addition of manufacturing facilities necessary for the production of both passenger cars and trucks in greater volume than ever before.
>
> The management's decision to introduce genuine postwar models as quickly possible was based on the conviction that the company stood to gain much from being the first to give its customers the advantage of advancements both in design and production methods accumulated during the war and which, in total, represented substantial progress. It is quite evident from the public's reaction to the 1947 Studebaker...that this decision will prove to have been one of the most significant in the company's history.[13]

They were entitled to boast, for Studebaker's dynamic new image was firmly cemented with that decision to commit the $11 million required to tool the first all-new line of postwar cars in America. In so doing, Studebaker outdistanced its established competition by one-and-a-half to four full years and grabbed the public's imagination in a market where appearance is often far more important than reality. An impressive 161,498 cars were built during the model run, about two-thirds of them Champions. Production was, of course, restricted for all manufacturers that year, but Studebaker's market share increased to slightly over 4%—a heady level, indeed, by South Bend standards—and was to remain there for nearly five years.

The decision to move aggressively with America's first all-new postwar cars was only part of the plan. The second, and equally critical, part—

expanding Studebaker's manufacturing facilities—was completed, as well, by the end of 1946. The company had spent $16 million to double its capacity to around 300,000 cars and trucks per year. At that level of volume, Studebaker could be solidly profitable. Production had run at around 50 percent of capacity—at best—in 1946, though there were hopeful signs, to be sure. In January, 1947, the company built 16,263 vehicles, the greatest number in any one month since the halcyon days of August, 1928, and a rate that represented about 65 percent of capacity. The company also announced plans to purchase from the government the Chicago plant in which it had built Cyclone aircraft engines during the war.

Up north, a plant was acquired at Hamilton, Ontario, to enable the company to assemble Studebaker cars there for the Canadian market in the spring of 1947 (and, presumably, for British Commonwealth export markets, as well). The company was forced to do this because of unexpected action taken by the Canadian government to severely restrict the importation of cars and trucks from the United States. Canada was experiencing a critical trade imbalance and draconian import restrictions were the response. Not surprisingly, this placed a special burden on the smaller manufacturers, but even mighty General Motors was hard hit. Buicks and Cadillacs were unavailable in Canada for several years as a consequence. The Canadian authorities appear to have offered some dispensation to the smaller auto makers who had no production facilities in Canada but Studebaker management was clearly taking no chances.[14]

In addition, agreements were reached with foreign distributors that promised the prospect of building Studebakers in various other countries. Clearly, Hoffman and Vance were not forgetting Studebaker's pre-war success in the export markets. They did, however, miss out on perhaps the greatest single opportunity of the postwar era when they passed up a chance to acquire distribution rights to the famous Volkswagen "Beetle."

The Volkswagen had been developed before the war by Ferdinand Porsche at the behest of Adolf Hitler as a "people's car"—hence the name—on the order of the Model T.[15] It did not enter production, however, before the outbreak of hostilities. Afterwards, the facility in Wolfsburg, Germany, came under British occupation. It looked to be about as hopeless a mess as anyone could imagine. The Beetle itself, although a work of genius, was eccentric; the Nazi association was regarded as an almost indellible stain; and the plant had been nearly obliterated by Allied bombing. The British put the facilities back into partial operation mainly to create "make work" for the local labor force, and then tried to dump the operation on just about every auto manufacturer in Europe and America. Ford, Renault, Humber and several others all rejected the chance to have it under almost any terms, or even as an outright gift.

Richard Hutchinson, head of Studebaker's export operations, learned about the Beetle and apparently became quite entranced with it. He acquired an offer from Wolfsburg promising distribution and manufacturing rights for North America and took the proposal to Vance, who turned it down flat. Vance didn't even want to see the car, although one was reportedly shipped to South Bend for testing. Nothing more was ever heard it.

In desperation, the British went so far as to offer the plant to the Russians—Wolfsburg was a mere six miles from the Soviet Zone and a slight redrafting of the map would have solved the problem very neatly—but even the Russians, who were looting Eastern Germany wholesale, turned-up their noses at the poor Beetle. Realizing then that they were stuck with it, the British decided to make the best of a bad lot, so they hired a former Opel executive, Heinz Nordhoff, to run it. Nordhoff didn't think much of the Beetle, either, but, like most of his countrymen, he was out of work and had a family to support...and the rest, as they say, is history.

Meanwhile, back in America, the demand for new cars, in general, and the appeal of the new Studebakers, in particular, enabled the company to break a series of records during the 1947 calendar year. The total car and truck production of 191,451 was the best in South Bend's history, and bettered the 1946 performance by nearly 60 percent. During the year, all existing company records for daily, weekly and monthly production were broken, and production in the final three months of the year made it the best quarter in Studebaker history. Meanwhile, dollar sales volume reached a peacetime record of $268 million and profits reached a record $15 million.

In this era, industry was under tremendous pressure from critics who complained about the "excessive" profits being made by American business from war contracts and from the postwar seller's market. Part of this was anger (genuine or feigned) with anti-big-business politicians, while part of it was prompted by radical elements, particularly in the labor movement, who missed few opportunities to attack the "greed" of big business. This had been a major element in the face-off General Motors experienced with the UAW during its 1945-46 strike and businessmen across the nation were feeling the heat. Most of them felt it was a bum rap, to put it mildly.

Studebaker management was no different and went to great lengths to understate (where possible) or downplay (where they had no other choice) their actual profits. For example, company financial statements in this period invariably reported previous profits for the war years as they had originally been reported, i. e., after deductions for excess profits taxes, conveniently ignoring the fact that virtually all such taxes had been refunded to the company later on. This had the effect of understating actual profits retained from 1942 to 1944 by about two-thirds and there is really no way to characterize this other than as a conscious effort by Studebaker management to cook the books for public relations purposes. Even the $15 million profit in 1947, which represented a fairly modest 5.6 percent on sales, was quoted in the annual report in its after-tax version: $9.1 million, or 3.4 percent on sales. Just to make sure no one missed the point, the annual report then went on to explain:

> In other words, the corporation's profit in 1947 represented approximately three and one-half cents in the sales dollar. This modest ratio of profits to sales is of particular significance in view of the widespread belief that industrial profits are excessive. Certainly in the case of Studebaker the profit margin is well below what could be called excessive.[16]

The statement was true enough, but the fact that the company felt compelled to make it spoke volumes about the challenges it felt it confronted. If this particular issue was a bit of a fraud, however, real ones remained.

Allocation problems and shortages of critical materials continued to bedevil the company. A considerable quantity of the steel Studebaker was able to buy in 1947 was so-called "conversion" steel. Rough ingots were purchased from one steel mill, then shipped to another steel mill for rolling and then to a third for final processing. This was effective enough as an emergency measure, but proved a costly way to obtain critical steel supplies. In a message to stockholders issued in March, 1948, Hoffman and Vance noted this ongoing dilemma and the company's solution for it:

> Throughout 1947, steel and iron were the controlling factors in automobile production, not only for Studebaker but for the entire automobile industry. There was no substantial improvement with respect to these two critical materials during [1947], nor is any in sight. The outlook has been further clouded by [President Truman's] request for Congressional authority to control the distribution of iron and steel. As a consequence, in order to safeguard maintenance of present production schedules and priced the basis for possible further increases in 1948, the company acquired as of December 31, 1947, the assets of the Empire Steel Corporation of Mansfield, Ohio.[17]

The purchase cost the company $7.4 million—cash. It was deemed well worth the expense in order to ensure Studebaker at least a measure of security in its steel sourcing.

If the company confronted a host of problems, it continued to boast of its stable work force. Indeed, this was to become a constant theme in company publicity and advertising in years to come. At the end of 1947, 17,698 men and women were employed by Studebaker.[18] The average length of service among workers in South Bend was ten years and the turn-over rate was less than one percent—an absolutely extraordinary figure in an industry where 15 percent and 20 percent rates of turn-over were not considered exceptional. Studebaker's record of safety on the job was worthy of note, too. In the main facility in South Bend, for example, the number of days lost due to on-the-job accidents in 1947 was 5.1 per million man-hours, down from 7.8 million man-hours in 1946. This was about half the industry average of 12.1 per million man-hours.[19]

Yet, there was another side to the labor story, one that did not reflect as well on the company. To put it bluntly, it cost too much to build a Studebaker car or truck. Hoffman and Vance were determined to maintain "friendly" labor relations, but what this mostly meant in practice was that they didn't stand up to their workers and demand a level of productivity that would keep the company on an even footing with Detroit. James Nance, who was fated to head Studebaker for two tumultuous years during the following decade, noted its effect on Studebaker's cost structure:

> During the war, everybody's costs got out of line on that cost-plus government program. Afterwards, the well-run companies—like General Motors—took a strike and got their production cost situation back in line. But, Studebaker did not take a strike and was stuck with these costly wartime production standards, and, as a result, they were just not competitive.[20]

In this period, for example, all the auto producers paid their workers on some sort of modified individual or group piecework plan. Shortly after the end of the war, though, Studebaker instituted an incentive system for its factory workers that was not tied rigidly to productivity. The result was that in no time at all Studebaker workers were being paid an average of 22 percent more than their counterparts in Detroit. In the nature of things, the deck was stacked against an independent producer all things being equal, but Hoffman and Vance permitted a labor situation to fester that tilted the playing field decidedly to Studebaker's disadvantage.

So, Studebaker's costs were significantly higher than those of the Big Three, or even of the other independents. There is ample evidence that Hoffman and Vance were well aware of this and of the bind in which it placed their company. One solution would have been to go to the mat with their workers and demand terms that were more in line with the industry norm, but this would have meant risking a strike (such as the brutal one endured by General Motors in the winter if 1945-46), and Hoffman and Vance simply didn't have the gumption to do that. A second solution would have been to compensate for the company's higher labor costs by boosting productivity, but there were daunting obstacles to that idea, such as the aging facilities in South Bend and the inherent disadvantages an independent producer bore in comparison to the volume efficiencies of the larger companies. The third solution was simply to sell more and more cars and trucks—to "make it up on volume," as the old saying goes—while judiciously raising prices whenever possible.

Hoffman and Vance clearly opted for the third solution and, in the postwar seller's market, they could get away with it. In a normal market, an automobile manufacturer's main challenge is selling, i.e., convincing consumers to buy its products. In the years immediately following the war, however, almost anything that was built was as good as sold the moment it rolled off the final assembly line and the big challenge was production. Hoffman and Vance proved that they were very good at building cars, but the day would come when normal conditions would return and they would have to prove as adept at selling them.

It light of this, Hoffman's departure from the corporation in April, 1948, was disturbing. He left to head the Marshall Plan and later directed the Economic Cooperation Administration in Washington. Still later, he put in a stint as head of the newly created Ford Foundation. Vance, who assumed the presidency in addition to his position as chairman of the board, was a manufacturing man. Hoffman had been the salesman and marketing whiz. Now that Studebaker was approaching a period when Vance's talents would be relatively less important and Hoffman's relatively more so, Hoffman was leaving. Indeed, Vance's assumption of both top jobs made his control of the company's destiny virtually undisputed. If there was anyone in South Bend who was bothered by this, nothing was being said aloud.

The fundamental dynamic of manufacturing "big ticket" items such as passenger cars is that once the break-even point is reached, every car sold above that level earns enormous "incremental" profits for the company. But, the reverse is also true. If a manufacturer's volume falls below that level, every unit not sold produces a huge incremental loss. By failing to address Studebaker's poor productivity—indeed, by letting it get progressively worse—Hoffman and Vance were allowing the company's break-even point to inexorably rise and, thus, making the company absolutely dependent for its survival upon maintaining volume at the daunting level of the early postwar years.

Of course, at this juncture the pent-up demand for car and trucks was still enormous, the 1947-series cars had been phenomenally successful, and as late as 1947-48 it was still possible to charge premium prices to car-hungry consumers. That this game could only continue as long as the abnor-

1948 Studebaker Commander.

mal conditions of the postwar marketplace continued seems not to have worried Hoffman and Vance inordinately. Like latter-day Messrs. Macawber, they apparently operated on the theory that "something would turn up" and that—somehow—they would manage to keep volume high enough to pay the bills, even though volume was already running at unheard-of levels by historic Studebaker standards.

And, indeed, at the end of 1947 Studebaker still had large backlogs of orders for new cars, although there were growing signs that supply was beginning to approach demand throughout the industry. The 1948 new model production change-over was completed in November, 1947, with virtually no downtime. This achievement was not surprising considering that the 1948 Studebakers were nearly indistinguishable from the wildly successful 1947 models. The main visual differences were limited to refinements—new bumpers on the Commander and Land Cruiser, and the addition of a horizontal grille bar to the Champion, for example—but convertible body types were added to both Champion and Commander lines, as well. There was talk of a station wagon, too, but none ever materialized.

Doubtless the opinion in South Bend was that there was no need to tamper with a winner and the facts bore this out. A total of 233,457 cars and trucks were sold in 1948, an all-time record. Actual production consisted of 166,755 cars and 67,982 trucks. Sales reached $383.6 million in 1948, while profits more than doubled to $32.3 million before taxes.

The 1949 Studebaker models, in turn, were essentially continuations of the highly successful 1948s. Again, the Champion received most of the attention, with a new egg-crate grille that more closely followed the Commander design, and the engine was stroked a little bit more to produce an even 100 horsepower. Inside, all Studebakers benefited from redesigned instrument panel controls.

The trucks, on the other hand, were entirely new in terms of their styling and even had a new plant. The company had purchased from the government, for a fairly modest $3.6 million, the Chippewa Avenue facility in which it had built Wright Cyclone aircraft engines during the war. All truck production was relocated there by the Spring of 1948 and the new R-series models followed soon thereafter.

Before the war, trucks had been little more than an after-thought. A meager 5,078 had been built in 1941, a high figure by Studebaker's prewar standards but one that barely showed-up on the charts compared to other truck producers. World War II changed all that. South Bend cranked-out an astonishing 197,000 trucks during the war and—given the pent-up de-

1949 Studebaker Champion.

mand for trucks after the war—the company realized undreamed-of levels of peacetime sales, as well. In 1946 and 1947, the company held about a 4% market share. The modern and handsome redesign of the R-series models done by Bob Bourke raised this to nearly 5%. In fact, the Studebaker truck line had a higher penetration in its market segment than did Studebaker cars, a happy situation that would continue for several more years.

The seller's market continued into the year, but the nagging allocation and supply problems of 1946-48 were finally resolved. As a result, the ability of Studebaker to build both cars and trucks was limited only by its capacity—and Vance was more than happy to oblige. Production was, after all, his strong suit and he proved it with the amazing total of 304,994 cars and trucks that were built during the calendar year. Of these, 239,900 were passenger cars and 64,971 were trucks. The Canadian plant at Hamilton, Ontario, accounted for 12,996 cars, while the Los Angeles assembly facility produced 33,760. Dollar sales reached an unheard-of $473.1 million—just shy of half-a-billion dollars—and profits hit $44.8 million.

Part of the reason for the hike in profitability was the fact that the company was able to cease buying "conversion" steel. The purchase of Empire Steel was paying off in a big way and was reflected in the bottom line. By the end of 1949, however, the steel situation had stabilized to such an extent that the company was able to obtain all it wanted through normal channels. Accordingly, the steel-making part of Empire Steel was sold off

1949 Studebaker R-series three-quarter ton pickup.

and a new company—Mansco, Inc.—was organized as a Studebaker sub-sidiary to carry on with the non-steel-making parts of Empire's business. Overall, Studebaker had made $1.9 million net profit on its investment in Empire Steel, not counting the money it was able to make by virtue of the increased auto and truck production Empire's steel made possible.

Amongst all the good news, labor provided a sour note, both at Studebaker and at one of its largest competitors. The General Motors strike in the winter of 1945-46 had been the longest in the history of the industry. Then, in January, the second longest—a three-and-a-half month shutdown—began at Chrysler Corporation. When it was finally over, the total cost for all sides was estimated at nearly $1.4 billion and the company lost almost half-a-million units of production, but management was willing to do what it had to do to keep its costs in line, no matter the short-term price.

Contrast this with what happened when Studebaker experienced its first official strike (as opposed to the occasional wildcat actions that had occurred at various times throughout its history), also beginning in January. The reason the union called the strike was especially disturbing. In addition to protesting the discharge of forty-three workers in violation (it was alleged) of established grievance procedures, the union was angry about a study of overtime methods on the part of management. Vance, it seems, had at last become motivated to do something about the runaway piece-work labor rates in the factory. The UAW local was obviously not about to cooperate in any efforts resolve the problem on any but its own terms and, therefore, the way the strike ended was perhaps most disturb-ing of all: after two days, Vance simply threw in the towel. *Plus ça change...*

The first major change in the landmark postwar Studebaker design came in 1950 with the celebrated "bullet nose" models. The annual report to stockholders, issued in March, 1950, described it thusly:

> Since the introduction of our first models of postwar design in 1946, we have gained recognition as the industry's style leader. We made no major changes in these cars until the third quarter of last year when we introduced our 1950 models. These newest cars, while carrying on the basic design of our first postwar models, feature a complete change in frontal appearance and fender treat-

1950 Studebaker Commander.

ment, as well as an improved ride and greater handling ease. That they are enjoying a high degree of public acceptance is apparent from the fact that in the five months after their introduction, our dealers in this country delivered a greater number of passenger car at retail than in any similar five-month period in our history.

In the very near future we will offer as optional equipment on our passenger cars, a new fully automatic transmission. This new transmission is the result of nearly 15 years of research and experimentation by our own engineers as well as the engineering staff of the Borg-Warner Corporation which will produce it for us. We consider it, and many impartial observers have adjudged it, superior to any automatic transmission on the market.[21]

The 1950 "bullet nose" cars are still controversial. Considered by many to be bizarre—that's one of the kinder descriptives used—they are often cited as one of the reasons Studebaker began to decline as an auto producer. Yet, wild as they may have been, they were also wildly popular in their day and still have a vociferous cult following. Even their detractors must admit that no Studebakers ever built were more distinctive.

Or, more distinctively "Loewy," in a sense, for there were two Raymond Loewys. The great designs commonly associated with his name are the 1953 Starliner and the 1963 Avanti, in other words, cars noted for their clean lines and restrained use of ornamentation. Nearly all the cars he designed for Studebaker were done in a similar vein. The cars he designed and had built for his own use, on the other hand, were often something else entirely. There was a series of such custombuilt cars, stretching from the 1930s on into the 1970s, and they often featured strange proportions and ornamentation of the gaudiest kind. In that, they formed a stark counterpoint to the elegant simplicity of his finest actual production designs. The "bullet nose" Studebaker is almost unique among his production cars as being an example of the "private" Loewy.

Even so, it almost didn't see production, for it was one of two competing restyles presented to management. Exner, working from the engineering department, did the other proposal, but Vance preferred Loewy's. Exner left shortly after that to accept an offer to head Chrysler's moribund design department. Cole, his patron, went into semi-retirement at more-or-less the same time and was replaced as chief engineer by Harold Churchill. Ironically, Loewy himself had mixed feelings about the "bullet nose"—or at least about they way it turned out. Years later he recalled:

> It started in a quarter-size clay model as a purely experimental sports car idea. As happens in such cases, the designer takes liberties with the wheelbase, the track and, mostly, starts with a low chassis. Designers must be given freedom of expression; it maintains...creativity. Unhindered by restrictions, we had a slender, racy-looking job with a lean, streamlined front end. It looked like a slender fuselage, fast and graceful. Then someone wished to see it adapted to the existing high and short chassis with a tall engine. The result was a bulbous, rather clumsy, fat automobile. Aesthetically, I never liked it much, but the customers did.[22]

They did, indeed. The 1950 model run proved to be the high watermark of Studebaker as an auto producer. A remarkable total of 334,554 cars and trucks rolled from the lines, by far the largest volume Studebaker would ever achieve. In June, the all-time monthly record was attained when 35,353 cars and trucks were built.

Sales were bolstered by the introduction early in the calendar year of a lower-priced Custom Champion and by an early introduction of the Borg-Warner automatic transmission. Prices for the Custom Champion started at $1,414, which placed it squarely in Chevy and Ford territory. The company did, however, correctly predict a softening of profits in 1950. It noted:

> The upward trend in our profit margin will be reversed this year. We started 1950 with production running at a record pace. Our schedule for the first quarter calls for the assembly of a greater number of passenger cars and trucks than in any previous three-month period and 30 percent more than in the initial quarter of 1949. Effective February 1, 1950, however, we made reductions in the list prices of all our passenger car models ranging from $82 to $135, so as to strengthen our competitive position.[23]

In fact, the dollar value of sales rose only slightly to $477 million and profits actually slumped to $39.1 million. After tax income fell from $27.6 million in 1949 to $22.5 million in 1950. In explaining this surprising result in what was the best year in the history of the automobile industry up to that time, Vance noted:

> The decline in income between 1950 and 1949, on approximately the same volume of total sales, was due primarily to (a) increased federal taxes, including a new excess profits tax, and (b) a substantial loss in scheduled production in the fourth quarter of the year due to model change and to labor difficulties incident to the establishment of work standards on new 1951 models.[24]

In other words, Studebaker's Achilles Heel, its runaway labor costs, remained a cause for deep concern with top management. As had happened so many times before, though, Vance and his team were utterly unable to muster the courage to do anything meaningful about them. Quite the contrary. Instead of cracking down, they signed a comprehensive pension plan in 1950 covering all hourly workers and a new five-year wage agreement that granted the UAW's long-demanded automatic cost-of-living increases—not, of course, tied in any way, shape, or form to corresponding increases in productivity. And, Studebaker's costs continued to mount.

Vance was still hoping to make it up on volume. So bullish was he at this point, with the plant operating at or near capacity for nearly four years, that the construction of a new assembly plant in New Brunswick, New Jersey, was contemplated. Even the realization that the postwar seller's market was winding down as production throughout the industry at last approached demand failed to be translated into any visible move toward retrenchment in South Bend.

Despite this activity, the 1949 annual report to stockholders, which was issued during the second quarter of 1950, struck a cautionary note:

> The new year [1950] started with the industry still accelerating its rate of production. First quarter schedules were at a higher rate than last year's and if maintained would result in a greater output for 1950 than for 1949. At the same time it is quite apparent that the bulk of the pent-up postwar demand has been satisfied and that the automobile market from here out will be closer to normal. As a result, the consensus in the industry is that the present rate of production cannot be maintained for long and that production of passenger car and trucks for the year will fall short of the 1949 total.

The advent of the Korean War in June of that year made it official. The war didn't come soon enough to put a damper on the 1950 model year, but its effects would be felt with the 1951 models that were nearly ready to enter production. Studebaker, a company that had seen so much war and contributed so much to the defense needs of the nation, would do so again.

In June—the same month the war started—the first contract for heavy-duty military trucks was assigned by the government. These would be essentially the same types of trucks the company had supplied during World War II. A few months later, Studebaker was instructed to begin acquisition of the equipment necessary for the production of J47 turbo-jet aircraft engines designed to power the B47 bomber. The engines were to be built under license from General Electric, which developed it. The New Brunswick plant was earmarked for this project. Civilian passenger car production would have to wait.

The 1951 model year was increasingly clouded by the war, then reaching its peak. It was an uncertain period with memories of the radical dislocations of the early 1940s still fresh. It wasn't just paranoia, either. The government had gone into the car business again, issuing price controls and allocating materials, although not so onerously as in the years immediately preceding and following World War II. There was constant talk of a cessation of civilian car production, though nothing came of it in the end. Civilian passenger car production was restricted, however, and price controls wreaked their predictable havoc on profits; the prices manufacturers were allowed to charge invariably lagged behind increases in the costs of material and labor. In a letter to stockholders in March, 1952, Vance noted:

> The automobile industry, as a whole, has always done business on a very narrow profit margin. In 1950, Studebaker's margin was 4.72 per cent of sales. Such a small margin of profit can be protected only by prompt adjustments of selling prices to compensate for increases in costs. There were substantial increases in costs during 1951, for which the Office of Price Stabilization would not permit either prompt or adequate adjustments in selling prices. It was largely because of this situation that Studebaker's profit margin declined to 2.51 per cent of sales in 1951.[25]

Despite the problems in the industry, and the fact that tens of thousands of customers had been shipped half-a-world away, Studebaker recorded its best year ever in 1951 in terms of dollar sales and its second-best in terms of unit production. A grand total of 285,888 Studebaker cars and trucks were built. The industry as a whole was down 19 percent, so Studebaker managed to maintain a stable 4 percent of the market. Revenues came to $503.3 million, while profits slumped again to $23 million.

This was an ominous trend, if anyone had cared to notice it. Unit pro-

Above, 1951 Studebaker Commander and, below, the Studebaker V8 engine.

duction of cars and trucks in 1951 was down barely 6 percent from what it had been in 1949, but profits had dropped by nearly half. To be sure, price controls and materials restrictions imposed by the government had played a part, and management preferred to cite that as the cause for the company's weakening performance, but the festering labor problems were an even more important factor. General Motors' profits, for example, had declined only 23 percent in the same period, while Packard's had suffered by a mere 1 percent. Something deeper than temporary dislocations prompted by the Korean War was at work in South Bend.

Regardless, the company continued to pay fat dividends. Payments to stockholders had been about 21 percent of after-tax profits in 1949, then rose to 35 percent in 1950 and to 56 percent in 1951 as earnings declined but payments to stockholders remained more-or-less constant. The percentage would decline slightly to 49 percent in 1952, but Studebaker seemed determined to maintain its reputation as a "stockholders" company, i. e., as a company that gave top priority to paying consistent dividends regardless of fluctuations in profitability. It was a policy that made Studebaker stock popular, but carried long-term risk that the company could be vulnerable to a sharp economic downturn or to a major marketing blunder.

These were factors that should have been of critical importance to an independent manufacturer and, above all, to one that had spent itself into bankruptcy only twenty years before. Studebaker's liquid assets taken as a percentage of net sales declined from 23 percent in 1946 to only 11 percent in 1952. General Motors, in contrast, had liquid assets taken as a percentage of net sales of 14 percent in 1952—and General Motors was a much bigger company. General Motors reported $7.5 billion in sales in 1952 to Studebaker's $586 million, while General Motors' liquid assets totaled just over $1 billion to $64 million for Studebaker.[26]

The 1951 models were modified somewhat in appearance from the 1950s. Essentially, the "bullet nose" was toned-down a bit. The most important news, though, was the advent of Studebaker's high-compression, overhead-valve V8 engine. An expenditure of $13 million on capital improvements in 1950 had principally been invested in this powerplant.

The high-compression, overhead-valve V8 had been pioneered only two seasons previously by Olds and Cadillac, and its appearance in a South Bend product put Studebaker at the forefront of automotive engineering trends. Designed by a team of engineers headed by Eugene Hardig, the V8 displaced 232 cubic inches. Not only was it one of the first of the modern V8s from any manufacturer, it predicted the future trend toward "small block" V8s that really began to gather speed with the introduction of Chevy's first V8 four years later.

In retrospect, however, Studebaker's V8 posed problems that would prove insurmountable later on. The engine was laid-out in such a way that it could not be bored out to any great extent for increased displacement. As one of the smallest of the "small block" V8s it was terrific, but there was another trend that was about to hit, as well. This was the trend toward "big block" V8s sparked by the industry horsepower race that struck in earnest in the mid-years of the decade. In time, even Chevy discovered that it had to supplement its "small block" engine with a larger design, but Studebaker would find itself out of the running because there wouldn't be enough money left to follow suit. But, that was all in the future.

As minor as the changes had been in 1951, they were even less dramatic in 1952. The war had dragged on into its third year, restricting the availability of chrome, copper, white sidewall tires and cars in general. The "Korean War chrome" on these 1952 cars has been a bane to old car enthusiasts for years; it is almost unheard-of to find a 1952 car with decent bright work. The copper under-layer had been deleted and the depth of the chrome surface had been reduced. So, in sum, the roads of America were filled with fewer Studebakers in 1952, and most of them had blackwall tires and chrome that was either bad or was soon going to be.

The 1952 Studebakers were never supposed to have been. Originally, all-new bodies were scheduled to have been announced for the company's centennial celebration in 1952. They were delayed until 1953 by wartime dislocations, however, and so the 1951s were hurriedly spruced up to replace them with a facelift utilizing many of the soon-to-be-seen 1953 styling cues. It is for this reason that the 1952 models were a bit awkward in their appearance, as is generally the case when styling cues from one design are grafted onto another. Rarely are the results entirely satisfying.[27]

An additional cloud hanging over the celebration was the deteriorating labor situation. A nationwide steel strike during the summer hadn't helped, but the really worrisome difficulties were, predictably, closer to home. Much closer. Vance privately grumbled that Hoffman's determination to have "friendly" labor relations at any price had saddled him with impossibly low productivity. Specifically, he confided to associates that inefficient work rules were going to cost the company $10 million in 1952 alone. Still, he didn't seem to be any better at doing anything about it than Hoffman had been.

To the good, Studebaker's military production continued to grow. For the year, military contracts accounted for 36 percent of total dollar sales volume, but reached 46 percent in the latter months of the year. A total of 231,837 Studebaker cars and trucks were built, a drop from 1951's total but in keeping with the general decline throughout the industry. Total revenues stood at $585.3 million and net profits rose slightly to $14.3 million.

None of the company's problems were on public display during the hundredth anniversary celebrations that year, of course. Studebaker was the first auto company to mark its centennial and it spared no effort in noting the occasion. The year was launched on February 16, 1952, the anniversary of the founding of the H. & C. Studebaker wagon business. At a gala dinner, national, state and local leaders honored the corporation. A commemorative medallion was cast in bronze and distributed. During the year a special centennial flag flew under the Stars and Stripes on masts at all of the corporation's plants and at dealers throughout the world. Studebaker was honored, or arranged to be honored, at numerous important events. The most notable of these was the Indianapolis 500 race on May 30, 1952, which was paced by a Studebaker. Not only that, but a pageant depicting the one-hundred-year history of the company was presented to race spectators, including everything from covered wagons to an array of historical Studebaker vehicles.

To cap it off, a Technicolor film, *The Studebaker Story*, was made to commemorate the event, and a company history was published: *A Century on Wheels*, by novelist and popular historian, Stephen Longstreet. In it Vance was quoted as follows:

> It's a changed world. Times are different. A hundred years ago people thought they were sure what the future would be. We no longer know or even think we know, and so Studebaker is geared to continue no matter what happens.

Alas, Vance's abilities as a seer, as the turbulent events of the next few months would all-too-amply demonstrate, were greatly exaggerated. The trouble began with the final event of the centennial year: the announcement of the 1953 models—the so-called "Studebaker Centennial Models of 1953"—in January and February, 1953.

When it launched the dramatically new 1947 models, it appeared that Studebaker had come into its own. And, indeed, the next five years proved to be the high-watermark of Studebaker as an auto producer. Market penetration remained stable at an impressive 4 percent of industry sales, while both production and profits soared to record levels. It had taken Hoffman and Vance fifteen years to push Studebaker to the heights. Alas, the 1947 line proved to be the last completely successful decision they ever made

Studebaker went all out to celebrate its centennial in 1952. Above, the UAW's Walter Reuther and Studebaker's Vance confer at a banquet. Below, the eight Wilks brothers were among the many family employee teams publicized during the event. Opposite, top to bottom: the centennial car and truck, and the Indy pace car.

and, when the downturn came in 1953, the descent was so rapid as to be dizzying. The collapse happened, relatively speaking, overnight and raised questions that historians have been struggling to answer ever since.

To be sure, the 1953 models were launched in an atmosphere of triumph. Studebaker had scored hugely with its first postwar cars and, so the thinking went in South Bend, was certain to do so again. Management projected production of 350,000 cars and trucks for the year. It placed particular hopes, of course, on the dramatically-styled new passenger cars. Noted the Annual Report to stockholders issued in February, 1953:

> In the spring of 1946, Studebaker introduced completely new postwar models of passenger cars at a time when all other automobile manufacturers were offering to the public only slightly altered versions of prewar cars. The resulting public interest in Studebaker products was an important factor in the progress which we made in the succeeding six years.
>
> For more than three years, our designers and engineers have been working on a new line of passenger cars of unique but very beautiful design. About a year a go, we concluded that 1953 would see a lifting, and later and ending, of government controls on production, and accordingly, we appropriated approximately $27,000,000 for tools and equipment required to produce these new models...
>
> In January, 1953, the new models, called the "Studebaker Centennial Models of 1953" were put on display, first to our dealers and later to the general public. We are happy to report that the reception accorded the new models, both here and abroad, has been even beyond our expectations and seems to be more than equal to the acceptance of our first postwar cars in 1946...The pacesetting design and engineering features of the Studebaker Centennial Models of 1953 constitute what the corporation believes to be another commanding step forward for Studebaker in the motor car industry.

In announcing the new cars, the company cited their low lines, re-

The impact of Studebaker designs on the postwar American public can perhaps best be indicated by the fact that Raymond Loewy and Harold Vance both made the cover of Time Magazine as a result—in 1949 and 1953, respectively.

duced center of gravity, improved weight distribution and redesigned suspension. Visibility, which was improved by around 33 percent over the 1952 models, was also noted, as was the mechanical power steering unit. This latter item was an answer to the trend toward power steering systems in the industry that had been sparked by Chrysler's first use of the technology in 1951. The Studebaker unit was, however, entirely mechanical in nature. In other words, it made no use of hydraulics as did other units on the market. The company naturally claimed this as an advantage and the system worked well enough in practice, but it was too expensive to manufacture and was soon discarded in favor of the GM-sourced Saginaw type.[28]

The existence of two different power steering systems was the least of it, though. Studebaker had built two almost entirely lines of *cars* for 1953, for the coupes and sedans shared very little other than their basic powertrain and odd pieces of trim. The reason this situation came about stemmed from the fact that the coupes were not supposed to have existed at all.

The original design program included only the body shell from which

Robert Bourke.

the sedans were built. Bob Bourke, working completely on his own in the styling studio, began the coupe sometime during 1951. Loewy saw it on one of his periodic trips to South Bend, liked it, encouraged its development and, eventually, touted it to Vance, who liked it, too. Vance may have been a manufacturing guy and dull as paste in most respects, but he had a certain appreciation for good design. In fact, Vance liked the coupe a lot and ordered its production. But, then the question arose of what to do about the other 1953 design that was being developed for the bread-and-butter sedan range. The two had to conform in looks. Since Loewy and Bourke were steadfast in their insistence that the coupe not be changed one iota from Bourke's final clay (and it wasn't in any significant particular), it was the sedan range that had to be modified. Unfortunately, adding the coupe's design cues after the fact to the sedans proved disastrous. The sedans turned out to be every bit as unappealing as the coupes were stunning.

If styling had been the end of it, the company might have been able to limit the damage. Alas, the engineering and manufacturing systems in place in South Bend turned out to be utterly incapable of handling the complex demands of building two different lines of cars at the same time.

To begin with, the assembly plant was simply not able to process all those parts. Bottlenecks developed from the first and grew so impossible that a new conveyor belt system had to be installed at a cost of two-thirds of a million dollars—but only after millions more had been lost due to production delays. And, of course, this chaotic situation did absolutely nothing to promote the quality of the early cars that were built and whose reputation for fit and finish was, to be kind about it, not good.

Even worse, South Bend's engineering and manufacturing people were swamped by the need to make all those different body parts go together on the same chassis. A system was in place for assuring such things, but it simply broke down under the strain. This unhappy fact became apparent in the most calamitous way imaginable when the components for the first coupe body moved down the assembly line...and wouldn't fit! As a consequence, the coupe had to be partially re-engineered in a crash program and at enormous additional expense. Meanwhile, still more sales were lost.

Worst of all, Vance and his management team had no concept of how popular the coupes would be. They based 1953 production schedules on the level of sales recorded in 1952 when the coupes and hardtops had accounted for about one quarter of the total. By the end of the 1953 model run, the coupes were hitting 80 percent of production, in part because of the dreadful sales of the sedans, but also due to their own immense appeal. Yet, throughout the model year, the coupes were in desperately short supply and, without question, tens of thousands of sales were lost simply because the factory couldn't build them fast enough.

As a direct result of this mushrooming nightmare, the company stumbled along for half the model year before it finally recorded its first monthly profit in April. Paul Hoffman hastily returned to South Bend in February to pitch in. On March 1st, he formally resumed a position as an

1953 Studebaker Commander Starliner.

officer, this time as chairman of the board, although it was announced that he would work in South Bend on only a part-time basis. Vance retained the title of president and chief executive officer.

It wasn't until about that time that production attained a level sufficient to satisfy dealer demand. Then, in May, a strike at Borg-Warner suddenly cut-off the supply of manual transmissions, which were still a very popular item with Studebaker buyers and production schedules had to be repeatedly cut back again. South Bend did not regain profitable production levels until July. Along the way, the company lost forty-four dealers owing directly to its inability to supply adequate quantities of cars.

When the smoke cleared, a total of 186,000 cars had been built. This was more than the number built in 1952, to be sure, but nowhere near the number that *could* have been built. The company recorded a miserable profit of only $2.7 million for calendar year—none of it, significantly, from the automotive operations. The situation was far worse than even that, however, for many of the company's expenses in 1953 had been amortized. Its cash position fell to a crisis level as the year staggered on and the company would have faced insolvency had it not been able to draw down a $100 million line of credit connected to its defense contracts.

Thus, only a few months after Hoffman and Vance had indulged in their orgy of self-congratulation at Studebaker's centennial dinner, they found themselves once again staring wide-eyed into the abyss.

Notes

The most important resources drawn upon in the writing of this chapter include Stephen Longstreet's official company history, *A Century on Wheels: The Story of Studebaker*, Raymond Loewy's *Industrial Design*, John Bridges' *John Bourke Designs for Studebaker*, and Richard M. Langworth's *Studebaker, 1946-1966*. Periodicals that proved to be important resources included various issues of *Mechanix Illustrated*, *Motor Life*, *Motor Trend*, and *Special-Interest Autos*.

[1] 1943 Studebaker Corporation Annual Report.
[2] 1944 Studebaker Corporation Annual Report.

[3] The status of the major producers as of December 31, 1945, appears below. Note that Ford Motor Company does not appear here because it was still a privately held company that issued no reports. (It would not go "public" until 1956.) Hudson's assets are estimated, but were at the same level for both 1944 and 1946, so 1945 is unlikely to have been much different. "Stock and Capital Surplus" includes the value of authorized but unissued stock and capital surpluses retained in the business. As with many accounting devices, much of this was no doubt done with smoke and mirrors, but, since the methods used by the various manufacturers were essentially the same, the numbers are valid for comparing the relative financial strength of the companies cited.

	Assets	Stock and Capital Surplus
General Motors	1,813,885,559	1,351,094,995
Chrysler	414,228,503	250,309,793
Packard	108,871,254	42,016,721
Nash	78,997,145	48,440,587
Studebaker	63,986,728	40,857,834
Hudson (est.)	55,000,000	n/a

[4] In contrast, the average number of man-days lost nationwide due to strikes in the 1935-39 period was only 17 million. It should not be forgotten, either, that, in addition to being the nation's largest auto maker, General Motors was also a key supplier of various critical components to the rest of the industry.

[5] 1946 Studebaker Corporation Annual Report.

[6] Langworth, *Studebaker, 1946-1966*, p. 19.

[7] Car Collector, August, 1979, p. 25

[8] In his autobiography, *Industrial Design*, Loewy included a professional-grade color art rendering of a cycle-fendered 1932 Hupmobile signed with his initials and the date, which was his usual practice: "RL 1932." The only problem with this is that the rendering was taken from the 1932 showroom sales catalog that was almost certainly prepared by the ad agency (using one of its own artists) in the latter months of 1931! Loewy, however exalted his reputation as a designer may have been, was not noted as a professional illustrator.

[9] Car Collector, August, 1979, p.26.

[10] Special Interest Autos, January-February, 1976, p. 44.

[11] Special Interest Autos, January-February, 1976, p. 44.

[12] Langworth, *Studebaker, 1946-1966*, p. 19.

[13] 1946 Studebaker Corporation Annual Report.

[14] Even while General Motors was given no quarter, Packard, for instance, which did not build cars in Canada, was allowed to continue shipping cars in at least limited quantities.

[15] The actual name of the car was the "Kraft-durch-Fruede Wagen," after the KdF, or Strength-through-Joy, Nazi-affiliated labor front. "Volkswagen" was the nickname until production started after the war. Then, it became official.

[16] 1947 Studebaker Corporation Annual Report.

[17] 1947 Studebaker Corporation Annual Report.

[18] This figure does not include 1,100 workers at Empire Steel.

[19] These figures were calculated from job accidents resulting in a worker being away from the job for one day or more.

[20] Langworth, *Studebaker, 1946-1966*, pp. 33-34.

[21] 1949 Studebaker Corporation Annual Report.

[22] Langworth, *Studebaker, 1946-1966*, p. 44.

[23] 1949 Studebaker Corporation Annual Report.

[24] 1950 Studebaker Corporation Annual Report.

[25] 1951 Studebaker Corporation Annual Report.

[26] Liquid assets here are defined as including cash on hand, current receivables, securities, and other negotiable instruments.

[27] Lincoln fell into the same trap when its new body was delayed from 1955 to 1956. The 1956 styling cues were grafted onto the 1952-54-series cars for the 1955 model year, and with much the same results.

[28] Ironically, General Motors had actually patented power steering in the early 1930s, but never put it into production because the depressed production levels at the time would not justify the investment. After the war, when demand was soaring, power steering wasn't needed to sell cars. It is hard to say how long it would have taken General Motors to get around to building it, if it hadn't been for Chrysler. The usually hide-bound Chrysler, showing unusual initiative for this era, waited patiently for the General Motors patents to run out, then moved quickly to put power steering into production in 1951. General Motors was suddenly in a position where it had to play catch up with an important innovation it had invented—literally. Such is the car business. Power steering appeared on Cadillacs in 1952, and, by 1953, most other General Motors divisions had it, too, and the rest of the industry was scrambling to play catch-up.

Overleaf, completed cars coming off the final assembly line in 1954.

EIGHT

The Packard Operation

It is in the nature of any industry to experience a process of consolidation over its life cycle and the automobile industry has been true to form. Within ten years after the first manufacturer was established in 1895[1], hundreds of would-be competitors joined the blossoming market. Eventually, more than two thousand names were added to the roll, the vast majority of them within the first two decades of the industry's existence.

Inevitably, a few companies proved to be more capable than the others. These few producers grew ever more successful and, as they did so, drove the weaker producers out. In 1920, there were about one hundred brands being produced. By the time the Great Depression struck at the close of the decade, that number had been reduced to around forty. When the Japanese paid their unanticipated visit to Pearl Harbor, only twenty-one brands from a mere dozen producers survived and only eight of these producers were of any real consequence.[2]

So, among the knowledgeable it was no secret that the automobile industry was consolidating. But, what did consolidation mean? Surely, the Big Three would survive, but what about the independents? Even in the heady days of the seller's market there had been talk about the need for the smaller producers to merge into larger entities that could operate on a more competitive basis. Nash's peripatetic chief, George Mason, was the principal booster for this view. His grand vision was to add a digit to the Big Three by putting all the major independents together in a giant combine in the manner of General Motors or Chrysler. Thus, as a member of a new Big Four, the consolidated independents could field a rationalized product program ranging from Studebaker (in the Pontiac-Dodge-Mercury volume-medium-priced segment, with a few models dipping down into the low-priced segment where Chevrolet and Ford reigned supreme) to Nash (in the Olds-De Soto mid-range-medium-priced segment) to Hudson (in the Buick-Chrysler upper-medium-priced segment) and, finally, to Packard (in the Cadillac-Lincoln luxury segment).

An immediate problem that Mason encountered was that companies rarely want to talk about consolidation until they have to. Nash and Packard discussed a merger in the 1940s, then A. E. Barit at Hudson and Vance at Studebaker were approached, but all were making cars (and money) hand-over-fist and gave Mason the brush-off.[3]

A fundamental fact of consolidation is that, almost inevitably, there is going to be a stronger partner and a weaker partner; rarely is there a coming together among absolute equals. For the top management of the weaker firm, the merger is likely to be seen, naturally enough, less as a business opportunity than as a loss of control, and as an almost certain loss of lucrative and powerful top-level jobs. After all, one of the prime benefits of consolidation is the elimination of duplications in fixed overhead; no company needs *two* chairmen, *two* presidents, *two* chief financial officers and so on. Bloodletting in the executive suites is, therefore, almost inevitable. Consequently, top management in the weaker firm tends to resist the idea so long as the company is strong enough to go it alone, which is precisely the time when a merger would produce the greatest benefit from a purely business point of view. Conversely, by the time top management is ready to bow to the inevitable, it is often too late.

So, Mason got nowhere preaching his merger Gospel until the market turned against the independents in 1953. Then, with Hudson on the ropes and Studebaker suddenly in trouble, the talks picked up speed. At that point, the president of Packard emerged as a key player.

James J. Nance had never had much to do with automobiles, other than as an ordinary car buyer, before accepting the job with Packard in March, 1952. After early training with National Cash Register, he had joined GM's Frigidaire division in 1927 and then had spent the ensuing twenty-five years selling appliances. And, he was a whiz at selling appliances. *Fortune* magazine once noted that he had "a bit of the revivalist speaker about him," while other contemporaries called him a "spellbinder" and claimed he could "charm the birds out of the trees."[4] At the time he left the top spot at General Electric's Hotpoint division in 1952, he was considered to be such a sizzling property that General Electric immediately bought 25,000 shares of Packard stock. If GE could no longer profit from his presence at Hotpoint, at least it could profit from the magic he was sure to work in his new job.

James J. Nance.

The move was not an impulse decision on Nance's part. He had been talking to Packard off-and-on for a couple of years—and, more importantly, Mason had been talking to him. In Nance, Mason at last found a ready convert. It was agreed between them that since Mason and Vance didn't get along, the proper strategy was a two-stage plan in which Nash and Hudson would merge, Packard and Studebaker would merge, and then at an unspecified later date the two merged companies would merge again. At that point, Mason would retire from active management and turn the whole show over to Nance. For his part, Nance became a True Believer. Years later, he told an interviewer:

> We agreed that Mason would take the Hudson-Nash end, and I would put Studebaker-Packard together, then we'd fold the two pieces together into one company. I wouldn't have gone into it just to take over Packard.[5]

Of course, Hudson and Studebaker hadn't been consulted about this grand scheme, but Mason and Nance were utterly convinced not only that it would work but that it was inevitable. Hudson, which had started losing money as early as 1951, was in obvious decline and was already being shopped around. It was an open secret that Queen Wilhelmina of the Netherlands, who controlled 11 percent of Hudson's stock, was anxious to sell. Studebaker would hold out for a while, perhaps, but its time would come, too.[6] That time came with a vengeance in the winter of 1953-54.

With the lifting of government controls and restrictions, the 1953 model year had started out at a great pace for virtually all automobile manufacturers. Then, overnight, everything went crazy, resulting in the most unsettled market conditions within the memory of industry veterans.

To begin with, the abnormal postwar seller's market had suddenly ended. It had looked as if the traditional buyer's market would return in 1950, but the Korean War aborted the process until the long-expected shift suddenly took place in the spring of 1953. So long as shortages lasted, any manufacturer could sell large numbers of cars—even one building a seriously deficient product (for reasons of engineering, styling, quality, etc.) or using a weak dealer network.

The effects of this were dramatically worsened by what came to be known as the "Ford Blitz" beginning in the fall almost as soon as the 1954 models were introduced. This was a damn-the-cost attempt by Henry Ford II to regain sales leadership from Chevrolet. In practice, it meant cranking up factory production schedules to their maximum possible level and dumping the excess cars onto Ford dealers in order to force up market share. Naturally, as soon as Chevy figured out what was going on it responded in kind. The poor Ford and Chevy dealers were given little or no choice. A truck load of unordered and unwanted cars would arrive, and the dealer would have to pay for them and then frantically dispose of them (often at a loss) in order to make room for the *next* truck load of unordered and unwanted cars that was sure to arrive momentarily.

Coming on top of the end of the seller's market, the blitz completely disrupted what was left of the normal rhythms of the automotive marketplace and, in particular, devastated the weaker competitive brands in the low- and medium-priced fields. So, with the market becoming saturated at about the time the 1954 models entered production and the Ford Blitz beginning shortly thereafter, several nameplates all but vanished from the sales charts. Hudson, Kaiser and Packard went into free-fall, while, among the Big Three, Chrysler suffered the worst, with sales and market share collapsing overnight by nearly 40 percent.

To defend against this, all Studebaker had to offer in 1954 was a thinly revised range of models that hadn't been very successful the year before. About the only visible difference was a series of slender vertical bars that were added the grille, while the only new model was the Conestoga station wagon. A wagon had been considered in 1947 or 1948, then abandoned. Now, with the growth of postwar suburban sprawl and two-car households, wagons had suddenly achieved a level of popularity that couldn't be ignored. Thus, the Conestoga, available in virtually every trim level offered in the sedans, plugged an important gap in Studebaker's product line-up—even if it was just about the homeliest wagon on the market.

[A stunning convertible prototype had been built at the factory, but production plans were killed due to concerns about body rigidity. Based on the already gorgeous Starliner hardtop body, the convertible was major opportunity missed, for convertible sales, like those of the station wagon, were growing stronger every year in the developing second-car culture.]

Most of the effort expended on the 1954 cars, however, showed-up on the inside. While "designer edition" cars didn't become a fad until the 1980s, the concept was taking root at this time. Dorothy Draper was doing Packard interiors, Kaiser had Marie Nichols, and, for 1954, Eleanor LeMaire was retained to work her magic on the Studebaker range. As a result, the 1954 interiors were dramatically more colorful and contemporary than the old-fashioned browns and grays that had been the staple for years. A leather interior option was even offered in the middle of the model run.[7]

Changes of a mechanical nature were extremely minor. The brakes were improved, the horsepower was slightly increased and a few other detail modifications were made. From an engineering standpoint, though, the new models were nearly identical to their predecessors.

Yet, Studebaker missed out on the biggest opportunity of all when it turned down its second chance to secure distribution rights to the Volkswagen Beetle. In the wake of South Bend's scorning of the first offer in 1946 or 1947, Volkswagen had been picked-up by one Maximillian Edwin Hoffman (or "Maxie" Hoffman, as he was more commonly known), a peripatetic presence in the world of European imports in the years following World War II. After coming to America as a Jewish Austrian refugee, Hoffman, at one time or another, wrangled the official distribution rights for almost every European brand worth selling in America—and quite a few that weren't. In 1953-54, the eccentric-looking Volkswagen was considered by most industry "experts" to be one of the ones that wasn't.

Even Maxie Hoffman—who had a reputation for being able to sell just about anything—hadn't been able to do much with the Beetle and, consequently, had actually dropped his distributorship.[8] Word of this reached an acquaintance, Richard Hutchinson, the head of Studebaker's export operations. Hutchinson, of course, had tried to "sell" the Beetle to Hoffman and Vance during the first episode, in the process becoming completely entranced by the car. This time, he met with Volkswagen officials, returned to South Bend in triumph with a signed distribution contract—and Vance refused to accept it a second time! Vance simply could not understand the potential appeal. In his opinion, the Beetle was too bizarre, too this, too that—just *too*. And, so, he refused to sign off for the corporation. In a very short while, the buying public would emphatically register its disagreement. American sales of the Beetle leapt from an almost invisible 1,139 in 1953 to 32,662 in 1955 and passed the 100,000 unit mark by 1960. How the fate of Studebaker would have changed with that one signature...

It wasn't the last time Studebaker would negotiate for distribution rights with Volkswagen or the last time it would cross paths with Maxie Hoffman, either, but that is moving us ahead of our story. As the 1954 model year began, South Bend was stuck with its own products and peddling *them* was proving to be a daunting challenge.

After the horrendous manufacturing problems of 1953 had been resolved, Vance had hoped that the 1954 model year would return the company to solid profitability. The cars were still new enough and most of Studebaker's direct competitors would be offering warmed-over 1953s, as well. It seemed a reasonable game plan. Nance had approached Vance in the latter months of 1953 with a proposal to enter into serious merger talks with Packard. After some initial conversations, Vance withdrew. Then, the bottom fell out.

As 1954 began, the red ink in South Bend surged to flood tide propor-

1954 Studebaker Champion Conestoga.

tions. Sales dropped alarmingly and the loss in the first quarter alone was $8.3 million. In response, Hoffman decided to return to work full-time. It was announced that his primary mission would be to lead the belated charge on bringing Studebaker's labor costs into line with the rest of the industry by getting rid of the piecework system and replacing it with a normal day rate. After much grumbling, the workers in South Bend actually voted themselves a pay cut, although, as events would demonstrate, it was too little too late and, from the company's point of view, the new terms were hardly all they were cracked-up to be, anyway.

The old piecework system, expensive as it had proven to be, at least defined objective standards of productivity and pay for the workers. With the new day-rate system, it would be up to management (through the shop foremen) to enforce subjective standards. This was something Studebaker's managers from the foremen on up were completely unequipped to do, either by training and by mindset, and so costs stubbornly resisted meaningful reduction. Gross over-staffing continued unabated and the losses mounted to an appalling $12 million in the second quarter. Worse, Studebaker's cash reserves were down to about $15 million. One or two more quarters like the second and the company would be insolvent. The merger talks with Nance resumed.

On April 6th, a report commissioned by Nance from Lehman Brothers was made public. Entitled, "Benefits of a Merger," it assessed the potential of a combination of Studebaker and Packard and reported, in part:

[It would be] a dignified combination of the two best names in the independent field. The combined lines are essentially complimentary and non-competitive. Studebaker covers the low- and low-medium-priced fields; Packard covers the upper-medium and high-priced fields. In addition, through the Studebaker truck line, the merged Company would be represented in the low-priced and high-volume segment of the trucking industry.[9]

The report noted a number of additional benefits, including the increased management and financial resources of the merged company, lower costs resulting from increased volume and the use of interchangeable parts, joint use Studebaker's East and West Coast assembly facilities, Studebaker's strong position in the export market that would give Packard increased access to those markets, and the efficiencies and increase in volume that would result from dual franchises at the dealer level.

On May 4th, Lehman Brothers delivered an addendum, "Suggested Basis of Consolidation," that recommended that the merger be structured as a takeover of Studebaker by Packard. And, in fact, the actual agreement between Studebaker and Packard signed on June 22nd stated, in part:

Packard desires to purchase, and Studebaker desires to sell, subject to the approval of their respective stockholders, substantially all the property and assets of Studebaker, including its name, business and good will, in exchange solely for shares of Packard

1954 Studebaker Champion.

voting stock and assumption by Packard of substantially all liabilities of Studebaker.[10]

A key element in the consolidation was a reported $70 million line of credit being extended to the new corporation by a group of banks and insurance companies. Reportedly, this promise of a quick cash infusion was the major inducement insofar as Hoffman and Vance were concerned. They knew that Studebaker couldn't survive without more capital and no other source was in sight.

The takeover required the approval of the stockholders of both corporations, of course, and that took another three months. There was much grumbling in both camps, but especially on the Packard side. A rump group of Packard stockholders even tried to block the deal. Eventually, though, their efforts went for naught and Studebaker-Packard Corporation formally came into being on October 1, 1954. Hoffman was named chairman of the new company, Vance was named to head the executive committee, and Nance assumed the duties of president and chief operating officer. In reality, Hoffman was already semi-retired and Vance had been kicked upstairs, so, for good or for ill, it was really Nance's show from that point on.[11]

A comprehensive program for the new company was quickly prepared under Nance's direction. It project a $9 million loss for 1955, a reduced loss for 1956, and a return to solid profitability in 1957 with the launching of entirely new Studebaker and Packard models on a common body shell. By 1958, the program predicted, Studebaker-Packard would be firmly positioned with about 4 percent of the market. It seemed reasonable at the time.

Almost immediately, though, this program began to come apart. The first storm warning came when Nance dispatched Walter Grant, Packard's chief financial officer who had assumed that position in the consolidated company, to South Bend to prepare a report on Studebaker's financial status. He returned to Detroit in a state of shock. What he had discovered was that Studebaker's real break-even point was not the 165,000 units per year given by Lehman Brothers—daunting enough as that was in light of South Bend's actual rate of production in 1954—but as high as 282,000! Studebaker had only exceeded that figure twice since the end of the war.[12]

Hoffman and Vance were extremely skeptical about Grant's report.

They argued that Studebaker had recorded a profit before taxes of $29.1 million in 1952 with vehicle production running at just under 200,000 units. It was a good point. Of course, much of that profit came from defense orders connected with the war in Korea and part of it was doubtless due to Studebaker's ability to charge relatively higher prices for its cars and trucks while supplies were restricted during the emergency. Neither of those factors were in play now.

Whether Grant's estimate was correct or somewhat overstated, Studebaker's break-even point was clearly too high and, as subsequent events would demonstrate, his analysis of the cause was all-too accurate. Even after Hoffman's exertions in the spring of 1954, Studebaker's real labor costs were still approximately twice the industry norm and getting them down would occupy a depressingly large amount of Nance's time over the next few months.

Nance hardly needed another crisis. Everywhere he looked things were going haywire. It started with the end of the war. Studebaker-Packard's lucrative defense business evaporated almost overnight. The phasing out of some contracts was to be expected, but the suddenness and totality of the actual cancellations was stunning. Nance calculated the loss in revenue (compared to his program projections) at a staggering $426 million. Charles Wilson, lately president of General Motors, was the new secretary of defense and his cuts seemed to be hurting the independents with special severity.[13] Lots of future fodder for conspiracy theorists there, although Wilson probably didn't comprehend the ramifications for Studebaker-Packard at the time.

Packard's body situation was turning into another disaster. Packard had stopped building its own bodies before the war, choosing to rely on Briggs, an independent body supplier whose main customer was Chrysler. This was fine until Walter Briggs died and his heirs were forced to sell the business to Chrysler in December, 1953, in order to satisfy the estate taxes.[14] Chrysler had no interest in building bodies for any other car company and sent a pink slip to Packard. By then, unfortunately, there were no independent body builders left that were big enough to handle the job the way Briggs had. Given little choice, Nance elected to buy the facility on Conner Avenue in Detroit in which Briggs had been making Packard bodies and, thus, have Packard go back into the body business for itself.

So far so good. Taking over the body plant should have been a net plus because it was a "turn key" operation and, all else being equal, it would have improved the efficiency of Studebaker-Packard by eliminating Briggs' profit from the cost of Packard bodies. But, Nance let himself be talked into moving the entire assembly operation into the body facility, too. Packards had been built in a sprawling plant on East Grand Boulevard for as long as anyone could remember. The East Grand operation was aging and costs there were certainly higher than Nance would have liked, but the place worked well enough and a quality product was being produced. The cost of the transfer of Packard assembly alone (not counting the cost of buying the Conner Avenue facility from Chrysler) has been estimated at $20 million, which was a) a huge and completely unnecessary expense in the critical summer of 1954, b) delayed the introduction of the vitally important 1955 Packards by months causing them to miss the crucial fall selling season, and c) set the stage for a nightmare collection of manufacturing and quality control headaches when they finally did enter production.[15]

The icing on the cake, at least insofar as Nance was concerned, was the sudden death of George Mason in October. George Romney assumed the reins at American Motors. Ironically, Romney—who later became governor of Michigan and, for a time, a power in national politics—had once been offered Nance's job. In 1948, he received offers from both Packard, where the board was already actively seeking a new chief operating officer, and Nash. The Packard position would have paid more and he was only being offered the number two slot at Nash under Mason, but Romney chose Nash because he thought it had the brighter future.

Almost immediately upon assuming the helm at American Motors, Romney let it be known that he had no interest at all in pursuing the final step in the grand Mason-Nance strategy by merging with Studebaker-Packard. Nance blamed Romney for the breakdown. Romney blamed Nance. In an interview given in 1981, Romney recalled:

> Nance kind of moved away from it. I concluded that he wanted to engineer this four-way merger himself.
>
> Mason and Nance worked out an agreement for a reciprocal

1955 Packard Caribbean.

buy-sell relationship. The understanding was that we would buy V8 engines from Packard and Packard would reciprocate by purchasing approximately an equal dollar amount of stampings from us. We had a new stamping plant over in Kenosha [Wisconsin].

Then, Nance, shortly after Mason's death, made arrangements to buy the Briggs stamping plant in Detroit. Well, I knew by that that he wasn't going to honor the understanding with respect to reciprocal purchases. So, I wired him within a few days after I took over and indicated that he was not honoring the understanding. And, that was the end of that.[16]

The problem with Romney's story is that the chronology doesn't jibe with the facts. Packard's crisis with Briggs arose nearly a year before Mason died. Nance's decision to buy the Conner Avenue plant was made shortly thereafter and the first 1955 Packard rolled off the new assembly line within a few days of Mason's death.

There was a more critical issue involved. Romney and Nance just didn't like each other. For years, Romney had been lost in the shadow of the peripatetic Mason, who, like Nance, tended to run a one-man show. Consequently, there were many in the industry who underestimated Romney. Nance was one of them. Again, Romney recalled:

> [Nance] was telling people—shortly after Mason's death and after I became head of American Motors—that I had just been an errand boy for Mason, and that I would be out and American Motors would be picked-up by Packard within a matter of months. I was told that by several people whom Nance had talked to. I don't think he thought I was capable of running the company.[17]

Alas for Nance, Romney *was* running the company and now had the power to see to it that the last stage in the four-company merger didn't go through. He wasted little time in availing himself of the opportunity. So, that deal was off and Nance was stuck with what he had whether he liked it or not. And, he didn't like it much. Years later he commented:

> I don't think [Studebaker] could have made it alone. I wouldn't have wanted them if I didn't see them as part of a bigger picture.[18]

Moreover, the pre-merger cooperation Nance had expected from American Motors—love without marriage, as one wit put it—mostly failed to materialize, as well. Mason and Nance had been actively discussing a common body shell for Nash-Hudson-Studebaker-Packard cars, but nothing more was heard about that idea after Romney took over. Studebaker-Packard did try to source parts and components through Kenosha, but the cost estimates coming back were almost always too high. An offer to buy six-cylinder engines to replace the aging Studebaker six—seemingly lucrative business from American Motors' standpoint—was rejected by Romney, who cited capacity restraints. Considering the dramatic success of the Rambler beginning in 1956, this may have been a wise move on Romney's part. Years later, he explained his actions to an interviewer:

> If we furnished the 30,000-40,000 six-cylinder engines to Studebaker, we would be short of sufficient engines for the ex-

pected Rambler sales volume in 1957. Expansion of present capacity would call for an expensive across-the-board investment in
machinery, equipment and considerable plant rearrangement...Our
difficulty was capacity, not a lack of willingness to produce engines for Studebaker if it were possible and practical to do so.[19]

An offer to have American Motors cast blocks for Studebaker-Packard
resulted in an estimate that was not only higher than Nance could get from
a foundry in Detroit, but came with an impossible nine-month lead time.
American Motors did buy Packard engines and transmissions for a while
until it could develop its own V8 in 1956, but then that business dried up,
too. And, so it went. For a variety of reasons, there would be little or no
long-term cooperation between American Motors and Studebaker-Packard.

As for Studebaker, Nance had bought in haste and he would now have
plenty of time to regret it. A question arises: Why were the Lehman Brothers figures so far off with regard to Studebaker's costs? The answer is disturbing because of what it says about the casual way in which the entire
merger had been handled. The figures were off because Lehman Brothers
hadn't done a formal audit of Studebaker's books. Normally, when it managed a merger Lehman Brothers (or any similar firm) would have done a
detailed audit of the books of both companies as a matter of course. But,
the plan for the Studebaker-Packard merger was based on unaudited figures because no merger was in the works when it was prepared and, therefore, Lehman Brothers had no legal responsibility for the accuracy of the
data (which, presumably, was either supplied directly by Studebaker or
indirectly by way of published industry sources that got their information
through South Bend). Nance accepted the figures at face value because, in
the good-old-boy culture that prevailed in the industry at that time, you
didn't go out of your way to question such things.

To be sure, there are old Packard hands who insist to this day that the
city boys in New York and Detroit were deliberately sold a bill of goods by
the country slickers in South Bend. Be that as it may, Nance's observation
that Studebaker couldn't have made it alone, is almost certainly true. By
the summer of 1954 the money in South Bend was all but gone and available credit was extremely limited, if not non-existent. In our times, Nance

has come under fire from many Studebaker partisans for this failing or that, real or imagined, with regard to way in which he ran Studebaker-Packard, yet the stark truth is that Studebaker wouldn't have survived at all if he hadn't been careless enough to buy it. It was mostly Studebaker—not Packard—that dragged Studebaker-Packard down. Despite the nightmare on Conner Avenue, Packard was still viable—although deeply troubled—as late as 1955. Nance unwittingly gave the South Bend firm a reprieve that it didn't deserve and arguably did so to the lasting detriment of his own company.

So, Grant was dispatched again to South Bend with the thankless assignment of getting Studebaker's costs down. In plain English, that meant persuading the union to use fewer men to do more work for less money. Not an easy sell. In the latter part of January, 1955, the union's answer came in the form of a wildcat strike. It was the first of eighty-five such job actions to follow during the calendar year and Studebaker was shut down for thirty-six work days in all before a new wage contract was negotiated. When the dust settled, the cost situation in South Bend was better—not by nearly enough, but better.

At one point Nance was called out to visit Hoffman at the latter's home in Palm Springs. "Don't you realize," Hoffman chastised, "this company is over one hundred years old and has never had a strike?" Replied Nance: "That's too damned long to go *without* a strike!"[20] Clearly, there was a fundamental difference in approach to labor policy. In March, 1955, Hoffman sent Nance a long letter instructing him like a schoolboy:

> It is quite possible that Studebaker-Packard can win a place for itself by being a little Ford or GM, but in the case of Ford notably, and GM to some extent, workers are numbers...If we should decide as a matter of fundamental policy to make a living fact of the slogan "America's Friendliest Factory," we would, of course, have to treat our workers as people.
>
> To succeed in making it this kind of company and to have the company recognized for what it is, your personality must be projected to your associates in management, our workers, our union officials, our union bargaining committee, our dealers and our

customers...There is still confusion in the organization as to what it is you are really seeking. It is my impression that our union officials and many of our workers believe that the company is no longer interested in them as human beings, that from now on they will be regarded simply as "labor" and dealt with as natural antagonists...There is, I believe, a great urgency to get under way with a program for communicating to all Studebaker-Packard people the kind of company you want Studebaker-Packard to become.[21]

It would be easy to make fun of Hoffman for the thoughts expressed in this letter. After all, it was his misguided efforts to create "America's Friendliest Factory" that saddled Studebaker with the excessive and unjustifiable labor rates that, according to one estimate, had cost the company a penalty of $30 million since the end of the war and had brought it to the brink of bankruptcy. To his credit, treating workers as human beings was a farsighted approach in that era. (It is by no means a universal practice even today.) Still, there is more than one way to abuse your work force. As the early labor leader, Samuel Gompers, once noted, "the greatest crime against the working man is a company that fails to turn a profit." Everything the workers desire must, of necessity, come from a company's profits. Hoffman tried to express his concern for his workers, in part, by caving-in to unreasonable wage demands and work rules that, ultimately, hurt the workers because they were more than the company could afford to pay. If Nance, who, in fact, had a reputation for caring a great deal about people, was being a hardnose in this case, perhaps it was because he had to correct—and very quickly and under the worst possible circumstances—the results of years of Hoffman's ill-considered "friendliness."

The tension between the people in Detroit and those in South Bend was almost palpable. The latter would come to refer to the 1954-56 period derisively as "the Packard Operation," and there was enough truth to the assertion to understand why. Hoffman and Vance had been shunted aside, while Nance ran the show with the help of key players, such as Grant, who were largely drawn from the Packard side. The new corporation was organized with semi-autonomous Studebaker and Packard divisions, but a general manager for the new Studebaker Division wasn't selected until August, 1955, when Harold Churchill, Studebaker's well-regarded chief engineer, finally got the nod. Packard people privately complained about the thinness of the executive talent available in South Bend, while Studebaker people felt as if they were living in an occupied country. Much of this was inevitable given the nature of the situation, but none of it helped the cause.

Meanwhile, the product continued to demand attention. The 1955 Studebakers were always intended to be an evolutionary development of the 1953-series design, but what the Loewy people came up with involved very little in the way of changes—entirely too little, in fact, in the view of Studebaker-Packard management. With sales collapsing, Studebaker's sales staff, in particular, pushed hard for more chrome and flash to bring the product more in line with what Detroit was offering. Since 1952, and in the face of plummeting sales, South Bend had done a complete turnabout in that regard, from wanting to be different to having an almost frantic eagerness to ape the Big Three in every detail. The chrome was only part of it; in the middle of the model run, a great deal of time and money was spent revising the windshield to give it the "wrap-around" look suddenly in vogue with the rest of the industry.

The entire Studebaker line for 1955 has come in for a great deal of criticism by modern-day writers and enthusiasts who contend that they were over-chromed and completely destroyed the beautiful concept of the Loewy design. There is some truth to this—at least to the extent that the Loewy design *was* put through a wringer—but, at least by prevailing Detroit standards, the chrome was applied with a fair degree of deftness and the line needed *something* new to attract buyers in a year in which many of Studebaker's most powerful competitors were offering entirely new products. If what was done failed to provide the answer, this writer has seen no evidence that the Loewy proposals, which involved thinly reworked rehashes of the 1953-54 look, were any better.

There was one new Studebaker model of some interest: the Speedster. It started out as a short run of twenty or so color-and-trim cars to add spice to the auto shows, but so much attention was attracted that it was made a mid-year offering. Most of these cars were done in blatant two-tone color schemes of lemon yellow and lime green, or three-toned riots of pink, white

1955 Studebaker President with, left to right, Vance, Nance and Hoffman.

and gray, but the Speedster also featured a beautifully crafted interior with an especially lovely faux engine-turned instrument panel. It made for a very appealing package and, although only 2,215 were built, it garnered much favorable publicity and was the genesis for the successful Hawk series that was to appear the following year.

Despite the concerted efforts of Hoffman, Grant and Nance, though, Studebaker still lost millions on the 138,472 cars and trucks that were built in 1955. Packard lost money, too, thanks to the start-up costs on Conner Avenue, but the real disaster was the flood of red ink washing through South Bend. In the end, Studebaker-Packard posted a staggering $29.7 million loss for the year, overall.

Yet, Studebaker was losing more than money. Its market share was collapsing, as well. True, volume slumped only slightly for the calendar year, but the industry as a whole was up sharply in what turned out to be the all-time best model year up to that time, so the Studebaker results represented a dramatic loss in market share for the third year in a row. The stark reality was that Studebaker's market penetration was barely one-third of what it had been as recently as 1952.

To be sure, there were external factors that greatly complicated Studebaker's position, such as the sudden end of the postwar seller's market and the Ford Blitz, that hurt all of the independent manufacturers. Yet, of the four major independent producers, Studebaker's loss between 1953 and 1955 was the most severe and Studebaker was the only one to post an actual decline in total registrations between 1954 and 1955.

Still, all of it can't have been Studebaker's fault. The actual registration figures for 1953-55 reveal another disturbing factor at work:

MAKE	1953	1954	1955	1954 vs 1953	1955 vs 1954	1955 vs 1953
Hudson	66,797	35,824	43,212	-46.4%	+20.6%	-35.3%
Nash	137,507	82,729	93,541	-39.8%	+13.1%	-32.0%
Packard	71,079	38,396	52,103	-46.0%	+35.7%	-26.7%
Studebaker	161,257	95,914	95,761	-40.5%	-0.2%	-40.6%
TOTAL	436,640	252,863	284,617	-42.1%	+12.6%	-34.8%
INDUSTRY	5,735,902	5,535,464	7,169,908	-3.5%	+29.5%	+25.0%

Compared to the other independents, Studebaker did slightly better than average in 1954 (compared to 1953, which, of course, was a disastrous

1955 Studebaker Speedster.

year in South Bend to start with), and somewhat worse than average in 1955 (compared to 1954). What is truly disturbing, however, is how poorly they did as a group. In 1954, the industry as a whole was down barely 3.5 percent, but the independents fell a whopping 42 percent. Furthermore, very little of this was recouped in 1955. While the industry showed a 25 percent gain in 1955 (compared to 1953), the independents were still down 35 percent as a group over the same period. To put it another way, if the independents as a group had done as well as the industry as a whole, they would have sold nearly twice as many cars in 1955 as they actually did. Clearly there was more going on here than Studebaker's own failings.

Whatever the causes, the mounting financial losses made any remedial action in South Bend increasingly difficult. In retrospect, it is amazing that there was a new Studebaker at all for 1956. As the 1955 model year began, Nance was still planning his remarkably ambitious program for 1957 that would have included a full range of new Studebaker and Packard cars built off one, highly interchangeable body shell. Within weeks, however, Studebaker was dropped from this program under a new "one plus" plan. Accordingly, the 1957 Studebakers would be facelifted yet again from the 1953 shell, while only the Clippers and Packards would be new.

Meanwhile, Loewy's staff in South Bend was hard at work on the 1956 Studebaker facelift, but what they were developing didn't sit well with Nance, or with Hoffman and Vance, either. As fate would have it, it was at just this time that Loewy's contract came up for renewal and Nance took the opportunity to effect a parting of the ways. It is unclear if this involved a "kill fee" of $1 million, as some sources have contended, but the annual fee for the services of Loewy and his associates was known to be running at that level. Nance may have been motivated in part by a desire to save on design costs, but he was genuinely disenchanted with Loewy's work. The "European" styling of the 1953-series Studebakers was getting most of the blame for the poor sales of those cars and the proposed 1956 facelift seemed to Nance to be more of the same. The Loewy-Studebaker-Packard relationship had become increasingly contentious as a result.

To replace Loewy, Duncan McRae was hired away from Ford and ordered to beef-up the in-house styling department in South Bend. His first job was to begin the process of getting rid of the Loewy people, then he

1956 Studebaker President Classic.

started building his team and got to work on a desperate effort to make the 1953 body shell do battle in an industry in which the smaller, narrower Studebakers had almost ceased to be viable competitors. In the end, McRae and his team, headed by Vince Gardner, worked a minor miracle. The 1956 Studebaker range was visually new and entirely up to date in most of its styling elements, although the size and configuration of the basic package was not—could not be—altered. Recalled Loewy stylist, Bob Bourke:

> Vince could do anything with his hands. He was pretty much a loner, but when fired up he'd put roller skates on his feet. Vince modeled the front and rear of the 1956 Studebaker sedans. He created a very nice, squared-off desk and a clean grille, and carried over the two flanking grilles from earlier designs. He worked like hell. Compared to [Loewy's] billings what he asked was next to nothing—about $7,500.[22]

The new Hawk series, which represented the final styling work performed by the Loewy staff, replaced the Speedster, although it was a more ambitious continuation of the same basic concept. The Hawks alone among 1956 Studebakers were relatively unchanged from the old look, which, wittingly or not, gave them a distinct identity from the rest of the line.

There were no less than four different Hawks offered: Flight, Power, Sky and Golden. All sported Mercedes-esque grilles. The Golden Hawk, at the top of the range, also featured the Packard V8. As a result, the Golden Hawk was very fast and very nose heavy, the handling being universally criticized by the motoring press. Still, it was widely regarded as the most impressive car in the Studebaker stable.[23]

Mechanically, 1956 was the year the Studebaker V8 reached its final stage of practical development. Bored out to 289 cubic inches, it remained, in that form, the work horse of the Studebaker car line for most of the remainder of the brand's existence. On the downside, the automatic transmission situation was a mess. The company had been buying its own unique automatics from Borg-Warner, but no longer had sufficient volume to justify the manufacturing costs. So, a cheaper, off-the-shelf unit was used on all 1956 models except the Golden Hawk, which used Packard's Ultramatic. But, Ultramatic was in the same boat. As the months ticked by in 1955, it became increasingly doubtful whether the Ultramatic facility could be justified and eventually the decision was made to shut it down after the 1956 model run. As a result, all Studebakers and Packards would be reduced to using store-bought transmissions for 1957.

1956 Studebaker Golden Hawk.

As the cash situation worsened, many interesting engineering ideas fell by the wayside. There was a rush toward fuel injection throughout the industry. Studebaker's engineering staff was working on a Bosch and Simmonds system, but work was stopped for lack of development money. The same fate befell programs to develop aluminum brake drums, disc brakes, and rack-and-pinion steering. Increasingly, Studebaker engineers were faced with having to make do with what they already had.

The most intriguing might-have-beens were a couple of engineering proposals from Porsche. Porsche has always been famed with the general public for its sports cars, but, within the industry, it has also been known for its consulting work for other manufacturers. In 1953 or 1954, it had undertaken a prototype for a possible Studebaker sedan. Known within Studebaker-Packard as the "Z-87" car, it used a 120-degree V6 engine and four-wheel-independent suspension.[24] The engine was designed to be either air- or water-cooled. A running prototype was built and shipped to South Bend for testing, but met with a decidedly cool reception. A report was prepared by Studebaker-Packard engineering under the aegis of the director of experimental engineering, John Z. DeLorean.[25] The report was highly critical of everything about the car that was distinctively European:

> Some excessive vertical shake was noted...There still remains considerable lateral movement and rear-end steering, with undesirable amounts of oversteer noted in moderate to hard cornering. There is uneven tire wear...The car steers quickly, but hard, and requires constant attention and correction for road wander. Crosswinds and slippery spots make driving tedious and rather dangerous...The radiator, grille, hood and deck slopes are quite steep and not in keeping with current American boxy-styling. The car is full width but rather short...It appears small and bug-like due to the sloping hood and squeezed-in rear fender treatment...This vehicle has a large amount of technical appeal, but a number of items need refinement to increase its overall appeal as a small car to the average American car buyer...The 1956 Champion or Commander is preferred to the Porsche [Z-87] for American driving...[26]

So, as might have been predicted, the Z-87 went nowhere. Porsche also proposed a compact car much like the "square-back" Volkswagen that was built in the latter 1960s. It, too, failed to spark much interest.

Also discussed in the winter of 1954-55 was a plan to assemble Volkswagen vans at Hamilton, Ontario. They were already being assembled under license in Studebaker's Belgian export assembly plant. Roger Bremer, in South Bend's product planning staff, recommended them to Nance for North American assembly, but, in the crisis year of 1955, the proposal got buried under the mounting debris and was never heard from again. Nance simply had too many other things on his mind.

As the New Year dawned in 1956, the situation at Studebaker-Packard was becoming increasingly desperate. Now, everything depended upon the dramatic new line of Clippers and Packards that were slated to be introduced in the fall using a common body shell. The projected tab was $50 million and a temporary finance committee was formed to negotiate the loan, headed by J. Russell Forgan, a long-time member of Studebaker's board of directors.

The first sign of the approaching crisis came in January when the committee met with strong resistance from the insurance companies that had been backing the corporation. Technically, Studebaker-Packard had a line of credit from which it could draw and all of Nance's plans assumed the availability of these funds. Their denial thus came as a terrible shock. Suddenly, Studebaker-Packard faced insolvency.

Overnight, the finance committee was transformed into a rescue committee and began exploring ways to save the company. Its first recommendation was to delay the launch of the new models and, in order to hold the Packard dealer body together, to facelift the 1956 Clipper as a stop-gap 1957 series to keep things going until the "real" 1957 models made it to production. This plan was soon abandoned as unworkable.

Finally, Ernst & Ernst, an industry consulting firm, was brought in for the purpose of preparing a detailed series of recommendations for consideration. Its report was ready in early April and consisted of three plausible options. The first called for moving Packard and Clipper production to South Bend, with the Studebaker continuing on the old body, the new Clipper being delayed until April, 1957, and the new Packard coming on stream in the fall of 1958 as a 1959 model. The second proposal called for dropping Packard entirely or trying to sell the brand to some other car company, although any suggestions as to who might be interested in such a purchase were notable by their absence. The third proposal called for the complete liquidation of the company, with an estimated cost of at least $45 million.

Nance was unwilling to consider any of these options at that point and began a frenetic personal campaign to enlist the help of other industrial companies, and not necessarily limiting his search to those in the auto industry, either. To be sure, General Motors, Ford and Chrysler were all approached, but so were International Harvester, Litton Industries, Textron, General Dynamics and Curtiss-Wright. The latter firms were all major defense contractors. One insurance company offered to make money available to Studebaker-Packard—if General Motors would guarantee the loan. GM declined. Ford was uninterested because it already had its plate full with the coming Edsel program, although it did offer to discuss selling the current Lincoln body dies to Packard when Lincoln was through with them in the summer of 1957. With that in mind, Nance set Packard's chief designer, Richard Teague, to work on 1957-58 Packards using the Lincoln dimensions. At the same time, McRae set about working up something similar with Studebaker sharing the new 1957 Ford shell. Nothing came of either project in the end. Meanwhile, Tex Colbert at Chrysler responded in terse fashion to Nance's approach. In a letter dated April 20th, he stated:

> When we examine our own situation, forward planning and the effects on Chrysler's corporate structure, we are unable to see any way that the merger or acquisition that you propose could be fitted into our plans to the mutual advantage of our companies and their stockholders.[27]

Washington was approached, as well. Defense Secretary Wilson refused to get involved, as did Treasury Secretary George Humphrey.[28]

Nance's desperation grew when he considered the dealer situation. Studebaker-Packard had had 2,178 dealers at the end of 1954, but only 1,523 of them remained by February, 1956, and they were jumping ship at the rate of 40-50 per month. Worse, this number included a disproportionate share of the better outlets, i.e., the ones that had other franchise options. At about this time, word reached Nance that Lincoln-Mercury was targeting Studebaker-Packard's best dealers. Nance sent a strong letter of protest and Lincoln-Mercury denied the allegation, but the attrition continued.

Studebaker-Packard stockholders were also becoming alarmed (as well they might have been) and Nance tried to reassure them:

> I am sure that you will recognize that premature public dis-cussion could seriously jeopardize plans. [We] have faced unusual difficulties, undertaken tasks with seemed overwhelming and car-ried on in trying circumstances with a degree of business and tech-nical competence, loyalty and devotion to duty which will prob-ably never be fully realized.[29]

In May, yet another study arrived, this one from Robert Heller & Asso-ciates. It recommended the liquidation of Studebaker-Packard and put the cost at a whopping $108 million. On the books, the company was only worth about $100 million. It is interesting to note that all of the plans that had come along had suggested either complete liquidation of, or some sort of semi-liquidation of, the autonomous Packard division. It was generally felt, apparently, that Studebaker, with its high volume potential, was the only truly viable division. Yet, Packard might have survived had it not gotten itself embroiled in the mess in South Bend. Now Packard was being written off and it was Studebaker that was getting the second chance. One wonders if Nance lay awake nights contemplating the irony of this.

Faced with the unspeakable situation that confronted them, Nance and the other members of Studebaker-Packard's board grasped desperately at the only proposal that offered any hope of salvation. This one had arrived on May 8th from Curtiss-Wright and, on its strength, Studebaker-Packard was able to negotiate a ninety day loan of $15.3 million from the banks in order to keep the company going while discussions continued.

In fact, the eleventh hour drama involved not only Curtiss-Wright Corporation, but (belatedly) the Eisenhower Administration and, most curiously of all, Daimler-Benz AG, the German manufacturer of Mercedes-Benz cars. How these three disparate players came to take an interest in

Studebaker-Packard is probably worth a book in itself, but it is easiest to make sense out of the tale if we begin with Daimler-Benz.

Daimler-Benz had had a long, if episodic, career in the United States. Benz vehicles were certainly sold in America in the 1890s, but it was Daimler, that made the first big score when American rights to Daimler vehicles were sold to the Steinway piano family in 1888.[30] Nothing much came of that, however, and Mercedes and Benz cars were seen only sporadically, with an estimated 560 Mercedes and Benz cars, combined, shipped to North America between 1901 and the outbreak of the First World War in 1914. Daimler (which later sold its cars under the Mercedes nameplate) and Benz were merged in 1927 to form Daimler-Benz AG, at which time the car became known as the Mercedes-Benz. Following the merger, the Mercedes-Benz Company was organized as a factory-owned distribution arm in the United States. Even then, perhaps as few as 200 Mercedes-Benz cars wound-up on these shores before the outbreak of World War II. In this period, Mercedes-Benz had a big reputation in America with the moneyed set—one that far outstripped the numbers of cars sold—but it was not until after the war that Daimler-Benz began to think in serious terms about shipping large volumes of cars to the United States.

There were various reasons why Daimler-Benz finally cast its gaze toward this side of the Pond, but the main one was the size and vibrancy of the American market, which far outstripped the sales potential of any other market in the world in the years immediately following the war, Europe included. So, in 1950, Daimler-Benz entered into discussions with—who else?—Maxie Hoffman.

In April, 1951, Hoffman was granted U.S. distribution rights.[31] A brilliant salesman, he seems to have shown a particular flair for cultivating big-name customers for Mercedes-Benz cars. Within a short period of time, the list included Bing Crosby, Marilyn Monroe, Zsa Zsa Gabor, Eddie Fisher and announcer Don Wilson (The Jack Benny Show, etc.). Hoffman hired no less a figure than Frank Lloyd Wright to design a showroom on New York City's posh Park Avenue, the first such automotive emporium in that exclusive part of town.

Despite his successes, however, Daimler-Benz was soon disenchanted with the way Hoffman treated his dealers (of whom there were perhaps forty by 1955), his run-of-the-mill customers and, most importantly, the factory back in Stuttgart. Hoffman personally owned the key showrooms in New York City, Chicago and Los Angeles, and more-or-less let the rest of the country fend for itself. He also took most of the profit on cars distributed through his dealers, leaving them with little incentive to market or service the product. In addition, Hoffman flatly refused to distribute the wide range of Daimler-Benz products other than cars: trucks, industrial engines and so forth. Recalled Heinz "Happy" Hoppe, who was to play a key role in the history of Mercedes-Benz in North America:[32]

> The customers suffered badly from Hoffman's sales structure, which landed them with a luxury automobile but offered them no prospects of reliable servicing for it. Daimler-Benz AG in Germany suffered, too, as its products' good reputation at the time of sale began to deteriorate because of poor maintenance. A flood of complaints soon set in, criticizing poor spare parts availability and servicing errors, but also warranty claim problems. All this led to continual disputes between Stuttgart and New York.[33]

Hoppe had been detailed in the latter months of 1954 by Carl F. Giese, his boss in Stuttgart, to open a U.S. office to market those Daimler-Benz products not being sold by Hoffman. The result was the creation of Daimler-Benz North America (DBNA). Although it was unsaid at the time, Stuttgart also hoped in time to find some pretext for yanking the cars away from Hoffman and giving them to Hoppe's new organization. Doing so, however, posed a host of problems. Hoppe recalled:

> Daimler-Benz AG still had no clear picture at that time of the best way to organize its American business affairs. There was anxiety, too, about tackling the American market alone, where the practices were quite different from those normally adopted at headquarters, where European thinking predominated. For psychological, financial and staff reasons, there was a certain reluctance to "go it alone" on this overseas market only ten years after the end of the war.[34]

In flailing around with the problem, Giese focused on several potential distribution partners, most notably United Aircraft, General Electric and Curtiss-Wright. Giese wanted a "non-standard" partner that could also distribute the other products made by Daimler-Benz, but United Aircraft and General Electric soon opted out of the negotiations, citing their lack of familiarity with the automobile business. That left Curtiss-Wright, which, as noted, was a major American defense contractor. In fact, Curtiss-Wright had voiced the same objection, but it was interested in a link-up with Daimler-Benz in order to secure cooperation with Stuttgart's expertise in aircraft engines and other items that might prove useful to its defense business. The cars, insofar as Curtiss-Wright was concerned, were something else entirely.

Roy Hurley.

Curtiss-Wright was headed by Roy Hurley. Brash, impulsive and a born wheeler-dealer, Hurley was as close to a self-made man as one could have found in American industry at the time. After stints in manufacturing positions with both Bendix and Ford, he took charge of Curtiss-Wright in 1949. The old-line manufacturer of aircraft components was a solid, if dull, pillar of the defense establishment whose best years were seemingly behind it. By 1956, however, Hurley had quadrupled sales and was beginning to diversify the company's operations. Still, it appeared that going into the car business was beyond anything even he had in mind.

Yet, suddenly Hurley did a complete about face and, if rumors rampant at the time can be believed, the explanation was that the Eisenhower Administration had gotten into the act. Suffering from a predictable case of the election year shakes, so the story goes, the Administration had belatedly come to its senses regarding the frightening ramifications of a Studebaker-Packard collapse and put pressure on Curtiss-Wright, using as leverage that company's myriad defense contracts. There is also evidence that Daimler-Benz played a key role, if only to spur Hurley's new-found interest in Studebaker-Packard from a point of view of a potential amalgamation with Mercedes-Benz cars. Indeed, Hoppe was certain that Hurley used the possible Daimler-Benz link-up as a negotiating tactic with Studebaker-Packard's lenders long before the deal with Daimler-Benz was signed. However it happened, overnight Curtiss-Wright had become very popular, indeed, and very interested in the car business.

Eventually, Hurley agreed to give Studebaker-Packard a quick capital infusion of $35 million in exchange for long-term leases on certain Studebaker-Packard facilities and the remnants of the Studebaker-Packard defense contracts. Hurley also assumed effective control, which allowed Curtiss-Wright to tap into some of the tax advantages of using Studebaker-Packard mounting losses against Curtiss-Wright's profits. Finally, Curtiss-Wright was given a generous stock option that would have enabled it to buy a controlling interest in Studebaker-Packard at fire-sale prices later on if the company could be turned around. The terms were stiff, but not unreasonable considering that Studebaker-Packard was effectively bankrupt.

1956 Packard Patrician.

The deal was accepted in principle on May 28th, formally signed on July 26th and was slated to take effect on September 1st.

Hurley's decision to discontinue Packard operations in Detroit in favor of the relatively high volume production in South Bend had been made known weeks before the formal ratification of the agreement. As a result, production in Detroit ended on June 25th. Forty-two cars were built that day, twenty-four Clippers and eighteen Packards.

Nance informed the board of his decision to resign as soon as Curtiss-Wright took over. Harold Churchill, the general manager of the Studebaker Division, was elected to replace him. It seemed a logical move. Most of Nance's key people had already left for greener pastures and the South Bend operations were, effectively, the totality of the company now. Nance then stayed on for another month or so without pay, working feverishly to find jobs throughout the industry for key Packard people.[35]

In later years, Nance was to become a favorite whipping boy for both Studebaker and Packard loyalists. Much of this was probably inevitable; somebody had to catch the blame. Yet, by any objective standard, Nance did remarkably well with the frighteningly bad hand he'd been dealt. As automotive historian, Richard Langworth, has noted:

> In assessing the Nance period at Studebaker, one must bear in mind the monumental problems it presented, no matter who was president. Nance was beset on all sides—by labor used to being coddled, by two managements wary of each other, by out-of-date products, by demoralized dealers, by inefficient, high-overhead plants. He was also deprived of the hook-up he expected with American Motors. But, above all, Nance...was thwarted by lack of the most essential commodity—money.[36]

In November, 1956, Nance, whose reputation as a manager and marketing expert was still intact, was hired by Ford Motor Company as corporate vice-president in charge of marketing. Within a year, he was reassigned to head the Lincoln-Mercury Division. A few months later, in the wake of the Edsel fiasco, this division was reconstituted as the Mercury-Edsel-Lincoln Division (M-E-L, for short). He, thus, found himself reliving a night-

James Nance during his Ford years.

mare as he endured the thankless challenge of burying yet another failed brand. He left Ford in August, 1958, reportedly after losing out in a corporate power struggle with Robert S. McNamara, who became Ford's president a few months later. By all accounts, Nance was delighted to be out of the car business. Eventually, he made a big success in a new career as a banker in Cleveland and that was where he spent the rest of his business life. As he noted in an interview in the 1970s:

> I welcomed the opportunity to run a bank. You can't do anything without money. Sooner or later everybody ends up at the bank.[37]

It was a lesson Churchill would learn soon enough.

Notes

The most important resources drawn upon in the writing of this chapter include, from the Studebaker side, Richard M. Langworth's *Studebaker, 1946-1966.* and, from the Packard side, Beverly R. Kimes' *Packard: A History of the Motorcar and the Company* and James Ward's *The Fall of the Packard Motor Car Company.* Further insights into the Packard side and into the career of James Nance were provided by the author's interview with Richard H. Stout. Heinz C. Hoppe's *Serving the Star Around the World* gave valuable insights into the important connection between Studebaker-Packard and Daimler-Benz, on the one hand, and Studebaker-Packard and Curtiss-

Wright, on the other. Studebaker-Packard papers in the author's collection provided still more material. Periodicals that proved to be important resources included various issues of *Car Collector, Motor Life, Motor Trend* and *Special-Interest Autos*.

[1] The Duryea Motor Wagon Company.

[2] General Motors, Ford, Chrysler, Studebaker, Packard, Nash, Hudson, and Willys-Overland. Graham and Hupmobile were on their last legs, although Graham would become the nucleus for Henry Kaiser's ambitious early postwar effort to crack the market. By the time Kaiser had acquired Willys in 1953, he was ready to throw in the towel on passenger cars. Profitable Jeep production continued until that operation was sold to American Motors in 1970.

[3] Interestingly, not even Mason seems to have had any interest in merging with the brash and eccentric Henry Kaiser.

[4] Kimes, p. 558.

[5] Studebaker-Packard papers, author's collection.

[6] American Motors officially came into being on May 1, 1954, as a result of a merger between Hudson and Nash. It was, in turn, acquired by Chrysler in the late 1980s.

[7] It was a sign of the times that the interior designers used for advertising purposes were all women. Fabrics and colors were considered "women's work" in that era. In fact, nearly all of the auto company designers were men, including those specializing in interior design, but, when the publicity mill started grinding, a member of the "fairer" sex was invariably trotted out.

[8] "It was my worst mistake," he later admitted.

[9] Langworth p. 74.

[10] Langworth, pp. 74-75.

[11] The actual stock transaction was complicated by the huge number of Packard shares outstanding: 14,491,340. These shares were consolidated into 6,440,455, which also became the total number of shares outstanding in the new Studebaker-Packard Corporation. A total of 2,898,268 of these shares were distributed to Packard stockholders on a five-for-one basis for shares in the new company. In other words, 100 shares of the old Packard stock was worth 20 shares in Studebaker-Packard. The remaining 3,542,187 shares went to Studebaker stockholders on a one-and-a-half-for-one basis: 100 shares of Studebaker brought 150 shares of Studebaker-Packard. Former Studebaker stockholders in this way controlled 55% of Studebaker-Packard.

[12] Studebaker had built 304,994 cars and trucks in 1949, and 334,554 in 1950.

[13] This was the same Charles Wilson who gained notoriety for his comment, "What's good for General Motors is good for America." Perhaps...but what

was "good" for America in this instance played havoc with Studebaker-Packard.
[14] At one time, Briggs had been a major supplier to Ford, as well. The Lincoln-Zephyr (1936-48), for example, had been built almost entirely by Briggs, with Lincoln supplying only the chassis and powerplant. By the time Walter Briggs died, though, Ford had taken its body production in-house. Briggs' heirs probably assumed that Chrysler would eventually want to do the same, hence another reason to sell-out to Chrysler while they still had a business to sell.
[15] At least Nance didn't have to pay cash for the Conner Avenue facility. It was taken-over on a lease-purchase arrangement.
[16] Studebaker-Packard papers, author's collection.
[17] Studebaker-Packard papers, author's collection.
[18] Kimes, p. 581.
[19] Langworth, p. 83.
[20] Langworth, p. 76
[21] Langworth, p. 77.
[22] Langworth, p. 81.
[23] Until you entered a fast corner!
[24] The Porsche internal designation was the Type 542.
[25] Yes, the same John DeLorean who later built the sports car.
[26] Langworth, p. 69.
[27] Studebaker-Packard papers, author's collection.
[28] It is interesting that the government didn't exhibit the same reluctance to lend a hand to Lockheed and Chrysler a few years later.
[29] Studebaker-Packard papers, author's collection.
[30] In 1898, most of the stock in the Daimler Manufacturing Company, as the Steinway-owned company was then known, was sold to General Electric. It was not until 1905, however, that the first complete Mercedes car was built in America in a factory at Steinway, Long Island—significantly, in the factory town built up around the Steinway piano works—and perhaps 60-100 were made before the factory burned down in February, 1907. Production was never restarted. The sole surviving American Mercedes now sits in the lobby of the Mercedes-Benz USA (MBUSA) headquarters in Montvale, New Jersey.
[31] Excepting only Alaska and Puerto Rico.
[32] Pronounced hop´-ee.
[33] Hoppe, p.64
[34] Hoppe, p. 67.
[35] John DeLorean was one. He was hired by Pontiac.
[36] Studebaker-Packard papers, author's collection.
[37] Studebaker-Packard papers, author's collection.

Overleaf, the Champ truck final assembly line in the latter months of 1960.

NINE

The Lark Ascendant

Harold Churchill was a long-time Studebaker loyalist. He had been one of the men who engineered the 1939 Champion and the World War II Weasel. The chassis Studebaker was still using was largely his work and, since 1955, he had been general manager of Studebaker Division. A modest man who enjoyed farming as a hobby, he formed a stark contrast to the fairly flamboyant characters who had run Studebaker for the previous half-century. Commented *Time* magazine:

> Unlike other auto chief executives, Churchill does not compete as a super salesman or financial whiz. He came up as an old-time, dirty-fingernail mechanic who still loves to tinker under an open hood.[1]

It wasn't just the personality of the president that had changed, though; the nature of the company had undergone a fundamental alteration. Throughout its history, Studebaker had been run by strong-willed men who were in the habit of dictating to their boards. To be sure, most companies have boards of directors that are little more than somnolent watchdogs, bestirring themselves occasionally to make appropriate noises for the sake of appearances, but remaining very much under the control of the chairman or president. This is the natural order of things (and is certainly the way any company's top officers would prefer to have it). When the

Harold Churchill.

Studebaker brothers ran the shop, they *were* the board, for all practical purposes. When Fred Fish came along, it was as a member of the family through marriage and he slipped into the presidency with scarcely a ripple. This might have been expected to change when the company went public in 1911, or at least when Erskine—the first outsider—became president in 1915. But, it didn't. Erskine ran the show like a benevolent despot—*usually* benevolent— and was only forced to kowtow to the board on one recorded occasion: in 1917, when he had to promise old J. M. Studebaker that the new automobile plant he had in mind would be built in South Bend. His successors, Hoffman and Vance, labored under the thumb of a court-appointed receiver for two long years, but then matters returned to normal. After 1948, when Hoffman began to devote his attentions to government service, Vance controlled the company as autocratically as Erskine ever had.

As the period of the receivership demonstrated, it is generally when a company is in financial trouble that its chief officers find their mastery of the domain challenged. Alas for Churchill, that was decidedly the case in the summer of 1956, and the remaining years of Studebaker's career as an auto producer were destined to be a tale filled with constant contention between president, board and outside lenders. Studebaker in its prime had always been a one- or two-man show; Studebaker in its decline became an industrial soap opera replete with chronic turmoil, heroes and villains, often bitter factionalism, and enormous frustration and uncertainty for those ostensibly in charge.

Now, Nance, Hoffman and Vance were off the board. Hurley, of course, was on. So, too, was Churchill along with his hand-picked deputies: A. J.

Porta (finance) and Sidney Skillman (sales). Hugh Ferry, the former Packard president, remained and a few others rounded out the cast of characters as the curtain rose on Studebaker's next act.

Churchill and Hurley were in agreement on the general direction Studebaker should take: niche marketing in the manner of American Motors. They were also of one mind with regard to Packard, for neither had any idea what to do other than that the Detroit-based Packard operation was dead. Beyond that, Churchill was hoping to keep the company afloat until something turned up—preferably Hurley's decision to exercise his stock option and merge Studebaker-Packard with Curtiss-Wright, for Studebaker-Packard desperately needed *somebody's* deep pockets. Hurley, on the other hand, seems to have been largely concerned with his new defense business and, conversely, not to have had much interest in Studebaker-Packard's automotive operations beyond occasional meddling and growling to reporters that if Churchill didn't turn things around pretty soon "a lotta people will just get fired."[2]

Churchill understood all-too-well the challenges that he faced, yet he possessed a deep faith that Studebaker could be saved and gamely set about doing his best. Under his leadership, a five-point plan for action was quickly developed for the beleaguered corporation and approved by the board:

1. Further reduction of costs of operations.
2. Disposal of [Packard] properties [in Detroit] and other surplus real estate holdings.
3. Establishment of Mercedes-Benz marketing organization.
4. Further development of our products to fit selective or less competitive markets.
5. Improvement of dealer organization and increase of sales of the corporation's cars and trucks.[3]

Everyone involved in the rescue operation of 1956 had written-off Packard. The only hope for the company was the relatively high volume potential that still existed in South Bend. Despite its capacity, though, Studebaker was far from being the most efficient manufacturer around, even after the blood-letting of the previous two-and-a-half years. Heinz

Hoppe of Daimler-Benz, who was to play a crucial supporting role in the unfolding drama, offered an illuminating outsider's view of Studebaker in the fall of 1956:

> In the first half of the 20th century, Studebaker had manufactured good, substantial passenger cars in the low and middle price brackets, but by [1956] its best times were definitely past...When I toured the automobile plant in September, 1956, we could see that the production methods were out of date.[4]

South Bend's nagging labor situation remained a critical obstacle to the company's survival. During one especially bad month in 1956, for example, the man-hours required to build a Studebaker soared as high as 200, or about twice the industry norm. From a high of perhaps a quarter-million units at the time of the merger, the break-even point was still stuck at an unrealistic 150,000 or so and Churchill was determined to force it down to a more manageable 80,000. Draconian cost cutting resulted in a drop in South Bend factory employment from 16,500 in 1956 to 8,000 in 1958—a feat accomplished, it must be emphasized, without a corresponding decline in Studebaker production.[5]

Nor did Churchill spare those at the top. He cut his own salary from $64,000—already unimpressive by Detroit standards—to $60,000 and slashed the executive payroll from $1.25 million to $350,000. Meanwhile, Packard assets in Detroit were liquidated at fire sale prices, both to eliminate on-going liabilities and to raise cash, and $3.5 million in Studebaker stamping work that had been sub-contracted was brought in-house. Expenses were drastically shaved as a result and the operating losses were diminished, but none of this addressed other fundamental problems: the loss of public confidence, the rapidly deteriorating dealer force, and the lack of a truly competitive product. Studebaker now had the image of a "loser," the high-quality outlets were fleeing and it was stuck face-lifting year-after-year a car that had never been very successful in the first place.

Total Studebaker sales in the nightmare year of 1956 slumped to 82,000 units, which could have been far worse, considering. Revenue came to $303 million, with a recorded loss of $43.3 million. That was bad enough, but special charge-offs and related expenses stemming from the closing of the Packard operations in Detroit cost another $60 million. On the other hand, a profit of nearly a million dollars had been recorded during November and December, and that served to bolster hopes for 1957. Still, even with the recent infusion from Curtiss-Wright, there wasn't money (or time) to do anything dramatic with the 1957 products. For months, the corporation's executives had been too busy fending off total disaster to give much thought to product planning and the plans they did develop usually became irrelevant almost as soon as the latest planning session adjourned.

As noted in the previous chapter, Nance's comprehensive concept of interchangeability between Studebaker, Clipper and Packard had first been pared back to the "one plus" plan that called for Clipper and Packard to share a new body, and for Studebaker to continue with a facelifted car derived from the 1953-series shell. Then, the fairly ambitious Studebaker redesign that Loewy's people had been working on in the early months of 1955 got scrapped along with Loewy and even Studebaker's stop-gap plans were thrown into turmoil. As for full interchangeability, it would have to wait until some unspecified point in the future when the company could afford it. Yet, fate—and finances—brought about interchangeability across the board a lot sooner than anyone would have imagined possible, for, with the Packard operations being liquidated in Detroit, everything built for the 1957 model year would now have to be facelifted off the existing Studebaker tooling.

Only minor changes were in evidence when the 1957 Studebakers were announced. Considering the disarray when they were in the works, however, any changes at all were surprising. The standard Studebaker line was freshened a bit and industry observers generally found the results pleasing. The most noticeable alterations, however, occurred in the Hawk range.

The 1957 Hawks are controversial with collectors. Some like them a lot, while some don't care for them much at all. The main cause for complaint with the nay-sayers are the tail fins bolted onto the rear fenders, but most contemporary accounts cited these models as being the best cars Studebaker built that year. At the top of the range was, as before, the Golden Hawk, while the collection of lesser Hawks at the bottom were replaced with a single model, the Silver Hawk.

1957 Studebaker Golden Hawk.

In mid-year, a special Golden Hawk 400 was added, featuring a beautifully-appointed leather interior in a monochromatic color scheme, which was quite unusual in a gaudy era noted for three-tone paint jobs and chaotic interior treatments. The "400" designation was reportedly chosen to indicate the low volume planned—i.e., only 400 units, although there are doubts even that many were actually built—but it was probably also a tip of the hat to the old top-of-the-line Packard series of the same designation.

Perhaps the best development with the Hawks, though, was under the hood. Because the Packard engine line was shutting down, it was necessary to revert to Studebaker engines. In the case of the Golden Hawk, this meant the 289 cubic inch V8. The 400 also came standard with a McCulloch supercharger (which was optional on the regular Golden Hawk) that raised horsepower output from 225 to about 275. Handling on the 1956 Golden Hawk had been dreadful owing to the weight of the Packard V8. Published road tests invariably noted that the 1957 editions were much better balanced driving cars.

Even more controversial than the Hawks were the "Packebakers"— the last-minute models cobbled together to keep the Packard name going. It was indicative of the incredible turmoil at Studebaker-Packard during the chaotic summer of 1956 that the decision that there should even *be* a 1957 Packard wasn't made by the board until August—in other words, until after 1957 models from competitive manufacturers were already in production and being shipped to the dealers. It has long been assumed that these cars were built in order to meet franchise requirements lest hundreds of former Packard dealers should decide to sue if they suddenly had no Packards to sell. There was probably some truth to this, although most of them were by then doing the bulk of their business with Studebakers, anyway. Yet, it was also true that there remained many within the company who hoped to see the big Packards return someday, so this decision should be understood at least in part as a stop-gap measure designed to keep the name alive until that could happen.

In any case, the 1957 Packard Clippers announced in the middle of the model run were all-too-clearly glorified Studebakers. Still, the amount of effort that went into them is even more astonishing than the effort that went into the Studebaker range. A great deal of work (and $1.1 million) was expended to make them at least *look* like Packards and, ironically, their exterior lines were very close to those of the design of what was supposed to have been the all-new 1957 Packards, albeit reduced in size and blended to conform to the Studebaker body. The instrument panel was copied from the 1955-56 Packard panel—although, of necessity, smaller and reconfigured to fit the Studebaker cowl—while the grille was done in the familiar Packard motif. Actual 1956 Clipper tail lights were fashioned into the rear fenders.

1957 Packard Clipper.

1957 models en route to dealers on a Studebaker car hauler.

Considering the crash nature of the program, the unsuitability of the Studebaker body, and the meager funds available, the results were fairly remarkable. The sales, were not, although the 5,000-odd units produced came pretty close to meeting the company's modest sales target. So, to that extent, the Packebaker must be considered at least a limited success.

Another last-minute idea proved to be much more significant, though: the low-buck Scotsman series. Basically a bottom-line Studebaker with all the trim removed and every possible piece of equipment deleted, it was designed to sell at the lowest price of any standard car line built in America. Windows featured rubber moldings to replace the stainless steel ones. Painted hub caps replaced the wheel covers. Even the grille was painted. The Scotsmans looked terribly plain, but sold surprisingly well, although one has to wonder how much money the company actually made off them. Never-the-less, they kept the line rolling, which was no inconsiderable accomplishment during those grim days, and a Scotsman half-ton pick-up truck was added later on. In addition, a Scotsman-related taxi cab was designed for fleet operators. Most important of all, though, it was the success of the Scotsman concept that got Churchill thinking seriously about the potential for a low-cost car of compact dimensions. Thus, the far more ambitious and important program that was to result in the 1959 Lark began with the Scotsman.

In the short run, Churchill pinned his hopes for new products on prospects of a deal between Daimler-Benz and Curtiss-Wright. As with all of Hurley's negotiations, this one seemed to drag on forever but it was at last signed on March 6, 1957. On that occasion, Hurley expansively promised his counterparts from Stuttgart:

> We, Curtiss-Wright, have supplied you with a ready-made sales network. Now all you have to do is sign on the dotted line and deliver 60,000 cars a year.[6]

It wasn't quite that simple, of course. Hurley's grandiose projection was based on the highly questionable assumption that every Studebaker-Packard dealer would sell two Mercedes-Benz cars each month, or 5,000 each month overall. In practice, most of the approximately 2,500 remaining Studebaker-Packard dealers were never given a Mercedes-Benz franchise. In 1957, only about 200 were allowed to sell the German marque and the number never rose above 430. Moreover, Maxie Hoffman had sold a mere 3,021 cars in all of 1956 and Stuttgart's entire output was then only

1957 Studebaker Commander.

about 80,000 cars per year. Still, the deal was attractive for the Germans and, most importantly, Carl Giese, Daimler-Benz's North American operative, wanted it. In one swoop, Mercedes-Benz cars would acquire a well-developed sales and service network throughout the United States.[7]

By this time, though, Hoppe, Giese's assistant, had become convinced that Giese was more concerned with building himself an empire in America and with fostering his own prerogatives than he was in advancing (or even protecting) the interests of Daimler-Benz. Giese, according to Hoppe, was imperious and dictatorial with subordinates and—more seriously—often failed to convey an accurate picture of situations to Stuttgart when doing so would lessen his own power over the American operations. Even with matters between Daimler-Benz and Curtiss-Wright moving decisively toward a conclusion, Hoppe was highly skeptical about the results Giese and Hurley were glibly predicting. Remarkably, he went so far as to try a risky eleventh-hour maneuver to head off the deal. He recalled:

> I persuaded Hans Klotz [Stuttgart's official negotiator], before the contract was signed, to visit Maxie Hoffman's imposing showroom on Park Avenue, and the dreary premises of the Studebaker dealer on 11th Avenue, to ponder the difference between them and work out for himself what was awaiting us after signing up with Studebaker.[8]

When Giese heard about the visit, he was furious and ordered Hoppe to stay away from New York City until the contract negotiations were concluded. The final deal effectively gave Curtiss-Wright importation rights to Mercedes-Benz cars for all of North America for fifteen years, the distribution to be handled by Studebaker-Packard exclusively through its dealers. A new company, Curtiss-Wright and Mercedes-Benz (CWMB) was created for the purpose, to be owned 60 percent by Curtiss-Wright and 40 percent by Daimler-Benz. Hurley would head CWMB, with Giese serving as his number two.

The agreement also gave CWMB rights to all Daimler-Benz licenses, patents and trademarks. The agreement, however, contained an escape clause that gave either party the right to terminate the agreement on Janu-

1958 Mercedes-Benz 300d.

ary 1, 1962, if CWMB sales had not, by then, reached $50 million per year.

Although it was unsaid at the time, one of the reasons Daimler-Benz was willing to assign rights for all licenses, patents and trademarks to CWMB was a nagging fear of political instability in Europe. In the wake of the Berlin blockade, the Hungarian uprising and left-wing political agitation in Western Europe, there were those in Stuttgart who wanted an insurance policy in the event Daimler-Benz was ever forced to leave Europe. If so, its future could continue in America.

In any case, notice of termination was given to Maxie Hoffman effective May 1, 1957, sparking yet another round of tortuous negotiations. During this phase, CWMB encountered unexpected hostility from equally unexpected quarters. Recalled Hoppe:

> Many customers, banks, and influential personalities in the USA were highly skeptical as to whether our expensive, top-quality passenger cars ought to be sold by the shaky manufacturer Studebaker, of all companies, with its unstable sales organization. This was precisely the view I had put forward. All too soon, it was to prove correct.[9]

The official sales plan agreed upon called for 43,000 Mercedes-Benz cars to be delivered to Studebaker during the period extending from April, 1957, to January, 1959. This number included 6,700 units of the top-end 300 sedan. The lack of reality inherent in this can be seen by the fact that worldwide sales of the 300 from 1957 until it went out of production in 1962 was a mere 3,152 units—or less than half the projected *annual* U.S. quota.

Total Mercedes-Benz sales in 1957 reached 3,150 units—only 129 more than Hoffman had sold the year before. Still, from Studebaker-Packard's perspective, the Mercedes-Benz marketing program immediately helped stem the flow of dealers, which at times had threatened to turn into a stampede. The downward trend in dealers bottomed out in October, 1957, and the number of Studebaker-Packard franchisees began to grow once again.

Over the summer, Hurley suddenly became enthused about the possibilities of another German car, the Goggomobil. This was the era when Volkswagen was soaring to prominence in America on the strength of its "Beetle"—the very car Studebaker had twice scorned—and this may have been what got Hurley thinking in that direction. Regardless, when Hurley became enthused Studebaker-Packard jumped, so Churchill was duly dispatched to Europe. There, he found a hopelessly inadequate sub-compact being built by a company that lacked the capacity to supply meaningful numbers of cars to Studebaker-Packard, anyway. So much for that.

Studebaker-Packard, for its part, had a roller-coaster year. Some months a little money was made, most months not. Net revenues slumped to $213.2 million in 1957, but the overall loss was brought way down, as well, and came in at a mere $11.1 million—bad enough, but comparative pocket change by the staggering standards of 1956. In part, this relatively encouraging news was a result of $17 million in overhead saved by Churchill's lay-offs in South Bend and Detroit. The corporation had to do a lot better than that, of course, but no one could deny that it was a huge improvement. In terms of model year production, Studebaker held up pretty well in a softening market with 74,738 cars being built. In his message to stockholders in March, 1958, Churchill concluded in a sober tone:

> Despite our progress, sales of passenger cars and trucks have not been up to expectations. At this writing, the automobile industry is feeling the effects of a nationwide business recession. Naturally, our program has been adversely effected by this widespread downturn in business. In my report to you a year ago, I stated that with continued improvement in our retail sales we could attain our goal of profitable operations. We have not attained this

goal. Management is exploring every possible avenue...The continuing cooperation of our employees and shareholders is appreciated.[10]

Despite its woes, the company was able to blaze a trail of sorts in the fall of 1957 when it became the first auto manufacturer to have a "stand alone" full-color advertising supplement in Sunday newspapers around the country. Touting the 1958 products range, the sixteen-page supplement was placed in newspapers with a combined circulation of sixteen million and copies of the supplement were supplied to Studebaker-Packard dealers for showroom distribution, as well.

The main subject of this novel promotion was the freshened 1958 Studebaker line. Duncan McRae, working with a ridiculously small budget, had somehow created an attractive new two-door hardtop roofline that was featured on both the Studebaker and Packard Clipper lines. In this, he had been heavily influenced by Virgil Exner's dramatic Chrysler "Forward Look" cars introduced the previous season, although he didn't copy them line-for-line as some writers have contended. (The difference in body dimensions alone would have rendered that impossible.) Less appealing quad head lamps were mounted at the front in keeping with the new industry styling rage. They looked odd, indeed, on the narrow Studebaker body, but were felt by management to be a requirement given the competitive demands of the marketplace. Recalled McRae:

> Since there was no money for fenders, we came up with a pod design that, looking back today, seems ridiculous. But, in the short period of time that was available, it seemed to give us something new-looking.[11]

Tail fins were added around back. As with the 1957 Hawks, they were bolt-on units and, as with the quad head lights, they were felt to be necessary in order to meet the competition but only served, once again, to emphasize the narrow Studebaker body. So, Studebaker was stuck in a no-win situation. If it retained its old look, it fell out of pace with competitive trends. If it moved to keep pace, the alterations only served to emphasize the basic lack of competitiveness of the body with which it was stuck.

As for the Hawk range, it remained virtually unchanged except for the 400, which was not revived, although the interior survived on a new Packard Hawk. The company scored a modest success with a new fleet vehicle: the Econ-O-Miler taxi cab. Derived from the Scotsman, the Econ-O-Miler quickly became the third-best-selling taxi in the large New York City fleet market. Studebaker trucks, now redubbed the "Haul of Fame" trucks, continued with few alterations and the production of military trucks continued at a rate of around 5,000 per year. The Defense Department was apparently determined to keep feeding the company defense contracts as a way of doing its share to boost its tottering finances. Better late than never.

The 1958 Packards proved to be the last to bear that once-great name and there were more than a few who wished the final effort had not been made. An oval grille had been decided upon at the insistence of Hurley, and it was featured on both the Clippers and the Hawk. Recalled McRae:

> [Hurley] had seen a Ferrari during one of his European trips and asked me to attempt to use the design theme on a Hawk. It was my opinion that we were doing a one-off special job for him, and I still believe that was the original intent.[12]

Somehow, though, the design ended up in production and came to be

1958 Studebaker President Starlite.

1958 Packard Hawk.

known around South Bend as the "Hurley" Hawk. The front end was described in various, more evocative, ways by the motoring press—"Ubangi-lipped," "fish-mouthed," etc.—none of them even remotely complimentary. The interior, as has been noted, was filched from the 1957 Golden Hawk 400, while the rear was mostly interchangeable with the 1958 Studebaker versions. Even there, however, someone couldn't leave well-enough alone. (McRae? Hurley?) The rear deck lid sported a fake wheel cover commonly referred to by automotive journalists as a "toilet seat." In short, the Packard Hawk was an answer to a question no one but Roy Hurley had asked or ever would. The standard models, featuring flashy new bolt-on tail fins and gaudier trim, were little better and barely 2,000 of the 1958 Packards of all types were built. It was a dismal end to the Packard story.[13]

In contrast, Mercedes-Benz sales at last seemed to be taking off. A total of 7,704 units were sold, a one-hundred-percent improvement over 1957. Despite this, Daimler-Benz was rapidly souring on the way its representation in America was being handled. Of those Studebaker-Packard franchisees who had been Packard dealers, there was some genuine ability to sell a car in the Mercedes-Benz class. The former Studebaker dealers, however, were, with few exceptions, proving to be utterly hopeless. Recalled Hoppe:

> Most Studebaker dealers had no idea how to tackle Mercedes-Benz sales. They had always operated at the lower end of the price

scale, with their premises in industrial and commercial areas...[Most] did no more than attach a Mercedes star to the front of their building. Let me quote the actual words of one Studebaker dealer: "I'll never sell a Mercedes here unless some half-wit comes along and wants one. But, I leave the star up there on the building because it raises my status in the area."[14]

Moreover, in selecting Mercedes-Benz dealers, Studebaker-Packard had in many cases not only chosen poorly, but too well. In Chicago, for example, there were at one point more Mercedes-Benz dealers than Cadillac dealers, despite the fact that Cadillac out-sold Mercedes-Benz by a margin of at least ten to one even in cosmopolitan urban centers. The result was an image-bruising price war.

As if the foregoing weren't sufficient, Studebaker mechanics at the dealer level were proving themselves to be totally out of their depth in repairing something as exotic as a Mercedes-Benz fuel injection system.[15] CWMB tried training programs, but the mechanics still failed because they saw so few cars they forgot the procedures when one did show up needing service. CWMB finally resorted to flying German mechanics into the United States for tours of duty at key Mercedes-Benz dealerships.

Yet, Daimler-Benz contributed mightily to its own difficulties through its unfamiliarity with American driving conditions and habits, its stubborn unwillingness to adapt in some cases, and its ham-handed attempts at emergency "fixes" in others that often turned out to be worse than the original problems. Recalled Hoppe:

> Mercedes-Benz models were just not available with the kind of equipment specification that people expected in this price category. The air conditioning that an American customer expected as a matter of course was quite unknown in Germany. Power steering was added to the 300d, but performed dreadfully, and an automatic transmission adapted by Borg-Warner to suit the car made it quite undriveable. Back in Stuttgart, [chief engineer] Fritz Nallinger clung determinedly to the standpoint that a Mercedes would lose its sporting character if it had automatic transmission.

His humorous contribution to the discussion was merely: "You'd better teach the Americans how to use a gear shift!"[16]

Yet, all of this seemed trivial compared to the increasingly desperate financial situation in South Bend in the early months of 1958. Once again, Studebaker-Packard was headed for bankruptcy. After about 6,000 Mercedes-Benz cars had arrived, Churchill exercised a provision of the contract and suspended deliveries for 90 days—but not before thousands of them were left stranded sitting up to their axles in snow and mud at various ports of entry, such as Baltimore and Houston. Hoppe was terrified that if title were transferred to Studebaker-Packard they would get caught up in litigation sure to result from the increasingly likely failure of the South Bend firm.

Giese flatly refused to listen to Hoppe's dire warnings and went so far as to order him not to have any contact with anyone at the home office. In retrospect, it is easy to understand why, for when Hoppe disobeyed this order all hell broke loose in Stuttgart. As a direct result, an emergency board meeting of CWMB was called in February, 1958, at which Giese was unceremoniously fired. Hoppe, as Giese's deputy, was almost fired, too, but he was saved by intercession on the part of Bob Guthrie, CWMB's attorney.[17] His law firm had represented CWMB from its inception and, later, represented Studebaker Corporation, as well. Guthrie knew of Hoppe's concerns, of the fact that Giese had ordered him to keep silent about them and of the genuine courage it took to disobey that order. When the dust settled, Hoppe was not only not fired, he was named to manage day-to-day operations for CWMB—in effect, named to be the chief operating officer of the company replacing Giese.

Hoppe's first decision was to drastically cut back on sales projections. His second task was to sell the thousands of cars already shipped that were sitting unsold. He succeeded at both tasks, but, in the summer of 1958, the deteriorating situation in South Bend suddenly came to a head. Devastated by continued losses made all the worse by a recession year, Studebaker-Packard faced insolvency. The first quarter loss of $6.2 was almost more than the company could bear and it was suddenly open to question whether it could survive to see the new Lark introduced that fall. Fran-

Heinz Hoppe, far right, at a meeting of Mercedes-Benz Sales (MBS). The others, left to right: Gerhard Korallus, Lon Fleenor (president of MBS), and an attorney.

tically, Churchill laid-off more workers and cut expenditures where he could, but the second quarter loss was even worse: $7 million.

Churchill had staked his hopes on completing the merger between Studebaker-Packard and Curtiss-Wright that had been implied in the 1956 agreement. As the months dragged on, though, and Studebaker-Packard failed to re-ignite, it became obvious that Hurley had no intention of exercising the stock option that would have effected that. The experience was extremely frustrating for Churchill. Hurley was buying the company, but he wasn't, he was running the show, but he wasn't. The only thing that was certain was that Hurley's act was wearing thin in South Bend.

If Hurley was clearly not going to infuse more money into Studebaker-Packard, neither, given the balance sheet, would any sane outside lender. That left Churchill with but one option. He sent an urgent plea to Daimler-Benz for a $7 million loan. The loan was eventually granted, but the price Daimler-Benz exacted in return was a complete renegotiation of the relationships between Daimler-Benz, Curtiss-Wright and Studebaker-Packard.

By 1958, Daimler-Benz, too, felt as if it had been put through a wringer by Hurley. The tantalizing sales and unheard of prosperity promised in the 1957 agreement had proven to be woefully unrealistic. Nor was Daimler-Benz at all pleased with the half-hearted way (as it saw it) in which Hurley had been promoting Daimler-Benz's non-automotive products. As was the case in South Bend, Daimler-Benz became increasingly convinced that

Hurley's only real concern was advancing the interests of Curtiss-Wright—
even at the expense of his alleged partners. In fact, Hoppe, Stuttgart's man
on the scene, had developed an intense distrust of the man.

In sum, both Studebaker-Packard and Daimler-Benz had, for their own
reasons, come to regard Hurley as a liability. They weren't in love with
each other, either, but what were they to do? South Bend urgently needed
a cash infusion and Mercedes-Benz products to bolster it at the dealer level,
while Stuttgart had no other retail organization in America and was not
yet prepared to go it alone. In this way, natural forces brought Studebaker-
Packard and Daimler-Benz together in opposition to Curtiss-Wright.

In August, South Bend dispatched a top-level negotiating team to
Stuttgart and an arrangement was hammered out. Had Hurley really possessed long-range plans that required either company, he could easily have
objected and thrown a wrench into the renegotiations, but he didn't. The
new agreement specified the following:

1) Curtiss-Wright would end its management contract with
Studebaker-Packard.

2) Curtiss-Wright would surrender all rights to Daimler-Benz
licenses, patents, and trademarks, as well as to the sales and distribution of Daimler-Benz products (excepting only large buses,
engines, and Unimogs).[18]

3) CWMB would be disbanded.

4) Studebaker-Packard would be required to set-up a new subsidiary—Mercedes-Benz Sales, Inc.—specifically for the sales and
distribution of Mercedes-Benz cars.

Curtiss-Wright, under terms of the reorganization agreement, not only
terminated its management contract with Studebaker-Packard, it also sur-
rendered the option to buy additional shares of stock that would have given
it control and paid $2 million for Studebaker-Packard's remaining interest
in the defense properties it had taken over in 1956.

Daimler-Benz advanced Studebaker-Packard a total of $7 million in
short-term loans—$6 million toward the purchase of Mercedes-Benz cars
and $1 million for spare parts. In addition, Studebaker-Packard was al-

lowed to cancel its outlandish commitment for 300-series cars. The 300s would continue to be imported, but only on a dealer-order basis.

Of course, none of this would have been final without the consent of Studebaker-Packard's lenders. Churchill confronted them with a Hobson's choice. They could either go along or lose their investment completely, but they had demands of their own that were to have far-reaching consequences.

As part of the refinancing package, notes payable by Studebaker-Packard to banks and insurance companies in the amount of $54.7 million were canceled. The lenders accepted in their stead secured notes totaling $16.5 million and 165,000 shares of Studebaker-Packard preferred stock. Although virtually the entire physical plant of the company was pledged as collateral, the deal was a good one from the company's perspective, and it was a clear indication that the lenders had given up any reasonable hope of seeing at any point in the foreseeable future the $38.2 million represented by the difference in the value of the new notes and the old.

The principal demand upon which the lenders had insisted was a reorganization of Studebaker-Packard's directors. Notable additions included Clarence Francis, the former chairman of General Foods, and Dr. Edward Litchfield, chairman of Smith-Corona Marchant. An interesting addition, however, was Abraham Sonnabend, the so-called "Marrying Sam" of the merger business, whose appointment was significant because a key component in the reorganization was a concerted push toward diversification.

In part, this was simple common sense. Thanks to its dreadful track record, Studebaker-Packard had an enormous backlog of losses. In the arcane word of accounting, these were potential assets of a sort because they could be applied against future profits and, thus, used to avoid tax liability. Since, however, the automotive operations were showing no signs of attaining profitability, the only way these assets could be used was the acquisition of profitable companies, i.e., by diversifying and using Studebaker-Packard's losses against *those* profits and gaining refunds on *their* previously paid taxes. In other words, the first goal of diversification was to, in effect, buy profits that could generate revenue by being used against Studebaker-Packard's losses.

So far so good, but there were many in the industry and, thanks to the reorganization, several now on the Studebaker-Packard board of directors, who were convinced that the automotive operations were doomed. With that thought firmly in mind, they were determined that Studebaker-Packard should diversify its operations as rapidly as possible into other profitable non-automotive ventures not only for the tax benefits, but to save the company by getting it out of cars entirely.

So, for various reasons a diversification plan was drafted and approved by the stockholders at a meeting held in Los Angeles on October 15, 1958. As the year drew to a close, Studebaker-Packard had been liberated from Curtiss-Wright, reorganized, and infused with some desperately-needed refinancing. Mercedes-Benz Sales, Inc., had been set-up to be a wholly-owned subsidiary of Studebaker-Packard, but Hoppe was named to its board of directors and continued to closely monitor operations.[19] Hurley was out and Studebaker-Packard's board had been reorganized with a new cast of characters that included practically no one who was a shareholder. As one of the new directors explained rather undiplomatically to *Fortune* magazine, a man might be stupid enough to be a director in a company he saw was no good but he wouldn't be stupid enough to own stock.[20]

In retrospect, whether this was the best way to approach Studebaker-Packard's daunting problems in the summer of 1958 can be debated, but clearly something had to be done. Public confidence and dealer morale had all but evaporated. Hoppe, who had to contend with this problem face-to-face in dealer-relation work on behalf of Mercedes-Benz, recalled:

> Sales of Studebaker's own models had slumped to such an extent that dealers feared for their survival. All their hopes were centered on the new Studebaker due in the fall.[21]

That new Studebaker was named the Lark. Acting out of a sense of desperation (the normal state of affairs in South Bend by this time), Churchill had ordered an emergency face-lift of the 1958 standard passenger car line. Inspired by the success of the Scotsman and observing the phenomenal revival of American Motors on the strength of its compact Rambler, which had shot from 55,000 units in 1954 to 186,000 in 1958, he decided to turn the Studebaker into a compact, too. Only about $8 million could be scraped together to pay for this, which is to say perhaps one-third of what a new

Eugene Hardig.

product line would have cost under normal conditions. Even at that, this sum was identical to the amount of the loan from Daimler-Benz plus the million or so saved by scrapping plans to restyle the Packard for 1959.[22] To understand why Churchill thought the Lark would work, it is necessary to understand the times.

The industry, in general, was reeling in 1958 and the medium-price segment was hit worst of all. The three million cars sold in the medium-priced field in 1955 collapsed to barely 1.2 million by 1958, a drop of 60 percent. No less than five medium-priced brands went under between 1957 and 1960: Nash and Hudson (1957), Packard (1958), Edsel (1959) and De Soto (1960). There is some evidence that General Motors considered dropping Pontiac, too. Thus, Studebaker-Packard, which had started from a position of near-terminal weakness, was faced with a declining market it could ill-afford. Model year production for the South Bend-built Studebakers and Packards combined were down about 58 percent from Studebaker's 1955 level, which was no worse than the industry as a whole but intolerable for a company in Studebaker-Packard's precarious condition.

The 1958 model year was not only a terrible one for the medium-priced field, though. In the entire industry, only two nameplates recorded gains: Thunderbird and Rambler. George Romney at American Motors added fuel to the fire with his aggressive advertising campaign for the Rambler, which was cleverly depicted as a common sense, socially responsible alternative to the chrome-laden "dinosaurs" being built by the Big Three.

Even the enthusiast press was turning on Detroit. To cite but one example, in its October, 1957, issue—the same one that introduced the Edsel to its readers—the lead feature in *Motor Trend* was an article entitled, "What's wrong with U.S. cars?" (According to the article, just about everything.) A slew of books and articles hostile to American automotive "culture" flooded the popular market, too, John Keats' celebrated, *Insolent Chariots*, being but the best remembered. There was an unmistakable anti-Detroit mood afoot in the land, it seemed, and everybody was jumping on the bandwagon.

In short, it was a bad time to be selling cars, in general, but a terrific opportunity for an "outsider" to make a score. While it was true that American Motors and Studebaker-Packard both moved bravely forward with their compacts as a way of making a virtue of a necessity, the timing couldn't have been better.[23]

Actual creation of the Lark was credited to Eugene Hardig. Hardig had joined Studebaker as a draftsman in 1918, then worked his way up through the engineering ranks. By 1955, when Churchill became general manager, he was named chief engineer. The Lark was perhaps his masterpiece. For sheer brilliance under incredible pressure, the program was almost unrivaled. Recalled a Studebaker associate years later:

> We'll never forget how Hardig, held back by lack of funds, designed the Lark with a blow torch and scrap metal. He's one of those real believers in the auto business. He burns with a bright blue flame.[24]

Purely from a conceptual standpoint—after the fact, of course—the Lark was surprisingly straight forward. Over two feet of front and rear over-hang was lopped off, a little new sheet metal was added and—*voilà!*—the "all new" Lark was the result. And, it was a rather nice compact, at that. If it seems absurd to turn a full-size car into a compact, though, it must be stated that the real absurdity was that for six years Studebaker had been attempting the exact reverse. It had started in 1953 with a body of truly compact dimensions, added two feet of over-hang to it, and tried to sell it as a *full-size car.*

The actual Lark line-up was simplicity itself. A mere four models were listed: two-door sedan, four-door sedan, two-door hardtop and two-door station wagon. The wagon was available in two-seat or three-seat versions, with the third seat facing rearward. The two-door sedan was offered in much plainer trim and was effectively the price leader of the line. All Larks were built on the same 108.5-inch wheelbase, except for the wagons, which used a slightly stretched 113-inch chassis. Two powerplants were available. The venerable 169 cubic inch L-head six was standard. It was rated at 90 horsepower. A 259 cubic inch V8 was optional and carried a rating of 180 horsepower. In V8 form, the Lark was a sprightly performer.

The company waxed enthusiastic about its new car. The advertising described the new Lark as:

> ...an automobile as fresh and new as the first breath of spring. It is unlike any other car because its proportions are uniquely, ideally suited to today's driving conditions. It strikes a smart, sensible balance between the five-eighths size foreign imports and the oversize U.S. models...It runs with the best of them and adds the advantage of economy. Its design will delight your eye. Its interior will flatter your good taste...In every respect, it is *the* car that meets the needs and tastes of our times.

If the words sounded a tad immodest, the company could be forgiven. It had been a long time since it had had anything to brag about and it wasn't going to miss the opportunity. Even the union chipped in, at least with words. T. Forrest Hanna, president of the UAW local, publicly pledged

1959 Studebaker Lark.

1959 Studebaker Silver Hawk.

the efforts of his members to make the Larks "the best-built cars in the world." Around South Bend, civic boosters staged parades, erected billboards reading, "South Bend Goes Up with the Lark," and distributed 60,000 stickers and 10,000 buttons publicizing the new car.

The Lark was joined by a Silver Hawk, the sole remaining model in the once expansive Hawk series. Why the Golden Hawk was dropped is unclear; it would have been simple enough to continue it over. In fact, the company intended to drop *both* Hawks, but encountered heated opposition from its dealers, who preferred to have at least one tried-and-true Studebaker product around in case the unknown Lark failed to catch on. In the end, the tail fins on the Silver Hawk were revised but, other than that, the model appeared much as it had in 1957 and 1958. The range of engines was the same as with the Lark and the Silver Hawk was available only in the pillared coupe body style.

A range of Lark fleet vehicles also joined the standard line-up. These included a panel wagon, a utility sedan and the Econ-O-Miler sedan. The panel wagon was essentially identical to the standard wagon except for body-color side panels that could be fitted to cover the rear windows behind the passenger doors. In this fashion, the wagon was turned into a smart panel truck in about thirty seconds. The utility sedan, in turn, was a Lark two-door sedan with the rear seat removed for increased storage area.

The Econ-O-Miler was more-or-less a continuation of the Scotsman idea, being a stripped-down Lark four-door sedan with all excess trim and bright work removed. It was offered at a price below that of any other Lark model and was also the basis for the Lark taxi conversions, in which form it was becoming quite popular with fleet buyers, attaining second place in fleet sales in the key New York City market in 1959, up from an already respectable third place achieved by the Scotsman-based version in 1958. The Scotsman was no longer offered to the public, though, because company planners had become convinced it was less effective at luring "conquest" buyers form other makes than it was at stealing probable buyers of more profitable Studebaker models.

On the international front, the company signed agreements to have Larks assembled in Australia and in Israel. In addition, the existing Canadian and Mexican subsidiaries reported greatly increased demand for cars, thanks to the appeal of the Lark.

Employment at South Bend rose with the success of the Lark, too. From an average of 8,175 workers in 1958, Studebaker-Packard reached an average of 11,307 workers in 1959. A new two-year labor contract was successfully negotiated with the UAW.

To say that Studebaker-Packard had a very good year in 1959 would be an understatement. It was a spectacular year, especially in comparison to the five horrendous years that had preceded it. Although net revenues for calendar year 1958 came to only $180.7 million and a loss of $13.4 million was reported—a larger loss than the one recorded in 1957—all the money, some $22.5 million, had been lost in the first three quarters. A profit of $3.7 million had actually been realized in the fourth quarter on the strength of the dramatically new Lark. Sales of cars and trucks soared from a pitiful 79,301 in 1958 to 182,323 in 1959.[25] The dollar value of those vehicles soared, too, from $180.7 million in 1958 to $387.4 million in 1959 and Studebaker-Packard Corporation reported its first ever calendar-year profit of $28.5 million. So, the Lark's effects were immediate and positive and with it now rested the desperate hopes of those in the company who still wanted to see the automotive operations survive.

The diversification campaign was beginning to gather steam, as well. Gering Products, Inc., and C.T.L., Inc., were acquired. The newly constituted Gering Plastics Division was located in Kenilworth, New Jersey, and was a producer of plastic materials and compounds used by other manufacturers to produce various plastic goods. The new CTL Division was in the growing aerospace industry. CTL had produced the nose-cone for NASA's first attempt to send animals into sub-space. Two lucky monkeys, Abel and Baker, were chosen for the historic flight, which took place on May 28, 1959. CTL, which stood for Cincinnati Testing Laboratories, was a leader in high-tech plastic applications.

In order to cash in on a good thing, the Lark's model range was expanded for 1960. The most exciting addition was the Lark convertible, but the four-door wagon may have been the more profitable new model. Other than these additions, however, the passenger car line-up for 1960 was little different than the successful one offered in 1959. The Lark was also available in two different trim levels, although you would never would have guessed it from reading the sales literature handed out in the showrooms. The Deluxe series was the cheaper and plainer of the two and, essentially, expanded the number of models available in base trim from one in 1959 (the two-door sedan) to four. Deluxe models included two-door sedan, four-door sedan, two-door wagon and four-door wagon. The Regal series in-

1960 Studebaker Lark Regal.

cluded fancier versions of the four-door sedan and four-door wagon, plus the two-door hardtop and convertible. Regal trim was more-or-less the same as that offered in the standard Larks in 1959 (with the exception of the two-door sedan). Except for the Econ-O-Miler, the fleet vehicle line offered in 1960 was the same as the standard line-up.

The motoring press continued to heap praise on the Lark. *CARS* magazine in its June issue voted the Lark the best of the compacts. In announcing the win, the magazine noted:

> Studebaker Lark now offers a convertible and a four-door wagon, giving it a uniquely complete line. Style remains the same as last year, cutting depreciation, and mechanical "bugs" have been eliminated. Our tests showed Lark to be a top-notch over-the-road car with admirable performance.

The most interesting new Studebaker in 1960, however—and certainly the most clever—was a truck. The Champ pick-up was added to the faltering truck line as a long-awaited replacement for the aging pick-up that had been around since 1949. The Champ was so neatly done that it was possible to overlook the fact that it was cobbled together almost entirely from parts already on the shelf. In the first place, it used the old 122-inch wheelbase pick-up chassis, with six-foot and eight-foot load boxes offered as before in both 5,000 pound GVW and 7,000 pound GVW ratings, respectively. Indeed, from the "B" pillar on back, the Champ was virtually unchanged from the old pick-up. From the "B" pillar forward, it was essentially the same as the Lark, with interior trim similar to that offered in Deluxe models. Even the instrument panel was interchangeable with the Lark. Only the grille (featuring bold, vertical bars) and the panel at the rear of the cab appear to have been original. In essence, a dramatically new and contemporary pick-up had been created simply by replacing the old cab with one cobbled together from Lark parts. It was a brilliant example of making the most of what you've got and showed that the company's creativity hadn't ended with the development of the Lark the year before. The Champ was introduced at the Chicago Auto Show in January, 1960.

Yet, the nation was gripped by a massive steel strike in the late-sum-

1960 Studebaker Champ.

mer of 1959. Churchill had seen it coming and stockpiled enough steel to keep the lines running. The 1960 trucks, however, were delayed and the strike turned out to be the harbinger of more bad news to come.

Unfortunately, things began to fall apart for the company once again in 1960. GM, Ford and Chrysler all entered the fray with their own compacts, and Studebaker simply didn't have the strength-in-depth to withstand Detroit's determined assault. Churchill had acknowledged this possibility in a letter to stockholders in March, 1960:

> The Lark now has several competitors, all three of the major Detroit producers having entered the compact car field. The Lark, however, is an excellent product with owner satisfaction at a very high level. It enjoys the added advantage of more than a billion miles of proven performance in the hands of customers. We recognize, however, that with increased competition, redoubled efforts will be required at all levels in the Studebaker-Packard organization to retain the benefits of the strong start we have made.[26]

It was, alas, prophetic. The company had sold 182,323 vehicles of all types in 1959. That number declined to 133,984 in 1960. It wasn't yet a rout, but it was ominous.[27] Revenues declined, as well, to $323.2 million and, worse, earnings all but vanished. A meager $708,850 profit was reported—none of it, significantly, from the automotive operations.

A serious problem serving to complicate matters was that, during the past few years, Studebaker had come to depend heavily upon dual franchises with dealers handling various lines manufactured by the Big Three. When Big Three compacts hit the market, many of these "duals" elected to drop Studebaker entirely. Between 1960 and 1961 alone, Studebaker lost 356 outlets, or over 14 percent of its total—and, many of the best.

Still, Studebaker-Packard had amply demonstrated that it could survive adversity. For the first four years of the corporation's existence it had had little choice in the matter and had lived to tell about more perils than Pauline. So, it was ironic that the sudden prosperity created by the Lark proved to be the almost insurmountable challenge.

The specific question that confronted the board in 1960 was what to do with the profits earned from overall operations in 1959. Churchill and Porta were insistent that it be plowed back into the automotive operations and used to finance a new body for the 1962 model year. They contended that the profits now being generated by the Lark would be sufficient to off-set the company's losses for tax purposes. This was particularly urgent, because the company had tremendous loss carry-forwards from 1955-57 that had to be used within five years. Initially, they won approval from the board for this approach.

Meanwhile, the diversification program continued apace. Yet, Sonnabend, who had come to the board with such impressive credentials as a merger specialist, had been responsible for none of the acquisitions actually made. His proposals for acquiring firms such as Manhattan Shirt and Revlon, had all been dismissed by the other directors as being inappropriate to an industrial company such as Studebaker-Packard and he became increasingly frustrated. Frank Manheim, a partner in Lehman Brothers, stoutly opposed Sonnabend and kept pushing for an expansion of Studebaker-Packard's relationship with Daimler-Benz.

Matters really took a turn for the worse with the acquisition of Gravely Tractor. There was nothing inherently wrong with the company, a manufacturer of lawn mowers and other yard equipment, but the takeover put Gravely's volatile chief executive, D. Ray Hall, on the board. He quickly

Clarence Francis.

proved to be a divisive influence.

As Lark sales softened alarmingly during 1960 and the automotive division again dipped into the red, the proposed new body for 1962 was scrapped in favor of a facelift and the future of the Studebaker car became a question mark once more.

The issue came to a head at the September board meeting. Byers Burlingame, the company's chief financial officer, reported that the automotive division was losing millions again, although he predicted a small profit for the year overall. As a direct result, Churchill was demoted. There appears to have been no animosity toward him personally, and he was allowed to retain both his position as president (for the time being) and his seat on the board, but, clearly, his solution for the company's problems hadn't worked. At the same time, Skillman, who had directed the Lark's sales effort, was fired and Louis Minkle was appointed to replace him.

Clarence Francis assumed the chairmanship and was officially designated as the new chief executive officer on an interim basis. He felt he was too old, though, to assume the obligation permanently and pushed for a talent search to find a suitable replacement.

That was Sonnabend's cue. He began politicking for his own selection. So, emphatically, did Hall, whose main contribution to the debate was that the whole show should be turned over to *him*. Unlike Sonnabend, Hall seems to have had no votes at this juncture other than his own.

Toward the end of November, the board met again to receive Burlingame's latest dose of bad news. At this meeting, the liquidation of Studebaker-Packard Corporation was actively debated. In the end, Minkle convinced them that a facelift for the 1962 model year, pegged at $3.5 million, would be sufficient to bolster the automotive operations in the short term, although even he was doubtful as to the long-term prospects.

A few days later, the board convened yet again and learned that Francis had found a candidate for chief executive officer: Sherwood Egbert of McCulloch Corporation. Hall vehemently object and again demanded the job for himself. The meeting adjourned in disarray.

A few days after that, the board resumed its deliberations only to hear from Francis that Egbert had withdrawn. That threw the situation into complete turmoil. Hall again demanded the job, this time backed by Manheim and Russell Forgan. Sonnabend, who had threatened to resign at the previous meeting, pressed his own candidacy, backed by Churchill and Porta. Sonnabend's candidacy was actually moved and seconded before the meeting broke up in confusion.

When the board resumed its debate on December 28th, it was in a highly contentious atmosphere that was not helped at all by Burlingame's latest tale of woe. A man who was notably conservative with his numbers, he was now predicting a whopping $28 million loss on the automotive operations in 1961. Sonnabend and Hall pressed their candidacies for the presidency once more, only to see the meeting thrown into utter chaos by Francis' announcement that Egbert had reconsidered.

That was too much for Churchill and Porta. Antagonized by Egbert's vacillation, they refused to support him, as, for obvious reasons, did Sonnabend and Hall. Francis was able to sway the other directors, but even he doubted that Egbert would accept the job with four of the twelve votes in opposition. He was wrong. When he left he meeting to phone Egbert with the news, Egbert's immediate reply was: "Let's go."

So, it was settled. By a vote of eight-to-two, Egbert was elected president and chief executive officer of the corporation. Sonnabend and Hall cast their votes against, while Churchill and Porta abstained. Sonnabend was livid at the turn of events and, as a parting shot, warned:

This company is doomed! The decision is ridiculous! The board should disband, get out! It is worthless![28]

Notes

The most important resources drawn upon in the writing of this chapter include Richard M. Langworth's *Studebaker, 1946-1966*, Michael Beatty, Patrick Furlong, and Loren Pennington's *Studebaker: Less Than They Promised*, and Donald T. Critchlow's *The Life and Death of an American Corporation*. Heinz C. Hoppe's *Serving the Star Around the World* gave valuable insights into the important connection between Studebaker-Packard and Daimler-Benz, on the one hand, and Studebaker-Packard and Curtiss-Wright, on the other. Studebaker-Packard Corporation papers in the author's collection, including annual Reports, brochures and miscellaneous publications, were also especially important source material. Periodicals that proved to be important resources included various issues of *Motor Life*, *Motor Trend*, and *Special-Interest Autos*.

[1] Langworth, p. 91.
[2] Langworth, p. 92.
[3] 1957 Studebaker Annual Report.
[4] Hoppe, p. 75.
[5] When this writer was doing research in South Bend in 1978, he encountered an old Studebaker hand who reminisced about working at Studebaker while he was going through college in the 1950s. He and a buddy, he said, worked the night shift. They brought a cot into the factory and alternated working the line and sleeping or studying. Meanwhile, of course, both were drawing full paychecks. He insisted this had not been considered exceptional behavior.
[6] Hoppe, p. 75.
[7] Mexico, Canada, and Cuba were also given to Studebaker-Packard in the agreement that was ultimately signed.
[8] Hoppe, p. 77. Klotz was a son-in-law of Ludwig Erhard, then economics minister in Bonn, later Chancellor of West Germany.
[9] Hoppe, p. 75.
[10] 1958 Studebaker Annual Report.
[11] Langworth, p. 99.
[12] Langworth, p. 99.
[13] Two years later, Churchill was approached by an outside group that wanted Studebaker-Packard to import Facel Vega Excellence sedan bodies from France, fit them out with left-over 374 cubic inch Packard engines, and offer them as limited edition Packards. Facel was a coachbuilder that had launched a series

of extremely interesting luxury sports cars and sport sedans on its own beginning around 1954. The Excellence, a four-door hardtop which used a Chrysler
V8 engine, was highly regarded by the motoring press. It was an intriguing
concept and Churchill was ready to try it until Daimler-Benz strenuously objected. That was the last realistic chance for any sort of Packard revival.

[14] Hoppe, p. 79.

[15] Fuel injection was just being introduced to America. General Motors, Ford,
and Chrysler all offered versions of it on a wide variety of product lines and all
had tremendous problems with reliability and service in the field.

[16] Hoppe, p. 80.

[17] This is the same Randolph "Bob" Guthrie who was destined to become chairman of Studebaker in June, 1963.

[18] The Unimog was—and is—a specialized all-terrain vehicle manufactured
by Daimler-Benz. Even Curtiss-Wright's reduced relationship with Daimler-
Benz AG was terminated a year later.

[19] Mercedes-Benz Sales, Inc. (MBS), however, only distributed Mercedes-Benz
cars; Hoppe's American organization, Daimler-Benz North America (DBNA),
which he headed and which had never ceased to function, would handle all
importation. The cars would then be turned over to MBS. Hoppe was especially pleased about this, for it gave DBNA its own significant source of income for the first time: It could charge 2.5 percent on every car it imported.

[20] It was at about this time that Frederick Donner, then president of General
Motors, was asked by a government investigator if the Big Three were trying
to put the independents out of business. Donner snapped back that if the question was in reference to Studebaker, GM hadn't driven *them* to the poorhouse,
they had driven themselves. A harsh statement, but essentially a true one.

[21] Hoppe, p. 79.

[22] According to minutes of the board, it was Hugh Ferry, the former president
of Packard, who proposed killing the Packebaker.

[23] Romney had made a major effort to keep AMC's large Nash and Hudson
lines going, and even commissioned a prototype from Pininfarina. AMC's bankers weren't any more anxious to pay for new cars than were Studebaker-
Packard's lenders, though, and Romney had little choice but to do the best he
could with the Rambler. As it turned out, that proved to be quite a lot.

[24] Studebaker-Packard files, author's collection.

[25] Company sales in 1959 included 160,826 Studebaker cars, 10,909 Studebaker
trucks, and 10,588 cars imported from Daimler-Benz and Auto Union-DKW.

[26] 1960 Studebaker Annual Report.

[27] In contrast, AMC actually increased both its sales and its market share.

[28] Critchlow, p. 174.

Overleaf, the body finishing area in the Avanti plant in 1963.

TEN

The Swan Song

Sherwood Harry Egbert was born in 1920 in Easton, Washington, in modest circumstances. His father ran a pool hall and barbershop, but young Sherwood started working at the tender age of twelve in order to supplement the family income. By that time, his father had opened a dance hall, but, when that burned down, the Egberts lived in a tent. Recalled Egbert in an interview with *Business Week*:

> We had to rough it for two winters. I stole coal from Northern Pacific railroad cars, and we ate plenty of stale bread with that old purple mold coming through.

Egbert was a determined man even then, though, and was so successful in high school athletics that he won a scholarship to Washington State University. There, he studied engineering, but dropped out after two years to go back to work as an engineer (despite his lack of a degree) with the Five Companies that built the Grand Coulee Dam. By 1942, when he enlisted in the Marine Corps, he had done a stint as an engineer with Boeing, learning the science as he went. In 1946, he joined McCulloch Corporation as the assistant production manager. McCulloch operated out of a Quonset hut at the time, but, by 1960, had grown to be a $70 million a year enterprise with Egbert as its executive vice-president. It was at that juncture that he came to the attention of Studebaker-Packard.

Sherwood H. Egbert.

On January 4, 1961, Egbert met with Studebaker-Packard's Executive Committee. Sonnabend's resignation was accepted and Egbert assumed effective control, although he wasn't formally named president of the corporation until February 1st. He had the full backing of the board—at least for a while. As Harold Churchill, who remained on the board as a "consultant," might have warned him, one could never be too sure about such things at Studebaker-Packard.

Egbert faced the seemingly impossible task of revitalizing an automotive operation that almost everybody in the industry, including its own board of directors, had given up for dead. It was Egbert's assignment to spread the company wide enough that it would no longer be vulnerable to losses from its automotive division and, although it was left unsaid, provide a way out of the automobile business entirely.

Egbert had taken the job because he relished a challenge. He certainly had one. Soon after his arrival, the board laid out a four-point program for the corporation:

1. To strengthen our competitive position in the automobile business;
2. To get an increased share of military business;
3. To set up and expand our International Division; and
4. To continue and expand our diversification program.

That the automotive operations remained at the top of the list was due in no small measure to Egbert's determination. He was quite willing to pursue an active diversification campaign, but he was, at the same time, unwilling to give up on Studebaker cars and trucks.

He immediately set about some of the more obvious tasks that had been long ignored. After viewing the plant, parts of which still had dirt floors dating from the wagon business, he ordered a general clean-up. With the help of idled assembly line workers and cans of left-over paint, nearly everything was repainted and refurbished.

He then turned his attention to the moribund dealer network. In August, in a whirlwind visit to some 1,300 of Studebaker-Packard's 2,036 dealers, he was amazed at the depth of their loyalty to Studebaker, but he was also frustrated by their lack of aggressiveness. He let it be known that Studebaker was on the move now and that any dealer unable to keep pace would have to go. He actually began to weed out the weakest dealers. This was a tough decision for a company with so few retail outlets (or "stores," in industry jargon), but one that he realized was essential in order to strengthen the few good dealers the company had. He noted in a letter to stockholders in March, 1962:

> [In 1961] we continued to weed out weaker outlets and replace them with stronger dealers... The number of dealers having been reduced to a low point in August [1961] through elimination

1961 Studebaker Lark.

1961 Studebaker Hawk.

of weak outlets, has now been increasing and concrete efforts are being made to build further on the strengthened foundation of existing representation. A number of company[-owned] retail stores have been established and more will be opened as the year progresses to provide needed representation in metropolitan markets.[1]

By December, 1961, the dealer total had risen to 2,102. Eleven factory-owned retail outlets were opened in Kansas City, Fort Wayne, New York City, Toledo, Tulsa, Memphis, Birmingham, Peoria, Indianapolis, Miami and San Diego.

He also addressed the fundamental problems back home in South Bend: negligible cash reserves, low productivity and the aging product line. The cash problem was not one that had an easy solution, so he set about acquiring companies that had large amounts of ready capital. In this way, he was able to slowly better Studebaker's cash position. Meanwhile, he did his best to peddle the 1961 Studebaker models.

The big news with the Lark in 1961 was the addition of a Cruiser four-door sedan. A more luxurious car than any previous Lark, it shared the

1961 Studebaker Champ.

longer 113-inch chassis with the wagons. This afforded it four inches more interior room (mostly rear seat leg room) than the base sedan. Other than that news, there was very little to report. All but the base Larks went to quad head lights, the Hawk sported a revised two-tone tail fin treatment, and trim was moved around on all models.

The model range was revised to the extent that the trim levels on the Lark were increased from two to three, while the number of models offered was actually reduced from eight to seven. It worked this way: the two-door wagon and two-door sedan came in the base trim level, the new Cruiser sedan featured a new luxury trim level, and all other models came with the equivalent of what had been the top trim level in 1960. The Lark Marshall was added to the fleet range as a specially-built police car.

Mechanically, the passenger car range was similar to the 1959 and 1960 models. The base six-cylinder engine was converted to overhead valves, which increased the horsepower rating to 112. While the block remained essentially the same, the head, manifold and, of course, the valve assembly were new. In addition, the Cruiser and Hawk were available with the larger 289 cubic inch V8 (rated at 225 horsepower) that had not been seen in several years. In an effort to stress the sporty nature of the Hawk, a floor-mounted, four-speed manual transmission was offered, as well. This was the same four-speed offered previously in the Corvette and was highly regarded within the industry.

The successful Champ pick-up introduced in 1960 was expanded into an attractive new line of light trucks for 1961. A new "wide box" or "spaceside" version was added, depending on which ad you read, featuring a wider box and sides that were more-or-less flush with the cab. It made for increased carrying capacity and a more stylish truck. In addition, stake and platform models were added. In all, it resulted in the most appealing line of half-ton and three-quarter-ton trucks Studebaker had offered in many a year.

Government sales continued to be an important element in the company's survival strategy and an office was established in Washington, DC, in order to better coordinate with officialdom, especially in the Defense Department. The company was rewarded with contracts totaling $37 million in 1961, including one contract for $27 million which represented the largest contract the company had been awarded since the Korean War. In addition to 5,000 military trucks, 6,000 Studebaker cars were sold to the General Services Administration (GSA).

On the international front, a Swiss subsidiary was established. Lark production was by that point underway in countries as disparate as Argentina, Australia, Belgium, Chile, Israel, the Philippines and South Africa. They accounted for 75 percent of the company's export sales in 1961.

Egbert got off to a good start. Within two months of joining the company, Studebaker sales rose smartly, some said as a vote of confidence in the new president. By May, the entire 1961 model run was sold out and Egbert announced plans to begin the 1962 run later that summer at an encouraging 62 units per hour.[2]

Despite this cheery news, the board was soon plunged into turmoil by D. Ray Hall, who charged that Egbert was becoming a dictator and ignoring the board's wishes. The other members of the board, however, whose wish list consisted primarily of turning a profit, were more than pleased with the directions things were taking and were not at all inclined to rock the boat. Edward Litchfield proposed a resolution backing Egbert and it passed with Hall's lone dissent.

Hall was hardly daunted by this rebuff, though, and came back in July with the startling news that he and his old nemesis, Sonnabend, had joined forces and laid plans with the Murcheson brothers of the Allegheny Corporation to buy up enough stock to gain control. When that transpired, Egbert, Litchfield, Francis and most of the other board members would presumably be dumped. It was at that point that Churchill jumped into the fray with a heartfelt expression of support for the job Egbert was doing. Hall was silenced—this time, as it turned out, for good—and nothing more was heard from the Murcheson bothers, either.

Egbert, however, was confronting another more deadly threat, for it was at about this time that he underwent surgery for cancer. He made a quick recovery, but it was unsettling news Studebaker-Packard scarcely needed. On top of that, a steel strike was in the offing, which forced the company to stockpile steel yet again. At the same time, the UAW had a contract up for renewal and a strike seemed increasingly likely.

In the end, net revenues in 1961 dropped a bit from 1960's pace, to $298.5 million, but Studebaker-Packard was able to report a profit for the year of $2.5 million. Part of this profit, however, was due to a favorable sale of the Gering Plastics Division to Monsanto Chemicals and (again) none of it came from automotive operations. A raft of new subsidiaries were acquired in the energized diversification program, including the Onan Division, the Clarke Division, the Schaefer Division, the Paxton Products Division and the Chemical Compounds Division (STP).

Onan was the world's largest manufacturer of gasoline and diesel engine-driven electric generating plants with an international customer base. Clarke was a leading manufacturer of mechanized floor finishing and maintenance equipment. Schaefer was one of the leading manufacturers of self-contained ice cream, frozen food and dairy cabinets. Paxton was a noted manufacturer of engine superchargers and, not incidentally, brought the Granetelli brothers (Andy and Vince) into the Studebaker fold. The Chemical Compounds Division of Paxton was famous for its STP line of engine additives and lubricants.

As for the Lark, which by 1961 was in its third year essentially unchanged, Egbert realized that something simply had to be done to spruce it up before the 1962 model announcement only a few months away. A

1962 Lark Daytona on the set of television's "Mr. Ed," which Studebaker sponsored.

major overhaul was out of the question, from considerations of both time and cost. A crash face-lifting program was, therefore, undertaken with suggestions solicited from Studebaker dealers. The stubby appearance of the original styling was mitigated by a longer-looking rear end design and a sassy new grille was copied directly from the Mercedes-Benz.

The model line-up was juggled, as well. New at the top of the range was the sporty Daytona series featuring two-door hardtop and convertible body styles. All Daytonas came standard with bucket seats. The four-speed manual was optional for those who preferred even sportier driving, as was a sliding sunroof for the hardtop.

Wheelbase was increased to 109 inches on two-door models, while all four-door models shared the 113-inch wheelbase with the station wagons. The base four-door sedan was, thus, increased in length by a substantial 13 inches, while two-door models were up by 9 inches. Most of this added length was in the rear end, which featured entirely new sheet metal and did much to alleviate the stubby appearance of the 1959-61 series models. Luggage capacity was likewise improved. All Larks now featured quad head lights. Transistorized radios and air conditioning were options.

The other dramatically "new" model was the Gran Turisimo Hawk.

Restyled by Brooks Stevens, the Hawk GT achieved its freshness largely through the legerdemain of a master designer. The only significant new stamping was the roof, a handsomely squared-off design in the formal style. The hardtop body style was revived, which further differentiated it from 1959-61 Hawks. The tail fins were deleted, to return it to the simplicity and cleanliness of the 1953 rear design, as were the bumper guards and the fake hood scoop that had been added along the way, while the side grilles were painted body color instead of chrome. Other than that, all that was really new consisted of various bits of trim and ornamentation: a new "classic" grille, a stainless steel panel to cover the ribbing on the rear deck lid, a new instrument cluster to dress-up the same old instrument panel and so forth. Probably never before or since has so little money been spent so effectively to create a new look for an old car. Better still, the Hawk GT was, by virtually all contemporary accounts, one of the handsomest cars on the road that year. Even today, a 1962 Hawk is a sure-fire head-turner. Whatever Egbert paid Stevens, he got his money's worth and then some.

Egbert knew too well, of course, that a few sheet metal revisions were a drop in the bucket compared with what was really needed to be competitive in the marketplace. Ultimately, something radical had to be done to

1962 Studebaker Gran Turisimo Hawk.

the entire line. In the spring of 1961 this was impossible, not only because a totally new line of cars would cost around $40 million, but also because of the inescapable fact that most of Studebaker's directors were not committed to the automobile business.

Egbert had been giving serious thought to a radical new car since late in 1960 during his initial discussions with Studebaker about the president's job. On one trip, during a lay-over at Chicago's O'Hare Airport, he bought some car magazines and, as he perused them, became convinced that Studebaker needed to produce something racy and European in order to bolster its sad image. As he recalled it later, somewhere between Omaha and Denver he grabbed some stationery and began sketching ideas.

What he intended to propose was a stop-gap model—not a complete line of cars, but a single dramatic new model that would bolster both Studebaker's dilapidated image and its sagging morale until the Lark could be redesigned or replaced. He realized, too, that to be successful, this stop-gap car would have to satisfy some pretty unrealistic requirements.

To begin with, it would have to be salable to the board. To have any hope of accomplishing this, it would have to involve relatively little money, and it would have to be truly exciting and compelling. Second, it would have to be in the dealers' showrooms as soon as humanly possible. The normal gestation period for an all-new model in the industry was three full years. Egbert boldly set his sights for an introduction at the New York International Automobile Show scheduled for April, 1962, scarcely more than a year away. Third, the new car would have to be a tremendous attention grabber with the public. It would have to almost single-handedly revive Studebaker's tarnished image among car buyers long enough for the real bread-and-butter lines to be designed and built. It would have to be able to serve as a draw to increase traffic in Studebaker showrooms, a vital job the aging Lark was no longer able to do unassisted. Finally, even if it were not a big money maker itself, it would have to at least pay for the costs of its own development. In all of this, Egbert instinctively knew that the car represented much more than just another vehicle in the Studebaker stable. With the automotive division well into its eleventh hour, the car represented perhaps the only hope for salvation.

On March 9, 1961, he asked Raymond Loewy to return to South Bend.

Loewy reported his impressions of their first meeting:

> He handed me a bunch of clippings about cars which he'd
> been carrying around, and asked me if I could do the design in
> two weeks...I did not know the man, but I read him through the
> sketches he handed me. I knew then that Egbert had a natural
> flair for design. I knew I was working for a man whom I could
> respect for his good taste.[3]

Within ten days, Loewy was hard at work on the project with three
assistants at a rented house in Palm Springs, California. These assistants
were his right-hand man, John Ebstein, plus Thomas Kellogg and Robert
Andrews. Andrews had helped design the "Step-Down" Hudson of 1948,
among other influential projects.

Working around the clock, the four men produced a finished one-eighth
scale clay model within two weeks. Loewy and Ebstein immediately departed for South Bend to present the model to Egbert. They also brought
with them a series of sketches by Kellogg of proposed interior treatments
and design details. Three weeks after his initial meeting with Loewy, on
April 2nd, Egbert was out in Palm Springs viewing the final one-eighth
scale clay and the final drawings.

Even before the one-eighth clay arrived back in South Bend,
Studebaker's styling and engineering sections had built a buck for a full-
size clay, and prepared a separate seating buck using the basic interior dimensions. Randall Faurot, chief of Studebaker's in-house styling division,
assigned Robert Doehler to do the actual work entailed in developing
Loewy's one-eighth scale model into a full-size prototype.

Up to this point the car did not have a name. Some of those involved
in the project referred to it as the "Q" car, others as the "Model X" car.
Later, it became known as the "X-SHE" car—the suffix standing for Egbert's
initials. Loewy himself used the Lark emblem in an early drawing. There
was considerable sentiment in South Bend for using the name "Packard."
Others suggested going back even further in Studebaker history and reviving the Pierce-Arrow name in honor of the other great luxury marque
that had been affiliated with Studebaker. It is not known for sure who first

came up with the name "Avanti." Andrews gave the credit to the D'Arcy Advertising Agency, while Loewy gave the credit to Egbert.

The first major issue to be resolved regarding the Avanti was whether to build it of steel or of fiberglass. Egbert favored fiberglass because of its successful use in the Corvette, which was the sort of car for which he was aiming. Gene Hardig examined the one-eighth scale model and agreed on the grounds that there was no practical way such a design could be built in steel. Loewy would later enjoy boasting that the Avanti was built without a single straight line, which was entirely true, but such a design of curves and compound curves was simply too complex for metal. The cost for each individual body would be greater with fiberglass, but the crucial tooling costs would be much less. Fiberglass was also dictated by the initial production schedule of 1,000 units per month, substantially below the 1,700 to 2,000 units considered the minimum economical run for steel.

As originally conceived by Egbert, the Avanti was to have been a two-seater, in the fashion of the previously mentioned Corvette. It was Hardig who made the decision to turn it into a four-seater. Egbert concurred and so the Avanti became the first of the new breed of sporty "personal" cars that was to revolutionize the industry following the introduction of the fabulously successful 1965 Ford Mustang.

The influence of the Avanti upon the Mustang has never been fully investigated. Ford public relations people claimed at the time of the Mustang's introduction that it had been designed closely after the original two-seater Thunderbird. It made for good advertising copy, but the specifications and the chronology raise other possibilities. The Avanti was formally introduced in April, 1962, or almost exactly two years prior to the introduction of the Mustang. The Mustang, following a more normal development program, was in its early design phases at this point. The timing, together with the unconcealed curiosity of Ford people at various early showings of the Avanti, suggests that at least some cross-fertilization must have taken place.

There were several interesting connections in the two programs. In the first place, both companies were attempting to build sporty cars "on the cheap" using existing platforms. For Studebaker, the platform was, of course, the compact Lark. For Ford, the platform of choice was the essentially similar, compact Falcon. The front and rear bumpers on the 1965 Mustang are very similar to the highly unusual bumpers that appeared on the Avanti. Both used 289 cubic inch V8 engines. When the exaggerated front over-hang to the Avanti is discounted, the dimensions of it and the Mustang are within an inch or so of each other right down the line. This is not to say that the Mustang was a slavish imitation of the Avanti. For one thing, the Mustang was aimed at an entirely different price point.[4] Still, there is no industry in which competitors are more preoccupied with each other's doings than the American automobile industry. In Detroit, there are few genuine coincidences.[5]

By dint of skill, dedication and a great deal of overtime—twelve to fourteen hour days were the norm—Doehler and his styling crew were able to complete the full-size clay, including chrome detailing but not paint, by April 27th. This was barely forty days since Loewy and his group had begun work on the project in Palm Springs. Such speed was almost unknown in the industry and it created an atmosphere of tremendous excitement among all those involved. It seemed as if Egbert and his car were pulling Studebaker out of its fatal dive by sheer enthusiasm.

On that same day, April 27th, Egbert showed the Avanti clay to the board of directors. Ebstein recalled that the clay model received a "standing ovation." So, as Egbert had hoped, they were greatly impressed by both the quality of the design proposal and Egbert's utter confidence that the car was the answer to Studebaker's automotive problems. The blessing for actual production was granted.

With the project officially on, work was undertaken to convert the clay mock-up into reality. Doehler set to work on interior design, Hardig set about the engineering tasks in earnest and the production people began making molds from the mock-up to send off to Molded Fiberglass Products Company of Ashtabula, Ohio. Molded Fiberglass had been forming fiberghass panels for the Corvette for many years at that point and was the only company with any broad experience in automotive fiberglass applications. It was hoped that by relying upon their expertise Studebaker would be able to avoid most of the problems in using the new material.

Egbert and Loewy were very concerned about the details of the interior design. Kellogg's initial sketches had sported aircraft-type overhead controls and full instrumentation. Egbert, who was big on aviation himself, insisted upon an aircraft level of designed-in safety throughout the car. Thus, the instruments were lighted at night in red, not the white or green then standard in the industry. Red lighting, common in aviation, reduces the stresses of night vision and has since become popular throughout the auto industry. It was also at Egbert's behest that the unique Avanti roll bar was incorporated into the design. That, plus recessed controls and padded everything, made the Avanti interior not only attractive in appearance, but also among the safest ever installed in a production automobile up to that time.

Within about six months of the presentation of the full-size clay to the board, orders went out to suppliers for the interior parts, excepting those that Studebaker felt it could produce itself. Meanwhile, Hardig had been feverishly at work on the mechanical aspects. No money had been budgeted for a new chassis or drive train, of course, so he began rummaging around the Studebaker parts bins to see what he could find to "make do." The fiberglass body with its relatively low rigidity required a strong frame. Hardig chose the reinforced X-member frame then being used on the Lark convertible. As originally conceived by Egbert, the Avanti was to have had independent rear suspension, but this was dropped due to the expense. Instead, the Avanti used front coil springs from the Lark heavy duty police package and rear leaf springs from the Lark station wagon. Heavy duty, adjustable shock absorbers were also added by the time the Avanti went into production.

When it came to power, Hardig was stuck with the same venerable V8 engine Studebakers had been using since 1951 and which for several years had been out-bored, out-powered and generally out-classed by nearly every other manufacturer in the industry. At its best, the engine, now bored to its practical maximum of 289 cubic inches, developed a paltry 225 horsepower with the aid of a four-barrel carburetor. Yet, Hardig had to do his best to turn it into a fire-breather. For want of any reasonable alternatives, he resorted to some basic hot rod techniques: increased compression ratio, more valve lift and so on. The real improvement, however, came from an optional belt-driven centrifugal supercharger acquired from Paxton, which Egbert had just bought. With the company came not only the much needed

Raymond Loewy, left, and Sherwood Egbert with an early Avanti.

supercharger technology, but also (as noted previously) the company president, Andy Granatelli. Granatelli subsequently proved to be a master when it came to promoting the Avanti's high performance potential.

The standard unsupercharged engine, known as the "R1," was capable of moving the Avanti at a pretty decent clip, thanks to the car's light-weight fiberglass construction. Studebaker at first refused to supply horsepower figures for the obvious reason that it was unable to compete with Detroit's 400 cubic inch monsters in that department, but it has since been established that the R1 engine produced approximately 240 horsepower. The supercharged R2 put out close to 300 horsepower.

Egbert had specified that the Avanti should have superior braking capabilities. Hardig discussed this problem with the Bendix Corporation. He came to the decision that caliper disc brakes were what the Avanti should probably employ, but an actual order was not given to Bendix until February, 1962—for May shipment. Bendix was in no position to completely engineer and tool an entirely new type of braking system in that short a period, so it arranged to manufacture under license from Dunlop the same disc brakes that had been stopping Jaguars for several years.

Avanti was not the first American-built car to have disc brakes. Crosley and Chrysler had used different types as early as 1949, but it was the Avanti that employed the first truly modern discs in America and it was the Avanti that convinced Detroit to give them serious consideration.

Against all odds, Hardig managed to take these diverse scraps and pieces and turn them into a genuinely competitive chassis. Toward the end, though, as the program crept further and further over the budget, several unplanned economies were necessitated. One of the most obvious was the wheel covers, which used left over dies from the 1953-55 models and were painted to look like mags.

The interior that was originally planned called for unique Royalite moldings (similar to fiberglass) throughout, but cost restraints resulted in these being replaced by carpeting and by individual vinyl sections that were padded, pleated and sewn together. At least in Ebstein's view, this cutback saved the interior from being "alarmingly over-designed."

Meanwhile, the general situation within the company seemed to be improving, too. By February, 1962, cash had increased from $21 million to around $50 million. This was due, in large part, to the success Egbert had had in diversifying Studebaker-Packard's operations. Four companies were acquired in 1962. Domowatt, S.p.A. in Italy in January, Trans International Airlines (TIA) in October, and Franklin Manufacturing in November. Domowatt was a leading manufacturer of refrigeration equipment and gave Studebaker an entré into the expanding European Common Market. Trans International Airlines was a military contract air carrier. Franklin was a leading manufacturer of refrigerators and freezers supplied under "private label" arrangements with big-name national retailers.

The total amount of sales generated by the company's diversified subsidiaries (including the North American distribution of Mercedes-Benz cars) was now in excess of $100 million and included most of the profitable business the company was doing. The automotive operations, which were still losing money despite the success of the restyled 1962 products, were accounting for a diminishing share of the company's overall sales. This, of course, was precisely what the board of directors had in mind, but the change was fairly dramatic.

In 1959, the company had done 82 percent of its sales in Studebaker cars and trucks. By 1962, that portion was down to barely half. Of the $365.4 million in net sales in 1962, 53 percent came from North American automotive operations, 31 percent came from acquired divisions (including Mercedes-Benz distribution), 11 percent came from defense contracts and 5 percent came from international sales of cars and trucks. It was only on the strength of the diversification drive that Studebaker was able to post a slender profit for the year of $2.6 million, or less than 1 percent on sales.

Studebaker's worldwide sales of cars and trucks rose to 99,476 units in 1962 (up from 92,434 the year before). Of this number, 83,090 were cars and trucks sold in the United States, 7,812 were cars and trucks sold in Canada, and 8,574 were export units, mostly Larks sold as unassembled vehicles to foreign assemblers with whom the company had reached agreements noted previously. Of the American sales, only 5,840 were trucks and fully 10,000 of the cars went to fleet buyers. The Studebaker taxi had dropped to fourth place in New York City sales, but there were still more than 1,000 Lark taxis plying the streets of Gotham and Studebaker continued to do around 10 percent of the business in that small but lucrative market. The Canadian assembly plant at Hamilton, Ontario, was at this point assembling both Larks and Hawks, and there was discussion within the company of the possibility of assembling the forthcoming Avanti there, as well, although this never came to pass.[6]

It was especially disheartening that the automotive operations should have remained in a "loss" condition despite the increase in sales during the 1962 model year. A major cause was nagging low productivity in South Bend which stemmed, in turn, from two main factors: antiquated plant and equipment, and Studebaker's traditionally shortsighted labor policies. Without ample cash Egbert couldn't do much about the factory, but he did try to lay down the law to the labor unions. The result, beginning in January, 1962, was the longest strike, and only the third official (as opposed to wildcat) walk-out, in Studebaker history.

The main point of contention with the union was "personal" time for washing-up and so on. For twenty years, personal time had been pegged at 39 minutes per shift. This contrasted with 24 minutes at General Motors and Ford, and Egbert—who calculated that this generosity on the part of the company had cost it $30 million over the years—was determined to

1963 Studebaker Avanti.

bring it in line as he saw it.[7]

The strike lasted thirty-eight days and included some harrowing moments, such as one occasion when Egbert and a striker came to blows. In the end, personal time had been cut back to 34 minutes and the company had won a few other minor concessions. This was not precisely what management had had in mind, to be sure but, never-the-less, it did give a labor contract somewhat more in line with the industry norm. In a report to Studebaker-Packard stockholders, Egbert tried to put the best face on it:

> It was our firm purpose during the negotiations to secure a contract which would materially improve our competitive position on labor costs. This was accomplished in part while still granting a wage increase for each of the next three years and providing certain improvements in employee benefits. The new agreement provides for the elimination of five minutes of clean-up time upon completion of 1962 model production, and it enables us to make more productive use of the employees' working time.[8]

By early 1962, the first Avanti prototype was ready to be assembled. The strike caused some delays and Hardig remembered, "We put the first one together ourselves and smuggled it out to the proving grounds."

As the New York International Automobile Show drew nearer, the work in South Bend became more and more feverish while final details were added to two prototypes. One was sent to New York just in time for the April 21st deadline. It was kept under wraps until the 26th when it was unveiled. On the same day the second prototype was unveiled at both a shareholders meeting and at a press preview in South Bend. An airlift operation flew an Avanti prototype to 24 cities in 16 days as a dramatic way of introducing Studebaker dealers to the new car. A sign over the car in South Bend carried the slogan, "A new star is born."

It was at that same Studebaker-Packard shareholders meeting, incidentally, that the shareholders voted to drop "Packard" from the company's name. So, Packard was officially history, but the Avanti represented the hope of an exciting future and Egbert was determined to fan the fires as much as possible. Studebaker public relations personnel found themselves spending many evenings hard at work churning out press releases. Anyone who claimed to be a journalist was given an Avanti to road test. This caused some embarrassment for Egbert when three of them were wrecked in one week, but the publicity was worth it.

Egbert had diversified the company dramatically since assuming the presidency. Studebaker was now solidly in the black, with the exception of its automotive division. Still, even there things were looking up. The restyled 1962 Larks had been well received. The new Hawk GT, which had been restyled on a minuscule budget, had stirred quite a bit of favorable reaction. In the first six months, despite a strike that had kept the factory shut down for the first few weeks of the New Year, production was up 64 percent over 1961.

The Federal government continued to do what it could to bolster the faltering operations in South Bend. In March, a $21.6 million contract was awarded to Studebaker for the manufacture of 2,821 trucks by April, 1963. In December, a $32 million contract was awarded for an additional 4,192 trucks to be built by June, 1964. And now the Avanti had had a spectacular debut. Surely the situation was finally in hand.

Well, not quite. Grave problems would envelop the program even before the first Avanti rolled from the production line. The initial storm warnings came from Molded Fiberglass late in the spring. They were manufacturing the various body parts, approximately 130 in all. They had also agreed to assemble the bodies, but when they attempted to do so many of the parts refused to fit. Horrified Studebaker engineers rushed to Ohio to somehow *make* them fit, while at the same time sort out the sources of the problems. It wasn't easy. It was June before the first Avanti limped from the assembly line in South Bend and, in fact, the difficulties were never completely overcome. A program of running changes was instituted to attempt to keep up with the engineers as well as the service people in the field.

One of the most serious defects was discovered within a few weeks of the first production. The rear window would "pop out" at high speeds due to air pressure. The design was revised, but more valuable time was lost.

From the very beginning, sizzling performance had been one of Egbert's requirements for the new car.[9] He now assigned to Andy Granatelli the task of putting the Avanti through its paces. The Avanti was, of course, completely unsuitable for most racing activities, but, thanks to its splendid aerodynamic qualities, it was a natural for high-speed runs. Concerning its aerodynamics, Loewy later recalled an interesting encounter:

> The chief engineer of Porsche in Stuttgart asked me, "Loewy, how did you wind-test the Avanti?" I said, "Why do you ask?" "Well, we know a little here about streamlining and your Avanti is almost perfect, no parasitic noise at high speed, skin friction reduced to practically nothing." I said, "I didn't test it at all." He couldn't believe it. "No," I said, "I did it by feel and design intuition."[10]

As soon as an extra prototype Avanti could be made available, the three Granatelli brothers—Andy, Vince and Joe—were on their way to the Bonneville Salt Flats in Utah. Using a basically stock Avanti powered by an R2 supercharged engine that had been bored to 299 cubic inches, they set two major American class C records: a two-way flying mile record of 168.15 mph and a standing start mile record of 92.03 mph.

Unfortunately, though, production problems continued to plague the program. The initial target had been 1,000 units per month, but actual production did not even reach half that figure until January, 1963. Then, a strike at Molded Fiberglass in the latter months of 1962 threw another wrench into the works. When problems in Ashtabula continued unabated, Studebaker finally tried building the fiberglass bodies in South Bend, although without much success. Orders filled after the first enthusiastic showings were canceled by more and more buyers.

After the crash-program exertions with the Lark, Hawk and Avanti lines in 1962-63, the company still managed to come up with a few more surprises in 1963. The biggest of these was the Wagonaire station wagon, which the company touted as the "most versatile wagon on wheels." Basically, the company took the sunroof idea and put it at the back over the cargo area. In this way, and with the help of a new one-piece tailgate, the cargo area could be opened up to turn the Wagonaire into what was, in effect, a convertible pick-up truck for carrying out-sized loads, etc.

The model range was becoming a tad confusing at this point. At the top, of course, were the Avanti and the Hawk. The top of the Lark range included the Cruiser sedan and the Daytona two-door hardtop and convertible, all of which featured more-or-less similar interior and exterior trim. The Wagonaire was in a class by itself, while the mid-range Custom and base Regal lines were available in two- and four-door sedan body styles. Then, a "Standard" series was offered to fleet buyers who wanted a super-

1963 Studebaker Wagonaire.

1963 Studebaker Cruiser.

low-cost car. The Standard was a revival of the old Scotsman concept in two- or four-door sedan versions, with every conceivable bit of exterior trim and ornamentation deleted to bring down the sticker price. Studebaker promoted the Standard as the cheapest car of its description available for fleet use, which it should have been considering the level of content left in it. Curiously, all Studebaker options were offered with the Standard, including air conditioning.

All Larks featured new instrument panels and (on most) fancier exterior trim, although the looks were not greatly altered from the 1962 restyle. A dual braking system was standard equipment, disc brakes were optional. The engine line-up was also similar to that offered in 1963, although the 289 V8 was downgraded to 210 horsepower. This may have been done to make room for the supercharger options created for the Avanti that were also, technically, available on the Lark and Hawk.

Elsewhere in the corporation, however, things were turning sour. In August, a strike at Budd, a major Studebaker supplier, caused production stoppages on the new 1963 models. When the assembly line began moving again, it was discovered that the seals around the roof of the innovative Wagonaire station wagon needed to be redesigned. Egbert was forced to delay the 1963 model announcement by two weeks, but even then it was a long while before Wagonaires were supplied in sufficient quantities to dealers who had been looking to them to provide much of the sales thrust of the new model year.

An early shipment of Avantis on a Studebaker car hauler.

The financial situation was also worsening—again. Studebaker had started the year with over $50 million in cash, but the Avanti program had been expensive and, as the year ended, had returned nothing to the corporate coffers. January, 1963, saw cash down to dangerous levels once again: approximately $24 million in a company that was doing close to $400 million in annual sales.

Trans-International was looking more and more like a total failure and the Franklin acquisition was turning into an albatross, as well. In particular, the company had borrowed $25 million to clinch the Franklin deal and the credit thus used up was making it that much harder to borrow money for future automotive development.

Egbert had planned to launch a dramatically new line of cars for the 1964 model year. Loewy was hard at work in Paris on two competing neo-Avanti designs that were also possible 1965 or 1966 models. Not really Avantis, they were designed to take Avanti design themes and bring them to the standard Studebaker line, using the existing Lark inner body shell and running gear. Pinchon-Parat, a Parisian coachbuilder, had been retained to develop running prototypes and these were well along. Egbert had also commissioned an interesting series of 1965, 1966 and 1967 prototypes from Brooks Stevens, and these, too, were being built in prototype form.

The problem was that a new range of cars for 1964 would cost something close to $20 million (even with carry-over components) and what the Franklin mess hadn't done to complicate the possibility of raising that much money had been taken care of by the botched start-up of the 1963 line.

There was little enough that Egbert could do to stem the tide. In fact, the board was quietly developing what was known as "Plan X," which called for the complete liquidation of the automotive operations. Matters came to a head at the board meeting in January, 1963. Two options were discussed: the substantially new Avanti-esque range upon which Loewy had been working, on the one hand, and getting out of cars completely, on the other. Egbert won that one, but, as sales softened, the banks insisted that in order to get the funds required for its new models the company would have to put up all of its diversified divisions as collateral. That was too much even for Egbert and so the 1964 plans were pared back to the several millions it would cost for a facelift of the existing Lark.

Francis stepped down as board chairman in June. His replacement was Randolph "Bob" Guthrie of the prestigious New York law firm of Nixon, Mudge, Rose, Guthrie and Alexander, which also, of course, represented Daimler-Benz North America (DBNA).[11] He immediately set about making a detailed assessment of the future of the automotive operations. His conclusion was that there wasn't any—unless the reskinned 1964 line took off, and he didn't see much hope for that. Egbert disagreed, but it was clear

1964 Studebakers.

to everyone that the banks weren't going to advance the company another dime for new cars if the 1964s failed to make a spectacular success.

On the other hand, despite the Franklin and Trans-International fiascoes, the diversification drive had proven to be such an overall success that—for the first time—the company could seriously consider the possibility of continuing on without the automotive operations at all. That realization was a turning point, for it opened up the viable possibility of a partial liquidation.

Meanwhile, production commenced on the 1964 models in August. Despite the comparatively pal-

Randolph "Bob" Guthrie.

try sum spent on them, and even though the interior and the chassis remained much as they had in 1963, the Larks looked surprisingly fresh. The idea was to give the Larks a longer and wider look, and, in that, the redesign was largely successful. The series names were juggled once again—one wonders if anyone (in or out of the company) could keep them straight by this point—and consisted of the Cruiser and Daytona at the top, the mid-range Commander (replacing the Custom) and the low-end Challenger (replacing the Regal). The Wagonaire rounded out the Lark line-up. Quad head lights were standard on the Cruiser, Daytona and Wagonaire, while the Commander and Challenger reverted to single head light units.

Despite detail refinements, the Hawk and Avanti were largely unchanged. Alterations to the Avanti included squared headlight bezels, a grille covering the front air intake opening and an extra set of vents on the left side of the cowl. Avanti production changes were not always made with precision, though, and there are some cars titled as 1964s that still have the round bezels which remained available as a no cost option. The major change to the Hawk was an attractive half-vinyl roof option.

1964 Studebaker Avanti.

The company had stopped advertising horsepower ratings across the board because it couldn't keep up with the mega-figures being quoted (sometimes fancifully) by its Big Three competitors. There was only so much that could be done with a small-block V8. The 1964 models did, however, offer a range of Jet Thrust variants known by the designations R1, R2, R3 and R4. The first two were 289 cubic inch jobs, while the latter two were bored out to 304.5 cubic inches. The R1, which was standard on the Avanti, was a normally-aspirated four-barrel engine, while the R2 and R3 versions were supercharged. The R4 was listed as a normally-aspirated engine with dual-four-barrel carbs, but it is not known if any were, in fact, installed in production cars. The company touted the R-series options as "the Super Series Studebakers" in which "130 mph is merely incidental." In truth, any of the upper R-series engines had to have delivered daunting performance in a car as small as the Lark.

The R3 and the R4 engines were developed largely through the efforts of the Granatelli brothers. Both used Studebaker 289 blocks bored out to an absolute maximum 304.5 cubic inches, at which point the cylinder walls were almost thin enough to see the pistons going up and down. Both engines had reworked heads and much larger valves. The supercharged R3 was unofficially rated at about 335 horsepower, but a properly tuned one

1964 Studebaker Avanti.

was said by Andy's brother, Vince, to be capable of close to 400 horsepower. Only nine R3s were built by the factory, although a few R3 conversions were earketed on an independent basis on the part of Paxton. No R4 engines were installed in regular production Avantis, although one reportedly made it into a Lark prototype.

Buoyed by these new engines, Studebaker decided to try for some additional performance records in the summer and fall of 1963. They were timed to coincide with the introduction of the 1964 models. An entire fleet of Studebakers was involved this time, from the lowliest six-cylinder Commander to the exalted R3 Avanti. Just to add some special excitement, the Granatellis also put together a mind-boggling R5 Avanti, known as the "Due Centro," equipped with twin superchargers. The R5 used the semi-standard 304.5 block. A special grind camshaft was used, ground to Paxton Products specifications. A magneto ignition system supplied the spark. The induction system utilized dual Paxton superchargers, one for each cylinder bank, paired with a single Bendix fuel injection system. (This was the

Studebaker Avanti "Due Centro" during a speed run in Utah.

system originally developed for the Novi V8 racing engines.) The engine ran a dry sump oil system with an oil reservoir and oil cooler. The R5 was redlined at 7,000 RPM and developed approximately 575 horsepower.

First, an R2 Avanti, sponsored by Sears and using ordinary All-State Guardsman 6.70x15 tires, was driven on four fast coast-to-coast trips. New York-to-San Diego was done in 52 hours and 6 minutes. Los Angeles-to-New York was done in even less: 49 hours and 36 minutes. The car was then brought to the Bonneville Salt Flats in October where Joe Granatelli, using the same engine and tires, made a run of 147 mph.

Then Andy, with three passengers, made a leisurely run at nearly 143 mph. After that, the team got down to serious business with the entire fleet. Speed records in the flying kilometer ranged from 59.8 mph in the six- cylinder Commander to a stunning 196.62 in the "Due Centro" Avanti. All in all, using twelve cars over a period of five days, 72 USAC records were set in half a dozen different classes.

In addition to Granatelli's efforts, Studebaker was still a hot topic with the media. In September, the company announced that it had managed to place an Avanti on the popular television program, "The Price Is Right," as a grand prize. This was supposed to heighten public awareness of the Avanti (and of Studebaker, of course) in the weeks stretching from mid-Septem-

1964 Studebaker Gran Turisimo Hawk.

ber through mid-October. Concurrently, a special "Avanti Inventory and Retail Program Contest" was announced for the dealers.

Not that any of it did much good. Sales, which had started to fall in the summer of 1962 after the first excitement over the Avanti began to wear off, continued their downward trajectory. Nothing Egbert or his people could do as 1963 wore on seemed to be able to reverse the tide. Automobile production in 1963 was barely half what was considered a reasonable break-even point and, worse, was sinking fast. The company's cash position continued to inexorably worsen, too, and reserves declined to frightening levels. By the end of the year they would reach a paltry $8 million, perhaps one-fourth of what a company the size of Studebaker required just to function normally. The non-automotive divisions continued to grow and produce solid profits, but the ailing automotive operations gobbled them all up—and more besides.

In October, with an 86-day supply of unsold cars at the factory and in dealer hands, the production lines were stopped. In early November, Egbert, tired and ill with his cancer, went on leave of absence. Then, on November 25th, he resigned.[12]

Byers Burlingame, the chief financial officer since 1961, was named to succeed Egbert. Burlingame had got his start with Packard in 1925, then spent his career on the financial side of the business, first with Packard and, later, with Studebaker. It was he who had been given the miserable job of liquidating Packard's Detroit assets. By all accounts, he didn't want the presidency and it is easy to understand why, for he realized it meant that he was about to go through the same thing again in South Bend.

On December 4th, Burlingame sent a letter to Studebaker dealers:

> It certainly is no news to you that we are losing money in the automobile business. When that happens— to you, or to us—there is only one thing to do and that is to pull your belt in tight—and real tight...This means we will regulate automotive production in accordance with orders received.
>
> With our factory inventory in control and production limited in this way, we can still supply your orders with reasonable promptness. However, let me point out to you that both you and

we need an increased volume of sales to operate profitably and to keep your supply lines current.[13]

Translation: Studebaker would no longer build cars without firm dealer orders. The company had been filling lags on the line with cars built "on spec" that the zone offices then had to foist off on the dealers, usually at distressed prices. This was great for the dealers, but ruinous for the company. A more subtle message in the letter was that continued Studebaker production might depend on the ability of the dealers to generate sufficient orders to enable South Bend to run the lines profitably. Three days later, on December 7th—a Saturday—the other shoe dropped. Union leaders were called in to hear the news that production would be halted in South Bend. The following Monday, the official announcement was made:

> Byers A. Burlingame, newly elected president of Studebaker Corporation, announced today adoption by the board of directors of a long-range program for continued production of Studebaker automobiles.
> This new program involves the shifting of Studebaker's primary base of automotive manufacture to the corporation's modern assembly plant at Hamilton, Ont., Canada...The high productivity and efficiency of the Hamilton plant should permit continuance of Studebaker's automotive activities on a profitable, although more restricted, basis...[14]

The announcement was upbeat, probably in order to avoid shaking public confidence in the company. That same day, a telegram signed by Burlingame was sent to all Studebaker dealers:

> Official press account of PM December 9 and December 10 will make clear an unequivocal statement Studebaker staying in automobile business with manufacturing being moved at a later date to Canadian plants in Hamilton, Ontario. Fullest details being airmailed to you. I feel strongly this move placed us on sound basis to build for the future.[15]

Two days later, however, Burlingame sent an upbeat message to Studebaker dealers that, considering the experience and savvy of its recipients, seems rather curious:

> I am sure that you are all as excited and pleased as we are that finally a solution to our difficulties has been reached...
>
> As you can appreciate, this is most unhappy news for the people of South Bend, but for the Corporation as a whole—for its shareholders, and for its dealer and its customers, it spells the best possible news. We are going to stay permanently in the auto business on a basis that unfortunately may not keep pace with your requirements at first, but which has a solid foundation on which we can grow rapidly and profitably over the years...
>
> We feel sure we can count on your continued support in making this planned growth of Studebaker a solid success.[16]

Excited and pleased? Planned growth? One wonders whether Burlingame was kidding the dealers or himself. It was left for Louis Minkel, Studebaker's marketing chief and president of its Automotive Sales Corporation subsidiary, to explain to the dealers in grisly detail what the decision would really mean to them:

> We will continue to manufacture certain component parts in South Bend to supply Hamilton and we will continue final assembly in South Bend as long as we have sufficient flow of orders to maintain full production. In the meantime, Hamilton production will be stepped up as rapidly as possible.
>
> The volume of our truck business has fallen off to the extent that it is no longer profitable for us to operate that line and a similar situation exists with regard to the Avanti. That plant will, therefore, be closed and production of all trucks and the Avanti will be discontinued as soon as we have assembled the cars for which we now have orders.
>
> The Canadian plant will be able to assemble all of the model cars which we are currently producing with the exception of the

Avanti and the Hawk...

This shift in operations is, of course, a terrible blow to South Bend and its neighboring communities. All of us involved in this decision regret that it has become necessary. The surest way to convince the public that we are going to stay in the automobile business is to operate profitably and this we could not do under the circumstances in South Bend...[17]

So, the Lark would continue on in Canada for the time being, but the Avanti and the Hawk were dead. On December 31, 1963, the last Studebaker Avanti—serial number R-5643—was built and the automotive assembly lines in South Bend fell silent forever.

Many workers refused to believe it. Rather like the reaction of those who had become used to living with a chronically ill relative, there had been so many bad periods followed by so many recoveries that they had come to believe that Studebaker would survive anything. Commented one veteran as he left the plant for the last time:

Just before I checked out I went up to the second floor and walked along the empty assembly line. Everything was still in place and I thought, "We could start production tomorrow."[18]

For South Bend, there would, indeed, be a tomorrow—and a surprisingly prosperous one, as it turned out—but it wouldn't involve Studebaker. The company's last automotive gamble, the Avanti, had, in hard commercial terms, been a failure.

Without a doubt, though, the Avanti ranks as one of the most significant cars produced in America in the postwar era. It was the first car in this country to have modern disc brakes. It pioneered the concept of designed-in safety that the government later picked-up with a vengeance. Its aerodynamic wedge shape, which seemed so astounding at the time, is now the norm. Far more than a pretty face, it was immensely influential. If the Avanti proved to be Studebaker's swan song, it was an unforgettable one.

Notes

The most important resources drawn upon in the writing of this chapter include Richard M. Langworth's *Studebaker, 1946-1966*, Michael Beatty, Patrick Furlong, and Loren Pennington's *Studebaker: Less Than They Promised*, and Donald T. Critchlow's *The Life and Death of an American Corporation*. Heinz C. Hoppe's *Serving the Star Around the World* gave valuable insights into the important connection between Studebaker-Packard and Daimler-Benz. Studebaker-Packard Corporation papers in the author's collection, including annual Reports, brochures and miscellaneous publications, were also especially important source material. Periodicals that proved to be important resources included various issues of: *Automotive News*, *Avanti Magazine*, *Car & Driver*, *Cars & Parts*, *Esquire*, *Motor Trend*, *Road & Track*, *South Bend Tribune*, *Special-Interest Autos*, and *Turning Wheels*.

[1] 1961 Studebaker-Packard Annual Report.

[2] The 1961 run was "sold out" in the sense that the dealers had committed to purchase all the cars Studebaker-Packard planned to build. The dealers still had to move them at the retail level, of course, but their willingness to commit themselves was, in itself, an encouraging vote of confidence in Egbert's leadership.

[3] Studebaker-Packard files, author's collection.

[4] One wonders how the fate of the Avanti—and of Studebaker—would have changed had the Avanti been pegged toward the same volume market segment as the Mustang.

[5] The actual comparative dimensions are as follows:

	1955 Thunderbird	1965 Mustang	1963 Avanti
Length:	175.3	182.0	192.4
Width:	70.3	69.0	70.4
Wheelbase:	102.0	108.0	109.0

[6] And, what a pity, too. Assembly of the Avanti in Hamilton might have changed the course of that model's history in intriguing ways—and, perhaps, that of the company's automotive operations, in general.

[7] This was a curious issue, since personal time was 37 minutes at Chrysler and 40 minutes at American Motors. The supposedly super-efficient Canadian operation at Hamilton, Ontario, allowed 61 minutes!

[8] 1962 Studebaker-Packard Annual Report.

[9] As the Avanti's problems continued to pile up, about the only pleasure Egbert managed to derive from the car was behind the wheel at speeds that often approached 130 mph—and this on the public highways in and around South Bend. This activity did not endear him to the local police.

[10] Loewy, p. 15.

[11] Please refer to Chapters Eight and Nine for more about Guthrie and DBNA.

[12] Egbert finally succumbed to his illness on July 30, 1969.

[13] Studebaker Corporation papers, author's collection.

[14] Studebaker Corporation papers, author's collection.

[15] Studebaker Corporation papers, author's collection.

[16] Studebaker Corporation papers, author's collection.

[17] Studebaker Corporation papers, author's collection.

[18] Beatty, Furlong, and Pennington, p. 48.

Overleaf, the first 1965 Studebaker ready to be shipped to the United States, with Gordon Grundy, left, and manufacturing director W. A. Moeser.

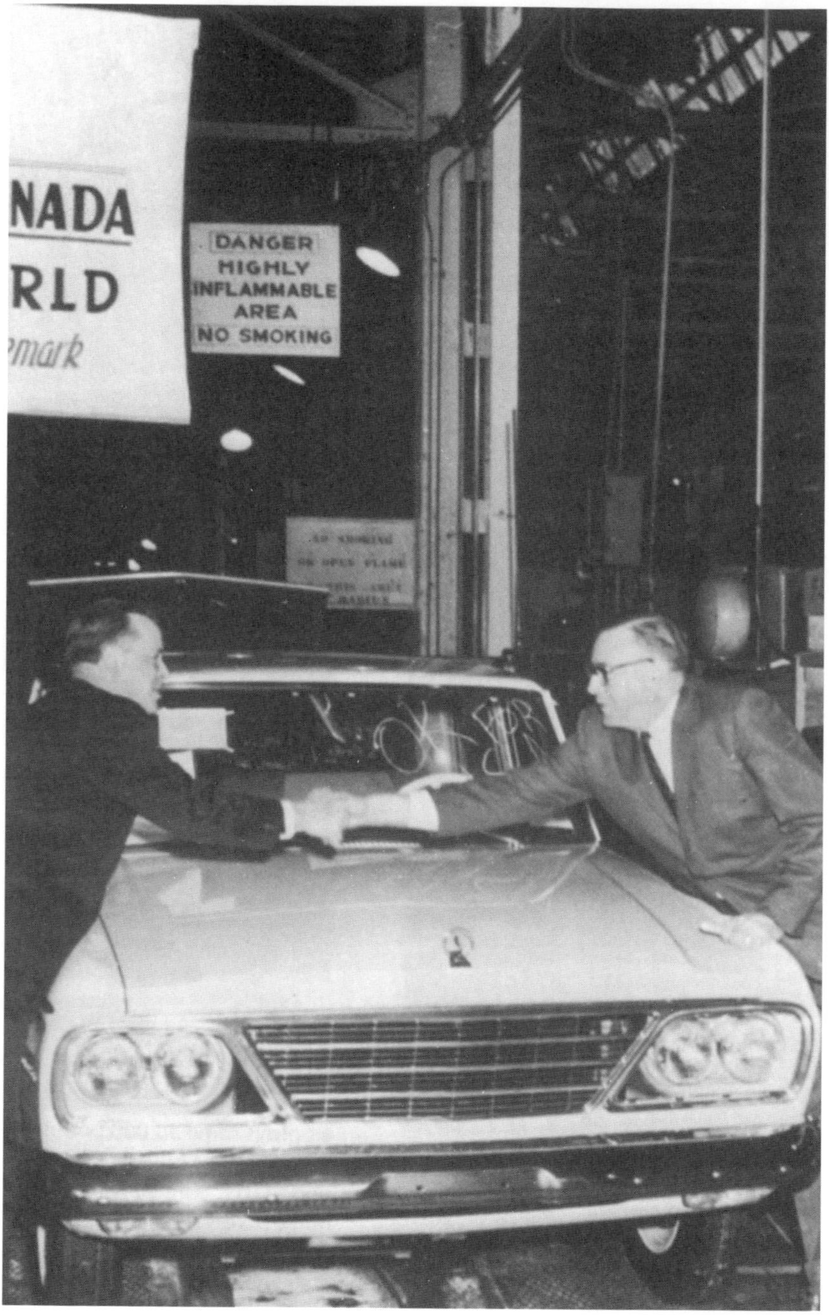
NADA
RLD
DANGER
HIGHLY
INFLAMMABLE
AREA
NO SMOKING

ELEVEN

Metamorphosis

With the start of the New Year, only government contract work continued in South Bend, and only then in order to complete contracts already in hand. Production of "Zip" vans for the Post Office continued for a time, but the contract for five-ton military trucks was eventually sold.

When the dust settled, Studebaker reported net revenues of $403.3 million in 1963. Car production dipped to 67,918, down from 86,974 in 1962, and the corporation reported an operating loss of $16.9 million. The automotive division, for its part, had lost more than $25 million during its final year in South Bend, not counting the $64 million set aside to pay for the closing of the various automotive facilities and properties in the United States. Even though much of this latter sum must have involved "paper losses" (write-offs for undepreciated facilities and equipment no longer useful to the company and so forth), one does not simply turn out the lights and walk away from a giant industrial operation. It can cost a fortune just to quit. Adding it all up, the posted loss for the year ended-up at a staggering $80.9 million.[1]

Given the magnitude of the crisis, it is difficult to see how the directors had any other responsible choice. A board's first obligation is to see to it that its company survives and survival in December, 1963, was in doubt so long as the failing automotive operations continued. Not even a company approaching half-a-billion dollars in sales volume is a bottomless pit of money. The real wonder is that the end didn't come any sooner. The board had, in fact, been patient far beyond the bounds of sound business sense.

Since its inception as Studebaker-Packard Corporation, the company had made only one meaningful profit—in 1959—and the automotive division had lost money every single year with the sole exception of 1959. The total over-all corporate losses had mounted to over $113 million by the end of 1963. The automotive division's losses were, of course, much greater and they were getting worse rather than better. No company could possibly continue on in that fashion indefinitely.

Sherwood Egbert had given the automotive division an exciting reprieve, but, when production difficulties turned the Avanti into a financial disaster and Studebaker's other product lines began to slide perceptibly, the outcome was inevitable. Many Studebaker enthusiasts blame Egbert for this, contending that the botched Avanti effort drained away capital that could have been used for the mainstream products. What these people miss is the fact that Studebaker was already effectively dead as an auto producer when Egbert signed on in 1961. Indeed, his primary assignment from the board was to speed diversification so that the company could afford to get out of cars entirely. The board wouldn't have spent the sum required for a new standard car line even if such a sum could have been raised—and, indeed, had already refused to do so. Egbert understood this, even if his modern-day detractors don't seem to grasp the point.

Despite a couple of notable misfires, the diversification drive had been everything for which the board had hoped and, all things considered, probably the best anyone could have achieved. If the Studebaker car was dead (or close to it), there were only but so many miracles that could reasonably be expected from one man. Egbert had done his best and that proved to be good enough to save the company.[2]

As *Ward's*, the industry trade journal, observed:

> The future portends well for Studebaker Corporation, even though its history as the oldest producer of "vehicles" in the United States came to an end in 1963...It had become quite apparent that the automotive division had become something of a millstone to the corporation's other eight diversified divisions, all of which were operating profitably.

That was putting it gently. The 1963 Studebaker annual report issued in March, 1964, also attempted to put the best face possible on the retreat:

> The basic difficulty in South Bend was insufficient volume of sales. Our facilities there were such that there was no way to reduce our costs so that a profit could be made upon such volume. The Canadian plant, on the other hand, is relatively modern and it can be operated at a profit on a much lower volume. Therefore, we have decided to live with the sales we have rather than to continue to hope they will improve. Let us make it clear, however, that all of our automotive problems are not solved. Many new problems arise, including finding new sources for some components, maintaining competitive prices on reduced production volume, reducing our sales force in the United States, and the like.[3]

The report went on to make it clear that, while automobile production would continue, the future of Studebaker was not going to be dependent upon automobiles for its well-being:

> Studebaker has now moved into a new period in its corporate history. It is now a diversified company of which only one of its many activities is the manufacture of automobiles. This difference is more than mere semantics—it represents a fundamental change. Other divisions of the corporation now rival the sales volume of the automotive division. For example, the sales of our Franklin appliance division could possibly exceed automotive sales in 1964...The heavy losses from the automotive division are now ended. While it still has its problems, Studebaker has emerged from a period of crisis as a solidly diversified corporation with a sound earning potential.[4]

Gordon E. Grundy, who had been head of the Canadian subsidiary since 1958, was named the new head of the Studebaker automotive division and immediately announced plans to expand Hamilton's capacity to 30,000 cars per year. While the Hamilton facility had had a break-even point of around 7,000 cars per year, that was based on being a satellite assembly point for the main automotive operation in South Bend. With South Bend shuttered, all the overhead would be dumped onto the Canadian operations and the break-even point would inevitably rise. By most accounts, though, Grundy really believed that Studebaker's automotive operations could continue on a permanent basis in Hamilton.

Most of the 1964 Studebaker line was continued through to the end of the 1964 model run. The Hawk and the Avanti failed to make the cut, as has been noted, and the low-buck Challenger line was also dropped in order to "halt production of vehicles which lacked volume movement," but there were a couple of compensating gains. The Cruiser had not been previously assembled in Canada, so it was a new offering to Canadian buyers. Likewise, a two-door Commander Special with a high-grade Daytona-like interior was sent south to American buyers for the first time.

It is unclear, in retrospect, why the Hawk was not continued. As the 1962 annual report made clear, the Hawk had been assembled at Hamilton during the 1962 model run and—at least by implication—into the 1963 run, as well. Furthermore, there is every indication that Studebaker dealers wanted it to continue. The Avanti was an easier call as it had only been assembled in South Bend and its assembly facility was unique and incompatible with the Lark facilities in either South Bend or in Hamilton. The

The Studebaker plant at Hamilton, Ontario.

Avanti *could* have been continued, but only by retaining the unique Avanti facility in South Bend or by physically removing it to Hamilton and re-establishing it there. Given that the Avanti had never earned a dime, it is hardly surprising that no Herculean efforts were made to save it in December of 1963.

Gordon Grundy.

As it turned out, the corporation reported a profit of $8 million in 1964. While it was unreported how much—if any—of this profit came from the down-sized automotive division, the Hamilton plant produced 17,614 cars—up 115 percent from the 8,190 built there in 1963. A total of 27,648 cars were sold in the United States during 1964, but perhaps half this number included cars built in the United States and still in factory or dealer inventories when the lights went out in South Bend. On the diversification front, corporate debt was reduced by $18.4 million, in part due to the sale of the Mercedes-Benz Sales, Inc., distribution organization to the parent company, Daimler-Benz.

Since the reorganization of 1958, Heinz Hoppe had been intentionally building up a sales organization within Daimler-Benz North America (DBNA) for the purpose of an eventual takeover of sales and distribution responsibilities from Studebaker. Although it is doubtful whether this long-term plan was ever expressed to South Bend, it was clearly understood in Stuttgart. There was, however, still considerable trepidation on the part of key people at Daimler Benz with regard to managing a sales and distribution organization in North America. So long as Studebaker did reasonably well, simple inertia promised to maintain the relationship as it was

As Studebaker continued its deterioration in the early 1960s, however, little money was available for long-term investment in the automotive operations, Mercedes-Benz included. Hoppe pressed South Bend again and again to invest more in service and parts facilities, and in service training.

Jane Kmita, Miss Dominion of Canada, with a 1964 Studebaker Daytona.

It never happened, or at least never at the level Hoppe considered necessary for the future development of Mercedes-Benz cars in North America.

Matters were destined to come to a head eventually and the cessation of automobile production in South Bend sparked the final confrontation. The appointment of Bob Guthrie as Studebaker's chairman that summer meant that someone sympathetic to Daimler-Benz's problems was running the show. It also meant a delicate balancing act for Guthrie, who, despite long-standing ties to Daimler-Benz, was duty-bound to protect Studebaker's interests and see to it that South Bend got a good settlement.

After months of sometimes contentious negotiations, a termination was agreed upon by all parties in December, 1964. Studebaker received $3.8 million in compensation for the seven years remaining in the distribution agreement and Daimler-Benz won the right to control its own destiny in North America. A new distribution entity, Mercedes-Benz North America (MBNA) was created, with Heinz Hoppe entrusted with day-to-day management. For "Happy" Hoppe, it was a happy day, indeed.

The eight year relationship between Studebaker and Mercedes-Benz had been a tortuous one, and one that had a profound effect upon Studebaker-Packard Corporation and, later, Studebaker Corporation. It was also a vitally important period in the history of Daimler-Benz in North America. The new organization, Mercedes-Benz North America (MBNA), has represented Daimler-Benz products in the United States ever since.[5]

It is interesting to note that while Studebaker and Daimler-Benz may have agreed to an amicable divorce, many Studebaker dealers in the United States and Canada continued to represent Mercedes-Benz cars. For many of them, it was the only profitable line they had left. MBNA, for its part, was only too happy to continue the relationships so long as the dealers met MBNA standards. MBNA contacted 210 of the 430 Mercedes-Benz dealers that existed at the time of the termination, offering them a continuing relationship. Of that number, 195 accepted MBNA's terms and became the core of the new Mercedes-Benz dealer network, and many of the largest Mercedes dealers in North America even today—if their origins are traced back far enough—started out with Studebaker or Packard.

As for Daimler-Benz, Hoppe summed up the experience thusly:

> Despite many difficulties and setbacks, Daimler-Benz AG succeeded in establishing a firm base for its activities on the North American continent. For everyone concerned, this permanent confrontation with professionals from the local automobile industry was extremely instructive. We got to know the practices and also the weaknesses of the American market and were able, while Mercedes-Benz Sales was operating under the auspices of Studebaker, to build up a closely-knit team of well-qualified employees, who knew exactly what to do—and how not to do it. This was the end of our apprenticeship, and we now wished to take control of our own affairs.[6]

Meanwhile, thinly revised for 1965, Studebakers were marketed as the "Common-Sense" cars. This was an attempt to make a virtue out of the inescapable reality that the automotive division could no longer afford dramatic annual model changes. Cruiser, Daytona and Commander series designations were used. The Wagonaire was offered in high-trim (Daytona)

1965 Studebaker Cruiser.

and low-trim (Commander) versions. Since the two-door hardtop and convertible body styles were dropped, the Daytona was available only as a two-door "sports sedan." A vinyl roof, however, was standard on the Daytona and this was a first for Studebaker other than the partial vinyl top offered on the Hawk during its abbreviated 1964 model run.

The major development, however, was the switch to Chevrolet engines for the entire Studebaker range. This was necessary due to the shutting down of the foundry in South Bend. The 194 cubic inch, in-line, six-cylinder Chevy engine was standard, rated at 120 horsepower. The 283 cubic inch V8 was optional and carried an advertised rating of 195 horsepower. That was the good news. The bad news was that General Motors was charging about $130 per engine more than it had cost Hamilton to buy them from South Bend. This, in turn, raised the break-even point again. It now stood at 14,000 units per year.

While this was going on, Grundy was negotiating with Toyota for distribution rights for that firm's Japanese-built cars and light trucks. Nothing came of it in the end and the talks were broken-off in March, 1965, but, in retrospect, the potential for that idea was intriguing...to say the least.[7]

An approach was also made to Nissan but it, too, failed to produce results.

Grundy then came up with a plan that was stunning in its sheer audacity. Volkswagen was enjoying a period of immense popularity in North America, Canada included. As a foreign manufacturer, Volkswagen had to pay duty on every car imported. Domestic Canadian manufacturers, in contrast, were exempt from this duty, so Grundy proposed that Hamilton take over the distribution of Volkswagens in Canada, import the cars duty free, and split the savings with the parent firm in Wolfsburg! It was a sham deal from the start, a fact about which Grundy made no bones at all. Nothing would have changed except that Studebaker, not Volkswagen, would have been listed as the importer of record. Grundy never intended to take physical possession of a single car; it would have been a paper transaction, pure and simple, but one that, owing to Volkswagen's volume in the Canadian market, was potentially lucrative in the extreme. Amazingly, there were influential men in the government in Ottawa who saw no problem with this at all, who even supported it. They realized it was a clever fraud, but they also knew that the shaky Hamilton operation needed a solid rev-

1965 Studebaker Daytona.

enue base to guarantee its future and the Canadian jobs that went with it. Soon enough, alas, other voices were raised in Parliament, voices that regarded the entire scheme as more fraud than clever and thus forced an end to yet another of Grundy's ingenious ideas.

As 1965 wore on, it was becoming abundantly clear even to Grundy that his own board increasingly regarded the continued existence of the Studebaker car as a nuisance—at best. He was instructed not to sign any additional dealers or to replace any that dropped by the wayside. Nor would there be any funds available for a 1966 facelift.

Undaunted, Grundy managed a face-lifted 1966 line, anyway, and did so without a penny of assistance from the corporation. The face-lift was done by a former Loewy designer, Bob Marcks, who was then a partner in industrial design firm of Marcks, Hazelquist and Powers. Marcks' contribution consisted of new exterior trim, including the grille, and some freshening of the interiors.

The model range was reduced to five: Cruiser, Daytona, Commander (in two- or four-door sedan versions) and Wagonaire (available only in up-level trim). The engine offerings were increased to three; a 230 cubic inch six joined the two engines offered in 1965. A transistorized ignition system was made standard on all models, as was an ingenious new "Refreshaire" air circulation system that drew fresh air into the passenger compartment through the cowl vents and exhausted the old air through vents located above the tail lights.

Toward the end, the Hamilton operation was actually turning a small profit under Grundy's capable leadership. The money being made was not enough to interest the board, though. By that point, the automobile men were nearly all gone and Studebaker was a growing conglomerate run by New York financiers far more concerned about the price of their stock than they were about the cars they were building. For them, the very existence of the Canadian operation was an embarrassment that wouldn't go away.

Early in 1966, Grundy requested a laughable sum of money for a proposed 1967 restyling—reportedly less than $30,000—and was informed by way of response that there would *be* no 1967 Studebaker. Grundy soldiered on, regardless. A few weeks later, the board decided to force the issue. In a telegram dated March 4th—notable for its clarity, if not its accuracy—

1966 Studebaker Daytona.

Studebaker's 1,500 remaining dealers were informed of the decision:

> Because of heavy and irreversible losses being incurred by the automotive division, automobile production and distribution to be permanently discontinued. Letter to follow promptly concerning financial assistance. Sincerely regret necessity to cease operations, but loss position permits no other course of action.[8]

In fairness to the board, the automotive division was probably costing it money in indirect ways. Since the corporation was now primarily engaged in building an industrial conglomerate, the price of its stock was of considerable importance. Stock was used, in whole or in part, to buy other companies. Anything that depressed the value of that stock, such as the lingering existence of the Studebaker car, could be costing millions in terms of higher prices the corporation had to pay for its acquisitions. From the point of view of Studebaker's directors, this was a proper—and serious—

concern. Despite any modest operating profits in Hamilton, they were convinced that the automotive division was costing them dearly.

So, profitable or not, the curtain was finally rung down on the Studebaker car on March 5, 1966. Only 524 were built during March and only 2,045 during the first three months of 1966.

Of course, it is difficult to see how Studebaker production could have continued for long without any research and development efforts, of which there were none of any meaningful scope in Hamilton. After South Bend folded, there was no Studebaker engineering department worthy of the name and no design staff at all—nothing to support the continued development of the automotive products in a way that would have been essential to keep them viable in the future. In that sense, at least, the Hamilton adventure was doomed to fail before it even began. Whether there was a way to save the Studebaker car in the post-South Bend era is open to debate, but the way it was handled in 1964-66 was definitely not it. In retrospect, it seems probable that the board got precisely what it wanted: an automotive division that went out with a whimper instead of a bang.

A dozen years later, when the author began the Studebaker research that ultimately resulted in this book, Bob Guthrie, the chairman of the board when the lights went out in South Bend, was the only hold-over from that era still on the board. Studebaker-Worthington, as the corporation was then known, was a successful conglomerate that controlled thirteen subsidiaries manufacturing industrial equipment and was reporting more than $1 billion in annual sales. A casual visitor to its main offices, decorated in Early Twenty-First Century Decor, on the 49th floor of the gleaming Dag Hammarskjold Plaza in New York City, would have been unaware that there had ever been a Studebaker car.

Then, in the merger-mania years of the late-1970s, Studebaker-Worthington itself was gobbled-up and the honored Studebaker name disappeared forever from the roles of major American businesses. Studebaker-Worthington was acquired buy McGraw-Edison in 1978. McGraw-Edison, in turn, was absorbed by Cooper Industries in 1985.

Cooper Industries was a Houston-based diversified manufacturing company that produced electrical equipment, tools and hardware and automotive products. In October, 1998, Cooper's automotive products operations were sold to Federal-Mogul Corporation for approximately $1.9 billion. The operations included Anco wiper blades, Champion spark plugs, and Moog steering and suspension components, among other things. Somewhere in those "other things" was all that remained of the once mighty empire that Hoffman and Vance organized in 1935 as the Studebaker Corporation (Delaware).

Notes

The most important resources drawn upon in the writing of this chapter include Richard M. Langworth's *Studebaker, 1946-1966*, Michael Beatty, Patrick Furlong, and Loren Pennington's *Studebaker: Less Than They Promised*, and Donald T. Critchlow's *The Life and Death of an American Corporation*. Heinz C. Hoppe's *Serving the Star Around the World* gave valuable insights into the important connection between Studebaker-Packard and Daimler-Benz. Studebaker-Packard Corporation papers in the author's collection, including annual Reports, brochures, letters and miscellaneous publications, were also especially important source material. Periodicals that proved to be important resources included various issues of: *Automotive News, Avanti Magazine, Car & Driver, Cars & Parts, Esquire, Motor Trend, Road & Track, South Bend Tribune, Special-Interest Autos, Track & Traffic, Turning Wheels.*, and *Ward's*.

[1] As the 1963 Annual Report to stockholders explained, the $64 million was pledged to cover "anticipated losses on disposal of South Bend automotive property, plant and equipment, and for estimated cancellation costs, inventory write-downs, and other cost related to the discontinued operations." The figure included $20 million for "properties including tooling" and $14 million for inventories. The latter presumably included parts and supplies that were rendered useless by the cessation of the automotive operations in South Bend. The former was almost entirely a paper loss, i.e., no cash was paid out directly as a result of the closing of the South Bend factory, while much of the latter probably fell into this category, as well.

[2] It is worth noting, too, that to a great extent the continuing popularity of Studebakers as collectibles is due to the seemingly deathless enthusiasm for two products: Egbert's Avanti and, to a lesser extent, Egbert's Gran Turisimo Hawk. Who cares about Nash or Hudson anymore? People under thirty don't

even recognize these once-honored names, much less the likes of Graham, Hupmobile or Peerless. As a collectible, Studebaker has eclipsed in popularity virtually every other American independent brand save Packard. Give Egbert a substantial share of the credit for this, too.

[3] 1963 Studebaker Corporation Annual Report.

[4] 1963 Studebaker Corporation Annual Report.

[5] It did, however, recently change its name. In April, 1999, following the DaimlerChrysler merger, MBNA became Mercedes-Benz USA (MBUSA).

[6] Hoppe, p. 96.

[7] Grundy was reportedly convinced that the failure of the Toyota negotiations was due to meddling by one of Guthrie's law partners: Richard Nixon.

[8] Studebaker Corporation papers, author's collection.

Overleaf, painting an Avanti II body in 1979.

TWELVE

Postscript

The Studebaker era was over. That the Avanti had had a tremendous effect upon the company is hard to deny, although certainly not the one intended. Yet, the Avanti—whose very name signified moving forward—would continue to do just that. Indeed, the Avanti managed a feat achieved by only one other design in American automotive history: It survived the demise of the manufacturer that created it. The other design was the "coffin nose" Cord of 1936, which for a few seasons was revived in modified form by Hupmobile and Graham. In the case of the Avanti, revival came at the unlikely hands of South Bend Studebaker dealer, Nate Altman.

Altman and his partner, Leo Newman, had been selling cars in South Bend for three decades. In fact, their store was the second largest Studebaker dealership in the United States. As Altman contemplated the Avanti sitting on his showroom floor in that depressing winter of 1963-64, he became more and more convinced that something had to be done to save it. The Avanti was such a dramatic design departure that he felt its demise would have been not just a tragedy, but almost a sacrilege. In short, he was so entranced with the car that he simply refused to admit that it had to die. So, in one of the great stories in automobile history, he brought the Avanti back to life through sheer force of his own determination.

Altman's initial plan was to knock on doors in Detroit until he found an established manufacturer capable of seeing the wisdom in taking over production of the Avanti where Studebaker had left off. None did. No one, it seems, wanted any part of Studebaker. Altman even tried tiny Checker Motors in Kalamazoo, Michigan, builder of the famed taxi cabs. When Altman tried to present his case, Checker's crusty president, Morris Markin, turned on him, exclaiming, "How can you come here and ask me if I'm interested in such an ugly car?"[1] That was the turning point for Altman. The major manufacturers all thought he was crazy and now the president of Checker, which built one of the homeliest cars on the market, was calling the Avanti ugly! The idea that had been brewing in the back of Altman's mind now became the only alternative. He and Leo Newman would produce the Avanti themselves.

At first glance the idea seemed absurd. They had no factory, no workers, no dealers and no working capital committed to such a venture. Every few years, it seems, someone somewhere announces a new, specialty entry into the automobile market. The odds against the success of such a venture are outrageous. But, Altman was no babe in the woods. He knew that an independent company built around the Avanti would have real advantages not usually available to a newcomer.

First, the product already existed and, largely because the Avanti had generated such enthusiasm within the corporation, Studebaker might be willing to surrender its rights and equipment for pennies on the dollar. Second, because the Avanti was constructed of fiberglass, it was ideal for low-volume manufacture. Third, a dealer network did exist. Studebaker was still in the car business and many Studebaker dealers could be expected to want to continue to offer Avantis if it were put back into production. Finally, the Avanti had attracted an enormous amount of interest with the public and was already becoming something of a cult car, which could only benefit a revival. If there was ever a situation in which an "outsider" had a chance, surely this was it.

In February, 1964, Altman and Newman bought six buildings in the old Studebaker complex, with a total of 500,000 square feet of floor space. One of the buildings had been used for final finishing of the original Avantis. Next, Altman asked Molded Fiberglass, of Ashtabula, Ohio, which had supplied the original Avanti bodies, if it would be willing to do the same for an Avanti revival. Robert Morrison, the company president, replied that if Altman and Newman were game, he was, too. In point of fact, Molded

Fiberglass still had about 150 Avanti bodies that it had been stuck with when Studebaker suddenly ceased production. Obviously, Molded Fiberglass had a vested interest in working with the new venture.

Still, in order to make the Avanti's revival a reality, Altman knew he would need the help of a qualified engineer. So, he approached Studebaker's former chief engineer, Eugene Hardig, with a proposition that Hardig assume similar responsibilities for the Avanti's successor. Hardig, always direct, jumped out of his chair, pointed a finger at Altman, and yelled, "Get the hell out of here!

Nathan D. Altman.

You're crazy and you're wasting my time!" Altman did leave, but not before saying to Hardig, "You've spent your life being told to cut corners, to save $50 so a car could be made cheaper. Here's your chance to build the best possible car without worrying about that."[2]

At the same time, Altman was attempting to persuade Studebaker to strike a deal for the rights, tooling, parts, etc. Studebaker executives, convinced of the futility of attempting a revival, tried to persuade him to reconsider, but his mind was made up. Eventually, Studebaker relented, and Avanti Motor Corporation was organized with initial capital provided by Altman, Newman, their attorney, Altman's brother Arnold, and various other family and friends. All rights and equipment needed to manufacture the Avanti were bought on July 1, 1964, along with parts and equipment for Studebaker trucks. The rights reportedly cost Altman $25,000, but this figure is probably in addition to the cost of the parts and equipment. It was felt that dealing in truck parts would offer enough of a financial cushion to carry the company through until profitable automobile production could commence. It was typical of the conservative approach Altman was using.

The idea of reviving the Avanti may have seemed crazy, but Nate Altman was a hard-headed Hoosier businessman who was determined that no one was going to get hurt by Avanti Motor Corporation.

Hardig, too, reconsidered. After a sleepless night pondering Altman's proposal, Hardig called to say he should be counted in. On September 9, 1964, he was officially appointed vice-president in charge of engineering for the new company.

It soon became apparent, however, that more capital was required. Altman went to the St. Joseph Bank & Trust company, where he and Newman had banked for years and requested a $75,000 line of credit for the new company. The loan committee turned him down flat. Everyone in South Bend, it seemed, was against anything even remotely connected with Studebaker. Altman then made a personal plea to the bank's president and a personal friend, Richard Rosenthal, who reluctantly agreed to the loan.

The first Avanti II was built on July 22, 1965, and formally introduced to the public in South Bend on August 2nd. A few months later, Altman returned to Rosenthal—with considerable trepidation—to ask for another line of credit five times as large as the first. Rosenthal approved it instantly, then changed the subject. Altman was dumbfounded. Rosenthal then explained apologetically that, like everybody else in South Bend, he hadn't

1968 Avanti II.

thought Avanti Motor Corporation would ever produce any cars at all.

Suppliers were also a real problem during the first few months. Robert Turpin, the company's purchasing man, would spend hours on the phone trying to convince them that the Avanti II was a real car that was really going to make it to production. Slowly the doubts were erased. Altman's prompt payment policy on bills didn't hurt, either.

Meanwhile, Hardig was hard at work on the car itself. From the first it had been obvious that alterations in the original Avanti would be required before the Avanti II could reach production. The major problem was with the engine. Since the supply of Studebaker powerplants could no longer be assured, a substitute would have to be found that would provide the necessary level of performance and yet be easily adapted to the existing body. Hardig's choice was the 327 cubic inch engine used in the Chevrolet Corvette. The Chevy engine was considerably lighter than the Studebaker V8 it supplanted, but, because it was slightly taller in production form, it was necessary to raise the front fender line of the Avanti II about two inches and to add a filler piece to the front wheel cut-outs. This gave the Avanti II a distinctly different appearance from the Studebaker version. The impudent rake of the original was replaced by a somewhat more civilized stance.

Unlike Studebaker, Avanti Motor Corporation was not seeking a performance image *per se*. The Avanti II was, from the first, aimed at the luxury car buyer who wanted something different, i.e., sort of a "gentleman's" grand touring machine, rather than a car aimed at the hot rod set. Still, the level of performance was roughly equivalent to the optional R2 Studebaker powerplant and considerably faster than the standard R1. In addition, the lighter Chevy block led to better weight distribution and handling.

Inside, the Avanti II defied Detroit tradition, for it was available in literally any combination of fabrics the customer cared to bring in. For those customers who did not wish to supply their own, the factory had some 400 selections on hand. The range of exterior finishes was equally expansive; an Avanti II could be painted in any color obtainable from the paint manufacturers. All this was possible because of the unique type of assembly method Altman and Hardig instituted.

All the bothersome questions—"If Studebaker couldn't make a go of it, how can you? Etc."—presupposed that the Avanti II would be mass produced just as the Studebaker Avanti was supposed to have been. Altman and Hardig realized that this was nonsense. Instead of attempting to build thousands of Avanti IIs each year for the mass market, they would carefully hand-build a few hundred—if that—and sell them to the cognoscenti, or to those luxury car buyers who wanted something unusual and were prepared to pay for it. The price would be set at whatever level was necessary to ensure profitability.

As dedicated as Altman was to the Avanti, he was determined to make money, and he liked to note that there were two ways to achieve that in the car business: to be the biggest or to be the smallest. Knowing he could never be one of the big boys, he intentionally set about creating the smallest car company in America. In doing so, he was determined to run Avanti the old-fashioned way, with methods and equipment that, to be sure, looked back to the Nineteenth Century more than they did forward to the Twenty-First. This concept, which was deliberately labor-intensive and minimized capital investment, seemed to Altman to be the only rational one for a company building a couple of hundred specialty cars annually.

Of course, this concept also made it extremely difficult to effect significant product changes from year to year, but, as Altman had no intention of changing the Avanti more than absolutely necessary, this didn't pose a problem, either. Nate Altman loved the Avanti just the way it was and was convinced that enough American car buyers would agree with him to render the operation profitable for the long-term. And, it should be noted, the Altman operation did indeed prove to be consistently profitable. While it is not known precisely what the Altmans invested in the Avanti, their investor group surely made several million dollars over the 18 years they ran it. According to information distributed by the company in 1983, Avanti Motor Corporation had recorded a profit every year of its existence up to that time. In fact, in its *worst* year prior to 1983, the company had recorded a profit of $100,000.

Initially, Molded Fiberglass assembled all Avanti II bodies in Ashtabula and then shipped them to South Bend. As soon as it could, Avanti Motor Corporation assumed this responsibility. By the mid-1970s, the entire car was assembled in the Avanti II factory, although Molded Fiberglass continued to manufacture the individual body parts. Avanti Motor Corpora-

1970 Avanti II.

tion was, never-the-less, manufacturing more and more of its own components as the years went by. Many suppliers were happy to sell the tooling
since it relieved them of bothersome low-volume work. The factory, for its
part, found that it preferred to have control over as much of the process as
possible. Often, when the supply of a particular part ran out, several years'
worth was manufactured and stored until needed. In this way, the factory
was not only able to oversee the manufacture of the parts, but it was also
able, in many cases, to secure some of the economies of volume.

Hardig insisted from the first that Avanti Motor Corporation be run
"one hundred percent" the same as a major manufacturer with regard to
engineering and development. That was not to say, of course, that Avanti
Motor Corporation had the same resources as a major manufacturer. In
particular, increasingly onerous government standards for safety, emissions,
and fuel economy, began to plague the company almost as soon as the first
Avanti II rolled off the jerry-rigged "assembly line" in South Bend. Altman
managed, in April of 1968, to have the company listed officially as a "low-
volume" producer and, therefore, exempt from the more threatening Fed-

eral rules and regulations, but it was a problem that had no permanent cure and came back to haunt Altman and his successors again and again.

The factory was forced to stop offering a manual transmission because of certification difficulties and no Avanti IIs were sold in California during the 1977 model year, due to the expense of complying with that state's complex certification procedures. Fortunately, the Federal government was generally more understanding. Avanti IIs, owing to their Corvette engines and the similarities in running gear, were successfully certified as Corvette derivatives—a much simpler process than certification from scratch.

Marketing methods also evolved through the years. The first Avanti IIs were sold "loaded" with every available option. If a customer didn't want a particular option, he had to specifically delete it. This had the unintended effect of making the car's price seem more formidable than necessary. By the late 1960s, Avanti IIs were beginning to be sold in the same "base price plus options" fashion as was the typical Detroit practice.

Another major marketing change also occurred in the late 1960s with

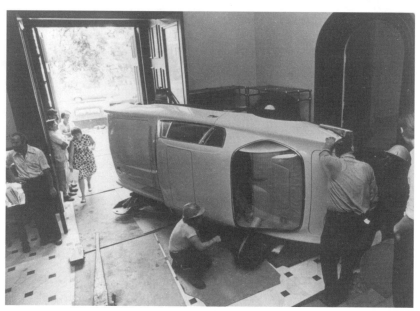

It wasn't easy getting an Avanti II into the Renwick Gallery in Washington, DC, for the Smithsonian's Raymond Loewy retrospective exhibit in 1975!

the phasing out of the dealer network. At first, and logically enough, Avanti IIs were sold through many former and soon-to-be-former Studebaker outlets. In 1965 and 1966, perhaps 70 percent of Avanti II output went this route. Inevitably, however, many of these dealers began to disappear and others began to prove inadequate. So, volume outlets handling other makes were signed on. It was difficult, however, to maintain a high level of enthusiasm at the dealer level for a car that sold in very modest numbers. Worse, it tended to appeal to connoisseurs, rather than to typical luxury car buyers. The Avanti II was the sort of car that sold itself, but it didn't do so often enough to suit the typical dealer mentality.

Eventually, Altman discovered that most customers preferred to buy their cars directly from the factory and that most leads came as the result of word-of-mouth advertising. So, by the mid-1970s, Avanti Motor Corporation had evolved into perhaps the only significant auto maker in the world with virtually no dealers and very little in the way of active marketing. In most years, it still sold all the cars it could comfortably produce.[3]

Avanti Motor Corporation did, indeed, do pretty well for itself. Altman built a astonishing record of stability. By the late 1970s, 120 people were employed in the Avanti plant and the company had never had a lay-off. As for the customers, 50 percent of them were repeat Avanti buyers. Remarkably, no Avanti had ever been recalled.

The first sign that Avanti Motor Company might face an uncertain future came in April, 1976, when Altman fell ill with pneumonia. On April 19th, he died. His brother, Arnold, who had been an active participant in the company from the beginning, assumed the reigns. Leo Newman was still intimately involved in company affairs, as was Gene Hardig. Hardig, however, was past his prime and had become a virtual recluse.[4] Newman was getting older, too, and died on March 20, 1980. Arnold Altman, a shy man who never possessed the vision or drive of his brother, was increasingly isolated at the helm. The company seemed to drift. By 1980, tired and under pressure from the Newman and Altman families to sell their holdings, Arnold Altman began listening with increasing interest to the ideas of an Avanti enthusiast named Steve Blake.

A "character" of sorts, the thirty-eight-year-old Blake was a Washington, DC, real estate developer and self-described "car nut." Blake had been

1979 Avanti II.

an Avanti fan for several years. In 1975, he bought a new one—his second Avanti—and made the "pilgrimage" to South Bend to take delivery. The delivery process, handled personally by Nate Altman, turned into dinner. By dessert, Blake had made his first offer for the company. It was refused. Sometime after Nate Altman died, Blake approached Arnold Altman. Recalled Blake:

> I called him and told him I wanted to buy his company and he hung up. I made over a hundred calls before they quit hanging up on me. They were *not* nice.[5]

Then, one day in 1980 Arnold Altman didn't hang up. The price: $4.3 million. Coming up with the money took Blake two years. In the end, the buy-out was financed, in large measure, by the First Source Bank of South Bend. Of that, perhaps as much as 75 percent was guaranteed by the Indiana Economic Development Authority. First Source also supplied $1 million to the new company in the nature of a revolving loan. The remainder of the purchase was supplied by Blake and other investors.

Avanti Motor Corporation was officially sold to Blake on October, 20, 1982. From the first, there was no doubt that Blake was determined to run Avanti aggressively and in his own fashion. He hit South Bend like a whirlwind determined to change everything. His plans included modernizing the car, the facility itself, and even the fundamental way of doing business. Activity of that nature had not been seen since the frantic development of the original Avanti itself.

Although the 1983 models were locked-up when he assumed control, Blake didn't take long to make his presence felt. The first "new" Avanti to result was the 20th Anniversary Edition announced mid-way through the 1983 model year. This model presented a wealth of innovative styling ideas and represented the first fundamental change in the original Avanti design. The purpose, as Blake saw it, was to give the twenty-year-old classic a "Euro" look befitting a contemporary GT automobile. The most obvious feature was the composite, resin-molded bumper design. Done in body color, these bumpers highlighted the dramatic look. Furthermore, all Anniversary Edition models were finished in a decidedly unusual Avanti color: black. The interior featured black leather trim. Each car included 20th Anniversary plaques on the glove box door and on the front fenders. An advertised 25 of the Anniversary Editions were supposed to have been built, in all, at a sticker price of $34,995. Blake commented later that he could

1982 Avanti II.

have sold four times that many.[6] One other significant action taken shortly after Blake assumed command was a name change: the "II" was dropped and, once again, the car was simply the Avanti.

Yet another major effort undertaken in the 1983 model year concerned dealer development. Despite the Altman experience, Blake was convinced that the lack of qualified dealers was holding Avanti back. To spearhead his ambitious goals, Blake hired C. R. "Dick" Brown to manage dealer development. Brown was Mazda's first American manager in the 1970s and later handled dealer development for the DeLorean Motor Company. In that capacity, he was responsible for recruiting 345 dealers from coast-to-coast. Brown was also charged with general marketing responsibilities, and expected to participate actively in financial planning and strategic planning. By June of 1983, about fifteen new dealers had been signed, mostly on the West Coast. By September, the number had risen to twenty-four.

In April, the UAW attempted to organize the plant. The attempt failed by a vote of 51 to 29. Blake blamed it on his needing to take a tough line in

1983 Avanti 20th Anniversary Edition.

order to get the work force in shape despite "labor resistance":

> I had to replace 30 percent to 40 percent of the work force
> when I came in. Not the older guys, not the craftsmen, but the
> younger guys. A lot of them had gotten into bad habits. They didn't
> love cars enough. They didn't want to work.[7]

Still, Blake's peculiar management style was also beginning to take a toll. Blake himself described his method of management as "irrational, illogical and messy," but defended it on the grounds that a little disorder is necessary in any aggressive, forward-thinking organization:

> [We need] people who get things done—entrepreneurial
> people, fanatics, people driven to get the job done. I want people
> who don't have clocks—aggressive, goal-oriented risk-takers.[8]

More ambitious still was Blake's racing effort. He spent $20,000 preparing an Avanti for the Daytona 500 in January, 1983. Against all odds, the car did surprisingly well. Although it failed to win, it was in fourth place for a while and finished at 27th. The fact that it actually finished the race in one piece—which 49 of the 79 cars entered failed to do—was accomplishment enough in Blake's eyes.

The 1983 20th Anniversary Edition was followed in 1984 by a similar Touring Coupe. Unlike the Anniversary Edition, the Touring Coupe was offered in a range of colors: red, white, blue and silver. Black was avoided in an effort to differentiate the Touring Coupe from the Anniversary Edition, although an additional three or four were reportedly done up in black anyway, apparently in response to customer requests. The Touring Coupe differed from past Anniversary Edition practice in other ways, too. "BBS" wheels were fitted, as were Goodyear Eagle GT performance tires. The special, leather steering wheel was "signed" by Zora Arkus Duntov, the father of the Corvette, and multi-adjustment Recaro seats were standard.

The regular 1984 models featured a significant increase in standard equipment level, necessitating a hike in the asking price to $31,860—a 28 percent increase in one year. In a way, this hearkened back to the original

Avanti II days when cars were sold completely loaded with every available option. Yet another portentous change was in the way Avantis were painted. A new Ditzler Deltron urethane paint was introduced on 1984 production. This paint was supposed to give a deeper, "show car" appearance "while providing unequaled durability."

Following the special edition coupes, Blake next launched an even more dramatic departure from existing Avanti design: a convertible. Where this idea came from is unclear, but it may have originated with Raymond Loewy. It is known that Loewy sent Blake a proposal to design a convertible. The actual convertible project, however, was done through the Straman Company in Costa Mesa, California.

The most ambitious, and potentially far reaching, plan Blake launched, however, was for a car that, as fate would have it, was never built: the Avanti GT. The GT was eloquent testimony to the depths of change that Blake sought in order to prepare the company for what he regarded as its future. Blake commented at the time that the first week after the buy-out he "took an '82 for a drive and I said, 'Omigod, I need some help.'"

Although the basic looks and basic powertrain of the two-decade-old Avanti were retained, the entire chassis—indeed, the entire concept of what a grand touring car meant—was re-thought and re-engineered. The GT was built off a new frame that, together with body alterations, lowered it to a mere 48 inches—six inches less than the standard Avanti. At the same time, the tread was widened and fenders were flared out in response. These changes had the beneficial effect of dramatically lowering the center of gravity for improved handling and cornering stability. In addition, independent rear suspension was added, as were rack-and-pinion steering and rear disc brakes. The transmission was a Borg-Warner five-speed manual. Body and frame modifications, and use of a Corvette aluminum differential case, together shaved off 400 pounds of weight. Blake reportedly sunk $250,000 in the program before mounting problems with Avanti Motor Corporation ground everything to a halt in the spring of 1985. Only one prototype was known to have been built.[9]

In 1983, Avanti Motor Corporation attained its all-time peak production year, with 289 cars built and some $8 million in sales. Unfortunately, the unprecedented level of production was accompanied by an alarming decrease in quality. Blake's rush to expand had, in all-too-many ways, been—as he himself had noted—irrational, illogical and messy. Worse, fundamental changes in methods and materials were often made with little or no prior testing. The new paint system instituted for the 1984 models was a disastrous case in point. The Ditzler Deltron urethane paint may have possessed all the virtues the company claimed for it, but it failed spectacularly in one critical respect: it would not bond to the Avanti body panels. Within weeks, angry buyers of 1984 Avantis were descending on the factory with a litany of paint-related horror stories. "Sometimes," Blake noted years later, "you could pull the paint off a whole door; it was unbelievable." A year later, Blake himself admitted that the company had been forced to repaint 270 cars, many of them several times over. The paint was, of course, the factory's responsibility under warranty and the time and expense of dealing with virtually an entire year's production gone bad broke the company's back.

In February, 1984, the First Source Bank dealt the company a critical blow when it cut off the flow of funds from the revolving credit line. As its cash position fell ever deeper into crisis, the company stopped manufacturing stocks of replacement parts, and began stiffing creditors large and small.[10] In October, the company filed suit against PPG Industries (the parent company of Ditzler) for $2 million in damages stemming from the paint catastrophe. Still, Blake and his cohorts tried to soldier on.

The first harbinger of approaching disaster occurred shortly after the New Year. On January 24, 1985, the First Source Bank obtained a $3 million prejudgment against the company's assets, charging that its loan was in default. Armed with a court order, bank representatives swept onto the company's property and seized cars. The day following the seizure, after Blake and the bank managed to smooth things out, the prejudgment was dismissed by the court and the cars were returned. The national publicity stemming from the action, however, crippled the company's resuscitation efforts. Overnight, sales collapsed.

On June 28th, the company filed for bankruptcy under Chapter 11 of the Federal Bankruptcy Code. The actual bankruptcy filing was precipitated by the filing of a Federal tax lien by the IRS. The largest unsecured creditor was General Motors. A reported $250,000 was owed for engines

leaving Indiana ... under Chapter 11; for Detroit site

Stephen H. Blake.

and other components. In addition, there were 567 other unsecured creditors listed in the bankruptcy filing.

Under court rules, the company was obligated to file a plan for reorganization. In desperation, Blake began negotiations with the Detroit Development Board for a $10 million refinancing plan. This plan, which would have involved moving Avanti Motor Corporation to Detroit, called for $5-6 million from the Detroit Development Board, an additional $2 million line of credit to be arranged through a Detroit bank, and $1.5-2 million from a new investor group. In the end, however, the Detroit Development Board declined. Banks in Detroit similarly refused to get involved.

The original date set for filing of the reorganization plan was September 30th. The company asked for, and received, an extension until November 25th, but Blake was removed by the court from day-to-day control over the company's affairs. Then, on October 30th, all hourly employees were indefinitely laid off and only a handful of people remained in parts and service, and in the front office.

On November 25th, the company proposed to the court a reorganization plan that called for a public stock offering in the early part of 1986 to fund a new company: Avanti USA Motorworks, Inc. It was projected that this offering would raise "at least" $2.5 million. Despite the bankruptcy filing, Blake was still wildly upbeat about the company's fortunes. He predicted that within five years the company would offer no less than four different models and be building 1,800 cars per year. Projected model production, in this scenario, would consist of 399 convertibles, 201 GTs, 800 roadsters and 400 of an all-new four-door sedan. The traditional Avanti coupe would be phased out.

The court had until January 16, 1986, to approve the company's reorganization plan. It did not do so, perhaps influenced by warnings about the proposed stock offering from the Securities and Exchange Commission (SEC). First Source Bank, as the only secured creditor, immediately moved to seize the company's assets with the intention of selling them to the highest bidder effective March 30th.

Several years later, in an interview, Blake summed up the challenges he confronted at Avanti thusly:

> I bought a mom-and-pop company that was building a 20-year-old car on a 40-year-old chassis with 70-year-old workers in a 100-year-old plant.[11]

The winning bid on the assets of Avanti Motor Corporation was submitted by Michael E. Kelly, a former South Bend resident then living in Dallas, Texas. The bid was for a reported $722,000—or, around $3.5 million less than Steve Blake had paid three-and-a-half years earlier. On April 30th, Kelly assumed control of the company. Renamed the New Avanti Motor Corporation (NAMC), it displayed its 1987 models to the automotive press corps on September 4th and sold its first car on September 22nd. By February, 1987, 90 cars had either been built or were in some stage of production. Best of all, after the tumultuous Blake years, were reports from customers and dealers of a return to "Altman standards" of quality.

In many ways, though, the ego-driven Kelly seemed like Steve Blake reincarnate. He had the same general ideas regarding the direction the Avanti should take in order to be competitive in the 1980s, i.e., away from the car's classic design roots and toward a "soft luxury" approach. In addition, Kelly was possessed of similar ambitions to turn

Michael E. Kelly.

the Avanti into a major competitor in the international luxury GT market.

NAMC almost immediately announced a new model intended for the upcoming 1987 model run: the Luxury Sport Coupe. Essentially a coupe with a nine-inch stretch, it was designed to afford more rear seat leg room. The price listed was an Avanti high: $55,900. The original coupe, now re-named the Classic Coupe, was offered at $29,995, while the Sport Convertible was listed at $39,995. Inside, the instrument panel and console received its first restyling since 1962. Underneath, all models featured a new frame and new suspension components, thanks to a decision to build the Avanti off of the Chevrolet Monte Carlo SS chassis. In fact, the 1987 Avanti was, when you got right down to it, a Monte Carlo with a custom body.

Kelly and his new team had discovered a host of problems when they assumed control of NAMC. One was the increasing age of the chassis components, some of which dated back to the 1950s. Parts were getting harder to come by and some components were badly in need of updating. NAMC was facing the same daunting, and perhaps prohibitive, costs in bringing the chassis up to contemporary standards that had bedeviled Blake. Worse, NAMC faced increasingly difficult government certification standards.

1988 Avanti.

Then, despite many years of supplying components to Avanti, General Motors refused to continue the relationship. Having been badly burned in the bankruptcy and facing increasing problems of its own in the mid-years of the decade, General Motors was in no mood to risk another round with a little company it had probably given up for dead, anyway. So, cut off from continued assistance from its former patron in Detroit, NAMC hit upon the unlikely strategy of buying completed Monte Carlos from a local South Bend Chevrolet dealer, scrapping the bodies, and using the rest. Kelly defended this process so eloquently that it almost seemed sensible:

> Frankly, we save a great deal by purchasing the entire car...If we did buy piece-by-piece each suspension/frame part, we would easily exceed the cost of the car purchased as an entity. We do spend time modifying the frame to fit the bodies. Most importantly, the EPA is comfortable as the car is first just that, a car. We have, upon purchase of the entire car, EPA certification and product liability.[12]

Early in 1987, Kelly announced that NAMC was looking for a new plant site in which to build a proposed four-door Avanti. Then, on April 30, 1987, he announced that the Cafaro Company, in Youngstown, Ohio, had purchased an equity stake in the New Avanti Motor Corporation. Kelly predicted that Avanti would be building cars at a rate of 1,000 per year by the winter of 1988. Then, he dropped the real bombshell:

> In March of this year, we positively determined that our South Bend facility could not facilitate a one-thousand car build and we began seeking locations and opportunities for a second plant site to hand-craft two new Avanti models—a four-door luxury touring sedan and a limousine...[13]

In short, Avanti would be moving at least some of its operations to Youngstown, with the stated goal of producing touring sedan and a limousine models there in time for the 1988 model year. Cafaro, it seems, had a site available in one of his industrial developments—the Ross Industrial

1988 Avanti LSC.

Park—and Youngstown had a mayor with, as Kelly characterized it, "a burning desire for Avanti and a willingness to do everything possible to make a second plant for Avanti a reality."

The deal had been the result of the work of a number of energetic citizens in Youngstown. Numbered among them was, of course, Cafaro, but the list also included Mayor Patrick J. Ungaro and State Senator Harry Meshel. In order to cement the deal, Ungaro had even gone to South Bend to woo Kelly with promised direct grants that ultimately reached $750,000, plus another $50,000 in job training subsidies. Ungaro had returned home with the deal in his pocket and a promise from the company that Avanti would employ 450 workers in Youngstown by September, 1990. On May 14th, the State of Ohio approved the first of the promised grant money— $450,000 to level buildings adjacent to the proposed Avanti plant.

That the Youngstown area, devastated by steel plant closings, had a plentiful supply of available workers was not in doubt. In August, when the new plant announced it was ready to hire the first 165, hundreds of job seekers were lined-up outside. In all, 11,000 employment applications were received. On the 16th of that same month, workers in South Bend were told the old plant would close and were given two-week's notice. In fact, the last Avanti built in South Bend left the factory on September 18, 1987, marking the end of one hundred thirty-five years of Studebaker-related vehicle production along the banks of the St. Joseph.

In addition to the new plant, an Avanti factory dealership was established nearby. In early December, 1987, Avanti dealers were treated to a preview of a "Silver Anniversary" coupe featuring black-out trim, ground effects and a lowered front end. This model had initially been conceived as a special run of 25 cars to celebrate twenty-five years, but the projected number was later increased to 50. It was decided to supercharge it and several supercharger manufacturers were contacted. Paxton, run by Joe Granatelli, was enthusiastic and got the business.[14]

In many ways, however, the spring and summer months of 1988 seemed to old Steve Blake watchers like *déjà vu* all over again.[15] A steady stream of grandiose pronouncements spewed forth from the company. In March, 1988, Kelly announced plans to buy a manufacturer of superchargers in Texas and relocate the operation to Youngstown within two months. In mid-July, plans for an Avanti two-seater sports car were announced. Then, in late-July, it was announced that the company would import the Puma, a Brazilian sports car, for distribution in the United States. Nothing again was ever heard of any of these projects.

Then, in September, Kelly suddenly resigned when Cafaro bought the rest of the company's assets. Unfortunately, Cafaro said, he and Kelly didn't see eye-to-eye on what sort of car the Avanti should be. Another reason may have been that Kelly was simply too thinly capitalized to keep up with the ambitions of the well-endowed Cafaros.

John J. "J. J." Cafaro, thirty-seven, purchased Kelly's 47.5 percent share of NAMC on September, 1, 1988, and promptly renamed the company the Avanti Automotive Corporation (AAC). Cafaro was the scion of a wealthy family in Youngstown, which, according to *Forbes*, owned the seventh-largest real estate development company in the U.S. worth half-a-billion dollars.[16] Cafaro and his team were described by *American Way* magazine:

> Cafaro is a guy who, by his own admission, doesn't know a spark plug from a carburetor. His wife, Janet, (Avanti's Chairwoman of the board) and 25-year-old Greg Lowry are the new Avanti design team.

Cafaro was apparently using family money to fund his purchase of

John J. Cafaro.

Avanti and his ambitious development plans for it. Cafaro sometimes claimed he had invested $10 million. At other times, the figure given was $15 million. Eventually, the quoted figure rose to $20 million and, on at least one occasion, to $24 million. No one seemed to know how much the Cafaro family had really invested. Still, it was obvious that large amounts of money (by Avanti standards, at any rate) were being poured into the business.

Central to the Cafaro effort was expansion of the Avanti dealer base. Gary Fielding, appointed vice-president for product and dealer development, increased the number of franchised outlets from 33 in 1988 to 45 by January, 1989. It was Fielding's announced intention to have at least "one hundred damn good, solid dealers" by the early 1990s. At the same time, Fielding announced that the company would build 350 cars in 1989, 500 in 1990 and 1,000 by 1991. The existing models were the coupe ($37,982) and the convertible ($47,982), but the heart of this expansion strategy was to be a new four-door Luxury Touring Sedan (or, "LTS").

On August 12th, however, 170 of the 200 employees were suddenly laid off. Two weeks later, the company was given a two-year reprieve by the National Highway Traffic Safety Administration (NHTSA) on coming government safety standards. These involved wavers on passive restraints, i.e., air bags and/or motorized seat belts. The company pleaded "substantial economic hardship" and described itself as "struggling." Yet, in late November, Cafaro was again waxing enthusiastic about its prospects:

> I think the future of Avanti is so bright it's scary. We are sitting right now in Youngstown, Ohio, with what can truly become the American alternative to Jaguar, Mercedes and BMW.[17]

As *Forbes* noted in a 1989 feature story, Cafaro made it "sound so easy one wonders why there aren't dozens of thriving specialty automakers."

In the latter months of 1989, the company announced a comprehensive marketing and advertising strategy designed to produce solid growth for the brand in future years. Then, the first four-door Luxury Touring Sedan was built in August, 1989. It used a simplified fiberglass casting process that was designed to reduce the labor content in the car. Involving a one-piece body mold, the company claimed that the man hours required to build an Avanti dropped from around 1,000 to 750. Actually, the sedan featured two processes that were new to the Avanti: carbon fiber composites and Kevlar. Carbon fiber composites were used for the roof, roof pillars and door beams (which were formerly of steel). These composites also replaced the traditional Avanti rollbar. Kevlar was used for the floor pan, bumpers and other high-stress components.

The Luxury Touring Sedan was based on the Chevrolet Caprice and, in so doing, underscored a major ongoing problem for the company, i.e., the lack of its own chassis. The 1987-89 cars had been based on the Monte Carlo platform and the system of using "borrowed" Monte Carlo mechanicals had apparently worked well, but the Monte Carlo was taken

1989 Avantis.

out of production after the 1988 model run. In the end, the decision to use Chevrolet mechanicals made the company as vulnerable with respect to available componentry as it had been with Studebaker componentry— which was why the switch to the Monte Carlo chassis had been made in the first place. Now, with the Monte Carlo out of production, the company was forced to switch to the larger Caprice. But, the Caprice was in its final year in 1990, too, and was scheduled to be superseded by another, completely re-engineered Caprice for the 1991 model year. So, the Avanti would have to be re-engineered yet again. In response, Cafaro determined (as had Blake before him) that the solution was for Avanti to assume the added burden and expense of developing its own chassis. In July, 1989, Callaway Advanced Technology, in Old Lyme, Connecticut, was hired for a reported $500,000 to handle the design and engineering.

The plan was for the coupe and convertible to undergo similar redesigns for 1991. The 1991 models would have the Callaway-engineered chassis and, according to the company, would also have a front end redesign. Meanwhile, the 1990 production schedule was supposed to have included three models: convertible, coupe and Luxury Touring Sedan. Nearly all sources claim that only sedans were actually built in 1990, although photographs of convertibles under construction have been published.

Many Avanti enthusiasts were outraged by the sedan. Tom Kellogg, one of the original designers, took a more positive view:

> When I saw the car, I was surprised by how nice it looked. I think it's one of the best-looking four-doors to come out of Detroit. Frankly, if I had the bucks, I think I would have gotten one.[18]

Road & Track magazine, in a review of the "1990" convertible (perhaps a prototype), took a more jaundiced view of Avanti styling changes:

> The modern Avanti's shape looks somewhat blurred next to an original; excessive roundness takes the latest version perilously close to plastic-toy status. This could be blamed on the plastic bumpers, but changes wrought to produce the bodies in larger molds don't help, either. New is good; old is better.[19]

By March, 1990, with dealers screaming for four-door models, plant employment was back up to the 200 mark. On the 23rd, Cafaro personally conducted a plant tour for dozens of leading local businessmen and government officials. On that occasion, Cafaro announced further plans to expand and talking about the possibility of hiring an additional 130 workers. In May, however, with sales of the sedan stalling, the layoffs commenced again. By December, only about twenty people were still on the payroll and only ten cars had been built since the layoffs restarted.

The Callaway chassis was supposed to have been available in March, 1990. By June, 1990, the company's estimate of the launch of the Callaway chassis had been pushed back to January, 1991—and only on a special order basis, at that. The company was likewise downplaying the future role of the classic Avanti coupe. By the late-summer of 1990, as sales of the sedan languished and the company's finances deteriorated, the Callaway chassis was indefinitely shelved. According to published accounts, Cafaro welshed on bills submitted by Callaway. Cafaro was quoted as saying, "I put myself into an engineering hole; now, I'm trying to dig out."

Gary Fielding, who quit in March, 1991, blamed the company's troubles on the decision to halt coupe and convertible production in order to focus energies and resources on the sedan. When that occurred, according to Fielding, "the cash registers stopped ringing." Why the company's fortunes had been bet on this new, untried model in the first place was something of a

1990 Avanti Luxury Touring Sedan.

mystery. Barry Toepke, who directed AAC's outside public relations and advertising efforts, recalled that the story he had heard "was that some of the Cafaro's friends said, hey, if there was a four-door version we'd buy it—that was their market research."

The stream of complaints by disgruntled dealers and customers regarding warranty claims that began with the Blake regime, continued with the Cafaro company. Complained one authorized repair shop in 1989:

> Under the Altmans, prompt payment for warranty repairs was effected. This is not the rule [today]. As I review the past, the Avanti buyer was KING. Currently, Avanti owners question whether they have a valid warranty.[20]

The company attempted a reorganization in 1991 and a few "1991" convertibles were reportedly delivered. What these consisted of is difficult to establish. They may have been leftover 1989-90 models, or cars built from existing parts. In any event, these 1991 convertibles used the same Caprice mechanicals as the sedan and the same composite/Kevlar manufacturing process. Priced at $65,964, they were reportedly being built on a "custom order" basis only.

Worse, eight lawsuits or judgments had been filed against the company since October. One creditor, with a $64,500 judgment in hand, found it still couldn't collect because all of the company's assets were already encumbered. The litigants eventually included the company's advertising and public relations agencies. It was rumored that Cafaro was interested in selling and a group of South Bend investors was reportedly interested in buying, but the outstanding claims against the company made any sale difficult—if not impossible—to effect.

The company's troubles were made all the worse by government passive restraint standards. The waver granted in 1989 was due to expire with the 1992 models, so any Avanti effort at that time would have required additional expenditures for the complex engineering and manufacturing alterations necessary to accommodate either air bags or motorized shoulder harnesses into the existing design. If Cafaro decided to develop a unique Avanti chassis, the ugly specter of government certification came into view.

And, as if that were not enough, the nation's economic picture looked decidedly bleak. The bruising recession of 1990 had continued into 1991 (and would do so into 1992, as well). Unlike in past recessions, where people with money seemed to be relatively less effected, luxury car sales across the board were hit hard by this one. Established makers were suffering mightily—U.S. Rolls-Royce sales, for example, collapsed from 1,200 units per year to fewer than 400—and there seemed to be little room for wannabes.

As if to confirm that the Cafaro family had given up on the Avanti, J. J. Cafaro bought a mansion in the Washington, DC, suburbs in August of 1991. In following months, with the plant still idle, it was announced that a public health center would be moving into the Avanti showroom in Youngstown. Then, in August of 1992, a fire in the Avanti factory seemed to rule out any possibility of resuming even limited production. Two years later, news accounts reported that the factory staff was down to one caretaker. Reportedly, he was ready and willing to build Avantis from left-over parts, but was finding no takers.[21]

As Nate Altman had noted, there were two ways to make money in the car business: to be the biggest or to be the smallest. Knowing he could never be big, he figured out a way to be profitably small. In contrast, Blake, Kelly, and Cafaro each had ambitions for growth that were probably unrealistic, perhaps impossible. In Cafaro's case, the repetition was on an even grander scale, with the results correspondingly worse. The decision to build the four-door sedan was poorly conceived and probably doomed to failure, but the decision to concentrate the entire fortunes of the company on this untried new model proved utterly calamitous.

The original loss on the Avanti by Studebaker has been estimated at as much as $20 million, although $10 million seems like a more believable figure. In contrast, Nate Altman and his co-investors turned a profit of several millions—no one really knows how much—in the eighteen years they ran the shop. Blake, on the other hand, lost at least $5 million in two years, while the Kelly/Cafaro losses must have amounted to at least that much. Indeed, if Cafaro's highest stated investment figure is correct, the combined Studebaker/Blake/Kelly/Cafaro losses approached $40 million, although Cafaro's higher figures were probably public relations puffery designed to promote the image of the company (and, probably, of J. J. Cafaro himself). Overall, the Avanti most likely cost its sponsors around $20 million, taking into account the probable Studebaker losses but ignoring the profits of the Altman years which have never been accurately reported.[22]

Critics of the Altmans—and there are more than a few—contend that it would have been impossible to continue to do business their way indefinitely. This line of thinking goes that the market and/or the government would have, eventually, demanded modernization that Altman production methods and rates were incapable of supporting. In Blake's words, you couldn't have gone on forever with "a mom-and-pop company that was building a 20-year-old car on a 40-year-old chassis with 70-year-old workers in a 100-year-old plant." That may have been true, but it did not automatically follow that the solution was to rip everything up and recast it on a grandiose scale. It just may be that there *was* no solution, that the best that could be hoped for was that the Avanti would be able soldier on for a few years until events caught up with it. Nothing lives forever.

As it was, the Avanti managed to outlive most of its patrons. Sherwood Egbert, who resigned from Studebaker while the original Avanti was still in production, was the first to go. He died on July 30, 1969. Nate Altman died on April 19, 1976, followed by Leo Newman on March 20, 1980. On July 15, 1986, Raymond Loewy died in Paris at the age of ninety-two. Eugene Hardig died on February 6, 1987, at the age of eighty-five. On April 5, 1991, Robert F. Andrews died at the age of sixty-eight. In September, 1992, the Avanti factory in South Bend was raised as part of a multi-million dollar Studebaker Corridor Renewal Area. On June 2, 1993, Steve Blake died of bone cancer at his home in McLean, Virginia. He was forty-eight.[23]

The Avanti, too, was dead and with it died the sole survivor of the Studebaker vehicle line that had lasted 139 years. Of the original Studebaker Avanti hands, Tom Kellogg is the only one still active. Perhaps he summed up the Avanti best of all:

> You rarely get a project like that. We had the bounds, the chassis, and engine, but no further restrictions. So, for days we just went wild, playing back and forth from sketches to three dimensions and back to sketches. If this car were designed today, it would have the same personality. It would be based upon a more mod-

ern chassis, simpler, lower, with state-of-the-art trim. But, it would have the same personality...You see, this isn't a styled car. It's a design. And, a design, to me, goes beyond styling.[24]

Yet, the Avanti design, apparently, possesses even the power to go beyond the grave. No sooner had the Cafaro operation folded than yet another Avanti revival—of sorts—began, thanks to the exertions of Avanti enthusiast Jim Bunting.

Bunting, a retired advertising executive from Lancaster, Pennsylvania, was given to attending Studebaker and Avanti meets in various parts of the country. At one such event, he chanced to make the acquaintance of Kellogg. The two struck up a friendship and, soon, Bunting had arranged with Bill Lang, a Harrisburg hot rod and custom car builder of national repute, to convert Bunting's Studebaker Avanti into a two-passenger coupe according to a design supplied by Kellogg.

One thing led to another (as it so often does with enthusiasts). As the two-passenger conversion was nearing completion, Kellogg sent Bunting yet another design along with a jocular note saying something to effect of, "Let's do this one next." That second design became the genesis for the AVX, for what Kellogg had proposed—and what Bunting immediately accepted—was the undertaking of a modern car based on Avanti design themes. The year was 1993.

In response to Bunting's enthusiasm for the project, Kellogg quickly supplied a series of drawings. Notes Kellogg: "We used the same design criteria on the AVX as we did on the Avanti." The design criteria included the distinctive Avanti no-grille front end, pronounced forward rake, "Coke bottle" side sculpting, wedge shape, and large, round headlights.

As the design progressed, it became necessary to select a platform. Several were considered, but the then-new General Motors F-body was ultimately chosen. Specifically, the Pontiac Firebird Formula / Trans Am was deemed most appropriate for the project. The AVX name was designated because the Cafaro interests still owned the rights to the Avanti name and refused to sell it at a price Bunting was willing to consider. AVX stood for AVanti eXperimental.

The original idea was to produce one car. That vehicle was built during the winter of 1995-96, then shown at several Studebaker and Avanti meets to wide acclaim and the idea of transforming the AVX from a one-off into a production car began to take seed. The design was refined again by Kellogg, this time with limited production in mind and the first production prototype was shown at the June, 1997, International Studebaker/ Avanti meet in South Bend, Indiana. AVX Cars was off and running.

It took about 280 hours to build an AVX, a rather dramatic improvement over the 750 hours that went into a Cafaro-built Avanti. The exterior body panels were made of high-grade fiberglass, then fitted to the Firebird structure. (The Firebird itself is manufactured in much the same way, with doors panels that are also fiberglass, for example.) Bunting had about $200,000 invested in all, including custom molds and the other bits and pieces necessary to enter limited production. To be sure, this was a mere drop in the bucket compared to what it would cost to build a similar car in Detroit—General Motors probably spends more than that on executive stationery—but the technology and low volume involved made it all feasible.[25]

Since the AVX was intended to be essentially custom-built, any number of options were theoretically available. In fact, the options were mostly limited by the customer's taste and bankroll. A couple of exotic engine options even featured Paxton superchargers—a nice Avanti-esque touch. Bunting claimed that 650 horsepower was possible with the top-end AVX-

1998 AVX.

1999 AVX convertible.

4 Performance Group. (The standard GM 5.7-liter V8 was rated at 285 horse-power.) Bunting noted that this option "is not for the faint of heart," although whether he was referring to the performance or to the $20,779 additional cost was unclear. What was clear was that going that fast was going to cost plenty (and the twenty grand didn't even cover speeding tickets and attorney's fees). It is unknown whether any of these AVX-4 cars were actually built before the company ceased production.

The cost of the basic conversion was listed at $33,900—for coupe, T-top, or convertible—not including the cost of the Firebird Formula or Trans Am. A would-be AVX owner could supply his or her own, or AVX would do it and tack the cost onto the price of the conversion. The total tab came to something over $60,000. Bunting planned to sell perhaps 20-25 cars a year, a figure that appeared plausible considering that the Avanti II regularly achieved a production rate of 100-200 cars for vehicles that—allowing for inflation—were similarly targeted and priced.

Then, in December of 1999, came another twist in the story. John Seaton, a Georgia businessman, bought out not only Bunting's interests, but Cafaro's in the old New Avanti Motor Corporation, as well, and announced a new company named the Avanti Motor Corporation (AMC). This was the same name the company had when it was revived the first time around in the 1960s. Not only that, but it will have the same chairman, Michael Kelly, who was behind the second revival in the 1980s.

This time the resurrection is being attempted in Villa Rica, Georgia, about 40 miles West of Atlanta. Seaton, who will be chief executive officer, presided over a ribbon-cutting ceremony at AMC's new 75,000-square-foot factory and predicted that the company would hire 50-150 employees by the middle of 2001 and projected annual production of a new Avanti model at 300 units per year.

If plans work out, the new Avanti will essentially be a continuation of the AVX, but, thanks to the deal with Cafaro, the Avanti nameplate will be back on it officially. While Seaton declined to reveal details about the company's finances, he insisted that AMC has "sufficient capital to get this car back into production."

Whether this latest revival succeeds or fails, it is clear that Sherwood Egbert and Raymond Loewy gave the world a timeless design that promises to continue the influence of Studebaker for generations to come.

Notes

An important resource drawn upon in the writing of this chapter was interviews by the author with Arnold Altman (of Avanti Motor Corporation), Steven Blake (of Avanti Motor Corporation), Reeves Callaway (a key vendor to Avanti Automotive Corporation), Thomas Kellogg (one of the original designers of the Studebaker Avanti and the principal designer of the AVX), Bill Lang (production manager of AVX Cars), Roger Penn (the only Avanti II dealer to handle the marque throughout its entire history), and Barry Toepke (who handled outside public relations for Avanti Automotive Corporation). Periodicals that proved to be important resources included the *American Way, Automotive News, Avanti Magazine,* the *Chicago Sun-Times,* the *Chicago Tribune,* the *South Bend Tribune,* and the *Youngstown Vindicator.* Also significant were brochures and miscellaneous publications of the Avanti Motor Corporation, the New Avanti Motor Corporation, the Avanti Automotive Corporation and AVX Cars.

[1] Avanti Motor Corporation papers, author's collection.

[2] Avanti Motor Corporation papers, author's collection. Altman was wrong about one thing. At the typical car company, engineers sweat blood to save not just dollars, but pennies.

[3] Roger Penn, in Northern Virginia, was the only Avanti II dealer continuously established throughout the brand's active history.

[4] When the author visited the factory in the summer of 1978, Hardig was still working, according to Arnold Altman, but was unwilling or unable to have contact with the public.

[5] Avanti Motor Corporation papers, author's collection.

[6] Some sources claim 26 were actually produced.

[7] Avanti Motor Corporation papers, author's collection.

[8] Avanti Motor Corporation papers, author's collection.

[9] The engineering of the GT was largely done by Herb Adams, a former General Motors engineer who had played an important role in muscle car development in the 1960s, most notably with the 1969 Pontiac GTO Judge and Firebird Trans Am models.

[10] The original deal with Newman and Altman had called for Blake to own the rights to certain Avanti and Avanti II parts, which the company would continue to supply to Newman and Altman. As the company's financial picture darkened, however, the manufacture of spare parts was reduced, then halted, leaving Newman and Altman in the lurch (as well as many owners of Studebaker Avantis and Avanti IIs).

[11] Avanti Motor Corporation papers, author's collection.

[12] Avanti Motor Corporation papers, author's collection.

[13] Avanti Motor Corporation papers, author's collection.

[14] Only 29 Silver Anniversary coupes were actually built.

[15] Noted with appropriate apologies to Yogi Berra.

[16] The Cafaros claimed a net worth of about twice the *Forbes* estimate.

[17] Avanti Motor Corporation papers, author's collection.

[18] Avanti Motor Corporation papers, author's collection.

[19] Avanti Motor Corporation papers, author's collection.

[20] Avanti Motor Corporation papers, author's collection.

[21] Reeves Callaway, in an impromptu interview as this book was being written, told the author that he had been eventually been paid in full and that, in the end, Cafaro had proven to be a "class act" in dealing with his creditors. Callaway also described a recent encounter with Cafaro in a Washington, DC, restaurant: "I saw a cloud of cigar smoke and J. J. Cafaro was inside."

[22] When the South Bend operations were discontinued in December, 1963, the company took a write-off of $20 for all "properties," including tooling. This did not mean that everything in South Bend taken together had cost only $20

million; it meant that the undepreciated value remaining on the books in December, 1963, was $20 million. Considering that automotive tooling and equipment is typically depreciated over a period of perhaps five years, the figure would include expenditures dating back to 1959. Much of the cost of the 1962 and 1963 restylings, most of the Avanti tooling and equipment costs paid out mostly in 1962, and all of the costs associated with the 1964 restyling would have been covered. It has been reported that the actual cost of the Avanti program up to the time production began was $3.5 million. This seems credible. Of course, there were subsequent "operating" losses stemming from the actual bungled production, the money spent on promotion and never recovered, etc. Still, it seems unlikely that the overall Avanti losses to Studebaker were much more than $10 million.

[23] As this book was going to press, word was received that the last members of the Newman and Altman families had sold their interest in Newman and Altman, the Studebaker parts supply house. The company will continue, but the sale represents yet another link lost with Studebaker's past.

[24] Avanti Motor Corporation papers, author's collection.

[25] Bunting heatedly denied this investment figure when it first appeared in a published article on rideanddrive.com, but refused to supply a "correct" one. The figure came from an interview with Bill Lang, who should have been in a position to know.

Overleaf, the Studebaker Centennial flag flying with Old Glory in 1952.

THIRTEEN

Why Studebaker Failed

Over the years, many explanations have been advanced for the precipitous decline and, ultimately, fall of Studebaker's automotive operations after World War II. There have been a number of reasons set forth. Among them, alas, one finds all-too-many unsubstantiated assertions and conspiracy theories. Yet, there are also several credible possibilities.

Looking at them overall, the explanations seem to be divided into two groupings: internal and external. In other words, there are those who contend that Studebaker failed due to its own mistakes or shortcomings, while others point to factors beyond the company's control. Among Studebaker enthusiasts and historians, the division between these two approaches is marked. At one extreme there are those who are convinced that it was all a conspiracy; i. e., that *they* put Studebaker and the other independents out of business as part of a carefully conceived plan and, by extension, that Studebaker couldn't have survived no matter how brilliant its products or strategies proved to be. At the other extreme are those who prefer to bash Studebaker and who insist that everything that went wrong was due to the stupidity or ineptitude of those minding the store in South Bend.

Postwar Quality Control

One theory that pops up frequently and seems to have a certain popularity is the assertion that Studebaker quality control was so poor in the postwar era that it eventually alienated Studebaker's customer base, both actual and potential. To the author's knowledge, there has never been a serious effort to prove this other than by reciting anecdotal evidence. As for the anecdotes, they seem to be mostly concentrated on the cars of the 1953-54 period and, significantly, are backed-up by contemporary accounts in the automotive press. Indeed, one can easily spot examples of sloppy fit and finish on 1953 cars even in glossy factory press release photos.

In general, though, the evidence indicates that the products emanating from South Bend in the postwar era, while not always perfect, were no worse than the typical American automotive products of the period. Moreover, Studebaker produced powerplants and other chassis components that, by all contemporary accounts, were consistently considered rugged, reliable and well engineered. If, at times, the standard of body assembly left something to be desired, the same could doubtless be said for most of Studebaker's competitors. Except for the afore-mentioned 1953 models— and for the most part early production examples, at that—one searches contemporary magazine road tests in vain for any indication that quality control in South Bend was regarded as an especially serious problem either by automotive writers or by car buyers. To the contrary, prior to 1953 and from 1955 onwards Studebaker quality was frequently cited for praise by automotive journalists, often in direct comparison to Studebaker's competition. The early postwar era was not, it should be noted, fondly remembered for top-notch quality in Detroit, either.

Tom McCahill, the dean of American magazine road test writers, frequently cited Studebakers for praise. In a 1948, in a review in *Mechanix Illustrated*, he wrote:

> If there's any place where pride in workmanship still exists in the auto industry, it's in the Studebaker plant. They build good honest cars to the best of their ability. And the public gets more than just an even break—it gets a fine car in the bargain.

To cite another example, *Car Life*, in its February and March issues in 1955, ran detailed road tests of Chevrolet, Ford, Plymouth and Studebaker cars. Its comments are revealing. Of the all-new Chevrolet, *Car Life* stated:

From a distance, it looks like a million bucks, but a close inspection...reveals...cheap and poor workmanship. Raw molding edges were the rule rather than the exception and the hood latch would make a good cutting tool for any workshop...The interior finish and design is even worse. We found screws either improperly driven home or with heads burred. Molding was forced into position and door insulating strips were poorly installed. Ventilating louvers were not screwed down tight, leaving an unsightly mess on the kick panels...Several of the controls were stiff to the point of actual resistance to operation. This was not due to "newness," but...to poor placement and cheap construction.

And, this was on top of the serious teething troubles many owners experienced with Chevy's first overhead-valve V8, which was also new that year. Moreover, the 1955-57 Chevys (that are such hot collectibles in our own era!) came to be notorious for being rust-buckets. As for the quality of the 1955 Plymouth it tested, *Car Life* was scarcely more enthusiastic:

The Plymouth's exterior finish and interior trim ruin its chances for best buy. [The exterior body] molding fails to fit [the] shape of curves and in many cases it has raw, cutting edges...The interior finish is poor, especially on the instrument panel where moldings have been squeezed into position.

In contrast, the Ford was rated highly:

Ford maintains its traditional fine finish...It gives the impression of quality construction both outside and inside. We could find no signs of shoddy workmanship in finishing, but were amazed to hear small parts drop off the underside of the dash where they had been improperly fastened.

The Studebaker President hardtop tested received the highest marks of all. *Car Life* had no complaints of any kind on the exterior quality and little but unblushing praise for the design and quality of the interior:

> The interior is nothing short of luxurious, with fine fittings and carefully blended color combinations...The owner of one of these cars has little to criticize on the general interior finish, which is quite the finest we have seen for some time.

Car Life's testers did note that one of the President's rear quarter windows failed to close tightly and that there were minor weather-stripping problems. The magazine added, though, that "none of these annoyances were really serious"—which in itself affords an insight into the prevailing quality standards of the day.

Quality was, indeed, a sometime thing in the industry back then and was likely to be a particular problem with major body changes. The Chevrolets and Plymouths were entirely new for 1955, which goes a long way toward explaining their poor showings. Studebaker had already been through the same cycle two years earlier and Ford was to repeat the process with the launching of its 1957 models. According to no less an authority than Lee Iacocca (who was a power at Ford Division at the time and should know what he's talking about), Ford Division products in the latter years of the decade suffered from horrendous quality deficiencies. Poor quality control has often been cited as a contributing factor in the Edsel debacle, as well, and was one of the problems that nearly killed Lincoln during the run of the 1958-60 series cars.

Chrysler Corporation may have plumbed the depths, though. During its Forward Look campaign of 1957 it experienced a quality control disaster that reached epic proportions and brought on the first of the recurring financial crises that were to plague that company for decades to come.

In short, if one had been looking for examples of slipshod workmanship back then, there would have been more than enough candidates. More to the point, while Studebakers of the era were surely far from flawless they hardly set any kind of enduring standard for shoddiness. It must be emphasized that the car buyer in the 1950s was not comparing Studebaker to the standards of quality we have today, or to some abstract concept of perfection. He or she was comparing Studebakers to the contemporary Dodges or Mercurys or Chevys for sale down the street, and by that standard the Studebakers were a far more attractive proposition.

Another dynamic that causes problems is the tendency of people to focus on the products themselves to the exclusion of everything else. The typical automobile enthusiast (from which source most of the second-guessing about Studebaker's fate springs) knows very little about marketing or the overall competitive pressures that existed in the industry in any given era—much less about high finance or industrial management technique. Therefore, he tends to believe that if a company succeeds it is because it is building better cars than its competitors and, conversely, if it fails it is because the products are deficient. But, this doesn't necessarily follow.

There have been many companies that went out of business despite building good cars, just as there have been many companies that made a big success building cars that were, by any objective yardstick, very poor. In the sixty-five years it built automobiles, Studebaker had it both ways. Arguably, some of the best cars it ever built were on the assembly line when the lights went out in South Bend in December, 1963. Conversely, the car that launched the company as a major producer—the E-M-F—was, by all accounts, an awful contraption. So was the Studebaker Six that followed, if no less an authority than Car Breer is to be believed. In fairness, most of the E-M-F/Studebaker competitors of the day were probably just as bad. Cars back then weren't very good by our standards. So, why did people buy E-M-Fs and Studebaker Sixes by the tens of thousands? Probably they did so because Studebaker was, at the time, one of the biggest producers with one of the most powerful dealer networks, because most of them were first time car buyers who were still relatively unsophisticated about cars and because their expectations were far lower

In sum, in assessing the reasons a particular company succeeds or fails the quality of its products is only one of many factors that must be considered and even that factor must be evaluated in relation to the prevailing standards of the day. Still, the ill-fated Chrysler Forward Look saga does demonstrate that notably bad quality control, even for a relatively brief period of time, can produce a serious backlash among car buyers. Chrysler quality, in general, had been regarded as at least average until 1957. Then, in a mad rush to satisfy demand for a very popular new line of cars, the quality was allowed to drop precipitously. It improved in 1958 and was probably back up to snuff by 1959 or 1960, but there remained thousands of people who swore they would never buy another Chrysler product and thousands more who were dissuaded from the attempt by hearing horror stories from those who had.

At least on the surface, there is a striking parallel between the Chrysler experience in the 1957-59 period and the Studebaker experience in 1953-55. Chrysler's corporate market share had been stable in the 16 percent range in 1955-56, then rose to 18.3 percent in 1957, only to collapse to a miserable 11.3 percent by 1959—nearly a 40 percent loss in market share in the two years following the disaster. After that, it took Chrysler several years and untold tens of millions of dollars in new products to regain the initiative it lost due almost entirely to the sloppy quality of the 1957-58 cars. Similarly, Studebaker's market share dropped by about half in 1954 and 1955 and, at that point, South Bend simply did not have access the millions required to buy it back. It is at least plausible that part of this decline could have been attributable to customer dissatisfaction with the poor quality of the 1953-54 models.

On the other hand, the parallel can be stretched too far. As we have seen in earlier chapters, the 1953 models themselves represented a significant drop in market share (in contrast to the temporary boost Chrysler experienced with its 1957 models), so the decline had started even before the word-of-mouth regarding the quality of the 1953 cars could have spread and, therefore, had to have gone deeper than the matter of fit and finish *per se*. Furthermore, we have also seen that all of the independents experienced severe drops in market share in the 1953-54 period irrespective of the intrinsic merits of the cars involved.

In sum, it is clear that quality was a liability for Studebaker in the 1953-54 period, but it is unlikely that it was the killer it has been made out to be by some. The bulk of the evidence indicates that Studebaker's quality reputation was, to the extent that it had any effect at all, an asset during most of the postwar period, while the poor fit and finish of the 1953-54 cars was only one of (and perhaps the least of) the problems that faced the company at that point.

Well, then, if Studebaker didn't produce bad cars, it must have been something else, something outside the corporation entirely. Perhaps "they" were responsible...

The Big Three Conspired Against the Independents

One of the oldest of chestnuts is that the Big Three drove the independents out of business. No one has ever turned up an iota of credible evidence that General Motors, Ford and/or Chrysler ever had any such intent. (And, it hasn't been for want of looking, either.) Following World War II, in fact, General Motors was so obsessed with government anti-trust actions—real and imagined—that it exerted major energy and resources in a variety of ways to keep the independents going. Kaiser-Frazer received a good deal of *sub rosa* assistance from GM, for example, as did American Motors in later years and, as we have seen, so did even tiny Avanti Motor Corporation. Meanwhile, Ford was obsessed in the 1940s and 1950s to the exclusion of all else (including, at times, common sense) with over-taking General Motors, while Chrysler, from the early 1950s, was too busy trying to save itself to focus on putting anybody else out of business.

In a sense, though, the charge was true. The simple disparity in size between General Motors and Ford, on the one hand, and the independents, on the other—a gap that would grow inexorably from the 1920s on—made it increasingly difficult for the independents (or even for Chrysler) to keep pace in a highly competitive industry in which not keeping pace was generally fatal. Because of their size, General Motors and Ford were able to establish trends in everything from styling, to engineering, to marketing— and just about everything in between—that the smaller companies failed to follow at their peril and all too often couldn't. General Motors and Ford were big enough, in fact, to define entire markets, as Ford did with the low-priced field in the teens, and as General Motors was to do with the medium-priced field in the 1920s and the luxury field in the 1930s.

Yet another considerable advantage the Big Three had over the independents was that they were big enough to survive their mistakes. One can rail on and on about the many failures of Hoffman and Vance in the years following World War II, but nothing they did wrong (or failed to do right) was any worse than the mismanagement that went on at Ford in the 1920s and 1930s, at Chrylser in the 1940s and 1950s and again in the 1970s, or at General Motors in the 1970s and 1980s. The difference was that the Big Three had the resources to first endure and then recover from their periods of ineptitude—although with Chrysler it was a close call, indeed.

This is a book about Studebaker, of course. Yet, in a sense, it is also a book about General Motors and Ford, for those two giants made most of the rules and set most of the standards for the world in which the independents struggled to survive. To understand why Studebaker failed, it is essential to understand the intense competitive battle that went on for forty years between Ford and General Motors, for it was this deadly-serious rivalry that defined the modern automobile industry and, in a meaningful sense, the diminishing role of independents such as Studebaker.

If Henry Ford was the manufacturing genius in the development of the modern automobile industry, Alfred Sloan at GM was the one who developed the modern management and marketing systems to go with it. In particular, Sloan recognized the fundamental changes in the market that took place after World War I and devised, to the lasting detriment of both Ford and the independents, a brilliant marketing strategy to exploit them.

The highly segmented market we know today did not always exist. In fact, in the earliest days of the industry, there were no recognizable market segments at all. There were just "good" cars and "bad" cars, although it was not always easy to tell which was which.

As the automobile began to be taken seriously as a means of transportation, however, two basic market segments quickly developed. The low-priced cars that were designed to sell to the ordinary citizen constituted one segment. This was the segment that Henry Ford brilliantly exploited with his fabulously successful Model T. Still, the Model T, for all its utility and affordability, was a fairly dreadful machine. Wags quickly claimed that the name "Ford" stood for "Fix Or Repair Daily," but people kept buying them because they were cheap and, if they required constant maintenance, they were at least easy to fix. Studebaker tried with only mixed success to reach this segment twice in the early years, first with the E-M-F and, later, with its spin-off, the Flanders.

On the other end of the spectrum was the quality car. These were cars designed for maximum performance, reliability and durability as those terms were understood at the time. A number of important competitors soon came into being. By 1910, Americans were already speaking of the "Three P's of Motoring"—Packard, Peerless and Pierce-Arrow. Together with Cadillac and Winton, these were probably considered the top five leaders in the quality field, although additional brands were important, as well, including Apperson, Chalmers, Franklin, Locomobile, Marmon, Stearns, Stevens-Duryea and a few others. The Studebaker-Garford and the Tincher struggled in this segment.

Yet, if Studebaker tried both low-priced cars and quality cars, it would have its greatest success selling what it termed (in a company publication issued around the time of World War I) "moderately-priced automobiles that could be built and sold in large quantities." This was the medium-priced field, the last major segment to come into existence in recognizable form. This occurred after World War I and there were several reasons.

One reason for the development of the medium-priced segment was the astounding success Henry Ford (and others) had achieved in extending automobile ownership to the masses of Americans. Prior to 1920, the vast majority of new car sales were to first-time buyers. Few people had ever bought a car twice. Inevitably, this game could only go on but so long; sooner or later the pool of prospects who had never owned a car would diminish below the level required to keep the manufacturers in business. True, there would always be people entering the market for the first time, but there would no longer be enough of them to keep the lines humming, much less enough of them to fuel the continued growth of the industry. Trade publications in the early 1920s were filled with anxious articles about the approaching market saturation that everyone knew was coming.

The second reason for the development of the medium-priced market was the nation's increasing prosperity. People had more money than ever before and they were living better than ever before. There was a lot of disposable income available for big-ticket items such as cars and installment buying, which had come into being around the time of the war, made it easier than ever to keep up with the Joneses, automotively speaking.

It was Alfred Sloan at General Motors, more than any other single individual, who figured out a way to deal with the problem of increasing market saturation, on the one hand, and how to get those ever more prosperous Americans to part with their money for new cars on a regular basis, on the other. Sloan's biggest worry was Henry Ford, who controlled nearly 60 percent of the market when Sloan assumed the helm at General Motors

Alfred Sloan, left, and Henry Ford.

in 1920. Ford's strategy was to concentrate on a single product line to the exclusion of all else. Sloan instinctively understood that this was no longer a valid approach in the maturing automobile industry of the 1920s

General Motors had been founded by William C. Durant in 1908, which just happened to be the same year Henry Ford introduced his revolutionary Model T and the year the E-M-F, which was to metamorphose in the Studebaker, appeared, as well. Durant was one of the very first to understand that the way to ultimate success was to blanket the market with a variety of brands. To do that required a highly complex organization that, unfortunately, was beyond Durant's management skills, but Sloan was able to take Durant's idea and make it work.

From the vantage point of 1920, it seemed to Sloan that the maturing automobile industry, abetted by increased prosperity and the development of installment buying, would induce increasing numbers of car buyers to raise their aspirations above the basic transportation level represented by the Model T. Thus, Sloan was convinced that the trend in the market strongly favored expansion of the medium-priced field. In fact, the share of new car sales going to the low-priced makes declined from well over 60 percent in

1920 to barely 40 percent by 1929. The Great Depression slowed this trend for a time but did not stop it.

Sloan also realized that this fundamental shift in the market would hurt Ford and be a boon to Ford's competitors. For Sloan, as well as for Erskine at Studebaker and all of Ford's other rivals, this was vital because Ford held such a strangle-hold on the industry at the time that real opportunity for the dozens of lesser auto makers could only come at Ford's expense. Fortunately for Sloan, Henry Ford was wedded to his Model T and was determined to make no important changes to it or even to supplement it with other models. The changing market conditions, however, signified a rush to better grades of transportation, i.e., toward cars that, due to Henry Ford's intransigence, would not be Fords.

Moreover, Sloan understood that General Motors had one other singnificant advantage over its arch-rival and over the other insurgents, as well—i.e., over companies such as Studebaker. Nearly all of the car companies were, in Sloan's word, "static." In other words, they built one car line in one price range. General Motors, with a number of lines in different price segments, was "fluid." As car buyers moved away from the basic level of transportation represented by the Model T, variety would be foremost on their minds and it stood to reason that the manufacturer that offered the greatest variety would stand to gain the most.

As a corollary to the above, Sloan was beginning to realize that those Model T owners who might be persuaded to want something a little better—i.e., a Chevy for a few dollars more—might, in time, become dissatisfied with their Chevy and want something better still. Extending this thought to its logical conclusion, General Motors could become the car company for millions of Americans who would move up or down the price scale as need or desire dictated without ever leaving the General Motors family. A young man buying a Chevy might be expected to become more prosperous in time and move on up through the ranks to an Oldsmobile, then to a Buick and, ultimately, even to a Cadillac. Chevrolet would have millions of customers who would never want anything better, of course, but the division would also cultivate hundreds of thousands of customers for Olds and Buick. It could work the other way, too. A certain number of well-to-do Buick households might need a less expensive second car, in which case Olds or Chevy would reap the benefits. Thus, General Motors would grow bigger and stronger and, by extension, its competitors would grow smaller and weaker. It is clear that Sloan was focused on the first half of this equation, but the consequences of the last part were no less real.

Sloan, who ran General Motors for nearly four decades, had far more influence on progressive men in the industry than is generally realized. Walter Chrysler—incidentally, one of Sloan's closest personal friends—virtually created Chrysler Corporation in GM's image by mimicking the strategy Sloan had developed in the early 1920s.

It is clear that this type of thinking was going on in Erskine's mind, as well, for he spent most of his last dozen years at Studebaker trying to do the same thing. Studebaker had been quite successful in selling medium-priced cars and, if Sloan was right, that market would continue to expand in the evolving market of the 1920s. But Studebaker was, again in Sloan's words, static. It couldn't take advantage of sudden shifts in buyer preference between the market segments, nor could it benefit from the inevitable movement of significant numbers of existing customers up or down the price scale. And, if it couldn't, it would grow progressively weaker relative to other companies such as General Motors that could. If Sloan wanted General Motors to be the sole car company for millions of buyers, it sounded, to Erskine, like a good idea for Studebaker, too. In the end, it didn't work out that way, of course, but no one can say Albert Erskine failed to see the hand-writing on the wall.

In fact, it had become clear to most American manufacturers as early as the 1920s that being fluid was not only good business, but a necessity in an ever-changing marketplace. There is also evidence that the idea had occurred to Studebaker a good deal earlier. In 1909, for example, the company was involved with Flanders, E-M-F, Studebaker Electric, Studebaker-Garford and Tincher brands all at once, although a couple of these were then moribund (see Chapter Two). By 1913, the decision had been made to concentrate on medium-priced cars under the Studebaker nameplate alone, but this restrictive strategy didn't last long after Erskine took over.

In 1923, Erskine came within a hairsbreadth of acquiring Maxwell-Chalmers, the company that Walter Chrysler was energetically rebuilding and was soon to turn into Chrysler Corporation (see Chapter Three). The result would have given Erskine the nucleus of a GM-type combine with Maxwell, Studebaker and Chalmers spanning most of the price spectrum.

When he was rebuffed on that deal, Erskine came back with another plan. The small Erskine was launched in 1927, followed a few months later by the acquisition of Pierce-Arrow (see Chapter Four). The failure of the Erskine brand was a setback, but the launching of the Rockne in 1932 finally gave Erskine three solid contenders that spanned the market: Rockne, Studebaker and Pierce-Arrow. It was due to the crushing weight of the depression combined with Erskine's fiscal irresponsibility, not to any failing by these three nameplates, that Studebaker fell into receivership in 1933.

After the bankruptcy, Studebaker again settled into the static mold, building medium-priced cars alone under the Hoffman/Vance regime. But, again, not for long. The Champion, introduced in 1939, was a limited, if reasonably successful, attempt to extend Studebaker's presence once again into the low-priced field (see Chapter Five).

Perhaps the final—and most curious—chance the company had to become successfully fluid occurred during World War II. When Edsel Ford died suddenly in 1943, there was apparently serious discussion in Detroit regarded the possibility of getting the government to lend Studebaker enough money to buy Ford Motor Company (see Chapter Six). The idea, alas, proved to be one whose time had not (and never would) come.

For a few years after the war, Studebaker enjoyed notable success until everything began to disintegrate all at once and it was forced to accept a takeover by Packard in 1954 (see Chapter Eight). So, once again, as in 1932-33, Studebaker (as allied with Packard) was a fluid company that spanned the market, but, once again, it was too late in the game to do any good.[1] In a stunning turnabout as Studebaker-Packard slid toward oblivion in the early months of 1956, then-president James J. Nance made a major pitch to sell the tottering enterprise to Ford Motor Company!

Nance's efforts to engineer a Ford takeover failed but, under the leadership of Roy Hurley, Studebaker-Packard was soon stalking other partners that would increase its fluidity. Rights to distribute Mercedes-Benz cars in America were secured within a few month's of Nance's departure (see Chapter Nine). Even after the lights went out in South Bend in December, 1963, and the Mercedes-Benz deal ended, efforts continued. Gordon

Grundy, then head of the automotive operations in Canada, tried hard to secure the Canadian distribution rights for both Nissan and Toyota vehicles (see Chapter Eleven). These efforts continued almost until the day the automotive division itself was given the axe in the spring of 1966.

It is ironic that Studebaker, which is regarded by most historians as a worst-case example of the pitfalls of remaining static (however they phrase it), flirted with plans and schemes to break out of its box repeatedly throughout its existence as an auto producer. That none of these efforts were successful goes a long way in explaining why the company ultimately failed.

Poor Productivity in the Early Postwar Years

Yet, Studebaker was also in trouble for reasons that were entirely homegrown. The most critical mistake made in the early postwar period was in deciding to persue a strategy of high volume instead of high productivity. The two are not mutually exclusive, of course; it is quite possible to do both, as General Motors amply demonstrated in this same era. But, General Motors was willing to take a four-month strike at the start of the 1946 model run in order to rein in its unions and keep costs down. Other manufacturers demonstrated a similar willingness to go to the mat with their unions when necessary, yet Hoffman and Vance wouldn't. To the contrary, they prided themselves in their "friendly" labor relations as evidenced by the fact that Studebaker had never had a strike.

That the company had never had a strike was patently untrue, as anyone who has read this far in this book will be aware, but it was a major part of the belief system in South Bend. Such beliefs, whether true or not, tend to take on a force of their own and this was the case with Studebaker. Since Studebaker had never *had* a strike, it must never *have* one, because good labor relations were equated with the absence of strikes and Studebaker must have good labor relations. The consequence of this was that Hoffman and Vance simply would not confront their union leaders with the one threat that showed they meant business and the leaders of UAW Local 5, understanding the implications of this all too well, had little incentive to help the company hold down labor costs or improve productivity.

Studebaker's lack of productivity cost it dearly. Albert Erskine had run the company onto the rocks in the early years of the depression by depleting Studebaker's capital through reckless dividends to stockholders. Hoffman and Vance accomplished much the same thing in the postwar years by recklessly over-paying their workers; i. e., by paying them more in wages than their level of productivity would justify. The effect was the same; the company was squandering its capital in ways that produced no results and left it vulnerable to unforeseen disasters that could only be successfully confronted with a strong capital base.

Studebaker and Chrysler both suddenly found themselves up against the wall in 1953. Both had made similar conceptual mistakes at the same time with their new products and suffered comparable damage in terms of sales. The critical difference was that Chrysler was able to arrange a $250 million line of credit and institute a crash program to prepare a completely new line of cars for the 1955 model year and Studebaker wasn't. The reason why Chrysler had options when it counted and Studebaker didn't was that Chrysler had protected its capital base and was, therefore, considered a good risk by commercial lenders.

Yet, Hoffman and Vance were not stupid, and they were well aware of the bind in which their labor policies placed the company, at least potentially. Their strategy was to accept the small unit margins that resulted from Studebaker's "good" labor relations and compensate by increasing Studebaker's volume and, when they could, by increasing the prices of Studebaker cars and trucks. In this way, Studebaker became absolutely dependent upon attaining and maintaining levels of volume in the postwar era that far exceeded anything the company had ever known. Amazingly, for a number of years the strategy worked, beginning with the landmark 1947 models introduced in 1946. Yet, those models themselves are a source of controversy.

The Decision to Build the All-New Cars in 1946

This decision has been harshly criticized by some Studebaker historians who reason that no automobile manufacturer needed a new car in 1946. To be precise, only one other major manufacturer even attempted to introduce an all-new postwar car before 1948. The sole exception was Kaiser-

1947 Studebaker Champion.

Frazer, which was starting from scratch and had little choice. In contrast, Hudson, whose cars had already been quite dated in 1942, continued merrily cranking them out through 1946 and 1947. Nash didn't make the change until 1949, while Packard, at the other end of the scale, didn't switch until 1951, although it certainly waited too long. Among the Big Three, Ford Motor Company introduced its postwar models in the early months of 1948 (as 1949s), General Motors retired its prewar bodies in stages in 1948 and 1949, and Chrysler—always a day late and a dollar short in this era—didn't join the party until the middle of the 1949 model run. So, with the Big Three, and even the other independents, biding their time, say Studebaker's critics, it was a ruinous waste of money for Studebaker to introduce new cars in 1946. Instead, the company should have husbanded every nickel until 1948 or 1949, and then met the Big Three head-to-head. As it was, according to the argument, Studebakers were fresh and exciting when those qualities were unnecessary to sell cars, and old-hat by the time the competition got tough.

It seems to this writer that the critics, while they have a point, miss a larger one: Studebaker *wasn't* one of the Big Three and there was little to be gained in being a follower. Simply mimicking General Motors proved repeatedly to be a prescription for disaster for an independent producer in the postwar era. The disparity in size between the Big Three and the independents was so huge that a company such as Studebaker couldn't hope to beat General Motors at its own game—or even Ford or Chrysler, both of which were running flat-out trying to keep pace with the mighty General.

If the brutally competitive auto industry can be compared to warfare, three essential military maxims bear consideration: 1) concentrate your forces, 2) strike where the enemy is weakest and/or where a blow is least expected, and, 3) above all, never waste your strength in direct confrontation with a stronger opponent. In short, bring your maximum strength to bear where it will encounter the least opposition. This was, in a nutshell, Studebaker's strategy in 1946. In the immortal words of Nathan Bedford Forrest, the Confederacy's brilliant cavalry commander in the Civil War, Studebaker "got there fust with the most"—and the rewards were enormous. Studebaker's market share rose by a third to the highest level the company had ever attained. Moreover, that high level of market penetration was sustained even after the Big Three introduced their all-new postwar designs. In addition, Studebaker, gained a reputation with car buyers as being a leader in the industry, which was no small asset for an independent producer. In contrast, Hudson and Nash took the advice of Studebaker's modern critics and waited until 1948 or 1949 to introduce their radically new postwar cars. These cars sold well enough, but—and, why is this surprising?—neither Hudson nor Nash ever got the boost from them that Studebaker did by being a leader.

It is ironic that Hoffman and Vance, who are justly criticized for their disastrous failings after the war, should be taken to task for the courage and foresight they showed with one of the most significant things they did right. Would that their next all-new line of cars had been as successful...

The Design of the 1953 Product Line

As it turned out, the 1953 models constituted the biggest single marketing mistake made after the war. These cars were once again styled by Raymond Loewy and his associates—meaning Bob Bourke, primarily—and the coupes and hardtops received, and continue to receive, much well-deserved critical acclaim. Regrettably, the rest of the line was less lovely.

The sedans were frumpy and the station wagons, added to the line in 1954, were almost homely (although there are doubtless some Studebaker enthusiasts who would take issue with this judgment).

The most obvious strike against them, and the reason most often cited for their failure in the marketplace, was that they were poorly conceived for the desires of the car buying public. They promoted the "European" concept of less bulk and greater space efficiency at a time when most consumers were thinking only in terms of longer, wider and heavier.

There was another problem, though, at once more subtle and more deadly. Even given the European concept, which may or may not have been a mistake, the design program was badly executed. Interestingly, it was General Motors that demonstrated in later years what went wrong with the 1953 Studebakers.

Like Studebaker in 1953, General Motors in 1968 decided to use different wheelbases for its two-and four-door "A-body" intermediate body types.[2] What prompted this was the traditional frustration of designers in trying to make two- and four-door models look equally appealing on the same wheelbase. A basic design that works for a four-door generally doesn't work so well for a two-door and vice versa. As a result, if a car is designed to look good as a two-door, it generally looks stubby on the same wheelbase as a four-door. Conversely, a car designed as a four-door looks stretched and ill-proportioned, as a rule, as a two-door. General Motors determined to solve this dilemma by using a short wheelbase for two-door models and a longer wheelbase for four-door models. It worked fabulously well. Unfortunately, Studebaker did precisely the reverse.

The final 1953 design started with the coupe, in which form it was, of course, stunning. The humdrum sedan body types, however, were then derived from the coupe, which would have tended to harm their proportions in any case, all else being equal. But, all else was not equal. Studebaker exacerbated the problem of developing a sedan from a coupe by putting the four-door models on a wheelbase that was actually *shorter* than that of the coupe! In other words, they did the exact opposite of what should have been done to ensure satisfactory proportions between coupe and sedan body types utilizing the same basic design, and the results, insofar as the sedans were concerned, were commensurately worse. The sedans lacked in abundance all the qualities that made the coupes so riveting. Where the coupes were long, low, relatively wide in relation to their height and, thus, sensuously proportioned, the sedans were too short, too tall, too narrow and, consequently, woefully unappealing. It would have been bad enough had the sedans merely shared the coupe's longer wheelbase.

Contrary to today's common wisdom, though, all 1953 Studebakers were not failures in the marketplace. The coupes and hardtops were huge successes. The public loved them and bought them in record numbers in comparison to any similar Studebaker body types ever built. Yet, an auto manufacturer does not live by coupes and hardtops alone, and sales of the standard sedan models—which, historically, had been the mainstay of any American manufacturer's program, Studebaker included—were disastrous. In an overall market that was up by 38 percent, production of Studebaker two- and four-door sedans dropped by a third. In contrast, production of hardtops and coupes soared 61 percent despite horrendous start-up problems and scheduling errors in South Bend that materially restricted their availability throughout much of the model run. To put it another way, had the sedans simply maintained their 1952 level of market penetration in 1953, Studebaker output would have been more than 40 percent higher than it turned out to be, the production problems with the coupes and

Harold Vance, behind the wheel, and Raymond Loewy with a 1953 Starliner.

hardtops notwithstanding. Of course, had the sedans been appealing, and had production problems not bedeviled the coupes and hardtops, the year could quite possibly have exceeded even the all-time record production in 1950. If any American auto company ever snatched defeat from the jaws of victory, it was Studebaker in 1953.

But, this was not all. Studebaker compounded the problem by building essentially two unique lines of products in 1953. Very little sheet metal was shared between the sedans and coupes; the company had, in effect, launched two new car lines that year. So, the sedans didn't turn out the way they did because they were locked into the coupe's body shell; they did so because the company wanted them to!

Dealing in "what ifs" is dangerous, indeed, with respect to Studebaker, but an intriguing possibility comes to mind. What would have happened had the company done the coupes as they did (with perhaps the addition of a convertible, which could have been spectacular[3]) and then taken part of the money spent on the sedans to restyle the 1952 models to harmonize with the new design themes? The 1947-52 series had a lot going for it. It was still as popular as ever in 1952, it was the right size for the needs of the market and, with the skills of Loewy and Bourke directed toward a thorough restyling, may well have had a few good years left in it. In this fashion, Studebaker might have had its cake and eaten it, too—and saved a pile of money in the bargain. It couldn't have done worse than the sedan range they actually built.

Still, that is hypothesis. The reality, which is beyond dispute, is that the 1953 products were overall disasters and, unlike Chrysler, Studebaker was in no position to borrow untold millions and start over. South Bend was forced to live with its mistakes and doing that proved impossible. Market penetration dropped in 1953 for the first time in fifteen years—by a full percentage point to 2.8 percent, then another point-and-a-half by 1955, to 1.3 percent, following a less than successful restyle of the original design. Studebaker had lost two-thirds of its market share in three years in what is unquestionably one of the most dramatic collapses by a major manufacturer in the history of the American automobile industry. Worse still, it had happened to a company utterly dependent upon maintaining what was, by historic standards, extraordinarily high volume.

The Failure to Recognize the Compact Car Market

It has been noted that Studebaker scored a huge success with its 1946 models precisely because it followed a plan General Motors and the other manufacturers didn't. The 1953 coupes were also notably successful for the same reason. Yet, Studebaker missed the development of the truly important market segment that came along in the 1950s: the compact car boom.

Nash had introduced its first Rambler compact as early as 1950, the Kaiser-Frazer-built Henry J came along in 1951, Willys re-entered the passenger car field with its own compact in 1952, while Hudson was planning the dimunitive Jet series for 1953. In addition, the British Morris and other wannabes from across the Pond were making a bit of splash in this same era. While it is true that none of these cars were setting the world on fire, they clearly represented the development of a new market that offered considerable potential.

The 1953 Studebakers, with their "European" lines and compact dimensions represented a move in the right direction, but South Bend was perversely determined to sell its smaller, more efficient cars head-to-head with the longer, lower, wider monsters so beloved in Detroit. And, it just didn't work. As it was, the 1953 sedans were neither fish nor fowl; they were too small to compete against the typical Detroit barges of the era, yet they were too big to exploit the growing interest in compacts.

It is ironic, indeed, that the 1959 Lark was a derivative of the 1953 body shell, for it showed dramatically what might have been done six years sooner. (See the photo comparison of 1956 and 1959 sedans on the following page.) What would have happened had South Bend pursued a three-prong strategy in 1953: 1) continued the 1952 full-size cars over with fresh restyling; 2) introduced the coupes as they were; and 3) added the sedans in roughly the 1959 Lark configuration as true compacts? The reworked 1952 models would have protected the existing customer base, the compact sedans (which could have been delayed for a year or two) would have put Studebaker squarely into the developing compact segment, while the coupes would have added icing to the cake by being the huge successes they were, anyway.

Admittedly, much of the above takes us rather more deeply into the

The compact 1959 Lark, top, and the "full-size" 1956 Champion.

realm of speculation than is probably wise. Still, the central point is an important one: Studebaker effectively abandoned its existing customers in 1953 and, worse, did so without moving decisively into another clearly identified market segment that had sufficient demonstrated potential to take up the slack. And, that was not, to put it mildly, a good idea.

The Lack of a Solid Presence at the Retail Level

In retrospect, it is clear that another critical—and generally over-looked—factor in Studebaker's decline as an automobile manufacturer was its inability to attract and keep top-notch dealers capable of maintaining the consistent high volume required by the Hoffman/Vance postwar strategy already noted. This weakness was not evident during the late-prewar years when volume expectations were much more modest, although the company's middling showing in 1940—despite the nearly new Champion—should have been a warning. Nor was it evident during the postwar seller's market when even second-rate dealers could sell all the cars they could get. The real crunch came in the summer of 1953 when two events transpired. The first was the end of the seller's market. The second, virtually concurrent, event was the launching of what came to be known as the Ford Blitz (see Chapter Eight). Taken together, the two events starkly revealed Studebaker's lack of competitive marketing muscle at the retail level.

The fact that Ford Motor Company and General Motors could get away with dumping cars onto their dealers, and the fact that Chrysler and the independents were almost powerless to counter this tactic, speaks volumes about the relationship between the various manufacturers and their dealers. To really understand this, however, it is necessary to understand how the dealers make their money.

A well-run dealer has three profit centers: 1) new car sales, 2) used car sales and 3) parts and service. Furthermore, this hypothetical well-run dealer can, if he has been around for a while and his facilities are paid for, earn sizable bottom-line income from the latter two profit centers alone. In other words, he can make enough money off the "back shop" and the used car lot to pay the bills without selling very many new cars at all. When the economy declines and people are holding onto their cars a little longer, or buying used cars instead of new ones, his profit in the back shop and the used car lot can actually rise. Naturally, he would *like* to sell lots of new cars if he could make good profits[4] doing so—the more the better, at least in theory—but the point is that he doesn't *have* to to stay in business.

The situation at the factory, however, is quite different. Although the manufacturers all have sideline businesses selling parts for older cars, the only profit center that really counts is selling new cars to the dealers. Given the enormous costs of developing products and operating the facilities in which to produce them, *the factory's break-even point is nearly always higher than the break-even point of the sum total of its dealers.* This fact is of enormous importance and well worth italicizing. What it means in the cold and unforgiving real world is that the dealers for any given brand of car can, theoretically, remain in business on an aggregate level of volume that would cause the factory to lose money and, ultimately, bankrupt it. Moreover, the less productive a manufacturer is, the more true this becomes and, to that extent, the Hoffman/Vance postwar strategy of buying labor peace with low productivity had made Studebaker a sitting duck for this dynamic.

Three pertinent examples illustrate the point. First, in an internal memo circulated through the company in the early months of 1956, Nance bitterly complained:

> We sweat and strain to produce and price our car competitively and then our dealers get $200 to $300 more than [the] competition. On limited volume, of course. In January, Studebaker dealers "creamed" the deals for a Variable Net of $374, while Chevrolet dealers were about $100...Since our dealer body, as a whole, has a breakeven point substantially below that of the factory, they bleed us to death, and have been doing it...for years.[5]

At the time the $6 millon loss for the first half of 1957 was announced, an unnamed Studebaker executive lamented: "If we can sell just one more car a month for each dealer, we'll be over the break-even point." But, as we have seen, the dealers didn't have to sell that car, which brings us to the third example: In 1958, in the depths of a recession in one of the worst selling years in memory and when Studebaker-Packard was at death's door after four years of nightmarish losses, America's Studebaker-Packard dealers actually recorded an aggregate net *profit* of $3.9 million! To be sure, there must have been some dealers who were losing money, but there were many more who were still making a fairly good living even as the factory was going broke.[6]

This crushing reality is the reason all the factories had (and still have) teams of zone "reps" whose job it was to motivate, persuade, cajole, hound and—depending on the factory's desperation and clout—threaten the dealers into taking more cars than they otherwise would. Unfortunately, the ability of the factories to do this effectively varied with the size of the club they could hold over their dealers. That, in turn, had a lot to do with the desirability of the various franchises and with why Studebaker failed.

Then as now, all franchises were not equal, for they differed dramatically in their profit potential. In 1952, the last year before the market saturated and the Ford Blitz began, the average number of cars sold per franchise stood as indicated in the chart on the following page.

In the typical community, the most desirable single franchises were Ford, Chevy and (owing to a combination of relatively high margins and relatively high volume) Buick. Surprisingly, Lincoln-Mercury heads the list here. Neither Lincoln nor Mercury was a top-ranked brand in its class, but the combination, or "dual" as it is known in the industry, made for a highly desirable franchise. This raises all sorts of qualifications that must be made regarding the rankings—and none of them improves Studebaker's already less than stellar showing.

Cadillac, for example, was perhaps the most profitable franchise of all if the dealer was located in a major metropolitan market. Part of this was due to the high margins and the relatively high volume per dealer in those markets, and part was due to the fact that Cadillac was never a "stand alone" franchise until 1967. Prior to that time, Cadillac was always dualed with another GM franchise, usually Oldsmobile. (The reverse was not necessarily true, it should be noted; not every Olds dealer carried Cadillac.) The average number of Cadillacs sold per dealer in the chart above is deceptive, too, owing to the division's practice of awarding many franchises in this era primarily as "service" points. At that time, luxury car sales were still disproportionately concentrated in the major urban centers. A Cadillac dealer in Cleveland was expected to sell lots of cars, but the dealer ninety miles away in East Liverpool existed primarily to service customers from Cleveland (or Pittsburgh or wherever) who experienced service problems on the road. The dealer in East Liverpool had the personal satisfaction of being able to drive a new Cadillac and enjoyed the enhanced prestige in his community that came with being the Cadillac dealer—which were not,

AVERAGE UNITS SOLD PER FRANCHISE IN 1952[†]

FRANCHISE	UNITS
Lincoln-Mercury	124
Chevrolet	112
Ford	110
Nash	94
Buick	89
Chrysler (Corp.) *	82
AVERAGE SALES PER FRANCHISE	79
Pontiac	63
Oldsmobile	56
STUDEBAKER	56
Cadillac	51
Packard	46
Hudson	41
Kaiser **	27
Willys-Overland	21

† This and the following charts and graphs apply to sales within the United States; Canada not included.
* The figures for Chrysler Corporation dealers are not broken down by brand. Every company-franchised dealer had a Plymouth franchise in addition to one or more of Dodge, DeSoto, and Chrysler.
** Kaiser includes Frazer, which had been discontinued after the 1951 model run, and Henry J.

by any means, insignificant perks—but he made his money off the lesser GM cars and trucks he sold. Thus, Cadillac's "sales" points did far better than the "average" number would suggest. In fact, for most metropolitan Cadillac-Oldsmobile dealers in the 1950s, the combination was almost a license to print money.

Moreover, in smaller communities the various medium-priced General Motors franchises were almost always dualed with Chevy, Cadillac, or each other in order to increase their strength. Those Pontiac and

Oldsmobile dealers that were not dualed with another General Motors car franchise were mostly limited to the large metropolitan areas where they had sufficient volume to make good money. Ford and Mercury were similarly handled in the smaller markets. And, as is noted in the footnote to the chart, the various Chrysler franchises were all dualed with Plymouth at this time, even in the major markets, and were dualed even more aggressively in smaller markets.

As if this weren't enough, Chevy, Ford and Dodge dealers all had lucrative truck franchises not reflected in the chart. General Motors offered the GMC Truck franchise, as well, which was usually dualed with Pontiac. Especially in the smaller markets where the Big Three franchises were aggressively dualed, dealer volume was aided enormously by the addition of these various truck lines.

In contrast, consider the poor independents. As the chart indicates, only Nash had a really solid dealer network, but even it wasn't strong enough to quite compete with the Big Three when dual franchises and truck franchises are taken into account and, on top of that, the unit profit margins were relatively low. Granted, in some cases there were duals in the smaller markets among the independents, too. Still, duals weren't nearly as effective with brands that competed head-to-head in the same price ranges and the independents were (save for Packard) all clustered in the lower-medium-priced field, with a few models dipping down into the low-priced field. Furthermore, among the independents only Studebaker offered trucks at all and the Studebaker truck franchise was never lucrative in the sense that the Big Three truck franchises were.

Not surprisingly, the most aggressive businessmen fought to get and hold the most lucrative franchises. If one of the top franchises in any given community suddenly came available, several suitors would be fighting each other to win it from the factory. In practice, that meant that the Big Three nearly always had the best representation. On the other end of the scale, it meant that the independents generally had to take what they could get, which often meant inadequate representation or, in the smaller communities, no representation at all. It also meant that GM and Ford dealers lived in real fear of their factories, while Studebaker dealers (and those allied with Chrysler and the other independents) lived secure in the knowledge

AVERAGE UNITS SOLD PER FRANCHISE IN 1954

FRANCHISE	UNITS
Ford	213
Chevrolet	188
Lincoln-Mercury	167
Buick	146
AVERAGE SALES PER FRANCHISE	113
Oldsmobile	105
Pontiac	87
Chrysler (Corp.)	70
Cadillac	64
Nash	54
STUDEBAKER	39
Packard	25
Hudson	24
Kaiser-Willys *	12

* Henry J had been dropped, but Kaiser had bought Willys in 1953.

that the factory needed them more than they needed the factory.

Moreover, the better the independent dealer, the more the imbalance was true. If a Studebaker dealer, for example, was truly top-notch, he would inevitably begin to harbor thoughts of treason. If he was that good, he knew he could make a lot more money selling, say, Buicks. So, for that matter, did Buick. If a Buick franchise came available, the top-notch Studebaker dealer would be sorely tempted to apply for it—if the Buick zone rep hadn't come to him first. This is, in fact, exactly what happened in the author's hometown in Ohio. In 1950—Studebaker's all-time record year, no less— the local Studebaker dealer jumped ship to take on the Buick franchise. If Studebaker couldn't hold onto such a dealer at the very peak of its success, one can imagine how difficult it became as the company began to decline.

Studebaker's situation did, in fact, begin to fall apart in 1954. The av-

erage number of cars sold per franchise is represented by the chart that
appears at the top of the previous page. During the Ford Blitz, the tremendous potential of the Ford and Chevy franchises meant that the factories
could force their dealers to take unwanted cars. As a result, Ford and Chevy
gained market share. Chrysler, to say nothing of the independents, simply
didn't have the clout to respond in kind. As a result, the local Ford dealer
was moving better than two hundred cars a year, even if he had to take a
loss overall, while the Studebaker dealer across the street was saying to
himself: "Why should I sell cars I don't make money on? Sure, I could sell
sixty cars a year if I wanted to give 'em away, but I'd only be building up
warranty headaches in the service department. I'm better off waiting for
thirty or forty customers who are willing to give me a decent profit."
Studebaker was powerless to do anything about it and that explains, as
succinctly as anything can, why Studebaker sales collapsed overnight by
40 percent in 1954.

The average new car franchise sold 79 cars in 1952. This rose to 147 by
1955, a gain of 86 percent. In the same period, the average Studebaker franchise dropped from 56 cars to 40, a decline of 29 percent. The Studebaker
performance was dreadful on its own merits, but absolutely stunning when
compared to the growing strength of the average franchise holder. The ramifications for Studebaker were just as stunning. If the average Studebaker
dealer had simply kept pace with industry growth between 1952 and 1955,
the company would have sold more than three times as many cars in 1955
as it actually did.

Of course, there were other factors involved in Studebaker's decline,
the unattractive design of the bread-and-butter sedans in the 1953-55 period being chief among them. Still, as Chevy was to prove the hard way in
1957 and again in 1959, strong dealers can sell a lot of unappealing cars. It
is, in fact, precisely when times are tough that the value of a strong dealer
body is greatest. For Studebaker, times got tough, indeed, beginning in
1953 and the company simply didn't have the clout at the retail level to
compensate for its other problems. After that, the downward spiral began
with dizzying speed. By 1955, with Studebaker's national market share
reduced to barely 1 percent, it was almost impossible for Studebaker to
attract or keep a top-notch dealer who had any feasible options.

The Abandonment of the Truck Market

Studebaker's trucks are usually covered only in passing even in "complete" histories of the company. It must be admitted that this volume is no different in that respect. In part, this bias toward the Studebaker automobiles is entirely understandable, for prior to World War II the trucks were little more than an after-thought even in South Bend. The company sold 5,078 trucks in 1941, a figure that was high by Studebaker's prewar standards but rated seven-tenths of one percent of the total registrations for trucks in the United States that year.

World War II changed the picture dramatically. As a truck producer, Studebaker was allowed—indeed, ordered—to keep the lines rolling. As a result, South Bend produced an astonishing 200,000 trucks during the conflagration and their reputation spread all over the world in much the same way the Studebaker wagon reputation had been fostered in America by the Civil War. As was noted in Chapter Six, Studebaker trucks were so ubiquitous in the Red Army that, for a time, the colloquial word for "truck" in Russian became "Studebaker"!

After the war—given its production capacity, its growing reputation and the pent-up demand for trucks—the company realized undreamed-of levels of sales. Market share rose from around 4 percent in 1946 (in itself

1954 Studebaker truck.

The Studebaker truck plant as it appeared in 1949.

fairly remarkable) to nearly 5 percent in 1948. The wonderful design of the all-new 1949 truck line boosted this to nearly 6 percent and the 7 percent level was exceeded in 1952. (It is certainly true that many of these trucks were destined for military duty at the height of the Korean War, but the same could be said for Studebaker's competitors.) Throughout the early postwar period, in fact, the Studebaker truck line had a higher market penetration in most years than did the much-vaunted Studebaker cars.

Yet, after the highly successful effort made with the 1949 trucks the company seems more or less to have forgotten about them. Thus starved for the investment needed to remain competitive, their sales went into a precipitous decline beginning in 1953. The figures are stark. Studebaker sold 58,985 trucks in 1952 for a 7.2 percent market share. This collapsed to 10,817 trucks in 1955 for a pathetic 1.1 percent share—a drop of 81 percent in volume and nearly 85 percent in market share in three years. That was even worse than the experience with the cars in the same period. Had the truck line simply kept pace with the industry, South Bend would have produced nearly 60,000 more vehicles in 1955 than it actually did.

Moreover, as has been noted above, having a solid truck line was a real boon to the dealer body. It gave them entrée to another market, and increased both their volume and their profits. In turn, this made it easier for the company to get and hold the better dealers, particularly in the smaller and more rural communities where Studebaker's retail presence was historically weakest compared to the Big Three and, therefore, precisely where it needed the most help.

In sum, South Bend's lack of investment in its promising truck side after the war represented yet another missed opportunity. It cost the company dearly by the mid-1950s when Studebaker suddenly needed every ounce of strength it could muster.

Conclusions

Throughout its history as an automobile producer, Studebaker was in a difficult position with survival always in doubt. The natural economic forces at work, which decreed that the strong would tend to get stronger while the weak would tend to get weaker, was a constant threat to any manufacturer not fortunate enough to be General Motors. Still, if the events of recent years have taught us anything it is that there is a place in the intensely fluid American automobile market for almost any number of competitors provided they have the skill and resources to take advantage of the opportunities that are always present. If, as some contend, it was "impossible" for a Studebaker to survive because no company but the Big Three had the strength to do so, why was it possible for a Toyota to storm the American market and establish a solid beachhead? Toyota was a mere fraction of Studebaker's size in 1945, or even in 1955.

In retrospect, it seems clear that Studebaker failed because of a fatal triple blow from: 1) the postwar strategy of tolerating low productivity in favor of high volume, followed by 2) the disastrous 1953 product line and 3) a weak dealer network that was unable to compensate for the crisis created by the first two. The decision to buy labor peace with low productivity only worked as long as astonishingly high volume was able to be maintained. The poor packaging of the 1953 line, the troubled start-up of production, the contemporaneous end of the seller's market, the Ford Blitz and the weak dealer network all acted in concert to rob the company of its precious volume overnight and, within a few short months, the company may well have been beyond resuscitation.

It is important to note that the end when it came was not the result of a gradual decline that knowledgeable observers had long predicted. Rather, it came as a sudden, unforeseen collapse that, even in retrospect, almost leaves one gasping in disbelief. The cataclysmic events of 1953 had a tragic dimension to them that was, in the literal meaning of a much-abused word, awesome. Even at a distance of nearly half-a-century, those events retain a dramatic impact that is comparable to other disasters of legend, such as the *Titanic*. One moment a great product of man's creative energy was sailing along toward a seemingly bright future and without a care in the world, and the next moment it was all over.

In 1952, Studebaker celebrated the conclusion of its first century of operations. A commemorative book published that year by the company concluded with the following paragraphs:

> The significance of Studebaker's first century is that in the ideas and ideals of those who today plan for Studebaker's tomorrow, we find a point of view not held by the men of younger companies. The men at South Bend live with a long-range outlook, and they make their plans for long periods of time. Each daily decision and action fit into the picture of Studebaker's future viewed confidently far ahead. Plans are never made on just a day-to-day or year-to-year basis. There is no opportunism. There is complete continuity of effort and purpose.
>
> Thus, confident in the tradition built through a century of trial and success, the men who today have charge of the affairs of Studebaker now see—in the words of Harold S. Vance—"a future much more intriguing than the past...a tomorrow that holds unknown but boundless opportunity."[7]

And, within a few months of the publication of those words, Studebaker had virtually ceased to exist as a viable vehicle producer. True, the company would struggle on for more than a decade, and there would be a couple of penultimate rises before the final fall, but it was really all over by the summer of 1953. When the downward spiral began in the early months of that year, it quickly assumed such momentum that it was simply beyond the ability and resources of the company to recover. That having been said, however, it must also be noted that the fall of Studebaker was not inevitable. It was a result of poor decisions in South Bend hastened by opportunities missed. It was a tragedy that need not have happened and in that may lie the greatest tragedy of all.

Notes

[1] As was noted in Chapter Eight, the Studebaker-Packard merger was intended by Mason and Nance to be the second step in a general consolidation of the major independents, which had commenced with the Nash-Hudson merger that took place in late-1953 and resulted in the formation of American Motors. Eventually, American Motors would have consisted of Studebaker, Nash, Hudson, and Packard.

[2] Chevrolet Chevelle, Pontiac Tempest/LeMans/GTO, Oldsmobile Cutlass, and Buick Skylark. The "G-body" cars—Chevrolet Monte Carlo, Pontiac Grand Prix, and Olds Cutlass Supreme—were also derived from the A-body.

[3] One was actually built and it was, in fact, spectacular.

[4] Or, "variable net" in Studebaker-Packard internal lingo.

[5] Langworth, p. 87.

[6] And, in fact, any number of Studebaker dealers survived long after the company stopped building cars entirely. Frost & French, the old-line Los Angeles dealer, was doing good business with service and used car sales alone well into the 1970s. Numerous other examples could be cited.

[7] Longstreet, pp. 120-121

Studebaker

Reference
Matter

Bibliography

Primary Sources

Avanti Automotive Corporation. Brochures, photographs and miscellaneous publications. Youngstown, Ohio.

Avanti Motor Corporation. Brochures, photographs and miscellaneous publications. South Bend, Indiana.

AVX Cars. Brochures, photographs and miscellaneous publications. Lancaster, Pennsylvania.

Breer, Carl. *The Birth of Chrysler Corporation and Its Engineering Legacy.* Warrendale, Pennsylvania, 1995.

Buehrig, Gordon M. *Rolling Sculpture, A Designer and His Work.* Newfoundland, New Jersey, 1975.

Chrysler, Walter P., and Boyden Sparks. *Life of an American Workman.* New York, 1937.

Chrysler Corporation. Annual Reports, brochures, photographs and miscellaneous publications. Highland Park, Michigan.

Conde, John. *American Motors Family Album.* Detroit, 1969.

Cooper Industries. Annual Reports. Houston, Texas.

Cravens, J. K. *Automobile Year Book and Buyer's Guide Illustrated.* Chicago, 1934.

Cravens, J. K. *Automobile Year Book and Buyer's Guide Illustrated.* Chicago, 1937.

Detroit Public Library, Automotive History Collection.

Drucker, Peter F. *Concept of the Corporation.* New York, 1946.

Drucker, Peter F. *The Practice of Management.* New York, 1954.

Erskine, Albert Russel. *History of the Studebaker Corporation.* South Bend, Indiana, 1918.

Erskine, Albert Russel. *History of the Studebaker Corporation.* South Bend, Indiana, 1924.

Everett-Metzger-Flanders Company. Brochures, photographs and miscellaneous publications. Detroit, Michigan.

Fischer, John. *Why They Behave Like Russians*. New York, 1946.

General Motors Corporation. Annual Reports, brochures, photographs and miscellaneous publications. Detroit, Michigan.

Hoppe, Heinz C. *Serving the Star Around the World*. Munich, 1992.

Hudson Motor Car Company. Annual Reports, brochures, photographs and miscellaneous publications. Detroit, Michigan.

Iacocca, Lido A. *Iacocca, An Autobiography*. New York, 1984.

Indiana State Archives, Indianapolis.

Khrushchev, Nikita S. *Khrushchev Remembers*. Boston, 1970.

Loewy, Raymond. *Industrial Design*. Woodstock, New York, 1979.

Longstreet, Stephen. *A Century on Wheels: The Story of Studebaker*. New York, 1952.

MacManus, Theodore, F., and Norman Beasely. *Men, Money and Motors*. New York, 1929.

Maxim, Hiram Percy. *Horseless Carriage Days*. New York, 1936.

Nash Motors Company. Annual Reports, brochures, photographs and miscellaneous publications. Detroit, Michigan.

Nash-Kelvinator Corporation. Annual Reports, brochures, photographs and miscellaneous publications. Detroit, Michigan.

New Avanti Motor Corporation. Brochures, photographs and miscellaneous publications. South Bend, Indiana.

Packard Motor Car Company. Annual Reports, brochures, photographs and miscellaneous publications. Detroit, Michigan.

Pfau, Hugo. *The Custom Body Era*. New York, 1970.

Salisbury, Harrison E. *To Moscow and Beyond*. New York, 1959.

Sloan, Alfred P. *Adventures of a White-Collar Man*. New York, 1941.

Sloan, Alfred P., Jr. *My Years With General Motors*. Garden City, New York, 1964.

Sorensen, Charles E. *My Forty Years With Ford*. New York, 1956.

Stout, Richard H. *Make 'Em Shout Hooray!* New York, 1988.

Studebaker Corporation (Delaware). Annual Reports, brochures, photographs and miscellaneous publications. South Bend, Indiana.

Studebaker Corporation (Indiana). Annual Reports, brochures, photographs and miscellaneous publications. South Bend, Indiana.

Studebaker National Museum Archives, South Bend, Indiana.

Studebaker-Packard Corporation. Annual Reports, brochures, photographs and miscellaneous publications. Detroit, Michigan, and South Bend, Indiana.

Studebaker-Packard Papers, George Arents Research Library, Syracuse University. Syracuse, New York.

Studebaker-Worthington Corporation. Annual Reports and miscellaneous publications. New York, New York.

United States Government, Federal Trade Commission. *Report on Motor Vehicle Industry*. Washington, D.C., 1939.

Used Car Statistical Bureau. *Market Analysis Report*. Boston, 1941.

Western Reserve Historical Society, Cleveland, Ohio.

Interviews by the author with Arnold Altman, Stephen Blake, James Bunting, Reeves Callaway, Thomas Kellogg, Semon E. Knudsen, Holden Koto, Bill Lang, Roger Penn, Richard Stout, Richard Teague, Barry Toepke.

Periodicals: *Action Era Vehicle, Advertising Age, American Way, Argosy, Autocar (G.B.), Auto Age, Automobile Quarterly, Automobile Show, Automobile, Automotive Industries, Automotive News, Automobile Topics, AutoWeek, Avanti Magazine, Boston Globe, Branham Automobile Reference Book* (various issues, 1918-1939), *Business Week, Car Classics, Car Craft, Car & Driver, Car Life, CARS, Cars & Parts, Chemical & Engineering News, Chicago Sun-Times, Chicago Tribune, Consumer Reports, Detroit News, Esquire, Forbes, Fortune, Handbook of Gasoline Automobiles, Horseless Age, Motor (G.B.), Hot Rod, Indiana History Bulletin, Indiana Magazine of History, Industrial Design, Mechanix Illustrated, Motor (U.S.), Motor Age, Motor Life, Motor Trend, Motor Trend Yearbook* (1955-61), *N.A.D.A. Used Car Guide* (various issues, 1934-67), *Newsweek, New York Times, Packard Cormorant, Pennsylvania Folklife, Popular Mechanics, Popular Science, Red Book National Used Car Market Report* (various issues, 1934-55), *Road & Track, Scientific American, South Bend Tribune, Special-Interest Autos, Sports Car Graphic, Time, Track & Traffic, True's Automobile Yearbook* (1953-60), *Turning Wheels, Wall Street Journal, Ward's, Washington Post, Youngstown Vindicator.*

Secondary Sources

Allen, Frederick Lewis. *The Big Change: America Transforms Itself, 1900-1950*. New York, 1952.

Barker, Ronald and Anthony Harding. *Automobile Design: Great Designers and Their Work*. Cambridge, Massachussetts, 1970.

Beasely, Norman. *Knudsen, A Biography*. New York, 1947.

Beasely, Norman and George W. Stark. *Made in Detroit*. New York, 1957.

Beatty, Michael, Patrick Furlong, and Loren Pennington. *Studebaker: Less Than They Promised*. South Bend, Indiana, 1984.

Bentley, John. *Oltime Steam Cars*. Greenwich, Connecticut, 1953.

Boyd, T. A. *Professional Amateur*. New York, 1957.

Bridges, John. John Bourke *Designs for Studebaker*. Nashville, Tennessee, 1984.

Brierly, Brooks T. *Auburn, Reo, Franklin and Pierce-Arrow versus Cadillac, Chrysler, Lincoln and Packard*. Coconut Grove, Florida, 1991.

Brierly, Brooks T. *There Is No Mistaking a Pierce-Arrow*. Coconut Grove, Florida, 1986.

Brinkley, David. *Washington Goes to War*. New York, 1988.

Brooks, John. *Fate of the Edsel and Other Business Adventures*. New York, 1963.

Bury, Martin H. *The Automobile Dealer*. Philadelphia, 1958.

Cannon, William A. and Fred K. Fox. *Studebaker: The Complete Story*. Blue Ridge Summit, Pennsylvania, 1981.

Catton, Bruce. *The War Lords of Washington*. New York, 1948.

Chandler, Alfred D., Jr. *Giant Enterprise*. New York, 1964.

Clymer, Floyd. *Those Wonderful Old Automobiles*. New York, 1953.

Clymer, Floyd. *Treasury of Early American Automobiles, 1877-1925*. New York, 1950.

Cohn, David L. *Combustion On Wheels*. Boston, 1944.

Colins, Herbert Ridgeway. *Presidents On Wheels*. New York, 1971.

Cornell Auto Publications. *Automobile Value Review*. Chicago, 1941.

Crabb, Richard. *Birth of a Giant*. New York, 1969.

Cray, Ed, *Chrome Colossus*. New York, 1980.

Critchlow, Donald T. *The Life and Death of an American Corporation*. Indianapolis, 1996.

Editors of Automobile Quarterly. *The American Car Since 1775*. New York, 1971.

Forbes, B. C., and O. D. Foster. *Automotive Giants of America*. New York, 1926.

Georgano, G. N., ed. *The Complete Encyclopedia of Commercial Vehicles*. Osceola, Wisconsin, 1979.

Georgano, G. N. *Cars, 1886-1930*. New York, 1985.

Georgano, G. N., ed. *The Complete Encyclopedia of Motorcars: 1885 to the Present*. New York, 1973.

Glasscock, C. B., *The Gasoline Age: The Story of the Men Who Made It*. Indianapolis, 1937.

Gustin, Lawrence R., *Billy Durant, Creator of General Motors*. Grand Rapids, Michigan, 1973.

Haddad, William. *Hard Driving, My Years With John DeLorean*. New York, 1985.

Hall, Asa E. and Richard Langworth. *The Studebaker Century*. Contoocook, New Hampshire, 1983.

Heasley, Jerry. *The Production Figure Book for U.S. Cars*. Osceola, Wisconsin, 1977.

Hendry, Maurice. *Cadillac: The Standard of the World*. Princeton, New Jersey, 1973.

Herndon, Booton. *Ford*. New York, 1969.

Josephson, Matthew. *Edison, A Biography*. New York, 1959.

Keats, John. *Insolent Chariots*. Philadelphia, 1958.

Kimes, Beverly R., ed. *Packard: A History of the Motorcar and the Company*. Princeton, New Jersey, 1978.

Kimes, Beverly Rae, and Henry Austin Clark, Jr. *Standard Catalog of American Cars 1805-1942*. Iola, Wisconsin, 1985.

Kuby, Erich. *The Russians and Berlin 1945*. New York, 1969.

Lacey, Robert. *Ford: The Men and the Machine*. New York, 1986.

Lamm, John. *DeLorean: Stainless Steel Illusion*. Santa Ana, California, 1983.

Langworth, Richard M. *Studebaker, 1946-1966*. Osceola, Wisconsin, 1979.

Langworth, Richard M. *The Last Onslaught on Detroit*. Princeton, New Jersey, 1975.

Leland, Mrs. Wilfred C., and Mrs. Minnie Dubbs Milbrook. *Master of Precision*. Detroit, 1966.

Leslie, Stuart W. *Boss Kettering, Wizard of General Motors*. New York, 1983.

Liddell Hart, B. H. *The Red Army*. New York, 1956.

MacMinn, Strother, and Michael Lamm. *Detroit Style, Automotive Form 1925-1950*. Detroit, 1985.

May, George S. *A Most Unique Machine*. Grand Rapids, Michigan, 1975.

May, George S. R. E. Olds: *Auto Industry Pioneer*. Grand Rapids, Michigan, 1977.

Moritz, Michael and Barrett Seaman. *Going For Broke, the Chrysler Story*. New York, 1981.

Nesbitt, Dick. *50 Years of American Automobile Design*. Chicago, 1985.

Nevins, Allan, and Farnk E. Hill. *Ford: Expansion and Challenge, 1915-1932*. New York, 1957.

Nevins, Allan, and Frank E. Hill. *Ford: The Times the Man and the Company*. New York, 1954.

Pound, Arthur. *The Turning Wheel: The Story of General Motors Through Twenty-Five Years*, 1908-1933. Garden City, New York, 1934

Rae, John B. *The American Automobile*. Chicago, 1965.

Ralston, Marc *Pierce-Arrow*. New York, 1980.

Riggs, L. Spencer. *Pace Cars of the Indy 500*. Ft. Lauderdale, Florida, 1989.

Scharchburg, Richard P. *Carriages Without Horses*. Warrendale, Pennsylvania, 1993.

Schönberger, Angela, ed. *Raymond Loewy: Pionier des Amerikanischen Industrie-Designs*. Berlin, West Germany, 1990.

Sedgwick, Michael. *Cars of the 1930s*. Cambridge, Massachusetts, 1970.

Sedgwick, Michael. *Cars of the Thirties and Forties*. New York, 1979.

Sedgwick, Michael. *Cars of the 50s and 60s*. New York, 1983.

Shuler, Terry with Griffith Borgeson and Jerry Sloniger. *The Origin and Evolution of the VW Beetle*. Princeton, New Jersey, 1985.

Spector, Ronald H. *Eagle Against the Sun, the American War With Japan*. New York, 1985.

Studebaker, Marvin F. *The Studebakers of South Bend*. South Bend, Indiana.

Turnquist, Robert E. *The Packard Story*. New York, 1965.

Ward, James A. *The Fall of the Packard Motor Car Company*. Stanford, California, 1995.

Weisberger, Bernard A. *The Dream Maker*. New York, 1979.

Wilkie, David J. and the editors of Esquire. *American Autos and Their Makers*. New York, 1963.

Young, Clarence H., and William A. Quinn. *Foundation for Living*. New York, 1963.

Index

Note: Members of the extended Studebaker family who were not directly involved in the management of H. & C. Studebaker, the Studebaker Brothers Manufacturing Company, or the Studebaker Corporation (New Jersey) are not referenced here, nor are individual models of Studebaker horse-drawn vehicles, automobiles and trucks. The same holds true for other brands associated with Studebaker: Garford, E-M-F, Flanders, Pierce-Arrow, Erskine, Rockne, etc. As this book is arranged in chronological order, finding individual models should not place an unreasonable burden on the reader, while including them would dramatically increase the length and complexity of this index without affording a corresponding increase in utility.

Adams, Herb, 433
Alfa Romeo automobile, 149
Allegheny Corporation, 355
Allis-Chalmers, farm equipment manufacturer, 109
Allison, William B., 15
Altman, Arnold, 409-410
Altman, Nathan D., 401-406-410, 427-428, 433-434
American Cotton Company, 93
American Motors Corporation, automobile manufacturer, 287-290, 309, 334-335, 346, 381, 443, 470
Andrews, Robert, 359-360, 428
Apperson automobile, 445

Ardsley automobile, 57
Association of Licensed Automobile Manufacturers (A.L.A.M.), 55, 79-81
Auto-Union-DKW automobiles, 346
Avanti Automotive Corporation, 421-428
Avanti Motor Corporation (I), 403-417, 426, 428, 433, 443
Avanti Motor Corporation (II), 432
Avanti USA Motorworks Corporation, 416
AVX Cars, 429-432, 434

Barit, A. E., 278
Bean, Ashton G., 183, 209, 211

Benidix Aviation Corporation, brake supplier, 363

Benny, Jack, 303

Bentley automobile, 149

Bergere, Cliff, 163

Blake, Stephen H., 409-418, 421, 426-428, 433

BMW automobile, 422

Boer War, 37

Borg-Warner Corporation, transmission supplier, 257, 272, 298, 328, 414

Bourke, Robert E., 192, 242-243, 255, 270, 297, 453, 456

Bowen, Lemuel, 56-57

Breer, Carl, 109, 112, 117, 119-125, 131, 155, 441

Briggs Manufacturing Company, 286-288, 310

Briggs, Eliakim, 15

Briscoe, Benjamin, 81

Brown, C. R., 412

Budd Company, parts supplier, 370

Buehrig, Gordon, 192, 204, 211

Bunting, James, 429-432, 434

Burlingame, Byers, 343-344, 377-380

Cadillac Automobile Company, automobile manufacturer, 53, 55-57, 64-67, 69, 81, see General Motors

Cafaro Company, 419, 429

Cafaro, Janet, 421

Cafaro, John J., 421-423, 425-427, 429, 432-434

Callaway Advanced Technology, 424-425

Callaway, Reeves, 433-434

Carter, Byron J., 38, 40, 44

Chalmers automobile and company, 445

Chanter, Arthur, J., 209-210

Chase Manhattan Bank, 168, 170

Checker Motors, automobile manufacturer, 402

Chemical Compounds Division (STP), Studebaker-Packard division, 355

Chevrolet, Louis, 57

Chrysler Corporation, automobile manufacturer, 6, 82, 124, 127, 132, 140, 154, 160-161, 168, 181, 192, 196, 207, 226, 236, 241, 256, 258, 268, 273-274, 278, 281, 286-287, 301, 309-310, 325, 341-342, 346, 364, 381, 440-444, 448, 451-453, 456, 459, 462-465; Plymouth automobile, 160-161, 226, 438-440, 462, 464; Dodge automobile, 79, 96, 188, 207, 226, 278, 440, 462, 464; DeSoto automobile, 226, 278, 334, 462, 464

Chrysler, Walter P., 6, 78, 82, 120-123, 155-156, 173, 217, 448

Churchill, Harold, 5, 240, 258, 293, 307-308, 313-316, 320-321, 324-325, 328-330, 332-335, 341-346, 350, 355

Cincinnati Testing Laboratories (C.T.L.), Inc., Studebaker-Packard division, 339

Civil War (U.S.), 11-12, 23-25, 466

Clarke Floor Machine Company, Studebaker-Packard division, 355

Cleveland automobile and company, 57, 61

Colbert, L. L., 301

Cole, Roy E., 154-156, 159, 182, 240-241, 243-244, 258

Continental Motors Corporation, engine supplier, 136-137, 148

Coolidge, Calvin, President of the

U. S., 158, 173
Cooper Industries, 396-397
Cord automobile, 163, 192, 204, 211-212, 401
Crosby, Bing, 303
Crosley automobile, 364
Curtiss-Wright Corporation, defense contractor, 301-302, 305-307, 315, 321-322, 329-331, 333, 346

D'Arcy Advertising Agency, 360
Daewoo automobile, 79
Daimler-Benz AG, automobile manufacturer, 302-306, 310, 316, 321-324, 327-333, 364-365, 372, 389-391, 398, 422, 449
De Luxe Motor Car Company, automobile manufacturer, 73, 82
DeCausse, Frank, 125
DeLorean , John Z., 299-300, 310
Delorean Motor Company, 412
Detroit Development Board, 416
Dietrich, Raymond, 136, 147, 173
Ditzler Color Division, PPG Industries, paint supplier, 414-415
Doehler, Robert, 359, 361
Domowatt, S.p.A., Studebaker-Packard division, 364
Donner, Frederick, 346
Dort, J. Dallas, 78
Draper, Dorothy, 281
Drucker, Peter F., 225, 230
Duesenberg automobile, 125
Dunkard religious movement, 12-14, 20-22, 29, 215
Duntov, Zora Arkus, 413
Durant automobile and company, 164
Durant, William C., 40, 43, 78, 114, 121, 217, 446
Duryea Motor Wagon Company,

automobile manufacturer, 80, 309

Eames, Harold Haydon, 38, 53, 61, 71, 73, 79-80
Earl, Harley, 125, 190, 204
Ebstein, Robert, 192, 359, 361, 364
Edison, Thomas Alva, 49-52, 79
Egbert, Sherwood H., 5, 7-8, 344, 349-352, 354-355, 357-363, 365-368, 370-372, 377, 386, 397-398, 428, 432
Eisenhower, Dwight D., President of the U. S., 302, 305
Electric Vehicle Company, automobile manufacturer, 38, 53, 80-81
Erhard, Ludwig, Chancellor of the Federal Republic of Germany, 344
Ernst & Ernst, industrial consultants, 300-301
Erskine, Albert Russel, 4-7, 85, 92-95, 100-112, 114-119, 121-125, 127, 129-131, 132, 135, 138-140, 146, 150-151, 154, 155-161, 163-172, 174, 178, 183, 197, 209, 314, 448-450
Erskine, Albert Russel, Jr., 172
Everitt, B. F., 64, 67-68, 70-71, 73, 81-82, 130
Everitt-Metzger-Flanders Company, automobile manufacturer, 41-42, 64, 68-77, 82, 85-86, 88, 95-98, 110, 128, 141, 158, 167, 174, 178, 441, 444, 446, 448
Exner, Virgil, 192, 202, 204, 240-245, 258, 325

Facel Vega automobile and company, 345-346
Faurot, Randall, 359
Federal Trade Commission, 171, 192-

195

Federal-Mogul Corporation, 397

Ferry, Hugh, 315, 346

Fielding, Gary, 422, 425-426

First Source Bank, 410, 415

Fischer, John, 223

Fish, F. Studebaker, 100

Fish, Frederick, S., 36-37, 39, 43, 52-
57, 59-64, 66-67, 70-71, 73-76, 85,
98-100, 103, 105, 114, 121, 141,
171, 174, 178, 209, 314

Fisher brothers, body builders, 43,
68, 72-73, 78, 177

Fisher, Eddie, 303

Flanders, Walter, 64-65, 67-68, 70-76,
82, 130, 141

Fleenor, Lon, 330

Flint automobile, 120-121, 131

Ford Motor Company, automobile
manufacturer, 53, 55, 67-69, 73-
74, 77, 79-82, 130-131, 141, 160-
161, 168, 187-188, 192, 196, 199-
200, 207, 224-227, 235. 247-248,
259, 273, 278, 280, 291, 301, 307,
309-310, 341-342, 346, 360-361,
365, 381, 438-440, 443-447, 449,
459, 462-465; Edsel automobile,
240, 301, 307-308, 334, 440, 452-
453; Lincoln automobile, 148,
164, 192, 195, 203-204, 207, 210,
274, 278, 310, 440, 462, 464;
Mercury automobile, 226, 278,
440, 462, 464

Ford, Edsel B., 203, 224-226, 449

Ford, Eleanor Clay, 227

Ford, Henry II, 227

Ford, Henry, 55, 58, 67-68, 74, 80-82,
101-102, 118-119, 131, 187, 217,
224-225. 444-445, 449

Forgan, J. Russell, 300, 344

Forrest, Nathan Bedford, 453

France, government, 215

Francis, Clarence, 332, 343-344, 355,
372

Franklin Manufacturing,
Studebaker-Packard division,
364, 371, 373, 387

Franklin, H. H., Manufacturing
Company, automobile manufacturer, 125, 164, 444

Frazer automobile, 462

Frost & French, Studebaker dealer,
470

Gabor, Zsa Zsa, 303

Gaeth automobile, 57

Gardner, Vince, 297

Garford Company, automobile
manufacturer, 53-54, 57-64, 80-82,
86, 95-98, 448

Garford, Arthur L., 54, 57-61, 63-64,
81

General Automobile and Manufacturing Company, automobile
manufacturer, 54-55, 57-59, 80

General Dynamics, defense contractor, 301

General Electric, home appliance
manufacturer and defense
contractor, 278-279, 310

General Foods, 332

General Motors Corporation,
automobile manufacturer, 77-78,
81, 113-14, 125-126, 137, 140, 154,
164-168, 173-174, 181-182, 186,
190, 196, 202-204, 207, 212, 225-
227, 230, 235-236, 247-248, 256,
262-263, 268, 273-274, 278, 286,
291, 301, 309-310, 341-342, 346,
365, 416, 419, 429-431, 433, 443-
450, 452-454, 459, 462-464, 468;
Chevrolet automobile, 160-161,

164, 186, 188, 200, 207, 235, 259, 263, 278, 280, 360-361, 392, 405, 408, 414, 418-419, 423-424, 438-440, 447, 460-462, 464-465, 470; Pontiac automobile, 78-79, 127, 161, 164, 188, 202, 207, 278, 334, 429-431, 433, 462-464, 470; Oldsmobile automobile, 68, 80, 154, 164, 188, 207, 263, 278, 447, 462, 464, 470; Buick automobile, 78, 96, 136, 161, 164, 192, 207, 226, 247, 447, 462, 464, 470; Cadillac automobile, 61, 67-69, 81, 126, 164, 186, 192, 202-203, 207, 210, 212, 247, 263, 274, 278, 328, 445, 447, 461-462, 464; GMC Truck, 463

General Services Administration, 354

Gering Products, Inc., Studebaker-Packard division, 339, 355

Giese, Carl F., 304-305, 322, 329

Goggomobil automobile and company, 324

Gompers, Samuel, 292

Graham automobile and company, 161, 309, 398, 401

Graham, George

Granetelli, Andy, 355, 362, 368, 374-376

Granetelli, Joe, 368, 374-376, 421

Granetelli, Vince, 355, 368, 374-375

Grant, Walter, 28%-286, 291-292, 294

Gravely Tractor, Studebaker-Packard division, 342

Gregorie, E. T., 203

Grundy, Gordon E., 383 384, 387 389, 392-394, 449-450

Guthrie, Randolph, 5, 329, 346, 372-373, 390, 396, 398

Hall, D. Ray, 343-344, 354-355

Halladay automobile and company, 177

Hanna, T. Forrest, 337

Hansen, Rasmus, 54-55, 81

Hardig, Eugene, 263, 334-335, 360, 362-364, 366, 403-407, 428

Harris, John F., 174

Heaslet, James, 61, 96, 103

Henry Ford Company, automobile manufacturer, 55

Henry, Guy, 112, 139

Hinds, Joe, 17-20, 39-40

Hitler, Adolf, Chancellor of Germany, 138, 220, 247

Hoffman, Maximillian E., 281-282, 303-304, 321, 323-324

Hoffman, Paul G., 5-6, 90-91, 127-128, 157, 177-183, 188, 195-198, 200, 208-209, 211, 215, 226-227, 236, 238, 240, 246-247, 250-253, 264, 271-272, 283, 285, 291-292, 294, 296, 314, 397, 443, 449-451, 453, 459-460

Hoover, Herbert, President of the U. S., 118, 165

Hoover, J. Edgar, 210

Hoppe, Heinz, 304, 306, 315-316, 322-323, 327-331, 333, 389-391

Hudson Motor Car Company, automobile manufacturer, 164, 193-194, 207, 235, 273, 278-281, 295, 309, 334, 346, 397, 452-453, 457, 462, 464, 470

Humber automobile, 248

Humphrey, George, 301

Hupp Motor Car Corporation, automobile manufacturer, 148, 189, 191, 197, 211, 273, 309, 398, 401

Hurley, Roy, 305-307, 315, 321-322, 324, 326-327, 330-331, 333, 449

Hutchinson, Richard, 248, 282
Indiana Economic Development
    Authority, 410
International Harvester, truck
    manufacturer, 301

J. P. Morgan and Company, brokers,
    76
Jaguar automobile, 363, 422
Jenkins, Ab, 128, 149, 160
Jordan automobile and company,
    164

Kaiser, Henry J., 309
Kaiser-Frazer Corporation, automo-
    bile manufacturer, 281, 443, 451-
    452, 457, 462, 464
Kellogg, Thomas, 359, 361, 424, 428-
    430
Kelly, Michael E., 417-419, 421, 427,
    430
Kelly, William E., 68, 73
Khrushchev, Nikita, Premier of the
    U. S. S. R., 222-223
King, Charles, 68
Klausmeyer, Otto, 156-157
Klotz, Hans, 322, 343
Knudsen, William S., 225-226, 230
Korallus, Gerhard, 330
Koto, Holden, 192, 243
Kuby, Erich, 222

Lang, Bill, 429-434
Lehman Brothers, brokers, 183, 283-
    285, 290, 342
Leland and Faulconer, automobile
    industry supplier, 55-57, 81
Leland Stanford University, 109
Leland, Henry Martyn, 40, 55-57, 67
LeMaire, Eleanor, 281
Litchfield, Dr. Edward, 332, 354-355

Litton Industries, defense contractor,
    301
Lockheed, defense contractor, 310
Locomobile automobile, 139, 444
Loewy, Raymond, 3, 189-193, 196,
    198, 200, 202-204, 210, 240-245,
    258, 269-270, 273, 293, 296-297,
    317, 358-361, 363, 368, 371-372,
    394, 414, 428, 432, 453, 455-456
Longstreet, Stephen, 265
Lowry, Greg, 421

MacArthur, Douglas, 219
Manhattan Shirt, 342
Manheim, Frank, 342, 344
Marcks, Bob, 394
Marcks, Hazelquist and Powers,
    design consultants, 394
Markin, Morris, 402
Marmon automobile and company,
    139, 164, 444
Marquette automobile, 164
Marriott, Fred, 78
Mason, George, 277-279, 287-289,
    309, 470
Maxim, Hiram Percy, 79
Maxwell, Jonathan, 68, 81
Maxwell-Chalmers, automobile
    manufacturer, 6, 81, 121-124, 132,
    449
Mazda automobile and company,
    412
McCahill, Tom, 438
McCulloch Corporation, 344, 349
McGraw-Edison, 396
McManus, Theodore, 66-67
McNamara, Robert S., 308
McRae, Duncan, 296, 301, 325-327
Meshel, Harry, 420
Metzger, William, 64-71, 73, 81-82,
    130

Milburn, George, 20-21
Minkle, Louis E., 343, 379-380
Mitsubishi automobile and company, 79
Mobile & Ohio Railroad, 92
Moeser, W. A., 383-384
Molded Fiberglass Products Company, fiberglass supplier, 361, 367-369, 402-403, 406
Monroe, Marilyn, 303
Monsanto Chemicals, 355
Moon automobile and company, 164
Mormon religious movement, 20-21, 27
Morris automobile, 457
Morrison, Robert, 402
"Mr. Ed," television show, 356
Munson Electric Motor Company, automobile manufacturer, 38-39, 44
Murphy, Edward, 43, 78
Mussolini, Benito, Prime Minister of Italy, 138, 173

Nance, James J., 5, 7, 278-279, 282-283, 285-292, 294, 296, 300-302, 307-308, 310, 314, 317, 449, 470
Nash Motor Company and Nash-Kelvinator Corporation, 164-168, 173-174, 207, 212, 273, 277-279, 295, 309, 334, 346, 397, 452-453, 457, 462-464, 470
Nash, Charles, 43, 78, 165, 168, 173
National Aeronautics and Space Administration (NASA), 339
National Cash Register, 278
New Avanti Motor Corporation, 417-421, 432
Newman, Leo, 401-402, 409, 428, 433-434
Nichols, Marie, 281

Nissan automobile and company, 393, 450
Nixon, Mudge, Rose, Guthrie and Alexander, law firm, 372
Nixon, Richard M., President of the U. S., 372, 398
Nordhoff, Heinz, 248
Northern Manufacturing Company, automobile manufacturer, 68, 75, 81

Oakland Motor Car Company, automobile manufacturer, 78, 164
Ohio State University, 109
Olley, Maurice, 186
Onan, Studebaker-Packard division, 355

Packard Motor Car Company, automobile manufacturer: 7, 77, 80, 109, 127, 164, 187, 192-193, 207, 210, 212, 262, 273, 278-279, 281, 283-285, 295, 377, 391, 398, 444, 449, 452, 462, 464
Panhard automobile, 204
Parker, Dorothy, 173
Paxton Products, Studebaker-Packard division, 355, 362, 375, 421, 431
Peerless automobile and company, 164, 398, 444
Penn, Roger, 433
Pierce-Arrow Motor Car Company, automobile manufacturer, 114, 139-142, 145-146, 148, 150, 160, 162-163, 170, 173-174, 180-181, 184, 192, 209-210, 212, 444, 449
Pinchon-Parat, coachbuilder, 371
Pininfarina, coachbuilder, 346
Pope, Alexander, 38, 53-54, 80
Porsche, Dr. Ing. h. c. F., AG,

automobile manufacturer, 299-300, 310, 368

Porta, A. J., 314-315, 342, 344

PPG Industries, 415

Puma automobile, 421

Rainer automobile and company, 57, 61

Reinhart, John, 192

Renault automobile and company, 248

Reuther, Walter, 267

Revlon, 342

Rickenbacker automobile and company, 125, 130

Rickenbacker, Eddie, 177

Rockne, Knute,(128, 157-159

Rogers, Will, 117

Rolls-Royce automobile and company, 186, 427

Romney, George, 287-290, 334, 346

Roos, Delmar G., 138-139, 160, 181-182

Roosevelt, Franklin D., 170, 174, 192, 210, 226

Rosenthal, Richard, 404

Royal automobile and company, 57

Salisbury, Harrison, 230

Schaefer, Studebaker-Packard division, 355

Sears and Roebuck, 376

Seaton, John, 432

Securities and Exchange Commission, 417

Selden, George B., 79-81

Skelton, Owen R., 109, 112, 117, 119-124, 131, 155

Skillman, Sidney, 315, 343

Slick, Thomas W., 117, 171, 178, 182-183

Sloan, Alfred P., 6, 217, 225-227, 444-448

Smith-Corona Marchant, 332

Sonnabend, Abraham, 332, 342-345, 350, 355

Sorensen, Charles, 225

St. Joseph Bank & Trust, 404

Stalin, Joseph V., Premier of the U. S. S. R., 222

Stanley automobile and company, 47, 78

Stearns automobile and company, 445

Stevens, Brooks, 357, 371

Stevens-Duryea automobile and company, 445

Straman Company, 414

Studebaker Brothers Manufacturing Company: incorporated, 25-26; fires, 28, 32; labor trouble, 30-31, 34; supplied carriages to Benjamin Harrison, President of the U. S., 32-33; Izzer buggy, 34; merged with E-M-F, 77; dissolved, 85

Studebaker Corporation (Delaware): incorporation, 183-184; recognizes UAW, 187-188; war production (WWII), 202, 205-209, 214-230, 240, 254; talk of Ford takeover, 224-227, 449; labor situation, 238, 250-251, 256, 259-260, 264, 283, 468; development of 1947 cars, 239-246; Empire Steel Corporation, 250, 255-256; war production (Korea), 260-261, 264, 272, 286, 467; development of 1953 cars, 264-265, 268-271; Indianapolis 500 race, 265-266; Ford "Blitz," 280, 459, 461, 465, 468; takeover by Packard, 279,

283-285, 397, 449

Studebaker Corporation (Indiana): incorporation, 85; bombing of New Jersey plant, 99; war production (WWI), 99-100, 105-108; liquidation of horse-drawn vehicle business, 111-112; Erskine automobile, 129-130, 135-137, 140, 142, 146-149, 159, 173, 449; purchase of Pierce-Arrow, 140-142, 145-146, 449; Rockne automobile, 155-162, 167, 174, 178, 184, 198, 245, 449; Indianapolis 500 race, 144-145, 150, 163; receivership, 170-171

Studebaker slogans, 4, 14, 22, 33-34,

Studebaker, Bill, 237

Studebaker, Clement, 14-16, 20-22, 25-26, 28-29, 32-33, 35-37, 39

Studebaker, Clement, Jr., 73, 85, 92

Studebaker, H. & C.: established, 16; supplied carriage to Abraham Lincoln, President of the U. S., 23, 129, 265

Studebaker, Henry, 14-16, 20-22, 24

Studebaker, Jacob Franklin, 14, 24, 27, 31-32

Studebaker, John Mohler, 14, 16-26, 29, 31, 36-37, 39-40, 43, 52-53, 62, 77, 85-92, 103-105, 166, 183, 209, 211, 314

Studebaker, Peter Everest, 14, 23, 25-26, 30-32, 35-37

Studebaker-Packard Corporation: 7; creation of, 279, 283-285; plan to merge with American Motors, 279-280, 287-290, 470; Curtiss-Wright management contract, 301-302, 305-307; end of Packard production in Detroit, 307; labor situation, 316, 338, 365-367, 450-451; reorganization of 1958, 330-333; development of 1959 Lark, 333-337; discontinuation of Packard brand, 334, 346; aborted Packard revival, 345-346; government contracts, 354, 367, 385; restyling of GT Hawk, 356-357; development of 1963 Avanti, 358-364, 366-367, 427-428; Packard dropped from corporate name, 367; ceasing operations in South Bend, 377-380; Studebaker car discontinued, 395-396; relations with Avanti Motor Corporation, 401-403

Studebaker-Worthington Corporation, 396

Stutz automobile and company, 164

Sun Yat Sen, 87

Taft, William H., President of the U. S., 62

Teagle, Walter, 183, 211

Teague, Richard, 301

Textron, defense contractor, 301

"The Price Is Right," television show, 377

Tincher automobile and company, 62-63

Tincher, Thomas, 62-63

Toepke, Barry, 426

Toyota automobile and company, 392, 398, 450, 468

Trans International Airlines, Studebaker-Packard division, 364, 371, 373

Turpin, Robert, 405

Underwood Typewriter, 93

Ungaro, Patrick J., 420

Union of Soviet Socialist Republics,

218-224, 248, 466

United Auto Workers, 187, 235, 248, 256, 260, 338, 355, 412-413, 450

Vail, Ralph A., 154-156, 159, 182

Vance, Harold S., 5-6, 127, 129, 158, 177-179, 182-183, 195-198, 200, 206, 208-209, 211, 215, 226-227, 236, 238, 240, 246-247, 250-253, 255-256, 258, 260, 264-267, 269-272, 278, 282, 285, 294, 296, 314, 397, 443, 449-451, 453, 455, 459-460, 469

Viking automobile, 164

Volkswagen AG, automobile manufacturer, 247-248, 274, 281-282, 300, 324, 393-394

Wayne Automobile Company, automobile manufacturer, 68, 75

White Motor Company, truck manufacturer, 6, 169-171, 181, 183-184, 209, 211

White, Walter, 169

Wilhelmina, Queen of the Nether-lands, 280

Willys-Overland Company, automo-bile manufacturer, 63, 81, 96, 113, 120-121, 139, 155-156, 159, 173, 182, 207, 209-210, 309, 457, 462, 464

Wilson, Charles, 286, 301, 309-310

Wilson, Don, 303

Wilson, Woodrow, President of the U. S., 102-103, 105, 131

Winton automobile, 445

Woodruff, Ernest, 183

Woodruff, Robert, 169, 174

Wright, Frank Lloyd, 303

Wright, Phil, 163

Yale & Towne Manufacturing Company, 93, 106

Zeder, Fred M., 96, 109-110, 112, 117, 119-124, 131-132, 139, 155